Real-World ASP.NET: Building a Content Management System

STEPHEN R. G. FRASER

Apress™

Real-World ASP.NET: Building a Content Management System
Copyright © 2002 by Stephen R. G. Fraser

ISBN (pbk): 1-59059-024-4
Printed and bound in the United States of America 12345678910
Trademarked names may appear in this book. Rather than use a trademark symbol with every occurrence of a trademarked name, we use the names only in an editorial fashion and to the benefit of the trademark owner, with no intention of infringement of the trademark.

Editorial Directors: Dan Appleman, Peter Blackburn, Gary Cornell, Jason Gilmore, Karen Watterson, John Zukowski
Managing Editor: Grace Wong
Copy Editor: Nicole LeClerc
Production Editor: Janet Vail
Compositor: Impressions
Artist: Kurt Krames
Indexer: Rebecca Plunkett
Cover Designer: Tom Debolski
Marketing Manager: Stephanie Rodriguez

Distributed to the book trade in the United States by Springer-Verlag New York, Inc.,175 Fifth Avenue, New York, NY, 10010
and outside the United States by Springer-Verlag GmbH & Co. KG, Tiergartenstr. 17, 69112 Heidelberg, Germany.
In the United States, phone 1-800-SPRINGER, e-mail orders@springer-ny.com, or visit http://www.springer-ny.com.
Outside the United States, fax +49 6221 345229, e-mail orders@springer.de, or visit http://www.springer.de.

For information on translations, please contact Apress directly at 2560 Ninth Street, Suite 219, Berkeley, CA 94710.
E-mail info@apress.com, or visit http://www.apress.com.

The source code for this book is available to readers at http://www.apress.com in the Downloads section. You will need to answer questions pertaining to this book in order to successfully download the code.

To my energy, Sarah, and bundle of joy, Shaina, with love.

Contents at a Glance

Contents

Chapter 13 Displaying Dynamic Content *387*

Chapter 14 Using a Workflow to Enter Content *427*

Chapter 15   Registered Users and Protected Content 473

About the Author

Stephen Fraser is the managing principal for Fraser Training, a corporate training company focusing on .NET technologies. Stephen has over 15 years of IT experience working for a number of consulting companies, ranging from the large consulting firms of EDS and Andersen Consulting (Accenture) to a number of smaller e-business companies. His IT experience covers all aspects of application and Web development and management, ranging from initial concept all the way through to deployment.

Stephen currently resides, with his beautiful wife Sarah and daughter Shaina, in beautiful Louisville, Kentucky.

Introduction

I've played with many of the commercial content management systems (CMSs) currently on the market, and many have certain qualities or features in common. There is one thing, however, that they all have in common: They are all overpriced.

Yes, they have hundreds of features. The fact is that when most Webmasters implement a CMS, they usually don't even come close to using half of the features provided by the CMS. Yes, a few Web sites are exceptions, but most don't need all the features and, unfortunately, they don't have anything available as a substitute, or so they believe.

This book will show that Webmasters have an alternative because it describes the ins and outs of a CMS. It goes as far as showing you how to build one of your own—CMS.NET. But even if you never plan to write your own CMS, this book and, in particular, CMS.NET will help you understand what is happening under the covers of its more expensive siblings.

Programmers (and I am one, so I can say this) like to make the world think that what they do is very mystical. In reality, it is actually very easy, if you have enough information and the right tools at hand. This book should be enough of a head start that most good programmers could, on their own, pump out a commercial-grade CMS in less than a year. Heck, I coded CMS.NET in just over three months while writing this book.

The quick development time can be directly attributed to the power of Microsoft's .NET and Visual Studio .NET. It saved me from many of the problems that occurred when I tried to develop an equivalent CMS using other, nearly as powerful, competitive tools.

What Is This Book About?

This book is about CMSs (I'm sure you figured that out from the front cover), but more specifically, it is a detailed programmer's look at what makes up, and how to develop, a CMS using Microsoft's new ASP.NET, C#, and the .NET Framework.

Ultimately, it is a book that shows how to build a fully functional CMS at a fraction of the cost of its commercial siblings. Even if you plan to buy a much more expensive CMS, this book will explain the internal details of a CMS and should help you make the correct decision when you make your purchase.

Who Is This Book Written For?

This book is for Web developers who want to learn the internal details of a CMS or who want to create a CMS of their own. With this book, a Web developer should gain a good understanding of how to build a CMS and where to find a lot of the code (prepackaged) needed to build one.

It is for Webmasters who want a more cost-effective way to maintain their Web content. This book will show that a Webmaster may, in fact, have another choice when it comes to his CMS.

It is also for any intermediate- to advanced-level Web developers who already have a basic understanding of the Microsoft .NET Framework and want to continue to expand their knowledge. It is designed to provide a lot of helpful coding hints using C#, ASP.NET, XML, and ADO.NET, within the Visual Studio .NET environment, in the area of server-side Web development.

What Is in This Book?

The following is a chapter-by-chapter breakdown of the book's contents:

Chapter 1, "So, What Is a Content Management System Anyway?" introduces the basic concepts of a CMS by breaking one down and explaining its most basic elements. The chapter then continues by describing some common features and benefits of most CMSs. Finally, it wraps up with a discussion on when a commercial CMS is really merited.

Chapter 2, "Version Control," covers version control, tracking, and rollback in detail. It shows how a CMS uses versioning, why it is important, and its benefits.

Chapter 3, "Workflow," covers workflows, a very important feature found in all CMSs. It shows what a workflow is, the roles it plays, and the benefits it provides to a CMS. The chapter also discusses some things that a workflow designer needs to examine when building the workflow.

Chapter 4, "Personalization," starts by defining personalization and walks through its objectives. It then explores many of the different types of personalization available on the market today. It covers two major issues of personalization: the law of diminishing returns and privacy. The chapter concludes with the roles and benefits that personalization provides to CMSs.

Chapter 5, "Basics of Web Architecture," first discusses Web architectures in general and their three layers: database, application, and presentation. Then it delves into the presentation layer in greater detail, showing how it is divided into server and client sides communicating using HTTP. The chapter then covers some of the more common client- and server-side technologies. It concludes by showing Web architectures using the .NET Framework.

Chapter 6, "ASP.NET, C#, and Visual Studio .NET," is a little refresher on C#, ASP.NET, and Visual Studio .NET. It is designed to get everybody on a level playing field when it comes to .NET Framework development.

Chapter 7, "Database Development and ADO.NET," covers all essential aspects of database development needed to develop a CMS system.

Chapter 8, "XML," covers in great detail some of the many ways in which a developer can access XML through the .NET Framework. It covers all facets of XML that are needed to build a CMS and, in particular, what is needed by CMS.NET.

Chapter 9, "A Quick Overview of CMS.NET," starts with a brief description of CMS.NET and then goes into how to install it. The chapter finishes off with a brief tutorial.

Chapter 10, "Initializing CMS.NET," covers the setup subsystem of CMS.NET. It starts by showing how to navigate from page to page. Then it discusses web.config and how to programmatically update and extract information from it. The chapter also shows how CMS.NET separates application development and database development with the use of database helper classes.

Chapter 11, "Getting Content into the System," covers the CURVeS (creating, updating, removing, viewing, and submitting) of CMS.NET's content management application. It shows how to break a Web page into frames and then revisits XML with the XML-driven NavBar (Navigation Bar). The chapter also covers error handling in some detail. It finishes by covering the Content database and its helper class.

Chapter 12, "Cookies, Authentication, Authorization, and Encryption," covers security—in particular, cookies, authentication, authorization, and encryption. It starts with a brief discussion of ASP.NET's security and then covers CMS.NET's security in more detail.

Chapter 13, "Displaying Dynamic Content," first covers the basics of what dynamic content is. Then it shows dynamic content in practice within CMS.NET's three-level dynamic navigation model. The chapter also covers both static and dynamic User Controls in detail.

Chapter 14, "Using a Workflow to Enter Content," covers role-based content administration. It describes CMS.NET's workflow and the roles it requires. It also discusses inter-role communication and e-mail alerts.

Chapter 15, "Registered Users and Protected Content," covers registering users and restricting content. It starts by describing why you might want to restrict content and covers the privacy policy Web page. It then covers user profiles and the two most common methods of retrieving user information: the quick blitz and the slow retrieval. The chapter ends by showing how to change CMS.NET to implement registration and protected content.

Conventions

I've tried to keep the number of different styles used in this book to a minimum. You didn't buy it for pretty icons, but rather its content (I hope). Here are examples of the styles used and explanations of what they mean:

- Important words and words being defined are in *italic* font.

- **Bold** font is use for things you must enter into an edit field.

- Code font is used for code, URLs, and e-mail addresses that appear in regular text.

Every once in a while I will include a Note, Tip, or Warning about something:

 NOTE   *Pay attention.*

TIP *Tricks that might help.*

WARNING *Danger ahead.*

Code that is highlighted in gray can mean one of two things: it is code that you need to enter yourself, or it is code of direct interest to you. Gray background code looks like this:

```
public Content(string h, string s)
{
    headline = h;
    story = s;
}
```

Otherwise, code has been autogenerated by Visual Studio .NET or it is something you have entered a while ago and has no bearing on what you are coding now:

```
<%@ Page language="c#" Codebehind="DCViewer.aspx.cs"
                    AutoEventWireup="false"
                    Inherits="Ch06Example.WebForm1" %>
<!DOCTYPE HTML PUBLIC "-//W3C//DTD HTML 4.0 Transitional//EN" >
<HTML>
```

Obviously, if some of the code is autogenerated and some is manually entered, you will find both styles in the code at the same time.

How to Reach the Author

I would like to hear from you. Feel free to e-mail me at `srgfraser@contentmgr.com`. I will respond to every e-mail that I can. Questions, comments, and suggestions are all welcome. Also, feel free to visit a copy of CMS.NET on the Internet at `www.contentmgr.com`. All registered users have the capability to author content on the site if they feel so inclined. Also, the `www.contentmgr.com` site is where the newest release of CMS.NET can be found, along with any user/reader contributions.

Oh, by the way, thank you for buying my book.

CHAPTER 1

So, What Is a Content Management System Anyway?

THIS SEEMS LIKE AN OBVIOUS QUESTION with which to start the book. Yet, the problem is that the answer, even if worded plainly, is far from obvious: A *content management system (CMS)* is a system that manages the content components of a Web site.

That's it. Seems simple enough, right? Why then, if you ask this question of two or more different Web professionals, do you get two or more different answers or, more precisely, two or more different "interpretations" of the preceding answer? The problem revolves around the ambiguity of the word "content" or, more accurately, the scope of the content or what portions of the content are contained under the umbrella of a CMS.

Another problem is that nowhere does this definition define what core functionality makes up a CMS. Most CMSs make their names by how many additional features they add. A true way of telling whether a CMS is any good is by gauging how well it does the core functionality that makes up a CMS. Without defining what the core functionality of a CMS is, there is no level playing field for measuring CMSs against each other.

This chapter will provide the information you need to determine what a content management system is, hopefully removing the ambiguity of the preceding simple definition . . . which brings us to the first major area of ambiguity.

What Is Content?

Most professionals will agree that *content* is the "stuff" (don't you love the technical jargon we software developers throw around?) found on a Web site. This "stuff" on a Web site can be broken down into two categories:

- The information—such as text and images—that you see on a Web site when you visit it

- The applications or software that runs on the Web site's servers and actually displays the information

1

Now comes the ambiguity. Some professionals will tell you that the domain of a CMS consists only of the information, whereas others will tell you that it consists of both the information and the applications. So, which definition is correct?

At first glance, one might say the all-encompassing definition is a more accurate explanation of the word "content." The question should be asked, though: Do you need to manage or can you manage the applications in the same way as the information? Many people would say no, believing that software developers should develop two different software systems—one that manages the information (that is, the CMS) and another that manages the applications—because the information is *what* is displayed, whereas applications determine *how* information is displayed.

What's more, the people who create and maintain these two different types of content are often as different as their work. The information developer tends to be more creative; the application developer is more technical (no offense to "creative" application developers). The most important difference seems to be that the workflows of information and applications vary considerably. (I explain more about workflows in Chapter 3, but for now, just take my word.) Different approaches, goals, users, and workflows, therefore, merit the building of two different systems. Forcing information and applications into the same model will cause unnecessary complexity for both the developers and the users of the system.

Developing a CMS that will work no matter the type of content (that is, information or application) requires the ability to maintain and follow the flow of two distinct workflows at the same time. It is true that the workflows of information and applications have many similarities—both create, change, approve, test, and deploy—but that is all they are, similarities. Very different skill sets are required in the role of creating information as opposed to creating an application, and the differences only widen as you continue through to the stage of deployment.

The workflows of information and applications are not the same either. Additional stages and tools are required in the workflow of an application. For example, there is analysis, design that is far more detailed, compiling, system testing, and release testing. Applications are far more intertwined with the Web site as a whole than is information. For many CMSs, the link between application and Web site is so interdependent that a shutdown of the Web site is required before deploying a new or updated application. Information, on the other hand, comprises distinct entities. It is possible to add, remove, and update information on a Web site without ever having to worry about bringing the Web site down.

In practice, you will find that most CMSs are not usually devoted to managing only application content or even a combination of information and application content. In most cases, CMS software developers focus on information management only and let other software developers build tools, such as source code management systems, to handle the application content.

With that said, many high-end, high-priced, commercial CMSs support the all-encompassing definition of content. Vignette and Interwoven are two such CMS systems. They both support practically any type of information content that can go on a Web site, as well as deployment of any custom applications. An interesting note about these CMSs is that they offer the application content management system as an add-on package. So, it appears that even they see the distinction between the two types of content.

Yet still, in light of all this, there is evidence that the industry is in the process of trying to merge all niches of CMSs together, bringing both information and applications under the same umbrella. The question is whether this merging will make CMSs all-encompassing or just create a large, integrated tool that handles all aspects of Web page development for which CMS is just one part.

I would hazard to guess that it is the latter because it would contradict the efforts of the rest of the industry, which is trying hard to do the exact opposite (that is, keep information and applications separate). Web site developers consciously make an effort to try to separate applications and information whenever they build systems. In fact, developers recommend that while using .NET, HTML (information) and the programmed functionality (application) should be in separate source code files. (We expand on this separation in the code when we start developing actual ASP.NET and C# programs in later chapters.)

This book will use the definition of content as being only the information and not the applications running it. If nothing else, using this definition of content will simplify the explanations and examples that follow and will enable you to focus on the key CMS issues without getting bogged down by exceptions to the norm. Know though, that even with this restriction in the definition of content, there is no reason why you cannot adapt the content of this book to build an all-encompassing content management system that addresses all Web site content.

Real-World Content

I have covered the theoretical definition of content, so now let's look at how all this comes into play in a real Web site, the MSNBC site (`www.msnbc.com`). This site, as you will see, contains both text and images; few sites *don't* have both. But this site has a lot more. Let's start with the cover page.

Why MSNBC calls this a cover page, as opposed to a home page like the rest of the industry, is beyond me. This is MSNBC's window into its Web site. You see a myriad of links to the actual content of the site. You are also bombarded with banner ads to the site's sponsors. The top half of the page is generic to all MSNBC users; the bottom half of the page, on the other hand, has content exclusive to me, or more specifically to my ZIP code. This user-specific content is known as *personalization*. (Chapter 4 covers personalization in more detail.)

You can also see that the left side of the page is made up of a navigation bar. You can find *navigation bars* (NavBars) on most Web sites. They allow a user to drill down to specific subtopics, making it easier for the user to select only the content areas in which he has interest. MSNBC uses image maps for a NavBar. Some Web sites use ordinary hyperlinks, and others use some sort of scripting language added to the hyperlinks to give the NavBar more life. Effects such as drop-down links or fancy animation can be achieved using scripting language, and they add some flair to a normally boring part of the page. (Chapter 11 looks at another way of handling NavBars using server-side scripting.)

To continue, the cover page you see is dynamically generated by the MSNBC server and then is sent over to my browser by way of the Internet. The site uses two types of links to its content:

- Image maps

- Hyperlinks

These links are usually in the form of a content title or a content title and teaser. *Teaser* is a term borrowed from the newspaper and magazine world; it refers to text and/or images designed to quickly attract the attention of readers and get them interested enough in the story to navigate to it.

The content that the links navigate to is usually stories or articles and is made up of text, images, audio, recorded video, and live video.

Let's navigate to the MSNBC top story. When you click the article hyperlink, a message will be sent to the MSNBC Web server requesting the article. The server would then dynamically generate the story and send it back to your browser.

Moving on, the story page, as you can see, is made up of numerous different types of content: the NavBar, a few banner ads, the story, images, and a video. The story itself is even broken into many different sections. An article usually consists of the headline, byline, dateline, source, teaser, body, tagline, and related links. As you may have noticed, content name types often derive from old newspaper and magazine names. This seems somewhat logical because journalists with newspaper or magazine backgrounds often write many of the articles, and the Web sites often model newspapers or magazines.

Mercifully, the format of most of the content sections on the MSNBC site is all text. You might have noticed that the different content types are displayed using a consistent pattern of different fonts, colors, and sometimes even backgrounds. Such displays of text in a CMS are often template driven. (Chapter 13 covers content formatting and templates in more detail.)

Also, here's a further comment about related links: Depending on the type of Web site you are building—in particular an e-commerce site—related links are also sometimes known as *up-* or *cross-sells*. These strategic sales tools give a user, who already plans to purchase an item, the option of examining and ordering a better model of the same item (up-sell) and/or the chance to look at all the item's accessories (cross-sell).

The content page has strategically located links to sponsors. These links are located where they will be most visible. You might have heard this location referred to as *above the fold,* meaning the top area of a Web page, which is visible when the page first loads. This phrase's origin, like many others in the Web world, comes from the newspaper industry, which the Web in its earlier years tried to emulate. In the case of the newspaper, "above the fold" points to area on the top half of the newspaper when it's folded in half. Since people have a tendency to scan the top of a page first to find things of interest, this area is considered better, as more people see it. Some sites randomly cycle through banner ads, and some target the specific user. Targeting the specific user is one more form of personalization, which I cover in Chapter 4.

Many CMSs provide the capability to have the content stay on the Web site for a predetermined amount of time. The length of time that the content remains on the site is set when the content is entered into the CMS. Depending on the Web site, the amount of time may range from a few hours to indefinitely. Once the allotted time expires, the content is automatically archived. Later, a user can search the site's archives to retrieve the article she wants.

What Is a Content Component?

As you can see, even a single Web site can be made up of many different types of content, such as text, image, audio, and video. It is far easier to work with each of these types of content separately than as one big chunk. The main reason is that it allows *specialization,* meaning you can use a tool designed specifically for that type of content. It also means a person can specialize in the skills she does best. For example, an expert at drawing images does not have to worry about writing the story.

CMSs rely heavily on the whole concept of small pieces of content. The term most CMSs use to represent these small pieces is *content component.* You might also think of a content component as an instance in which one of the content pieces makes up a story or article on a Web page.

The granularity of a content component is determined by the CMS being used and can be as granular as a headline, byline, dateline, source, teaser, and so on or as large as an entire story. Content components typically are stored in a repository using the same format. For example, a content component of the image type might be stored in a GIF-formatted file with a predetermined height and width. Content components should also be able to stand on their own. In other words, a content component will have meaning in and of itself.

Figure 1-1 should help you understand what a content component is. The left-hand portion of the diagram shows a complete Web page. The right-hand side shows the same page broken down into content components.

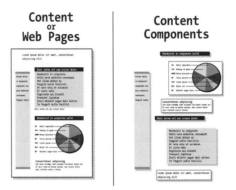

Figure 1-1. Content components

At the other end of the spectrum from a content component is a document. A *document* is often known as a file. It can also be thought of as a group of content components.

Document management systems provide the same functionality as a CMS except at the document level (or, in the Web world, at the Web-page level). They lack the capability to work with the details contained within the page. Instead, they deal with the entire page. Because of this, they lack the power and flexibility of a CMS. Still, document management systems sometimes get confused with content management systems and are promoted and sold as such. It could be argued that a document management system is a CMS with the content component granularity set at its maximum.

The CMS Elements

Typically, a CMS consists of a minimum of three elements: the content management application (CMA), the metacontent management application (MMA), and the content delivery application (CDA). Some CMSs have more elements, but all will have these three in some form.

The CMA manages the content components of the CMS. The MMA, on the other hand, manages the information about the content components. Finally, the CDA provides a way of displaying content components to the user of the Web site.

Content Management Application (CMA)

Simply stated, a *content management application (CMA)* manages the full life cycle of content components, from inception through removal. A CMA will create, maintain, and remove content components to and from a repository. The repository can be a database, a set of files, or a combination of both. The management process is sequential in nature and is accomplished using a workflow. The CMA is often thought of as the administration portion of the CMS.

The CMA allows the content author to develop content components without having to know Hypertext Markup Language (HTML) or understand the underlying Web architecture. This allows the day-to-day maintenance of a Web site without the constant need of a Webmaster.

All CMAs are multiuser in design, with each user having one or more roles through the life cycle of the content component. Many CMAs have role-based security, meaning users are only allowed to do the tasks allotted to them when they were added to the system. A small Web site with only a few people working on it may comprise a small number of roles, with each role having a lot of different tasks or functions that it can perform. For a larger Web site with more bureaucracy, there may be several different roles with very limited functionality. User roles are usually set up when the CMS is installed. Often you are presented with a list of tasks or functions when setting up a role, from which you select the specific tasks or functions that the role will have authority to complete. Some more advanced systems may allow the addition of new roles or changes after the system has been active for some time, thus allowing for a more dynamic, roles-based system that will evolve as the Web site organization changes. Chapter 12 discusses roles and role-based security in more detail.

The purpose of the CMA is to progress content components through their life cycle as quickly and efficiently as possible. At the end of each life-cycle stage, the content components should be in a more mature and stable state. Figure 1-2 shows some of the common high-level life-cycle stages that a CMA should address.

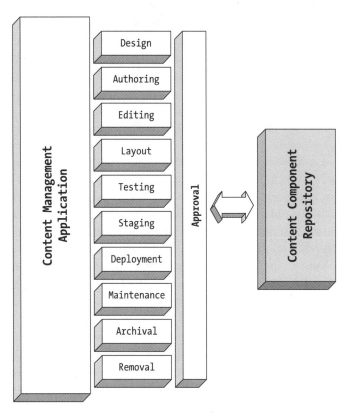

Figure 1-2. The content management application

Approval

Before any stage in the life of a content component is completed and the next is to start, someone with the authority to do so should approve the changes made to the content component.

The approval process will vary greatly between Web sites, even those Web sites using the same type of CMS. In large bureaucracies, a different person, role, or committee may be required, at each life-cycle stage, to approve content before it is ready to progress to the next stage. At the other extreme, a small Web site may have the same person approve his own work throughout the entire life cycle.

Design

This is where all the content components that will be published on the Web site are identified and described. In some CMSs, during this stage, the content components enter into the system as only placeholders, comments, and descriptions, which the authors complete later.

This stage often is not a built-in part of a CMS and is handled by a third-party tool. The plethora of third-party design tools on the market can handle this stage of a content component's life cycle. In many cases, you can save your money and not buy these sometimes-expensive tools because, quite often, a simple paint program will suffice.

Authoring

Authoring is the process of acquiring content components for a Web site. It not only includes writing a content component from scratch, but also acquiring content from other sources and then loading it into the system.

It is possible for a CMS to receive some of its content components from a content feed and then directly make them available to the site without human intervention. Some sites want this content to be stored in their repository for a certain period of time. Others flush it out of their system as new content is received.

However, having all your content provided in this way is a surefire way of killing your Web site because most users come to a site for its uniqueness. Having content that's the same as everyone else's is boring, and a smart user will just go to the source of the content and leave out the middleman (your Web site).

In most cases, it is better to load the relevant content to your Web site, put it into your repository, and then let your authors improve it before publishing it. Most authors will be able to enhance the value of the original content by adding things such as user opinions and more in-depth analysis.

Most CMS authoring systems are text based. Other media types—such as images, video, and audio—are often authored by tools specific to them outside of the CMS. These media are then imported as complete content components that cannot be edited by the CMS itself.

Editing

After the content component is created, it often goes through multiple rounds of editing and rewriting until all appropriate people with authority think it is complete, correct, and ready to progress to the next stage.

This circular process of a content component's life cycle is where most errors are likely to be introduced if the repository does not have a CMS. It requires careful coordination between author and editor because each author and editor may be able to overwrite the work of the other. This coordination is where CMSs excel and why any decent-size Web site uses them.

A CMS can mitigate this problem effectively by using content tracking (covered in Chapter 2) and workflows (covered in Chapter 3).

Layout

After all the content components are completed, they are arranged on a Web page for viewing. A good CDA should have no real say in the layout of a content component. What a CDA should do is provide a way to make suggestions to the MMA about the layout and location it prefers for the content component.

Some MMAs allow the CDA to provide information about internal formatting of the content components themselves. For example, they may allow a content component to specify that a section of text should be bold or italic. Usually, though, they will not allow the content component to specify things such as font, text color, or size because the MMA should standardize them.

Testing

Now that you have your content component ready for viewing, you should test it.

Many first-time Web site developers overlook this activity, assuming that if the site comes up in a browser it must be working. They quickly learn that this isn't the case when they hear from users about missing or bad links, images with bad color, images that are too big or that don't show up, and a myriad of other possible problems. Some Web developers are not so lucky, and users simply do not come back to their Web sites.

Testing a Web site involves activities like following all the hyperlinks and image map links to make sure they go where you want, checking to make sure images match text, and verifying that Web forms behave as expected. You should examine each page to make sure it appears how you want. Something that many testers fail to do, until it bites them, is view the Web site using different browsers; after all, not all browsers are alike. Be careful of client-side scripting and fonts because browsers handle these differently as well.

Staging

After the site has been tested and is ready to go live, all the finished Web components move to a staging server to await replication to production.

The goal of a staging server is to make the transfer to production as fast and painless as possible so as to not interfere with active users. On smaller Web sites, this stage is often overlooked or ignored due to the additional cost of having to buy another server. On these smaller sites, after testing, new content components usually move directly to production without any staging.

Deployment

Obviously, you need to move the content to your live site periodically; otherwise, your site will stagnate very quickly.

The deployment procedure can be quite complex depending on the number of servers you have in your Web farm and whether you provide 24/7 access to your site.

Maintenance

The content management process does not end when the content components are deployed to the Web site. Content components frequently need to be updated with additional or more up-to-date information. You also may find an occasional mistake that made its way through the content component's life cycle and that needs correcting.

> **WARNING**   *A word to the wise: Never perform maintenance directly on a live, deployed system. If you do this, you are begging for trouble. The correct approach is to walk the content components through the entire life cycle, just like new content. You will find, if nothing else, that the logging provided by the version tracking system, discussed in Chapter 2, will help keep your site well documented. More important, though, by following the full life cycle, you will be able to use the rollback functionality provided by version control. Chapter 2 covers rollback as well.*

Archival

Once a content component is outdated or has reached the end of its usefulness, it should be archived. Archiving does not mean that a user cannot get access to the component; instead, it is accessible by way of an archive search of the site.

The number of people who access your site only for your archives might surprise you. Many people use the Internet for research, and having a large archive of information might be a good selling feature for a site.

The archival process can be automated so that you do not have to worry about examining all the content components on your site for dated material.

Removal

If a content component becomes obsolete and cannot be updated (or there is no need to update it), the content component needs to be removed.

Though the removal feature is available, unless something happens as drastic as a lawsuit for having the content on your site, the correct route is to archive the content component and allow it to be accessed through archives.

What now seems useless may turn out to be a gold mine later. I used to have complete sets of hockey cards in mint condition for the 1972 through 1976 seasons, but I threw them out, thinking them useless. Ouch!

Metacontent Management Application (MMA)

In an ideal CMS, the content and the delivery of a content component should be kept completely separate, hence the separation of the CMS administrative side into the CMA and the MMA. Each specializes in different things: the content and the delivery of the content.

The main reason to keep the content and delivery separate is that the CMA and the MMA have completely different workflows and groups of people using them. Remember the earlier argument about information versus applications and whether they are both part of a CMS? Well, it appears that even within the information part of content, you are going to have different groups of people and workflows. This gives you even more reason to keep applications out of the CMS mix because applications will complicate things further.

The editorial staff is the primary user of the CMA. The workflow of the CMA, as discussed earlier, directly relates to the life-cycle stages of a content component. There is little or no reference to how the content is to be displayed by the CDA in the CMA.

The MMA, on the other hand, is used by the creative or site-design staff and has a life cycle related specifically to the setting up of information pertaining to how the Web site is to look and feel. In fact, the MMA process does not care at all about the actual content to be delivered.

Metacontent Life Cycle

The MMA is an application that manages the full life cycle of metacontent. You might think of metacontent as information about the content components, in particular how the content components are laid out on a Web site.

The purpose of the MMA is to progress metacontent through its life cycle. The process closely resembles that of the CMA but with a completely different focus: the generation of metacontent instead of content components. Just like the CMA, at the end of each stage, the metacontent should be in a more mature and stable state. Here are some of the common high-level life-cycle stages (see Figure 1-3) that an MMA should address.

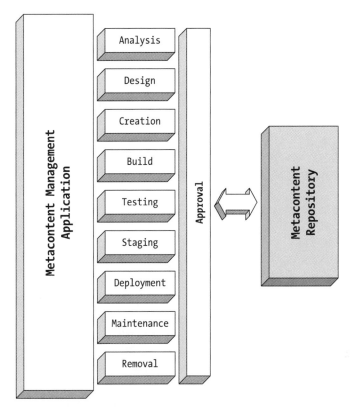

Figure 1-3. The metacontent management application

Approval

Before any life-cycle stage is completed and the next stage is to begin, someone with the authority to do so should approve the metacontent.

A committee or a board quite often does the approval of any major changes to metacontent rather than an individual, as you may find in a CMA. This is because any major change in the metacontent often has a significant impact on the look and feel of the entire Web site. The approval committee is often made up of representatives from all departments that have a vested interest in the Web site.

For minor changes, on the other hand, such as column adjustments or minor spacing fixes, an individual might have approval authority.

Analysis

Before making any changes to a Web site, some type of business analysis effort should take place.

Here are some common questions asked during analysis: What is the likely market response to the change? How will response time be affected by the change? Is the color-scheme change easy on the eyes? Is the layout too cluttered? Is the change really needed?

Analysis work is often done outside of the CMS because there are many good third-party tools to do Web analysis work. In fact, objective third-party consultants frequently do the analysis of Web sites.

Design

This describes the metacontent that will be deployed on the Web site, usually in great detail because the design often has to go through a committee to be approved.

Committees have the useful side effect of forcing the designer to be thorough because so many people want to make sure that what they want is incorporated and that they understand what others are doing (because it may affect them). Committees also, unfortunately, have the undesirable side effect of slowing the approval process as compared to individual approval.

Design frequently takes place outside the CMS. As with analysis, a plethora of third-party Web site design tools are on the market.

Creation

The creation of metacontent should always be based on the prior analysis and design work. Haphazard creation of metacontent is prone to failure. This is because metacontent is usually quite complex, and interaction with other metacontent frequently occurs. Without detailed analysis and design, many of the details will be missed, causing errors or, at the very least, a lot of rework.

Metacontent consists of any combination of templates, scripts, programs, and runtime dependency. Each of these is covered in detail in this chapter.

Build

Once all the pieces of metacontent are completed, depending on their type, they might need to be assembled together. In the case of .NET, most of the metacontent will be ASP.NET and C# files that require compiling.

This is a major difference between a CMA and an MMA because this stage usually requires a third-party tool outside of the CMS to complete.

Test

After the metacontent is created and built, it needs to be thoroughly tested.

Unlike content components, the testing of metacontent is extremely rigorous and cannot be overlooked at any cost. You will usually find that the testing of metacontent follows the standard software-development process: unit, string, system, and release test.

Stage

After the metacontent has been tested and is ready to go, it moves to a staging server to await replication to production.

The goal of a staging server is to make the transfer of metacontent to production as fast and painless as possible so as not to interfere with active users. On smaller Web sites, this stage is often overlooked or ignored due to the cost of buying another server; after testing, the metacontent is moved directly to production without any staging.

Deployment

Deployment is, obviously, the moving of metacontent to your live site.

The deployment procedure can be quite complex depending on the number of servers you have in your Web farm and whether you require 24/7 access to your site.

The deployment of metacontent, for many CMSs, requires the Web site to be temporarily shut down, hence the need for staging and a quick installation platform.

Maintenance

The life cycle of metacontent does not end when it moves to the Web site. Metacontent often needs to be fixed due to errors, tweaked for speed, or simply given a facelift due to a marketing decision.

WARNING   *A word to the wise (even though it was said earlier, I think it merits repeating): Never perform maintenance directly on a live, deployed system. If you do this, you are begging for trouble. The correct approach is to walk the metacontent components through the entire life cycle, just like new metacontent. By following the full life cycle, you will be able to use the rollback functionality provided by version control. With rollback, you can get your Web site back to its original stage before you introduce the new metacontent. This is very helpful, especially if the new metacontent introduces an even worse problem than the one you were originally trying to fix. Chapter 2 covers rollback in more detail.*

Removal

Once a piece of metacontent is no longer needed, it should be removed from the live site.

Removal is not the same as deletion; it is a good practice to keep old code in the repository. You never know when an old routine you wrote may be useful again or will be needed due to some unforeseen event.

Metacontent Types

The goal of the metacontent is to provide a simple, user-friendly, consistent interface to a Web site. It should not matter to the Web site user that he has selected text, a PDF file, an image, video, audio, or any other form of content component that the Web site supports.

The metacontent generated through the MMA workflow is any, or a combination of, the following.

Templates

These are usually in the form of HTML with placeholders for content components. Depending on the implementation, a template can even have
placeholders for other templates, allowing for a modular approach to developing
the look and feel of a Web site. Different types of content components may
require specific templates so that they can be placed on a Web page.

Scripts

A multitude of Web scripting languages are available today. Most CMSs support
at least one scripting language if not many. Scripting languages come in two
flavors: client side and server side. Client-side scripts run on the browser;
server-side scripts run on the server. Scripting is covering in Chapter 5 in
more detail.

Programs

Programs differ from scripts in that they are compiled before they are run on the
server, which allows them to be much faster. They also provide much more functionality than scripting languages because they can draw from all the
functionality provided by the operating system on which they are running. The
drawback is that they run only on the server side and, if used carelessly, can
cause slow response time due to slow network connections. There are now two
competing types of programming languages on the market: JSP/Java and the
.NET family of languages, the most prevalent of which will be Visual Basic .NET
and C#.

Runtime Dependencies

Though not directly related to displaying content components, this is also an
important part of the MMA. When the CMA adds content, it cannot be determined where or when it will be displayed. This being the case, you must be
careful when it comes to content links. Check dependencies to make sure content component links exist before enabling them. If you don't do this, your site
may have dead links, which are very annoying to users (to the point that
users may not return to your site if they encounter dead links too often).

Content Delivery Application (CDA)

The content delivery application's job is to take the content components out of the CMS repository and display them, using metacontent, to the Web site user. CMS users usually do nothing with the CDA other than install and configure it. The reason for this is that it runs off the data you created with the CMA and the MMA.

A good CDA is driven completely by the metacontent. This means that the metacontent determines what is displayed and how it is displayed. There is virtually an unlimited number of ways for the metacontent to determine what and how content components are displayed. It all depends on how imaginative the creative staff is at templating, scripting, and/or programming.

Because no display information is hard-coded in the CDA, the layout, color, spacing, fonts, and so on can also be changed dynamically using metacontent, just as the Web site's content can be changed using content components. This means that, with careful planning, a Web site does not have to come down even to change the site's look and feel.

The metacontent also determines the navigation through the Web site using hyperlinks and image map links. The only thing a good CDA needs to know about navigating the Web site is how to load the default start page and how to load a page by a correctly formatted URL address.

The CDA has only read access to the repository, thus providing security to the Web site because a user will not be able to change the content components she is viewing. Read access to files and databases also has the benefit that locking does not occur on the files or database records, thus allowing multiple users to access the Web site at the same time without contention. It also means that because the data will not be changing (unless by way of deployment), caching can be implemented to speed up the retrieval of content. Caching is examined further later in this chapter.

One capability that a CDA should provide to the Web user is a search function on the active and archived content components. Many good search algorithms are available. Their implementation depends on the storage method used by the repository. The type of searches can range from a list of predetermined keys or attributes to a full content component search. Searching is also covered later in this chapter.

What Is a Content Management System?

Okay, this chapter has come full circle. Here is our original definition: A content management system is a system that manages the content components of a Web site.

It makes more sense now, does it not? Let's expand this definition to what this book will use as the definition: A *content management system (CMS)* is a system made up of a minimum of three applications: content management, metacontent management, and content delivery. Their purpose is to manage the full life cycle of content components and metacontent by way of a workflow in a repository, with the goal of dynamically displaying content in a user-friendly fashion on a Web site.

If you are like me and find it easier to visualize what you are trying to understand, Figure 1-4 displays a simple CMS flowchart.

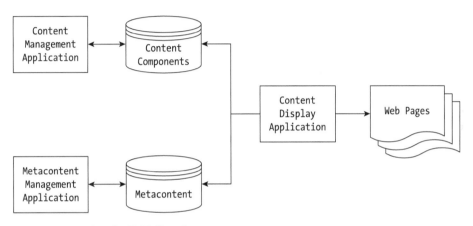

Figure 1-4. A simple CMS flowchart

As you can see, the content management application maintains all aspects of content components, and the metacontent management application maintains the same for metacontent. The content delivery application generates Web pages by extracting content components and metacontent from their respective repositories.

It's pretty simple, no? So why are people spending $500,000 to $1.5 million (or more) for a CMS? Well, in truth, it is easy to visualize, but those little boxes in Figure 1-4 contain a lot of complex functionality. It's what is in those three little boxes—and an assortment of additional elements linked to those boxes—that can cause the price tag to be so high.

Some Common CMS Features

Not all CMSs are created equal, but all CMSs should have a CMA, MMA, and CDA (maybe not using the same names, but at the very least the same functionality). The functionality may not be separated as laid out in this chapter, but the basic maintenance of the content components and metacontent, as well as the display of the content components using metacontent, should all be found in the CMS.

That being said, CMSs can include a lot more functionality, and many CMSs do. The more expensive the CMS is, the more functionality is usually available. The question you should be asking if you are on a tight budget and planning to buy a CMS is this: Do I need the additional functionality that this expensive CMS provides, or can I make do with less?

Many consultants will tell you to buy the expensive one now because, in the end, it will be cheaper. Pardon my French, but hogwash! More expensive only means the consultants can get more money for installing and implementing it. With technology today, anything you buy will most likely be obsolete before a year is up, if not in two. During that time, your expensive CMS will have gone through multiple releases. Unless you paid for those releases in advance or have a maintenance contact that gives you free updates, you will be paying through the nose to get those updates. In the long run, buying expensive is just expensive.

The better route is to buy what you need for the next year and can afford now, and then upgrade to more power when you need it and when you can better afford it. Most CMSs have routes to upgrade from their competitors' software. That probably will not be an issue, however, because the package you buy either has an upgrade path of its own or will have grown during the year and probably will have, by then, the functionality you need.

The real reason to buy an expensive CMS is that you need all the functionality in the CMS now, not because of some presumed need in the future.

The following sections examine some of the more common functionalities you might find in a CMS.

Standard Interface for Creating, Editing, Approving, and Deploying

There is no doubt that only having to learn how to do something once is easier than having to learn it multiple times. After you learn one part of the standard interface provided by a CMS, all you then have to learn for a new interface is the differences, which should only be the needed additional functionality to complete the task associated with that new interface.

This might seem like an obvious thing to have, but you will find that some CMSs don't have a standard interface. The reason is that a lot of software that is a CMS, or that contains CMS functionality, came from different packages that were merged into one. Each of these packages once had its own look and feel and has now been patched together in an attempt to make one coherent package. With time, the more mature packages have successfully created a standard interface, but some are still working on it.

Common Repository

Putting your content components and metacontent in one place makes them easier to maintain, track, and find. It also provides a more secure way of storing your data. Having your data localized means you have a smaller area to protect from intruders. The more your data is dispersed through your system, the more entry points there are for attack.

Some CMSs provide their own repositories to store your data. Others allow you to retain your existing repositories or have you buy or build your own and then extract from them.

The major factor you should consider when selecting a CMS is whether you already have a well-established repository or you are starting from scratch. If you are starting from an existing database, you may find it easier to implement a CMS that enables you to retain it as opposed to trying to import the existing repository into a CMS that uses its own repository.

A few CMSs still don't use a common repository. Instead, they provide a common controlling file, or the like, that keeps track of where your dispersed information is stored.

Version Control, Tracking, and Rollback

Keeping track of the versions of your content is a very important feature of any CMS. The importance of keeping track of content versions cannot be stressed enough, especially if multiple people will be accessing the same content at the same time.

Without a version-control system, it is common for versions of content components or metacontent to get out of sync. For example, author A enters a content component. Then, editor B edits the content component and approves it. Then, author A updates the original copy of the content component with some changes and overwrites editor B's approved content component. Suddenly, the content component is possibly inaccurate or is published with spelling, grammar, or other errors. With version control, this will not happen. Not only does the version control notify the editor of the changes, but it also tracks who made the changes.

Rollback is one added bit of security for situations in which something does slip through the content-approval process. It enables a CMS to revert to a previous stage before the erroneous content entered the system. This functionality is important enough that it gets a chapter of its own in this book (Chapter 2). That chapter covers version control, tracking, and rollback in great detail.

Workflow

All CMSs have a workflow. A key to a good CMS is how simple and flexible this workflow system is. Many CMSs provide the capability to create your own user-defined workflow, whereas others provide the standard hard-coded create, edit, approve, and release workflow. Some CMSs go as far as providing proactive notifications and an audit trail for editorial control and tracking.

It is quite common to have the workflow and version-control system tightly coupled. This provides a more comprehensive platform for managing the flow and staging of content among all the groups involved.

Because it is a key function of all CMSs, workflow is covered in detail in Chapter 3.

Dynamic Page Generation

This functionality is the key differentiator between content and document management systems. A CMS generates pages dynamically from a repository of content components based on the layouts defined by metacontent. In a document management system, complete Web pages are stored. The content of the pages is defined before the user ever accesses the Web site.

Dynamic page generation is the process of a CDA figuring out what content components and metacontent, when combined, satisfy the user's request. Using dynamic page generation can cause the exact same request by different users to generate completely different Web pages. This is because of other factors such as the time of the request, the ZIP code the user resides in, and other personalization settings. Dynamic page generation is covered in Chapter 13 and again in Chapter 15.

Personalization

This is probably one of the most abused terms when it comes to describing additional functionality in a CMS. It means anything from being able to write a user's name out when he reenters a site or navigates around it, to providing user-specific content based on personal preferences and navigational habits.

Personalization is a major reason why many people return to a Web site. At one time, seeing her name on a Web page was all that was needed for a user to come back. Now, with far more sophisticated users, you need a personalization engine built into the CMS that helps the user retrieve the information she wants, even when she is not looking for anything (in other words, a personalization engine that knows what the user wants and provides it without her having to request it).

There are so many different types and levels of personalization that Chapter 4 is devoted to this topic.

Cache Management

Before .NET, cache management would have been the scariest topic in this book, requiring multiple chapters just to explain it. Happily, I can tell you that it is handled, if you code properly, by .NET. This book explains in detail the correct way to code so that you don't have to worry about this nightmare.

What is *cache management?* It is the process of storing preconfigured pages in memory and on disk for faster retrieval. Most CMSs have their own version of this process in place so that common pages don't have to be repeatedly generated. CMS systems are often selected partially for their strength at cache management. But now, .NET—or to be more accurate, ASP.NET—is leveling the playing field in this area.

Content Conversion

Some of the more function-rich (you may also read this as expensive) CMSs provide the capability to convert files from one format to the required format of their repository. For example, they can convert Microsoft Word or WordPerfect into straight ANSI text or bring in Excel spreadsheets and load them as HTML tables without any special actions by the user.

This functionality allows a user to create content with his favorite tools, thus saving him the time of having to learn a new tool and then worry about how to convert his content so that it works in the CMS.

Search Integration

A lot of CMSs use third-party search engines to do their searches for them. Doing this makes sense because it allows the CMS people to specialize in the thing they do best, content management, while allowing a different group that specializes in searching to do that.

Some CMSs have their own built-in search engines. They often are not as advanced as what's available from a third party, but they have the benefit of saving the user money by not forcing him to buy a search program and then have to integrate it.

Monitoring, Analyzing, and Reporting Content and Web Site Hits

Known as *click-stream analysis,* the tracking of site usage is the process of analyzing how a user enters a site, how she leaves, and what pages she accesses between the two points. In the process, it provides information such as how many users access a specific page or what is the predominate start and end page of a Web site visit.

Monitoring Web site usage is essential for sales and marketing. Personalization engines often use it as well. Many CMSs don't have good reporting capabilities on Web site usage, which makes sense because site usage has nothing to do with content management and thus relies on third-party tools that specialize in Web usage analysis to provide it. Numerous third-party tools on the market do click-stream analysis and will, in most cases, provide more valuable information than the CMS does.

What Are the Benefits of a CMS?

In an ideal world, the CMS would be the core of all e-business infrastructures. The CMA would handle the creation, acquisition, maintenance, and retirement of all content components for the Web site. The MMA would handle the maintenance of the metacontent, which indicates how the content components are displayed. The CDA would handle the actual display of the content components. All three elements would provide hooks so that third-party features could augment the basic content management functionality, but everything would ultimately go through the CMS.

You might think of the CMS as the switchboard operator of a Web site. It receives all incoming content, puts it on hold (stores it in a repository), routes it to the appropriate Web page for display, and then finally closes the connection (archives or removes content).

The following are some of the more obvious and common benefits of having the CMS as the core of a Web site.

Control and Consistency

With a CMS, you can enforce such corporate Web site standards as fonts, styles, and layouts. All content enters the system without any formatting. It is up to the CMS, or more accurately the CDA, to format and display the content components maintained by the CMA, based on the metacontent provided by the MMA.

Authors can no longer change the look and feel of the Web site as they see fit. All content components they write must now go through the workflow provided by the CMS. If handled properly, the CMA process should remove any formatting provided by the author—other than things such as boldface and italics—and replace it with the corporate standards.

Global Web Site Update Access

Most CMSs provide the capability to access the editorial functionality from anywhere around the world by way of the Internet. This enables the editorial staff to work remotely, as long as each staff member has a computer and an Internet connection. This alone can be a major cost savings because Web site operators don't have to provide office space for their staff, who can work from home. Just think of the benefits for a news Web site. A reporter can be right at an event and, with an Internet connection, cover the story live.

The editorial staff member can only access the CDA Web site by way of standard HTML Web forms. This method is secure because of the role-based authorization used. The staff member can only access the functionality associated with his role. Because the content repository is stored behind the company's firewall, the data will not be accessible outside of the access provided by the HTML forms. As long as the password systems are not compromised at the highest levels, no damage will happen.

WARNING   *Please note that no Web site is truly 100 percent secure. Hackers are always finding new destructive ways of getting into Web sites. It is a sad thing that individuals enjoy destroying other people's hard work, but alas, it appears to happen way too often. It is best to consult a Web security expert if you want to get the maximum security currently available because her job is to try to keep up with the ways hackers do their destructive work.*

No Workstation Installation Is Required

Accessing many CMSs requires only a PC with any standard browser. Gone are the days when you had to install client software on all the editorial staff's workstations. The interfaces now are standard HTML Web forms that can be run on any computer—whether it is an Intel running UNIX, Linux, or Windows; a Macintosh running Mac OS X; or even a mainframe running MVS—as long as it can support a standard Web browser.

Adding or removing a person from your editorial staff is as easy as adding or removing his password from the CMS authorization database.

No Knowledge of HTML or Programming Is Required to Author Content

CMSs try to separate the content from how it is displayed. This will allow a writer to hone her craft and let designers do what they do best, which of course is Web site design. This benefit allows a Web site to hire the best writers and not just the best writers who know HTML.

Having knowledge of HTML will not hurt, though, because some CMSs allow boldfacing, underlining, and italicizing of text in the content component, and the best way to do that is directly in the component itself. An author should realize, though, that depending on the CMS, any formatting he may do is only a suggestion and may be removed during the component's migration through the workflow or by the CDA itself when it's displayed.

Multiple Concurrent Users

CMSs are client-server based, allowing multiple clients to access the server at the same time. Another way of looking at it is that this allows multiple people to work at the same time on the Web site. Each of these users can be doing any of the functions allowed by her role. This means that one user can be creating a content component while another is editing metacontent and a third is viewing content on the site.

Each user of the site can work without having to worry about someone else messing up or interfering with his activities. In fact, a user probably would not even be aware that someone else is working with the CMS.

Improved Collaboration

It is common for CMSs to have both version-control and workflow systems; therefore, it is even safe to have multiple people working on the same content at the same time. It is completely possible that one person can be writing some content while another is creating the graphics and a third is figuring out how best to lay it all out.

It is probably not a good practice to have two people editing a story at the same time because that would require the changes to be merged at the end. Typically, a content component should move seamlessly through the workflow, navigating back and forth between author and editor until it is in a condition to be approved by someone authorized to do so.

Content Component Reuse

It is usually a good idea just to archive a content component when it becomes old, outdated, or irrelevant, as opposed to removing it. The life of a content component may not always be over when you think it is.

For example, images can be reused without any changes in a different story if they match the other content components making up the story. Another type of reuse occurs when a story you have already covered in the past resurfaces. Having this information in the system may save an author time in research and, if nothing else, provides a good starting place for doing the research. Also, users interested in how a story developed may want to look at your archives to see past content components about the topic in question.

Having a well-stocked archive may bring many unexpected users to your site, especially those doing research.

Personalized Experience

One of the most obvious benefits of a CMS is that it provides the capability to add personalization. A CMS mixed with a third-party personalization engine, or even a CMS with its own simple personalization engine, can do wonders in attracting users.

People like being catered to. Entering a Web site that greets you by name will give you a cheap thrill, the first few times at least. Being able to set up a home page just as you like and having it still be that way when you get back is an even bigger thrill. Knowing that a Web site is helping you find the information you are looking for—or is providing you the information you want without having to do the searches yourself—should bring you back.

When Do You Need a Commercial CMS?

The first and most obvious factor in determining whether you need a commercial CMS is the amount of content your Web site contains. You need a CMS system when there are simply too many content components to process by hand. It is true that content management can help with even small Web sites, but you simply cannot justify the cost of a commercial CMS until the Web site is larger.

So, when is a Web site large enough to merit a commercial CMS? A large Web site is one that cannot be managed in the head of your Webmaster. This means that when your Webmaster can no longer quickly figure out where a specific content component is stored or when she can no longer handle all the incoming information, you might want to start looking around for a commercial CMS. A ballpark figure would be around 500 to 1,000 different content components.

Another clue that you might need a commercial CMS is when your Web site is made up of many different types of content components. If your site is made up of 500 to 1,000 text files only, it is easier to maintain than if it is made up of 500 to 1,000 content components of different types such as text, images, video, audio, and banner ads.

If your site has a lot of changes—even if your site is not that large—it may merit a commercial content management system. For example, if your site experiences 100 or more changes per week—in the form of additions, updates, and deletions—it may be too much to handle without a CMS.

The last thing you might want to look at is the frequency of Web site design changes. Design changes can cause major headaches for a Webmaster without a CMS. If your site has frequent look-and-feel changes, you might want to consider a CMS, especially if your site is starting to become large.

NOTE *This section is talking about commercial CMSs. With the release of this book, even small Web sites can benefit from a CMS like the one developed in this book. The return on investment (ROI) is much better on the price of this book as compared to the cost of a CMS, even for a very small Web site. If you follow along with this book and build one from the information found in it, you will have the groundwork for a decent homegrown CMS. When your site becomes large and profitable, you can move to a commercial CMS if you need to.*

Summary

This chapter provided a detailed introduction to what a content management system is. It discussed what content is, what a content component is, and what the most common elements of a CMS are. It then looked at what a CMS is as a whole and described additional common features and benefits. Finally, it wrapped up with a discussion of when you would likely need a commercial CMS.

The next chapter covers version control, version tracking, and rollback.

CHAPTER 2

Version Control

Version control, which also encompasses version tracking and rollback, is an essential capability of any good content management system (CMS), for it is the framework on which the content management application (CMA) and metacontent management application (MMA) stand. Without version control, a Web site would have a hard time maintaining its integrity. The process of randomly adding content components and metacontent to a site would, in the long run, most likely cause the Web site to run amuck or, at the very least, provide the Web site user with a very inconsistent viewing experience.

CMSs can implement version control in many different ways. Some CMSs rely on third-party version control packages. Most, though, have version control built directly into them. Version control usually is tightly coupled with the CMS's workflow system, often to the point where a user might not realize that there even is version control in the CMS.

You might be thinking that you only need version control for large Web sites with multiple designers, coders, and writers, but you would be wrong. Even for a Web site managed by one person, version control can add many benefits to a CMS.

This chapter covers all aspects of version control, explains its roles in a CMS, and then finishes up with some of its benefits.

What Is Version Control?

There are two different approaches to version control: an easy one and a complex one. The easy approach is available to almost all CMSs, including those that follow the complex approach. Using the complex one frequently requires the integration of a third-party version control system, or in the case of expensive commercial CMSs, the third-party version control system may already be repurchased and integrated. So what are these approaches?

Easy Version Control

Easy version control operates with the premise that only one person can have access to a piece of content at any one time (see Figure 2-1). This type of version control relies on keeping locks on the content. Basically, the process is that someone checks out the content from the repository, makes his changes, and then returns it to the repository. Then the next person has her turn at the content.

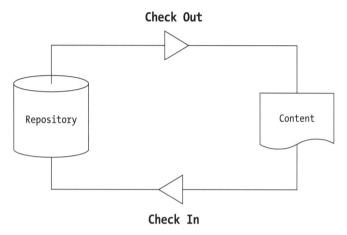

Check Out

Check In

Figure 2-1. Easy version control

In most situations, this process isn't as restrictive as it might seem. Think about it this way: An author writes some content, an editor edits it, and finally it is approved. In every step of this process, the next person in the stream did not need the content until the prior person finished with it.

Version control by this method is simple, easy to understand, and straightforward. As you will see in Chapter 3, easy version control is all that is needed to implement a workflow system.

Complex Version Control

Complex version control operates with the premise that anybody can have access to the content at any time as long as only one master copy of each piece of content exists (see Figure 2-2). Any checked-out version of the content is only a copy, and when the content is checked back in, all changes are merged with the master copy.

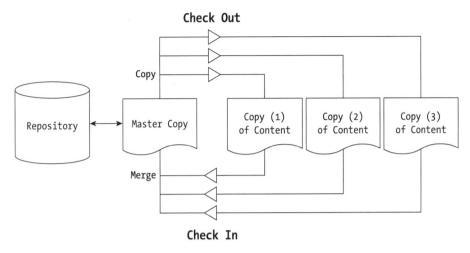

Figure 2-2. Complex version control

This process allows multiple people to check out a piece of content at the same time, make all the changes they think are necessary, and then check the content back in. The version control software then merges all the checked-in copies of the content with the master copy. The more advanced version control software often handles all the merging on its own or with a little help from the person who checked the content in.

Though complex version control seems to be more common in the expensive commercial CMSs, the only reason I could see needing this type of version control would be for a huge piece of content with multiple authors writing at the same time. Something like the online help provided by Microsoft comes to mind as an example of where complex version control could come in handy. I doubt, though, that Microsoft uses the version control built into its CMS to build the online help file. My guess is that Microsoft uses an add-on tool outside of the CMS and imports it when it is completed.

In most cases, simple version control should be good enough. The option is available, however, for those Web sites that do want this complex version control because many CMSs will allow you to integrate a complex third-party version control system. This type of version control is really more suited for writing software.

How Does Version Control Store Content?

Most text content, when checked into the CMS repository, is stored using *deltas*. This means that only the changes made between the time it was checked out and the time it was checked back in are stored. Storing by deltas is more efficient when it comes to disk storage because there is no need to have multiple copies of the same content stored in the repository, even if there are many versions of the content.

Because no complete copy of the content is stored in the repository, the version control software must also be able to build a piece of content using all its stored delta information. Thinking logically, this also means it is possible to check out any version you want. All the version control software would have to do is apply sequentially only the deltas up to the version requested.

Binary content, when checked into some of the more powerful CMS repositories, is sometimes stored using deltas, but due to binary file complexity, the binary content versions more often are stored as complete files. In this case, the checkout process simply has to grab the correct version of the binary content from the repository with no delta processing.

What Is Version Tracking?

Version tracking takes version control a step further. You can think of it as a process of notarizing the versions of the checked-in and checked-out content.

The main purpose of version tracking is to keep track of all information related to the changes that happen during the life cycle of a piece of content. This involves noting things such as when changes were made, who made the changes, what changes were made, and possibly why the changes were made.

Why would you want to go to the added effort of tracking all these changes? Doesn't this just complicate things? Why not just keep the most up-to-date version of the content in the repository and ignore the past versions?

Version tracking provides a protected running log or audit of who has accessed a piece of content. When someone checks in or out some content, her ID is automatically recorded. This is a very useful tool if you need to keep track of who did what to the content. This information, for example, could be used to figure out whom to pay for a piece of content. It could also be used to track down who caused damage to a piece of content, perhaps due to a hacker figuring out his password. Because you know which role is causing the damage, it is possible to delete the user or change the password.

It is possible, using a simple tool that shows the difference between two pieces of content, to figure out what changes have been made between versions. In fact, most version tracking systems have this functionality built right in. A better approach is for the person who made the changes to record them in the version control's built-in comment field while she is checking it back in. This information is added to the content's log file. Now, all someone has to do to see all the changes that occurred to a piece of content is to look at its log file.

Using this built-in login functionality also makes it possible to pass information back and forth between parties that are working together on the same piece of content. An added bonus is that the information links directly to the content, and there is no need to embed notes directly into the content. (Someone would have to remember to remove these notes before the content goes live.) This simple but powerful tool is very beneficial if used by an author and an editor to communicate what needs to be done to content before it can move to the approval stage.

The CMS can also use version tracking to track where the content is in the workflow and whether it has moved or is about to move on to the next workflow stage. To accomplish this, the version tracking system needs to add the current workflow stage and the current date and time to the information it stores during the content check-in process. Providing this information can be done in one of two ways: by changing the version tracking software to have these as input fields during check-in and checkout or by mandating a standard format in the provided comments field.

If you add the workflow stage and checkout date and time to the version tracking, the version tracking system will be able to show whether any content has somehow become stagnant in the workflow. To see if any content is stagnant, periodically have the CMS examine how long a piece of content has spent in its current workflow stage. If it appears to have spent too long in its current stage, the CMS can trigger some type of event, probably an e-mail, to notify you of the stagnation.

A feature of version tracking that could be useful is the capability to tag content as a version group. This will make all content with a particular tag part of the same version. For example, some Web sites like to release their content in groups or releases instead of releasing individual content as it becomes available. With tagging, version tracking enables a CMS to mark a set of content as a release, and then the CMS can deploy the release to the live site as one group.

What Is Rollback?

As previously pointed out, version tracking keeps track of all the changes made to a piece of content. *Rollback* provides the capability to change the current version of a piece of content or a tagged group of content back to its prior version.

A rollback is most often done on production-deployed content components and metacontent. A rollback of a Web site changes all the content back to how it was before it was updated.

The rollback process is usually safe because it takes all content and replaces it with a previous stable version. A rollback done on a Web site usually requires shutting down the Web site temporarily so that there's no chance of a user accidentally causing damage by using prerollback content. For example, if a user is entering data into a form when a rollback occurs, it is possible that, if the form has changed in the new version, the submitted information could corrupt the system.

You might be thinking, Why would someone want to roll the system back to an older version? Here is a possibly devastating example. Imagine you are the Webmaster for an e-retailer site that sells expensive memory chips, and your marketing brand says that you honor all sales on the site. One fine morning, your sales representative notifies you that hundreds of people are buying your normally $350-priced memory chips for $3.50. To save your company, you order an emergency rollback of the site to the previous version where the price was $350. Sound farfetched? Nope. Something very much like this has happened to several well-known e-retailers.

You can also use a rollback for less drastic reasons as well. An author may realize that his facts are wrong in an updated version of his story and decide to rollback to the previous version of the story. Correcting this version is easier than having to correct the current version.

The Roles of Version Control in a CMS

Version control has many roles when it is integrated into a CMS. All of these roles, one way or another, are related to coordination and/or efficiency gained by implementing the version control system. The following are three of the more visible roles of version control found in a CMS.

Enabling Team Collaboration

The primary role of version control in a CMS is to provide a better foundation for team collaboration. With the myriad of content components and metacontent that make up a typical Web site, it is virtually impossible for one person to build a half-decent Web site on her own.

During the process of building a good Web site, you will most likely need the skills of an artist, writer, lawyer, layout designer, coder, and many others. Few people have all these skills. True, for a small Web site you might be able to get by on the skill of one person, but then this site will probably be made up of only a handful of pages and have no real need for a CMS anyway. Heck, a person that manages a site this small probably isn't even going to read this book.

To build a good Web site, you will need the skills of multiple people. As anyone who has ever worked in a group can tell you, good teamwork is key to getting anything done. Version control is the first piece of the puzzle for getting team members to work efficiently together and not get in one another's way.

Assuming that the CMS you are using implements simple version control, as most CMSs do at a minimum, you can be assured that only one person is working on any piece of content at any particular time.

This may not seem like a big deal until you try to create a piece of content using more than one person at a time. Unless you have complex version control software, I can virtually guarantee that at least one of your content components will be mangled, except perhaps in the off chance that you are lucky enough to have a good editor to clean up after the two or more authors have finished their portions of the content.

Oh, did I forget to mention that while the editor is working on the content, the authors are not supposed to be making any changes? Unfortunately, without content locking, there is nothing stopping an author from making more changes to the content. Depending on when the author makes her changes, it is possible that—without proper coordination—the content that the editor was updating or the author was working on could be lost.

Now, add the complication that the authors, editors, approvers, testers, and so on can be anywhere around the world, in different time zones, and communicating using only e-mail, and you can see that coordination can quickly become a nightmare. You can simplify coordination by adding version tracking to your CMS arsenal. By using the check-in comments function, you can let the next person know exactly what you did with the content and what you expect the next person to do with the content—without having to open the content component itself. Not only is coordination eased, but also the content is fully documented so that, at a later date, someone can go back and see the changes as well as the flow the content went through to be deployed.

Enhancing Site Management

Something that has not been discussed so far about version control and version tracking is the assortment of reports they provide. A few of the reports focus on a range of information that an editorial site manager or Webmaster can use to help administer his site.

One report that comes in handy keeps track of all the content that each member of your staff has accessed or made modifications to. You can use this report to see which team members are most productive. You can also use it to see which team members let the most errors slip through if you cross-reference it with a content error report. This report can come in handy when it is time to do employee reviews because you have a running history of every task that each person did.

One of the most common reports is simply a list of all the content currently locked in the CMS, who has control of the lock, and when the lock was created. A site manager can use this information to figure out the number of content components in the pipeline, although by itself this does not provide too much help.

Now, if you tweak the information generated by this report a little, you will get a set of reports that can be really handy. By adding the current workflow stage to the standard information stored by the version tracking system, you now know exactly where all the content components and metacontent are in the pipeline. If you add estimated completion dates and times to the version tracking system, you now have powerful scheduling capabilities.

With the additional information, you can generate the following:

- *A report that enables you to organize the workload of the authors and editors:* This report shows which authors and editors are available, which are busy, and which will soon become available. With this information, you can schedule time as new content enters the pipeline.

- *A report that shows when content approval is pending:* This will allow you to manage the content-approval schedule. If there is a special piece of content that you need to streamline through the pipeline for some reason, you can set an event flag for when it is ready for approval. Then, when it hits the ready-for-approval stage, you can immediately forward it to the appropriate staff member to get it approved.

- *A report that shows when content is stuck in the pipeline for some reason:* It becomes readily noticeable that content is not flowing properly through the pipeline when the estimated completion date has passed and the content has not passed on to its next life-cycle stage. It is possible to set an event flag to notify the appropriate people of this event so that it can be resolved.

- *A report that shows when content is ready for deployment:* This report can be cross-referenced with what is later deployed to make sure that all content was deployed successfully.

Speeding Up Content Development

You cannot get authors and editors to work faster than they are physically capable of, but it is possible to shorten the time that content is in an inactive state, such as awaiting editing, corrections, approval, testing, or deployment. Minimizing time is accomplished by automatically generating an event to the system, notifying the CMS the instant that content is checked back into the repository. This event would trigger the creation of an e-mail, for example, to notify the next person in line for the content that it is now available to be worked on. Without this automated system, content developers could spend a considerable amount of time looking for—or simply waiting around until someone hands them—content to work on.

An advanced system might even be able to handle some events itself without human intervention. For example, an automated testing tool could be used instead of a person. If the confidence level is not high that the tool will catch all errors, it is still possible to use a human tester. This tester can have his workload reduced, however, because he will know that certain things have already been tested.

You can completely automate deployment so that after a piece of content passes its final approval stage, it is automatically deployed to the production Web server.

Benefits of Version Control and Tracking

There is, of course, version control's obvious benefit of helping a Web site avoid the chaos of having anyone changing anything at any time. As previously pointed out, content locking allows only one person to access a piece of content at any one time. Version tracking captures who accessed a piece of content and when and why it was accessed throughout its entire life cycle.

There are many other benefits of version control, and some of the more obvious need to be pointed out. Most of the following were noted earlier in this chapter—they are summarized here again.

Improved Communications

Version tracking allows you to automate the communication process between all the parties associated with a piece of content. The automatic generation and routing of e-mails when checking in a content component or metacontent, combined with the entering of all required communications into the version tracking system, should help ensure a smooth transition between all content life-cycle stages.

Version tracking also provides a complete log of all communications associated with each piece of content in one easy-to-access location. This makes all information about any particular piece of content available to anyone who is authorized and needs it.

Enhanced Workflow

Version control and tracking should work closely with the workflow system of a CMS. By providing content component and metacontent locking and logging, it helps encourage and maintain good workflow practices.

Each stage of a workflow has distinct starting and stopping points due to the locking functionality provided by the version control system. Because only one person is working on the content at any particular time, there is no overlap in the development process and thus no backtracking to get all parts of a piece of content in sync.

As pointed out earlier in this chapter, version control and tracking also can be used to automate portions of the workflow process to minimize human involvement.

Protected Repository

When you use version control, the only way to enter content into the repository should be by way of the version control system.

Using the check-in/checkout process provided by version control, you now ensure that shared content is not accidentally overwritten in the team environment required by a Web site.

Even if the version control system lets multiple people edit the same content, the content is still merged into a single version before being returned to the repository.

Enforced Structure

The environment for developing content is more structured and consistent among all stages of the content's workflow.

There is a consistent pattern of checking out content from the repository, making changes, and then checking the content back into the repository. There is no haphazard selection of content and no random entering of content back into the system.

Version control helps maintain the workflow structure. A person with a particular role cannot check out a piece of content until the content is checked in by someone else and is moved into a workflow stage where her role has the authority to check it out.

Reduced Number of Defects

As a result of the far more structured environment provided by version control for updating content, accidental errors caused by content overwrites, manual merging of content, or lack of communication between all parties maintaining the content will be reduced, if not totally eliminated.

Summary

This chapter covered in detail all aspects of version control. It started by describing the three parts of version control: control, tracking, and rollback. Then it covered what roles version control plays in a CMS. Finally, it wrapped up with the benefits of having version control in a CMS. The next chapter continues with workflows.

CHAPTER 3
Workflow

ARE ANY OF THE FOLLOWING ITEMS TRUE about your current Web content development system?

- You have a high dependency on paper.

- Your system is labor intensive.

- Frequently, many of your content components get lost or are delayed due to being temporarily misplaced.

- When content gets returned for fixing, the only way to know what needs to be fixed is by interrupting the person who returned the content component and asking him what the problem was.

- There is no way to track the status of your content components.

- The only way to find out what someone has to work on next is by asking the people on staff who usually route content if they are finished.

- Every staff member needs training about the rules of how content components are routed.

- The process of creating content components is never done the same way twice.

- Each new employee has a large learning curve to conquer before she can create a piece of content.

- There is no way to keep track of how much it costs or how long it takes to build a content component.

If several of these statements are true, most likely you are not using a content management system (CMS), your CMS does not have a workflow, or you are not using your CMS's workflow correctly.

The solution to these problems is using a good workflow system, and to put it bluntly, you will not be able to develop much of a Web site without a workflow to develop your content.

This chapter shows you how to alleviate all of these problems and describes everything you need to know about workflows.

What Is a Workflow?

You can apply a workflow to almost any business activity done by a group of people. Let's quickly examine what a generic workflow is before you delve into a CMS workflow.

The first step in understanding what a workflow is requires breaking the word "workflow" into its two parts—*work* and *flow*. By examining these two words, you begin to get a high-level understanding of what it means. The word "work" brings to mind groups of people trying to complete some type of task or activity. Each person is usually allocated a certain task or a set of tasks. The word "flow," on the other hand, brings to mind smooth, steady, constant, forward movement. The first thing you probably think of is a stream or a river.

Merging the words "work" and "flow" together, you get a group of people working together, each having tasks that run smoothly and in support of a common goal.

NOTE *A workflow is a set of tasks performed in a sequential or parallel manner by more than one person, with a goal of reaching a common objective.*

To have a flow, you have to have more than one task. There really is not any point in creating a workflow of one activity because that would simply be a single task. The tasks themselves can flow sequentially or in parallel. This means that one task can either lead to another or run at the same time as another. As the term "flow" suggests, the task must transition from one person to another, so a workflow must involve a group of people. The final outcome of a workflow is reaching a common objective or goal. This means that all the tasks will eventually join at a single endpoint (see Figure 3-1).

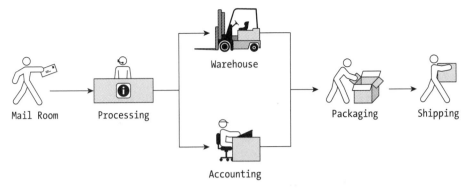

Figure 3-1. A simple order-fulfillment workflow

So, what then is a CMS workflow? It is simply the flow of all tasks done by the editorial and creative staffs that moves a content component or metacontent through its life cycle. In other words, it is the mapping out and completing of every stage that a piece of content goes through, from conception to retirement.

You might be thinking, or hoping, that there is only one such workflow. That, of course, would be too easy. Different types of content have different workflows. Some have long, detailed workflows; others have brief, simple ones. Fortunately, many of the workflows are very similar or can follow—or are forced to follow—a common workflow. You will explore some of the more common CMS workflows later in this chapter.

Workflow Components

Most CMS workflows are broken up into at least two components: the administrative component that creates the workflow definition and the actual engine that runs the workflow for the CMS. The names of these components will differ for each CMS, but the functionality should be available in some form.

Workflow Definition Application (WDA)

The *workflow definition application (WDA)* is the component of the CMS's workflow system that enables a user to create, modify, and delete the available workflows.

This component can add a lot of power to a CMS because it gives the CMS's configuration the capability to customize the way components are built by the editorial and creative staffs. Because a workflow can be configured however you want, the workflow can be defined exactly as it was done manually before the workflow was implemented. Learning curves in using the new system are reduced because users don't have to learn a new workflow. There will probably be less resistance to the workflow system as well. This is because the user will see the workflow system as a helpful tool instead of something that's changing how everything is done.

Many WDAs are implemented by dragging icons around on the screen, with each icon representing a different task or activity in the workflow. Once all the tasks are laid out, each task is then assigned a role in charge of completing it. The role can be a person or, preferably, a group of people. It can also be an automated role, in which the computer handles all aspects of the task. The final step in defining the workflow is specifying the notification process of the transition between tasks. For example, will an e-mail or a page be sent, or will the task simply be put on a list in the system so that the next person who logs on with the needed role will see it?

In some workflows, it is also possible to specify the version control necessary for the content at each task in the workflow. For example, can only one person have access, can multiple people with read-only privileges have access, or can multiple people with read *and* write privileges have access? (This last option can be dangerous.)

Some of the more powerful CMSs go one step further when defining the workflow. They enable the administrator to specify which data elements will be gathered or viewed for the content component or metacontent at each stage of the workflow.

Creating a powerful WDA is a costly, time-consuming, and difficult exercise, and thus not all CMSs have one. Because the workflow for creating a content component is similar for most component types, it is possible to hard-code some of the more common workflows and allow the administrator to pick the one (or the few) that matches close enough to the existing flow.

For a smaller Web site with few content component types, this might be the best way to go. A simplified workflow system often (but not always) means a lower CMS price tag.

Workflow Engine

After a workflow is defined and entered into the WDA, there has to be some way to make use of it in the CMS for it to be of any value. This is the responsibility of the workflow engine.

The *workflow engine* is the central hub of all activity in most CMSs. It will often provide most, if not all, of the functions discussed in the following sections.

Check-In and Checkout System

Most workflow engines work closely with a version control system.

Whenever content is to be used by the workflow engine, it needs to be checked out. The checkout process does one of two things, depending on the type of version control system (see Chapter 2). It either places a lock on the content so that no one else can change it or it creates a copy from a master version so that changes can be made in it and then merged back with the master later.

This checkout process even happens when the system first introduces a brand-new piece of content. The first thing the workflow engine will do is generate a placeholder for the content and then check out an empty piece of content.

When all changes are completed, the content needs to be checked back in. Again, the check-in process depends on the type of version control system used by the CMS. Either the check-in content will overlay the current copy in the repository or the content will merge with the master copy in the repository.

Interface for Content Entry

The first stage for most workflows is the creation of the initial draft of the content component or metacontent. A piece of content is usually created by entering the appropriate information on a Web form, which the workflow engine generates.

Usually, the first Web form that an author sees when entering the workflow is a list of all the content he has created and its status. From there, the author can choose to continue entering information about the last content he was working on, or he can create a new piece of content.

Viewing and entering an incomplete piece of content can only be done by the person(s) who created the story (and administrators with higher authority, of course). The Web form provides very little available functionality. Most often, the only fields available to the content creator are the content itself and the comment field, which provides information to the next role in the workflow.

The Web form will always have a way of stating that the content is finished in the current stage and needs to move on to the next workflow stage.

Interface for Content Editing

The next most common interface provided by a workflow engine is an interface to edit a prior role in the workflow's content. The most obvious example of this is from author to editor.

Similar to the author's starting Web form, the editing Web form brings up a list of content that has been edited by the editor and a list of all the content available to be edited. Depending on the workflow engine, this list of available content may be truly all the content available to be edited or just a list of content that has been allocated by the workflow engine to the editor.

The content edit Web form is very similar to the creation Web form, but it will have at least one additional feature: a way of sending the content back to the creator for further work. It will, of course, also have a way to move the content on to the next workflow stage.

Interface for Content Approval

Content approval is one of the most important but, unfortunately for many smaller CMSs, overlooked features of a workflow engine. Most workflow engines provide some way of having one or more authorized persons approve a piece of content.

The approval starting Web form differs from the creating and editing Web forms because it will not be cluttered with any content that does not need the immediate attention of the approver. It will contain a list of only the content awaiting approval.

The approval Web form does not provide a way to edit the content. Instead, it contains a way to view and approve the content as is or return it back to the previous stage, preferably with a comment about why it could not be approved.

Depending on how the approval process was defined in the WDA, the approval of a piece of content could be contingent on the approval of more than one person. If this is the case, the workflow engine will keep the content in the awaiting approval stage until all necessary approvals are made. Otherwise, after the content is approved by a person authorized to do so, it will move on to the next stage.

Interface for Content Testing

A feature-rich workflow engine might provide a way to test the content without having to leave the workflow environment.

Some workflows require that the content be moved to a test server to be tested. Sometimes this movement causes the piece of content to be taken out of the control of the workflow engine.

The capability to test within the workflow engine saves time because no importing or exporting of the content needs to be done. Because the content remains within the workflow engine, it can keep track of and control the content. When the content is exported, it could possibly be lost or corrupted.

It is possible to do much of the testing of a piece of content within the workflow engine itself, without having to move the content out of the engine's control.

It is even possible to have the test server and staging server within the control of the workflow engine.

Interface for Content Deployment

A workflow engine is supposed to handle the complete life cycle of a piece of content. Deployment is part of the life cycle. A workflow engine should provide a way to handle the deployment of all its content. A good workflow engine will do it automatically without human involvement.

There is always a chance that an error could occur when a piece of content is deployed to production. If this happens, the workflow engine provides a Web form that displays all the content on the system and any other information the Web site administrator thought necessary. For example, other information could include the date the content was deployed, the length of the content in bytes, the format of the content, and so on.

Interface for Content Archival

When a piece of content is no longer wanted on the main Web site, it should be archived.

The content archival process can be handled at least two ways:

- The first method is to provide a Web form that lists all the active content and then provide a way to specify which piece of content needs to be archived. A person who has the authority to archive content should probably be high ranking because there is usually no approval stage for moving content to an archive.

- The second method is to specify, during the creation of the content, how long a piece of content should remain active on the Web site. When the time expires, the workflow engine should automatically archive it. With automatic archival, a Web form should provide a way to extend or shorten the duration during which the content stays active.

Interface for Content Removal

As mentioned in Chapter 1, it is better to archive a piece of content and let it remain available than to remove it from the system. However, if you must remove the content, the workflow engine provides a Web form of all the content on the system and a way to remove each piece of content. Only a person with the highest permission level should have removal authority because the removal process can be very dangerous if given to the wrong person.

Some workflow engines actually remove the content from the system. Most just mark the content as deleted, and it remains hidden in a repository. Only someone with a high permission level can retrieve removed content that is hidden.

Content Movement or Update on Site Servers

A piece of content, during its lifetime, will reside on many different servers. Which server(s) it is on depends on its current workflow stage. Even though copies of the content may reside on many different servers, only one master copy of the content exists.

It is the job of the workflow engine to manage the content on the different servers. The workflow engine makes sure the appropriate servers are updated when a piece of content moves to a different workflow stage. The process of moving or updating the content from the master repository copy to a server should be handled automatically.

The most common servers that the workflow engine manages are the development, testing, staging, and deployment servers. It should not matter to the workflow engine that these servers may reside on different computers. All the workflow engine needs to know is that the content has moved to a new stage. If the stage requires that the content populate a different server (based on the information entered in the workflow definition application [WDA]), the workflow engine should automatically make a copy of the content in the master repository and place it across the company's network to the required server.

Content Status System

An important administrative feature of a workflow engine is that it knows in what stage every piece of content is in the repository.

All information about all of the content is available by way of a Web form. This form usually provides summary information about each piece of content as well as the capability to drill down into it for more details.

The form will show information such as the author, the editor, approvers, dates and times when content transitioned to a new stage, the current stage, the content size in bytes or words, and the content type.

You might think of a workflow engine content status system as a data warehouse of all the content in your system. In fact, it is possible to use a third-party data warehouse tool to handle content status if your CMS's workflow engine does not.

You can use the information provided by the content status system to aid you in many ways. For example, you can calculate the exact cost for a Web page and how long it took to get to the site. You can even calculate the content cost per word if you want because you know everyone who worked on the story (including the author, editor, approver, and tester), how long they worked on it, and when they checked the content in and out.

Event Notification System

The notification system is a key component to reducing time lags between stages in a workflow. Its purpose is to automatically generate e-mails or pages addressed to the next role that will be working with the content when it becomes available. A copy of the notification is also available when a person of that role logs on.

Another neat feature is that it can be used to continue to pester someone if she fails to complete the task in a specified amount of time.

A feature-rich workflow engine might even be able to route notifications to particular people based on workload and/or skill sets. User-specific notifications reduce the number of unwanted e-mails or pages sent to a person who is already busy or is unavailable for some other reason.

The event notification system is not essential to a workflow engine, but it is a very powerful feature when available. If a workflow engine does not have an event notification system, it will provide a similar functionality by notifying people when they log on of all the content available for them to work on.

Communication System

Feature-rich workflow engines will sometimes augment the communication capabilities provided by version tracking, as outlined in Chapter 2. Because of the distributed nature of editorial and creative staffs, direct face-to-face communication may not be possible. A good way to communicate is through the CMS workflow engine.

The workflow engine may provide features such as built-in e-mailing of comments or even a built-in real-time chat facility. Each of these functionalities, though, can be obtained for free by using tools like good old-fashioned e-mail, ICQ, AOL Instant Messenger, or MSN Messenger. Having them directly integrated into the workflow engine may simplify things because you can provide a common interface, but it can also become another complication because you are now forcing your users to know how to install and use these other tools.

The workflow engine is probably the only interface seen by most, if not all, editorial and creative staff members. For example, when an author enters her story into the CMS, she will be entering it through the workflow engine. When a change is required to the story, the workflow engine generates an e-mail that notifies her. When she makes the change, it is through the workflow engine. If the author wants to know the status of the story, again she will be using the workflow engine.

What Is a Workflow's Role in CMS?

A CMS would have little functionality if it weren't for its workflow because there would be no managing the life cycle of a piece of content. In fact, there wouldn't even be a life cycle. Instead, a CMS would simply be a storage facility for a Web site.

A workflow gives a CMS the capability to let content mature, under control, before it is presented to the Web. By following the life cycle provided by the workflow, your content is much more polished, accurate, and consistent.

A workflow has many roles in a CMS. Let's examine three of its most important roles.

Coordinating Content Development

By its very nature, a workflow provides coordination. By definition, it is a set of tasks performed to reach a goal. The goal in a CMS is to get a piece of content through its life cycle.

As you have seen, the workflow engine controls all aspects of a piece of content's life, from its creation to its archival or removal. The key to a workflow engine's success, however, is its capability to break the life cycle stages into small, independent, manageable pieces. This allows specialization on the part of the people completing these stages and, in turn, enables people to do a better job because they have to worry about fewer things.

It may seem kind of weird that I point out how well a workflow engine breaks up the development of content, when we are actually discussing how it coordinates content development. A workflow makes it easy for users because it takes all the hard stuff as its domain. That "hard stuff" is the coordination of all the pieces into which a workflow has broken the content's life cycle.

The first thing you notice about a workflow engine is that you—the author, editor, or approver—don't have to worry about how the content gets to you from within the CMS or where it is going after you have finished with it. All you have to worry about is doing the job required by your role.

The workflow engine handles all content routing automatically. No longer will any content get lost during the transition between stages. Moreover, with notifications, there are no delays because people will know immediately that they should start working on the content.

Users are provided all the tools necessary to do their job and a stable environment in which to do it. Users are notified when there is more work for them to do and when they are lagging. In other words, they have complete freedom to do their jobs and don't have to worry about anybody else's. In fact, all a user has to learn is his own job.

The workflow engine handles, equally well, the coordination of content development remotely or within a single location. The main reason is that location has no real meaning except as proximity to an Internet connection. Content modifications, event notifications, and even communications are via the Internet.

For those who hate office politics, a good workflow engine is a godsend because there is no office in which to have politics.

Managing Content Development

The workflow engine is a powerful tool when used correctly by a manager. It provides help in all four standard management functions: controlling, planning, organizing, and implementing. In fact, it helps so much that it can do several of the manager's tasks.

Controlling

Obviously, the workflow engine helps a manager control many aspects of the development of content, such as who does what task and when. A workflow engine can even free a manager from having to worry about this.

It is possible to program into the engine the capability to figure out who can do the task required and allocate it to that person if she is free. It is even possible for the workflow engine to distribute the work evenly based on factors such as byte size of the content, expertise level, or even vacation schedules.

Planning

The workflow engine provides all the information necessary to plan the future direction of the content development process. Based on past performance information, it is possible for a manager to know how long it takes for content to move through the workflow and when it is available for publication.

Almost exclusively, the workflow engine can handle this task as well. The manager now has time for the more important task of planning out what content should be added to the Web site.

Organizing

The manager uses the WDA to organize his personnel. The manager will get to know the strengths and weaknesses of his team and then, using this information, organize his roles in the workflow.

The workflow, by nature, organizes the order in which tasks are completed, thus allowing the task of creating content to be very repeatable. As a manager, you know that the content is being developed the same way every time. The fewer surprises in the life of a manager, the better—having a repeatable process goes a long way in that department.

Implementing

There is no question that a workflow engine helps put into operation the development of content for a Web site. It provides all the tools essential to build many—and, in very feature-rich CMSs, perhaps all—types of content.

So, do you still need a manager? Of course. Workflow helps the manager handle many tedious, day-to-day jobs so that she can do the more important job of making sure the content gets completed by her staff and ensuring that the people working with her are happy and work well.

Ensuring Content Control

Most workflow engines work very closely with the version control system, and the closer that the workflow and the version control are, the better. Almost everything covered in Chapter 2 could be repeated here because the features of version control are a big part of how workflow engines provide control.

To enable users of the workflow to be oblivious to other people working on the content of the site, strict controls need to be in place. When someone gets control of a piece of content, he should not have to worry that someone else is going to make a change to it that may cause all his work to be for naught.

The easiest way to ensure that a user has complete control of his content is to lock it from other people on the site (or at least lock out write access to the content). There really isn't any harm if someone checks out a piece of content for reading as long as she is aware that it is currently a work in progress.

Version control is the best means of providing locking to content, as you saw in Chapter 2. One of the neat features of a workflow engine is that the user can be completely oblivious to the fact that he is using a version control system. When he gets a piece of content to work on, it is checked out of the repository behind the scenes. When he is finished making all the changes to the content, he releases the content to the next person in the workflow, and as he does so, it is checked back in to the repository. It is the option of the workflow implementation as to whether it uses the version control's comments field to handle communication or provides its own equivalent.

Another feature of a workflow is that it controls which version of content is on each server. It is possible to have version 1 of a piece of content on the production Web server, version 2 in the development repository, version 1.4 in staging, and version 1.3 in testing. Why all these versions are distributed like this is immaterial. That it is possible to distribute it like this, though, is material.

Again, the capability to control versions like this is provided by the power of a version control system, which was covered in Chapter 2.

Building CMS Workflows

As previously pointed out, some powerful WDAs provide the capability to configure a workflow however you want. Having a piece of content go through eight different editors before it's ready for approval is perfectly within your rights as a workflow designer. (Personally, I would think you are nuts, but hey, it's your workflow.)

Workflows should be designed to streamline the building of content without erring on the side of recklessness. You should include all the roles needed to complete the creation of the task. Personally, I feel you should trust your people to do a good job. You did hire them to do the job, didn't you? Therefore, embedding multiple approval stages or unnecessary checks to make sure your people are doing their jobs correctly is a waste of resources. All it does is delay the release of the content.

If you feel the need to do a little micromanaging, do periodic spot checks. Most workflow engines give read permission to people with enough authority. Use this feature to do the spot checks. Don't change the workflow itself.

Let's take a simple workflow as an example and see some of the problems that a workflow designer has to muddle through.

Figure 3-2 shows a pretty standard and straightforward workflow used by small Web sites to create content: author, edit, approve, test, stage, deploy. This workflow makes the very big assumption that the author knows what content should be on the site. This workflow would probably work well for a small editorial staff with good internal communications.

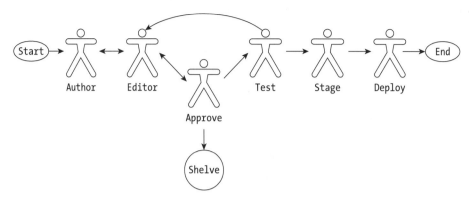

Figure 3-2. A simple, standard workflow

One thing you should note about this workflow is that it has the key role of approver in the middle of the workflow. This role is the safety value of the workflow; not only does this role have the option of returning content to the editor for rework, but it also has the powerful option of shelving the content altogether. You might be wondering why an approver would shelve a piece of content. The most common reason is a communication breakdown, such as the wrong type of story being covered or the same story being covered twice.

Using this workflow, it is possible—with bad communications—that a story may even go completely through editing before being caught. This is a complete waste of resources and explains why this workflow is really only usable by a small Web site.

Let's see if we can adapt this simple workflow to a slightly larger company. Larger companies quite often don't have the luxury of good communication among staff members, especially if the staff is primarily remote. The first thing you might want to try if you are designing the workflow is to see if you can reduce the waste of unnecessary stories being written and edited. To do this, you might make a slight change to the earlier workflow by adding two new roles: submitter and acquisitions. True, the role of submitter and author is usually the same, but it doesn't have to be, and the flow in Figure 3-3 makes this distinction. The acquisitions role takes in all the submitted content from the authors and then determines which ones will be covered. This simple step makes sure that the correct content enters the system and that there are no duplicates.

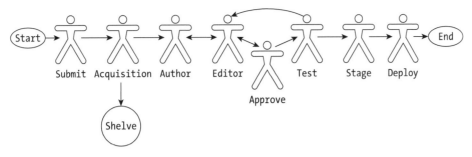

Figure 3-3. An enhanced standard workflow

As a workflow designer, you might have to add roles such as fact checker, legal department approval, different levels of editing, and so on. The possibilities may not be endless, but it might seem like it if you are designing the flow for a huge Web site. The key to good workflow design is keeping it simple and trusting your people.

Benefits of a Workflow

The benefits of a workflow are numerous. Though many are abstract, some touch your return on investment (ROI) directly. Here's a short list of some of the more obvious and important benefits:

- *Reduced cycle time:* Because all content-routing activities are automated, the transition time between roles is reduced. The next role in the workflow is notified immediately of available content, thus reducing the time a role spends querying the system looking for content on which to work.

- *Increased throughput:* Because people can now specialize in their own roles, they can improve their skills and not have to worry about doing the work of others.

- *Elimination of forgotten process steps:* Because the flow of the content is from one role to another, there is no chance that a step will be overlooked, unless it is done purposely.

- *Consistently repeatable process:* The workflow system imposes a consistent and repeatable process. Once defined in the WDA, the process of creating content will be the same until it is changed again.

- *User empowerment:* Users can now focus on their business skills, use them to the best of their abilities, and not have to worry about content-routing issues such as where to get their work from or where it has to go.

- *Automation of process steps:* The system can be streamlined by automating some of the more menial tasks, particularly in the areas of content routing and notification systems.

- *Improved business management:* Process metrics, ROI, audit control, and many other features that can enable continuous improvement are readily available, thanks to the content status provided by the workflow.

- *Process flexibility:* With a WDA, you can change your process to adapt to your changing business.

- *Process status tracking:* Nearly all aspects of the content's life cycle are recorded and available when needed.

- *Process cost tracking:* All the information is available, as previously pointed out, to be able to calculate accurately the cost of content development.

Summary

This chapter covered in detail all aspects of workflows. It started by describing what a generic workflow is and then what a CMS workflow is. It then covered in detail the two major components of a workflow system: the workflow definition application (WDA) and the workflow engine. Next, it looked at the roles that a workflow plays in a CMS. It then explained some of the things that a workflow designer needs to examine when building a workflow. Finally, the chapter wrapped up with a small subset of the benefits of a workflow.

The next chapter will start to explore the exciting area of personalization and how it affects—and is affected by—a CMS.

CHAPTER 4

Personalization

PERSONALIZATION IS ONE OF THE MOST written-about features of Web development. You can find an enormous number of articles on the subject, with new ones coming out every day. Why is there this fascination with personalization?

Personalization, like most Web technologies, is still in its infancy. Many ideas exist as to what you can accomplish by way of personalization. Some ideas can be implemented now; others need to wait for technology to catch up with dreams.

You can personalize a Web site in many different ways, ranging from the simple "Welcome back, Stephen" to the complex role-based and collaborative filtering. Each type of personalization is trying to address a different need in the Web site/user relationship. What is this relationship, and why is it so important?

Personalization is all about helping to build a relationship between the Web surfer and a Web site. There are millions of surfers out there. For a site to become successful, you need some of those surfers to become users.

How important personalization is to relationship building depends on what you read. There is quite a contrast in opinions; some writers say personalization is a waste of money, while others say you cannot have a Web site without it. This chapter covers personalization impartially and tries to explain why there is such a great range of opinions.

After reading this chapter, you will be able to make an educated decision about what aspects of personalization, if any, to implement on your Web site.

What Is Personalization?

For such a simple term, "personalization" gets a lot of play in the Web world. Most major Web sites on the Internet have, or are implementing, some type of personalization. For example, Chapter 1 described how MSNBC's Web site implements some personalization on its cover page by providing content based on the user's ZIP code. However, that is just one of many types of personalization.

Let's take a step back and define exactly what personalization is: *Personalization* is the process of using automated Web technology to generate and present individualized content based on the needs of a user. Not much to it, is there? The concept is hardly new. Salespeople have been using personalization for centuries. If you're like most people, you love going into your favorite store, where the salesperson already knows what you like and has whatever you are searching for ready for you to look at when you get there. Isn't it nice having a salesperson already know your size so that you don't have to repeatedly be measured and reminded that you are a little overweight?

The only difference between what your favorite store has been doing for years and what Web sites are trying to do now is that computers are doing the job of the salesperson. Personalization is a rather simple concept for a human to grasp, but implementing it on a computer, on the other hand, is anything but simple.

The circular process, which a Web site personalization system needs to automate, is straightforward (see Figure 4-1):

1. Collect all relevant data about the user of the system.

2. Match the data collected to the content of the Web site.

3. Determine the most important or relevant content to the user and give it higher priority.

4. Display the content in descending priority.

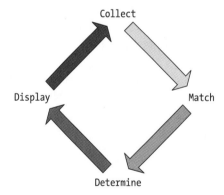

Figure 4-1. The personalization process

In theory, as a personalization system collects more detailed information about its users, it will become increasingly more accurate in matching the needs of those users to the information it controls in its CMS content repository.

The problem with this theory is that in many situations, more information is not necessarily better. In those cases, careful programming is necessary to get around the anomalies. For example, sometimes a user is looking for something completely different than what he normally looks for. Maybe the user is helping a friend find something. When this happens, two things can occur.

First, the user will probably get a little frustrated because it takes longer—possibly a lot longer—than normal to find what he wants because what he is looking for now is no longer near the top of the content. Instead, it is deeply buried in the hierarchical layers generated by personalization. This frustration, if it continues to happen on subsequent visits to the site, might cause the user to second-guess the usefulness of the site, especially if he was able to find the content somewhere else quicker.

Second, the information in the user record is now skewed because it has added this one-time, unusual transaction in the user's records. This information will probably cause some weird things to show up on the user's home page for a little while, at least until enough other information is added to the user's records to cause the weighting of the unusual transaction to become unsubstantial.

For a human salesperson, this one-time, unusual search made by his client will probably be forgotten by the next visit or brought up as a playful joke: "You shopping for your friend again?" The problem is that computers can have long memories if stored to a hard drive, and they have no sense of humor.

Personalization Objectives

Why go through all the problems of personalizing a Web site at all? You might be thinking that if you make the information available on the Internet, users will just come. If you think that, I'm sorry to have to burst your bubble, but there are millions of sites on the Internet, all of them trying to get the attention of all the uncommitted Web surfers out there. Many will have information just like your Web site, plus they may have the added hook of personalization.

Without some kind of edge, you will be one of many and will probably get lost in the crowd. You might figure out some other way to stand out from the crowd without personalization, but most Web developers claim it's personalization that gives them a competitive edge. In fact, it is the goal of personalization to give you this edge.

What are the objectives of personalization? They are very simple:

- Retain interest

- Build a relationship

- Get users to participate

Interest

Okay, the first thing you want for your site is to capture the interest of Web surfers. You can do this in many ways, but personalization is not one of them.

Still, let's pretend you can use personalization to capture interest. The most effective way to get surfer interest using personalization is to provide the content people want to see. However, you might be thinking, isn't that putting the cart before the horse? (If you aren't thinking that, you should be.) Unfortunately, yes it is.

How can you provide content specific to a surfer if you know nothing about her? The simple answer is that you can't.

If you remember the life cycle of personalization, the first step is to get information about the user. Getting information from a user requires some initial interest in your Web site, at least enough interest—depending on which type of personalization you implement—to have the surfer wonder about the site or fill in your preliminary user questionnaire.

Personalization cannot be used to try to ignite interest in your site. It can only be used to retain Web site interest. If your goal in personalization is to get people interested in your site, you are looking at the wrong technology.

How does personalization retain user interest? By itself, it doesn't. Personalization is just a tool you can have in your arsenal to help you keep users coming back. It helps tailor the content of your site to the needs of your users, with the intent of keeping them interested.

Simple personalization—such as having the Web site call the user by name, believe it or not—brings more smiles to faces than most other forms of personalization combined, at least for the first little while. Another personalization feature that is becoming quite popular is creating a My Yahoo–style site. These sites enable a user to configure his Web site however he wants. Quite often, these Web pages become the home page of the user. Unfortunately, creating a site like this is far from easy. Of course, you can always create a site that uses personalization as it is defined, having a site that provides the content that the user wants. I'm sure you don't think doing this is easy either.

You cannot just install personalization on your site and then hope for—voilà—instant interest. You need to figure out what is going to be unique about your site. Why are people coming to your site? What is going to keep your users coming back? No book can give you the answers to these questions. If you bought one that claimed it could, you might as well return it because your site would be anything but unique. You might find that the answers to these questions show that personalization is not going to help you, but most likely, some type of personalization will help.

Relationship

Relationships are a cornerstone of personalization. When you implement personalization, you are hoping to build relationships with your users. By definition, personalization provides something to the user, and of course, a Web site gets something in return. This is a relationship—a win-win relationship in fact.

The goal of a Web site is to have a user interact with your site. Some simple types of interaction include having the user read your content, click on any banner ads, and buy items from the Web site. Providing the content in a way that makes it easy for your user to do these activities could be your part of the relationship.

One-sided relationships don't last. Most users want to feel that there is something special about returning to a Web site or, more accurately, that the site provides them with some type of value. Relating to a Web site, or having a relationship with it, is one of the strongest bonds a user can have with a Web site. It is something that any good Web site should strive for.

Having relationships with users means having a continuous, guaranteed viewer base that you can use to further the goals of your site. To have this relationship, you must provide to users their perceived value of the site. Reread that last sentence carefully. The key words are "their perceived value." As long as users perceive that the Web site has value, they will most likely continue the relationship (see Figure 4-2).

Figure 4-2. Perceived value to a programmer

Like any other type of relationship, it takes time and trust to build a Web relationship. You must build a relationship in small, nonthreatening steps. For example, asking for a user's name on her first visit to your Web site is usually okay. On the other hand, asking for a user's home phone number will probably drive her away without any chance of a return visit. If the Web site takes any wrong steps, it may find that it loses some ground in the relationship or possibly loses the relationship completely.

Again, like interest, personalization does not guarantee a relationship with a user. It just provides the tools to establish and build one. You must understand what it is that the user wants in the relationship and then use the tools provided by personalization to help fulfill the user's wants.

Participation

Getting users involved in a Web site is an important part of personalization. The more a user participates in the site, the more opportunities a Web site gets to learn about him. And, as you now know, learning as much as possible about your users is the key to developing personalization that provides perceived value to the user. This retains interest in the site and keeps a user coming back, which is, of course, one of the key reasons for implementing personalization in the first place.

Having users participate in the Web site by sharing their personal experiences and opinions is a sure sign that the site is providing what users want. It is also one of the first steps in developing a loyal user community. A loyal user community will usually promote your site, and as the community grows, more fun can be had by all. And, as everyone knows, word of mouth (or of fingers, in this case) is one of the most powerful tools for promoting a Web site.

On the opposite side of the coin, negative word of mouth can kill a Web site. Word of mouth can grow exponentially. Therefore, it is beneficial to listen to your users and try to address all concerns as quickly as possible.

Again, personalization does not guarantee participation. You use it as a tool to get users to participate.

Types of Personalization

A site can use many different methods to provide personalization. Many Web sites differentiate themselves based on the factors of price and effort to implement. These are the wrong factors on which to base the type of personalization. The decisive factors you should use are as follows: the reason you want to implement personalization and what you are trying to accomplish by personalizing your Web site.

Although you can use personalization types individually, I submit that a better approach is to use multiple types of personalization together, building on the strengths of each.

Nominal Personalization

Nominal personalization is the simplest of all the different personalization types. All it really does is provide the user with a friendly greeting when she returns to the Web site. It requires the user of the site to answer a simple form requesting her name.

After the user enters the information into the form, the Web site creates a cookie (see Chapter 12 for more information), which is stored on the user's site and is retrieved by the Web site whenever the user returns. A Web site can handle the cookie in one of two ways. The first way is to store the information in the cookie itself and then, when the user returns to the site, retrieve the information from the cookie. The second way is to place a random and unique key in the cookie. When the user returns, the Web site retrieves the cookie and looks the key up in the repository of users, which provides the username to display on the Web site.

The first method is only good for storing the username. This is because the placement of any other information in the cookie is unavailable for the Web site's use because the Web site will not be able to access the cookie until the next time the user logs in. The first method also starts to infringe on the user's privacy, an issue that is covered later in this chapter.

Group Personalization

One of the easiest ways to handle multiple groups on a single Web site is by using *group personalization*. For example, a Web site for students might use group personalization to distinguish which grade a user is in. Once the Web site knows which grade the user is in, it can route her to the correct menus and Web pages.

Usually, group-personalized sites require some form of registration. The registration typically involves entering information on a form, which the site then stores in a user repository. The Web site administrator then verifies the information. If the user's information is satisfactory, she is e-mailed a username and password.

Two different approaches exist for handling returning users with group personalization. The first is similar to nominal personalization. A unique random key is stored in a cookie after the first time the user logs on using the supplied username and password provided in the e-mail. Each subsequent time the user logs in, the Web site retrieves the key from the cookie and logs the user in. Or, if security is an issue, it asks for a password. The second method forces the user to log in from a generic start page using the supplied username and password. No cookie is stored on the user's computer.

In both cases, privacy is protected because no user information passes over the Internet, other than in the case of the first method, in which a random key traverses the Internet.

Subscription Personalization

Subscription personalization provides a way for a site to send newsletters to users. It requires the user of the site to enter information into a simple form that requests an e-mail address to which the Web site can send the newsletter. Quite often, the Web site will send a test e-mail to the provided e-mail address, asking the user to verify that he is in fact the person requesting the newsletter.

Basically, with subscription personalization, a Web site is sending a newsletter to a target group of users who have an expressed interest in the newsletter's content. It usually includes subtle, or not so subtle, advertisements to encourage readers to make purchases from the Web site or a partner site.

On a very simple implementation of subscription personalization, typically in conjunction with nominal personalization, the newsletter is often used just as a way for the Web site to remind the user of its existence.

Intelligent Agent Personalization

An *intelligent agent* is really subscription personalization on steroids. It basically is a more elaborate subscription personalization Web site requesting more information from the user. From the information provided, the intelligent agent will generate a newsletter containing articles (or hyperlinks to articles) that it believes the user will be interested in, as opposed to a generic newsletter as produced by subscription personalization.

Some intelligent agents will only examine the content of their own Web sites. Other intelligent agents can become pretty elaborate and will send out spiders all over the Internet, searching for information that the user wants.

A *spider* is a little program that searches a Web site for content; if it finds any, it sends the content back to the requester. What makes a spider special is that it can locate hyperlinks and jump to a hyperlinked page recursively. In theory, a spider can search the entire Internet for something. When implemented, though, most spiders are restricted to the level for which they can recursively jump because it would take a very long time to search the entire Internet. More important, however, the memory requirements would be astronomical to run a nonrestricted spider because it has to remember where it went on a stack of some type.

Push or Webcasting Personalization

Push technology is very similar to subscription personalization and intelligent agents in that a user subscribes to receive information from a Web site. The big difference is that the information does not come by way of e-mail. Instead, it goes directly, at prearranged intervals via an unobtrusive transmission, to the user's computer from the push Web site.

Unlike normal Web browsing, the content comes to the user; the user does not have to go look for it. The basic procedure is to turn on the browser to receive the push transmissions, and then periodically the browser will display updated information without any activity on the part of the user.

The setting up of this content can get very elaborate, depending on the push Web site provider used. The process usually involves the user going through many lists of content type, selecting the topics of interest. For example, a user could select weather for her area, local and international news, information about her stock portfolio, and information about her favorite sports.

Notice that privacy is maintained at the level at which the user feels comfortable. Users have the choice to disclose as much or as little about themselves as they want. With this simple example, the push Web site knows information like in what ZIP code the user lives, in what stocks the user has an interest, and what the user's favorite sports teams are. With this information, the push Web site can place ads on the browser for stockbrokers in the user's area or tickets to local sporting events involving the user's favorite teams.

Customization

Customization often goes under the name of My Yahoo personalization. Figure 4-3 is the real My Yahoo from which the name comes. It is a Web site that enables a user to customize the look and feel and what sections of content he wants to display. This type of site often becomes a user's home page when he logs onto the Internet because it provides the daily information that the user wants and links to the Web sites he frequents.

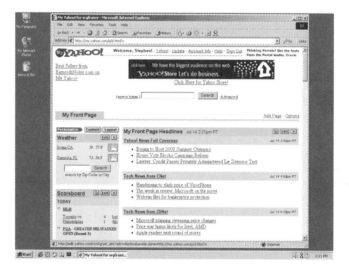

Figure 4-3. My Yahoo

Screen shot reproduced with permission of Yahoo! Inc. © 2000 by Yahoo! Inc. YAHOO! and the YAHOO! logo are trademarks of Yahoo! Inc.

Customization uses the same approach as group personalization when it comes to Web returns (that is, cookies or login). Not only user information is stored in the repository but also the layout of the home page, preferred content sections, hyperlinks, and any other information that the site enabled the user to customize.

Privacy is maintained because for this type of personalization, total anonymity can be retained if the site wants. The username does not need to be stored anywhere on the site to use customization. At the very least, however, customization usually is used in conjunction with nominal personalization.

Rule-Based Personalization

Rule-based personalization is a method of personalizing in which a Web site requests the help of the user to define what she is looking for from the Web site. This type of personalization requires the user to show some trust in the Web site because the user will be asked many different questions, some of which the user will not want to—or simply will not—answer.

Two schools of thought exist for setting up a user when implementing rule-based personalization:

1. The first approach is to get the user up and running as fast as possible so that he will be immediately productive. This method will instantly ask the user a series of targeted questions, each trying to help the Web site target which content to provide to the user. The user must have a true need for what this site is providing for him to willingly answer so many questions up front.

2. The second approach is to ease the user into the Web site by asking questions as needed. This method is frequently implemented by requesting information when there is an immediate need for the information. The user is aware of this need and therefore is not put off by the request. For example, when a user selects a sports link, the Web site could ask him which sports are his favorites before actually displaying the linked page. For more personal information, such as a street address, the site might only ask after the user has agreed that he wants something shipped to him. This method of setting up a user is less obtrusive and is more likely to succeed, especially if the user does not have an immediate need to use all the available functionality of the Web site.

The goal of both of these setup procedures is to create a complete profile of the user so that the site can generate content targeted to the user. When a user accesses the Web site, the personalization system will examine the profile of the user and see if any available information would be of specific interest to the user. It will then sort all the content based on weighting factors calculated from the answers provided to the questions it posted during the setup of the user's profile.

Privacy is maintained because the profile information never leaves the Web site. For a user to get access to the site, she would have to log in either with a username and password or with a cookie and, usually, a password.

Collaborative Filtering

The *collaborative filtering* method of personalization is by far the least obtrusive as far as the user of a site is concerned. In fact, if implemented correctly, a user may not even be aware that a profile is being made of her.

This method of personalization is based on the study of group behaviors. This means that if several users like something, the odds are good that the current user will as well. Another way of looking at it is that if a user starts a pattern that previous groups of people have already followed, it is likely that the user will be striving for the same end. Thus, a collaborative filter can look for patterns and, when it finds one, provide the next element in the pattern before the user actually requests it.

To implement collaborative filtering, the Web designer has to embed tags in each piece of content. *Tags* are developer-defined pieces of information that uniquely identify a piece of content. Then, as a user navigates through the Web site, the personalization engine records in its own repository all the information viewed and the pattern used to get there.

The biggest problem with collaborative filtering is that it takes time to seed the system with enough information to make it useful. The more people navigate the Web site, the more patterns the collaborative filter can determine.

Because it takes some time to get enough information into the system to make it provide any relevant personalization for the Web user, collaborative filtering provides two cheats. The first cheat is that a personalization system can load the data of another system, thus providing instant seeding. The second cheat is that many collaborative filters ask users directly about their preferences using Web form questionnaires without having to navigate there themselves. For example, a video store Web site might ask a user, after she buys a particular movie, what other videos she might be interested in that are similar to the one she just bought, instead of waiting for the user to navigate to them.

One of the key user benefits in collaborative filtering is that a user has complete privacy. Other than a randomly created unique ID key stored as a cookie, there is nothing to link the user to the data being collected. No names, addresses, or phone numbers are needed for collaborative filtering personalization.

Law of Diminishing Returns

It is important for all implementers of personalized Web sites to understand that the law of diminishing returns applies to personalization.

The law states that if one factor of production increases while the others remain constant, the overall returns will relatively decrease after a certain point. Thus, for Web site personalization, if more and more personalization systems are added to a Web site, at some point, each additional system will generate relatively less return on investment (ROI) than its predecessor did, simply because the system has less and less of the fixed amount of significant individualizations it can provide for a user. Figure 4-4 depicts this scenario.

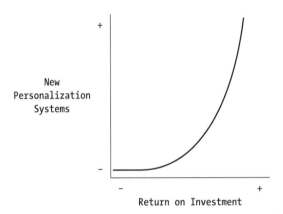

Figure 4-4. The law of diminishing returns

Another way of looking at it is that adding more personalization systems to a Web site is good until it reaches a certain point. After you pass that point, it simply is not cost effective to add any more personalization systems. To continue to add more is just a waste of computer capacity, disk space, bandwidth, developer time, and many other resources. For the addition of more personalization systems to become cost effective again, you need to add something more to be individualized. For example, a Web site could add new and different content areas or add a new newsletter.

A Web site must be careful to add only features and information that its users will perceive as having added value. Adding something that users don't see as having value is a waste of resources.

What this all boils down to is that all sites can use some personalization. What each site needs to find is the *sweet spot*, or the spot where personalization provides the best ROI. As I am sure you are aware, the sweet spot is different for every Web site.

Be wary of consultants who claim the answer to all your Web site problems is adding more personalization. Your problem might be—with your current significant individualization level—that you have too much personalization. Your Web site may have moved beyond the sweet spot.

Privacy

As I am sure you know or can figure out, privacy is a major issue when it comes to personalization. Personalization's goal is to provide individualized content. To do that, personalization systems need to know all about the user for whom they are trying to provide individualized content. The problem is all this personally identifiable information, or PII, needs to be stored someplace. If the PII is stored someplace, it is possible that someone whom the user does not want to see it might get access to it. In other words, someone could invade the user's privacy.

A solution available to some Web sites—to avoid the whole privacy issue and not request any PII on your Web site at all—is to rely solely on anonymous collaborative filtering. Unfortunately, this approach is really not that feasible for most sites and is not possible for personalized e-commerce sites in which name, address, and credit card number information is frequently required to purchase something.

So, what if you are one of the majority of sites on the Internet for which using only anonymous collaborative filtering is not an option? Are you out of luck and forced into the privacy fray? Yes, I'm afraid so.

If your Web site uses its PII for its intended purpose—that is, to provide individualized content to match users' interests—and if you can guarantee that the content will never leave your control, you should have no privacy issues. The hard part is convincing users that this is the case.

Getting users to trust a Web site with their PII is hard with all the horror stories floating around the Internet about hackers stealing credit card numbers or even Web sites selling the PII to whomever wants it.

The first step in building user trust is providing a clear and specific privacy policy for the Web site. The policy should be readily available for all to read. It should spell out exactly what PII is being collected, for what purpose the site will use the PII, and who has access to it. If you want trust, never have clauses in the policy such as "These are our current policies, and they may change in the future, so please check back here regularly." Once you have a policy, stick to it. If you do not, whatever trust you have built with your user base will quickly disappear.

Make sure the user has the capability to see (or, even better, to determine), in a secure fashion, exactly what of her PII is on the Web site. The site should also provide a way for the user to edit or delete the PII as she sees fit. It is fine to warn the user that the removal of a piece of PII may cause the personalization system to no longer work or to require its manual entry later, as in the case of a credit card number. You must remember that the user, not the Web site, owns the PII.

The Web site should provide to the user base some type of trustworthy third-party proof that the Web site is abiding by its privacy policies. A couple of certified organizations that provide this service are TRUSTe (`www.truste.com`) and BBBOnLine (`www.bbbonline.com`). A Web site might also use a new technology called P3P, or Platform for Privacy Preferences, provided by The Personalization

Consortium (`www.personalization.org`). This will establish protocols that let users control what PII information a site is allowed to know.

The last, and most important, thing that a Web site should do to build trust is always get the users' permission before you get or use their PII. At the same time, it might be nice to tell them why you need the PII.

Role of Personalization in a CMS

Personalization is not a mandatory component of a CMS, but because of the roles it plays when integrated with a CMS, it might as well be. Without personalization, a CMS is just a repository of content. With the roles that personalization provides, a CMS starts to offer value to the user. Because of its importance, most CMSs provide personalization or at least hooks so that third-party personalization systems can be integrated.

Let's examine some of the more visible and obvious roles that personalization provides to a CMS.

Building Relationships

A CMS is of little use if no one ever visits its Web site. By itself, a CMS is just a repository of content linked to the Internet. The information contained in the CMS is the reason users will initially be attracted to a Web site. Somehow, you have to find a way to get Web surfers to come across your Web site. Once a surfer is on your site, the layout, look and feel, and quality of content must draw him in for a closer look. If it does not, your Web site is doomed. The content itself may keep the surfer entertained for a while. Unfortunately, a CMS on its own has little it can do to retain a surfer and make him into a user in the long run. This is the role of personalization.

As discussed earlier in this chapter, personalization is a tool to help develop a relationship between a surfer and the Web site and make her into a user. It does this by starting a dialog between the surfer and the Web site. A well-laid-out personalization system will draw a surfer into the site, providing more and more value to the surfer in exchange for increasing amounts of information about the surfer. Somewhere during this process, the visitor to the site ceases being a surfer and becomes a user who will return regularly to keep her relationship with the site alive.

Personalization engines have at their disposal many different ways to maintain a relationship with the user. A couple of the more common ways are to slowly dole out the content or to continually add more individualized content.

If a Web site has only a limited or fixed amount of content, about the only way it can maintain a relationship is to not give everything to a user at one time.

Instead, the personalization system will have to keep track of the number of times the user has been on the site and slowly provide new links to content. This type of Web site is doomed to fail when it comes to building a lasting relationship. Without a new supply of content, users will sooner or later find everything they need and move on. In other words, they will perceive that no more value is being provided by the site. In actuality, the site may have a lot more to offer, but unfortunately, the perception of the user is the reality that the Web site must live by.

A growing Web site has a much greater chance of retaining a lasting relationship than a static Web site. Because the personalization system continually tries to determine what areas interest users, the CMS can tap into this information and help generate topics for the authors to write about. Having targeted content will play a major role in maintaining a relationship with the user. User interest and the perceived value of the site—because of the continually new content—should remain high.

As long as the user continues to perceive that the site is providing value, he will remain loyal to the Web site.

Matching Content to User Needs

Having the exact content that a user needs in a Web site repository is only half the story when it comes to personalization. A user never finding an article he needs is the same thing as not having the article in the first place. It is the role of personalization to act on behalf of the user and find the exact information the user is looking for. The less the user has to do to find the article, the better the user's perceived value of the Web site.

Most users do not have a lot of time to spend wading through myriad stories just to find the one they find interesting. A smart user will go to a Web site that helps her find the information. A simple search engine often will do just fine, but it would be better in many cases for a user to be able to come back day after day and see new, updated information relating to previous searches and have it show up as the top story. This is the role of personalization.

Most users realize that personalized service requires some input on their part. They expect to have to give some details about what they are looking for. Personalization systems need this information to build a user profile. The more details a user can provide for her profile, the better the profile will be.

The user profile is what drives the matching engine of personalization. Once the profile has all the details that the personalization engine needs, the personalization system can start making meaningful matches. The more detailed the profile, the better the chance that the correct content will be retrieved by personalization.

Good personalization systems can hide the fact that they are building user profiles. Collaborative filter personalization is exceptional in this regard because it never actually has to ask the user for any information. Basically, it just sits back and watches.

The key to a high-quality personalization system is to build a user profile with only information that is absolutely necessary to match the user to Web site content. Any information that a user thinks unnecessary to disclose must be justified before expecting any response from the user. It is often a deadly sin for a personalization system to require, as mandatory, any information that a user perceives as unnecessary or, even worse, feels is too private in nature.

It is essential for a personalization system to be as accurate as possible when it comes to matching content to user needs. Nothing annoys users more than spending valuable time answering questions posed by the personalization system and then getting nothing relevant in return. Wasting users' time is a surefire way to drive them elsewhere.

Creating Differentiation

A CMS, as far as a user is concerned, is just a repository full of text and images. They are a dime a dozen on the Internet. It is possible to differentiate a Web site using only the features of a CMS. Good layout and well-thought-out navigation are major contributors to having a Web site stand out. Personalization and the capability to target content to the user is how a Web site can really start to stand out.

Let's take the example of a moving company's site, which could be a rather boring Web site. Why pick one moving company Web site over another? Will you pick it because of the full-color picture of their moving trucks on their home page? I would think not. More likely, it is a combination of price and the services provided. A quality site will use personalization to help users decide—in their own interest, of course—that the company provides the best moving service.

The Web site might walk the user through a set of questions, all the while touting the strengths and weaknesses of competitors. At the end, it would provide a detailed, personalized estimate of the price of the move and all the special services they will include.

This is an oversimplified example, to be sure, but the same process can be done for almost any site. Using personalization, you can find out exactly what the user wants and then try to convince him that your site will provide it better than anybody else—you can provide content within your site hyping these exact things as strengths.

Benefits of Personalization

You might have noticed that personalization is not rocket science. Basically, you need to find out what a user wants and then provide it. Implementing personalization, on the other hand, can be a mammoth task. The benefits are well worth it, though.

Salespeople have been using personalization effectively for years. This is probably why Web builders have had no problem spending large dollar amounts on personalization; they perceive that they will get the same benefit from it as a salesperson would.

It is no coincidence that the benefits of personalizing a Web site are the same benefits that come with having a good salesperson.

You will also find that if your CMS is part of an e-commerce site, these benefits are even more impressive. They are discussed in the following sections.

Increased User Satisfaction

Users are getting the exact information they need with little effort on their part.

The following are two of the most obvious side benefits of having satisfied users:

- Users now become a great promotional vehicle. A user vouching for your Web site, to a friend or colleague, is probably one of the easiest and most effective forms of advertisement.

- Satisfied users are more apt to answer the questionnaires generated by the personalization system. This, in turn, means that the profiles of the users will be that much more detailed.

Lasting Relationships

A major strength of personalization is fostering relationships, which enables a site to generate content based on the profiles of similar users, knowing that the content will match a specific need of a group of users who will return to the site.

Having many lasting relationships with users means the Web site now has a solid user base with which to work.

Loyal Users

A loyal user spends a larger proportion of time on a site than the average user. He is also less likely to jump ship. Advertisers love it when a site has a proven loyal audience because it means the same users are looking at their ads for more time. This means you can demand a greater fee to advertise on your site.

Longer Site Visits

The longer the user remains on the site, the more time she allocates to replying to questionnaires, adding commentary, and even possibly creating feature content, all at no cost to the Web site.

Increased Market Share

Obviously, the larger your market share, the more you can demand from advertisers. It also means that more of what you are providing from your Web site is being distributed. This might also mean you have a chance to influence the market.

Learning More about the User

The more you can learn about your users, the more accurate your personalization will be. The more accurately your Web site meets the needs of current users, the better it can cater to the needs of new users, especially if collaborative filtering is being used.

Learning What Does and Does Not Work on Web Sites

With personalization, you learn what users like and dislike. It is possible to test some features and have the personalization system poll users for their thoughts about the new features.

Summary

This chapter covered personalization in detail. It started by defining personalization and then walked through the objectives of personalization. Then it explored all the different types of personalization available on the market today. Next, it covered a couple of issues: the first being that the law of diminishing returns applies to personalization and second being privacy. It concluded with the roles and benefits that personalization provides to a CMS.

The next chapter gives CMS a rest and begins your foray into .NET software development.

CHAPTER 5

Basics of Web Architecture

WEB DEVELOPERS LIKE TO MAKE THE WORLD believe that Web architectures are complicated and original. I guess Web developers have never heard of the client/server architecture, which has been around for longer than many Web developers have been alive.

The actual underlying architecture may differ, but in the perspective of a developer, many similarities exist between classic 3-tier or n-tier client/server architectures and current Web architectures. They both consist of three layers:

- *Presentation layer:* Handles the system I/O

- *Application layer:* Provides all the information with which the system works

- *Database layer:* Massages all the data handled by the system

The only visible difference between client/server and Web architectures is that the presentation layer for Web architecture is via a generic Web browser instead of an operating system–specific executable. The result of this difference is a whole new set of tools to enable this Web presentation layer.

Has Microsoft changed Web architecture, as we know it, with .NET? No, it has not. It has just simplified the process considerably. Program language is no longer an issue because Microsoft has introduced the common language runtime (CLR). More important, interprocess communication is now as simple as HTTP and XML. Still remaining are the well-tested and accepted presentation, application, and database client/server layers.

Most Web architectures derive from the same client/server root architecture, which this chapter covers briefly. The majority of this chapter covers the many different ways in which Web architectures can be implemented. A large portion of the chapter's material is .NET-specific because that is the focus of the rest of this book.

Basic Web Architecture

In simple terms, a Web architecture is all the hardware and software needed to get a Web site up and running. Hardware is the domain of operations. All you really need to know, as a developer, is that there is usually at least one computer (often called a *server*) to handle each of the layers discussed in the following sections. These servers are connected in a network so that they can communicate with each other. The actual protocols by which these computers communicate will depend on the implementation method of your architecture.

There is nothing difficult about understanding the software side of standard Web architecture because it really involves common sense. You need some way of interacting with the user, some way of manipulating the information required by the user, and finally, some way of storing the results.

Implementing the architecture, on the other hand, can be a lot harder. You can implement a Web architecture in many different ways, and each one of these implementations claims to be the best. I would argue that each has its weak and strong points, and in some situations, one implementation will excel over others, but in a different situation, another implementation may be better. At this point, there is no best implementation.

Let's first worry about what the architecture is before going into how it can be implemented. Visually, a Web architecture is not rocket science, as you can see in Figure 5-1. This is a simple 3-tier architecture broken down into the presentation layer, the application layer, and the database layer, with each layer corresponding directly to one of the three things needed in an architecture: interaction, manipulation, and storage.

Why break a Web architecture into these parts? It is for the same reason that you break down any task: to simplify it and enable specialization. Each layer of the architecture can be developed independently of the others as long as some upfront effort is made to allow communication between the layers. This communication must be bidirectional because data will flow back and forth between layers. Fortunately, the communication mechanism has already been developed for all major Web architecture implementations.

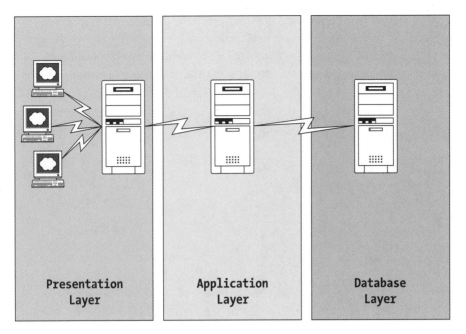

Figure 5-1. The 3-tier Web architecture

All architecture layers have some skill set similarities for development, but each also has a specific skill set of its own that requires special training to become an expert. The skills needed to develop elaborate graphical user interfaces (GUIs) are very different from those required to develop business logic, which then again differ from the skills needed to develop database record structures.

Because a developer only develops code specific to the layer, he does not have to worry about conflicts between layers as long as a developer abides by the defined application programming interface (API), both to and from the other layers. A developer can become an expert in his particular layer of the architecture and doesn't have to get bogged down with the details of the other layers.

A more complex Web architecture known as n-tier architecture is not discussed in this book, but many other good books do cover it. A simple explanation of n-tier is that it is just a 3-tier architecture with the application layer split up into more layers (see Figure 5-2). Breaking up the application layer into smaller parts enables more fine-tuning in performance and the distribution of the system onto more computers. This allows for more computer horsepower and leads to fewer bottlenecks due to the computation time of a given computer.

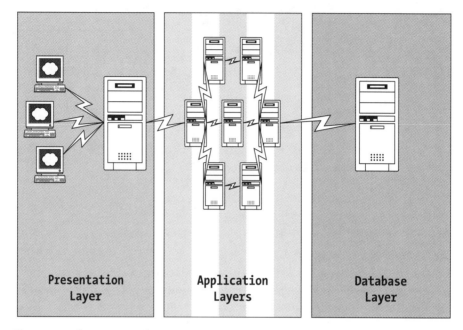

Figure 5-2. The n-tier Web architecture

What Is the Database Layer?

This layer's name kind of gives away what it is responsible for. Obviously, it is in charge of the storage and retrieval of any data into or out of some form of storage. This storage does not have to be a database; it could be a flat file or set of flat files, maybe in XML format, but it usually is a database. The type of database is usually immaterial because a Microsoft SQL Server database usually works just as well as an Oracle or Sybase database for most Web sites (if you are working in a Windows environment, anyway). What is important is the API provided by the implementation because it will determine how accessing information to and from the database is done. Usually, the API does not care which database it is connected to after it is initially configured.

The database for this layer is usually loaded and accessed from its own computer, and on larger Web systems, it often has a mirror copy placed on another computer in case problems occur with the master copy of the database or the computer itself.

The internal workings of this layer, and the database itself, are a mystery to the average programmer. You really don't have to concern yourself with how the data is stored. The most that developers have to do with this layer is set up the database, create and load the database schemas, occasionally generate reports, and regularly back up the database.

The most common methods of accessing data are ODBC, JDBC, ADO, and now with .NET, ADO.NET. All of these methods use SQL as the main language to read to and from the database. Only ADO.NET will be addressed in this book. It is covered in Chapter 7.

What Is the Application Layer?

This layer is where all the business logic of the Web system takes place. The main functionality of this layer can be broken into three parts:

- Get and send data to the database layer.

- Get and receive data from the presentation layer.

- Perform necessary calculations and/or data manipulations.

The application layer takes any data it gets from the database layer and reformats it to the needs of the user as defined by the presentation layer. ADO.NET has some handy functions to make this process very easy; Chapter 7 covers these functions.

The application layer will also take the information provided by the user through the presentation layer and format it to the needs of the database for storage. The data will often come from the presentation layer as a list of fields that just needs to be placed into the database layer using ADO.NET and SQL.

Much of the logic associated with many Web sites' application layers relates to interfacing with the other two layers. The most complex logic performed by this layer is the calculations and manipulations of data it does to handle the business logic of the site.

The application layer is commonly used to map the presentation and database together for transactions such as creating, reading, updating, and deleting. Another major function is to set up and send a SQL transaction to the database layer and then, after the database layer completes the transaction, receive the response back.

What Is the Presentation Layer?

Though not really any more important than the other layers, this layer gets all the glory because it is the only layer that a user ever sees. If a Web site is created properly, only operations and maybe the occasional administrator will ever have to work with the other two layers after everything is configured and working.

This layer is responsible for all user interfaces to the Web site. In most Web sites, even though it presents the logon and password screen, the presentation layer is not responsible for authentication and authorization. These functions are handled by the application layer, which should be hidden securely behind the Web site's firewall.

This layer will generate all dynamic Web pages and forms with the help of the application layer, but the user should not be aware that multiple layers or servers are being used to handle her Web visit. Text, images, audio, video, and whatever else a Web site has gets formatted and ultimately presented to the user through this layer, though the origin of these pieces of content is the CMS repository located in the database layer.

HTML used to be the only method of presenting content to the user through the presentation layer. More recently, two additional technologies, Java applets and ActiveX components, have also become the norm. Even with these two technologies, HTML is still necessary because it is the basis of all client and server communication, which is covered next.

What Are Clients and Servers, Web Style?

A Web architecture has many actual clients and servers. The basic definition of a *client* is a piece of software that requires the assistance of another piece of software to complete its appointed task. A *server* is a piece of software that provides this assistance. These two pieces of software are often located on different computers, but that is not a requirement.

In the Web world, the presentation layer is always broken into two parts. The first part is local to the Web site. The second part is on the user's computer. *Client/server* does have a more accurate definition in the computer world, as already pointed out, but in the Web world, when a developer talks about the client and server, it is this division of the presentation layer to which he is most likely referring. Here, the client is the user's computer and the server is the Web site.

Like any client/server architecture, bidirectional communication must be available between the client and server. In the case of Web clients and servers, this communication is always done by way of a TCP/IP network using HTTP.

What Is Client Side?

To use the Internet, a user needs a computer, any operating system (O/S), Internet access, and any Web browser. Believe it or not, this is everything that makes up the *client side* of a Web site (see Figure 5-3). (Unless, of course, the site you are accessing is using Java applets; then you would need the Java Runtime Environment, or JRE, as well. If the site uses ActiveX components, the O/S needs to be Microsoft based.)

Figure 5-3. The client side

The client side is purposely designed to be as generic as possible so that it allows the most users access to it. It should not matter whether you are a Mac, Microsoft, UNIX, or mainframe user as long as your machine has the core requirement of a Web browser.

Unfortunately, it does matter what platform or browser is used because each platform supports its own implementation of a browser and each browser is slightly different. Major visual differences, for example, are the default screen resolution, and font types, sizes, and colors. Something more worrisome is that each browser type supports different scripting languages or different versions of the same scripting language.

As a developer, you will have to wade through the myriad browsers and browser versions available on the Web today, each of which provides a slightly different version of HTML. Even worse, each browser supports different scripting languages or subtle-but-dangerous differences in the functionality provided under the guise of the same base scripting language. Because of all these differences, testing of a Web site must be thorough and done on multiple browsers and, if possible, platforms.

Fortunately, all browsers seem to support the same version of HTTP, thus allowing at least some subset of the transactions to occur between the client and server. If nothing else, an error of failure can be sent.

The client side in the perspective of a user is the only way to access a Web site. It allows the user to view dynamically all the text and images that the Web site has to offer. All the user has to do is enter the Web site's Uniform Resource Locator (URL) into her browser and then read the information presented on the Web site, click hyperlinks, and/or fill in any Web forms.

What Is Server Side?

The *server side* is everything that is not the client side, obviously (see Figure 5-4). In other words, it contains all the hardware and software that makes up the three layers of a Web architecture, except the parts found on the client side. This includes the database or content repository, any software that handles business logic, and any software that generates and sends information to the client side.

Figure 5-4. The server side

Unlike the client side, the server side is anything but generic. True, it will probably have a database server, application server, and presentation server, but after that, the sky is the limit when it comes to adding servers to the system. Larger Web sites will likely have redundant copies of each of these servers. In fact, many large Web sites will have what is known as a Web server farm, which is made up of many presentation servers (also known as Web servers, which kind of confuses things).

Another common feature on the server side is a firewall or, in some cases, several firewalls. A *firewall* is a piece of software or hardware that restricts further access to a Web site to the pieces of software or people authorized to do so. It is frequently one of the first forms of security added to a Web site and is usually placed in the middle of the presentation layer or between the presentation layer and the application layer. You might place it in front of the server side if you want to restrict access to the Web site right off the bat so that only authorized users can access the site.

Almost any part of the existing computer systems of the company providing the Web site can be integrated into the server side of the Web site. For example, the server side of a Web site will often integrate with back-end systems such as customer relationship management (CRM), enterprise resource planning (ERP), old legacy databases, and other applications. Integration is the meat and potatoes of a Web-consulting firm, and most employees are hired to perform these integrations.

What Is the Hypertext Transfer Protocol (HTTP)?

The Hypertext Transfer Protocol (HTTP) is a very simple protocol, and just like any interactive transaction, it is made up of two parts: the HTTP request shown in Listing 5-1 and the HTTP response shown in Listing 5-2. HTTP has been accepted as the standard for all Web interaction. The key to HTTP's swift and near-universal acceptance is that it is simple and yet still provides a complete solution.

HTTP Request

To initiate a transaction, someone must make a request to another party. The HTTP request does this on behalf of the Web browser and thus the user.

Seven different types of requests are available:

- DELETE

- GET

- HEAD

- OPTIONS

- POST

- PUT

- TRACE

The most common of these request types are GET and POST. In fact, you will probably never encounter the other five request types. It is so unlikely that this book does not even cover the other five types.

The GET transaction type is for a simple Web request. A browser executes it automatically when you type the Web site's URL into the browser's address field. The transaction sent by the browser is very simple. It is made up of three parts, the second two parts being optional.

First, the browser-built mandatory three-part request line is sent. This line will contain the transaction type (GET in this case), the Uniform Resource Identifier (URI), and finally the lowest HTTP version supported by the request. The Web browser then has the option to create request headers that follow the request line. Each request header is a key/value pair made up of three parts: the key field, followed immediately by a colon (:), followed by the value field.

In Listing 5-1, you see the request line with its three parts: GET, /index.html, and HTTP/1.0. These two request headers follow it: User-Agent and Host. The final section is unused in a GET transaction.

Listing 5-1. The HTTP Request

```
GET /index.html HTTP/1.0
User-Agent: Mozilla/4.0 (compatible; MSIE 5.0; Windows NT)
Host: www.contentmgr.com
```

The POST transaction is virtually the same as the GET transaction, except that after all the request headers, the browser appends a message body.

HTTP Response

After you are asked something, it is only appropriate that you respond. This is the job of the HTTP response transaction. It simply replies back to the browser that sent the HTTP request with the requested Web page, if it is able.

The format is very similar to the HTTP request. It is broken into three parts. The first part is the mandatory status line, which is also broken into three parts: the highest HTTP version supported by the response, a three-digit return code, and a human-readable version of the return code. The second part is some optional response headers and key/value pairs, similar to the request headers. Finally, the third part is the actual body of the message requested by the HTTP request. (The creators of HTTP seemed to like threes, no?)

In Listing 5-2, you find the response line with its three parts: HTTP/1.1, 200, and OK. These seven request headers follow it: Server, Date, Connection, Content-Length, Content-Type, Set-Cookie, and Cache-control. It is then completed with the actual HTML code (truncated in the listing to simplify things).

Listing 5-2. The HTTP Response

```
HTTP/1.1 200 OK
Server: Microsoft-IIS/5.0
Date: Thu, 12 Jul 2001 19:19:52 GMT
Connection: Keep-Alive
Content-Length: 1270
Content-Type: text/html
Set-Cookie: ASPSESSIONIDQQQGQGDC=MOFPDBPCPNIBACIBDCIOFCCL; path=/
Cache-control: private

<HTML>
  <BODY>
    (Actual index.html web page)
  </BODY>
</HTML>
```

Fortunately for all, a developer never has to actually create any HTTP of her own. Browsers and the server-side implementation language create it all automatically. The previous explanation is just for your reference so that you can better understand what is happening under the covers.

Web Programming before .NET

Web programming focuses primarily on the presentation layer of a Web architecture. Some of the technologies covered in this chapter do offer a complete solution encompassing all layers of a Web architecture. This is not essential for Web programming, however, because each architecture layer can be developed independently using its own technologies, as long as the layer provides the capability to communicate with the other layers.

Creating Web pages is where the fun is for a Web programmer. Any programmer (well, almost any programmer) can write business-logic programs and code that interfaces with a database, but it takes a special breed of programmer to build Web pages. To a Web programmer, working with text, images, video, and audio is far more exciting than crunching numbers and loading databases.

Creating Web pages can be done from three perspectives: the client side, the server side, or both. You will find that client-side and server-side technologies, on their own, have their strengths and weaknesses, but when used together properly, you can create an impressive and powerful Web interface to your Web site.

As I am sure you have figured out, client-side technologies run on the client computer controlled by the Web browser, and server-side technologies run on the Web site itself. One interesting thing that some Web programmers forget is that you can implement client-side technologies from within server-side technologies.

It would be a big mistake to assume that client side is better than server side or vice versa. You will find that at times one technology will work far better than the other one. As a Web programmer, you should know when it is more appropriate to use client-side technologies than server-side technologies and vice versa.

Now let's cover some of the more widely used client-side and server-side technologies.

Client-Side Technologies

Client-side technologies have the advantage of being run directly on the user's computer. There is no need to send HTTP transactions round-trip over the Internet to complete a task because everything needed to run it is local to the user's computer. This is due to the capability to run local response times for user interaction within the Web page, and these times are often significantly faster.

Client-side technologies can excel in the areas of Web-form validation, mouse-over text and image manipulations, and drop-down menus.

There are some problems, however, with client-side technologies. The biggest is the lack of control. There is nothing stopping a hacker from taking the Web page to his site and tweaking it to do whatever he wants it to do before it is sent back to the Web site. Because of this, authentications and authorizations must never be done using client-side technologies. Also, it is a good idea to have server-side validations on a Web form—even if you are implementing client-side validations—because it is possible for a hacker to send bad data to a site by bypassing the client-side validations.

Another problem with client-side technology is that it is reliant on the capability of the Web browsers to run it. If the browser does not support the client-side technology in use, it obviously will not work. As previously mentioned, browsers come in many flavors, not all of them equal. Some support certain scripting languages and not others.

 TIP *It is always a good idea to check the Web browser to see if it supports the client-side technology being used. If it does not support the technology, provide some way to fall back to a server-side technology. (Server-side technologies should always work because you have complete control.)*

You may also find that, with some client-side technologies, it takes a long time for the Web page to start on the client computer due to the amount of data that needs to be transferred over the Internet before it can start to run. You might find, at times, that you can overkill a Web page with client-side technologies. When you find that it takes longer to load a Web page on the client computer than the amount of time the user spends using it, you might be guilty of client-side overkill.

Hypertext Markup Language (HTML)

If you don't know what Listing 5-3 is or does, I recommend that you put this book down right now and learn HTML first. Web developers may be able to rely on HTML generators to a certain point, but eventually they will need to get their hands dirty and do some HTML coding. If you are a Web developer who has only used HTML generators, you may find the going tough because much of the remainder of this book assumes at least a basic coding knowledge of HTML.

Listing 5-3. Some Basic HTML

```html
<html>
  <head>
    <title>First Web Page</title>
  </head>
  <body>
    <h1><font color="red">Hello New User!</font></h1>
    <p><b>Please enter your name below:</b></p>
    <form method="POST" action="/admin">
      <table border="0" width="50%">
        <tr>
          <td width="75%" colspan="2">
            <p align="center">
            <input type="text" name="Text" size="50">
          </td>
        </tr>
        <tr>
          <td width="50%">
            <p align="center">
            <input type="submit" value="Submit">
          </td>
          <td width="50%">
            <p align="center">
            <input type="reset" value="Reset">
          </td>
        </tr>
      </table>
    </form>
    <p> </p>
    <hr align="left" width="50%">
    <h3>Enjoy the web site!</h3>
  </body>
</html>
```

Even though HTML is the origin of Web programming and has been around since the beginning of the World Wide Web, you cannot overlook it as a key client-side technology. In fact, you will not have much of a Web site without it.

You will find that all other client-side technologies rely on HTML for building a Web page. All server-side technologies generate HTML, which is then sent over to the user's computer to be run. HTML is always present on a Web page, even if it is only used as a means of letting the Web browser know that a different technology is going to take over the execution of the Web page.

Client-Side Scripting

The most common forms of client-side scripting are Netscape and Sun Microsystems' JavaScript (also known as ECMAScript), and Microsoft's JScript and VBScript. All provide basically the same functionality. The only real difference is their syntax. JavaScript, ECMAScript, and JScript are loosely based on Java, whereas VBScript is based on Visual Basic.

These scripting languages provide the capability to add logic to HTML so that it can be more dynamic. For example, scripting languages provide functionality such as input validation and mouse-over effects such as having text change color or an image change when the mouse passes over it.

When client-side scripts are used in conjunction with dynamic HTML (DHTML), it is possible to have a Web page change dynamically without having to send any information over the Internet back to the Web server, thus allowing for things such as drop-down menus.

Another important feature of client-side scripting is that it also provides basic coding logic, such as if-else conditions and looping. This provides a way to dynamically generate a page based on variables as opposed to having the Web page always appear exactly the same way.

However, not all is rosy with client-side scripting. Some browsers don't support scripting, only Internet Explorer supports VBScript, and there are a myriad of JavaScript flavors, each supporting a different subset of functionality set forward by the European Computer Manufacturers Association (ECMA), the international standards body.

When developing client-side JavaScript, a developer needs to be aware of which version of JavaScript the Web browser supports because each version may handle the script differently or possibly not at all.

Plug-ins and ActiveX Components

Plug-ins and ActiveX components are very similar in nature; they are designed to provide some extra pizzazz to a Web site. Plug-ins and ActiveX often add multimedia capabilities to a Web page, but they can actually provide to a Web page almost any functionality that a Web developer can dream up.

Plug-ins are a Netscape technology that give primarily multimedia vendors the capability to integrate their technologies with the Netscape browser. Users must search for and install plug-ins manually. Once installed, whenever the Netscape browser recognizes an input stream as targeted for a plug-in, it will relinquish control and let the plug-in take over.

ActiveX is a Microsoft technology, and it is actually a small program based on Microsoft's Component Object Model (COM) that is downloaded when needed—with user permission—and integrated into the Internet Explorer browser.

Both of these technologies depend on the hardware and O/S of the client computer on which they are running because they are compiled to a binary executable. The plug-in technology supports a much larger variety of hardware and O/Ss, but not all plug-ins are available for all supported hardware and O/Ss. ActiveX is primarily Windows specific, but Mac and UNIX also have some support.

Major concern is focused on ActiveX regarding security, however, because these small programs could potentially gain full access to the user's system. The same concern should also occur with plug-ins because they are also binary programs and can get full access to the user's system.

Java Applets

Java applets are small, downloadable applications that are hosted by a Web browser. Sounds very similar to plug-ins and ActiveX components, doesn't it? Applets enable a Web browser to become a full-blown GUI, not just formed with the few input options provided by HTML. Added to this, they are machine independent and have built-in security. Wow—where can I buy one? They are free as well. Now, this has to be too good to be true.

Yes, there are some catches. First, you have to download and install the Java Virtual Machine (JVM), though this is not a big deal because it comes bundled with the major Web browsers. Second, applets are interpreted on the client machine, so they are slower than native-machine plug-ins and ActiveX components. This is not really an issue with the advent of Just-in-Time (JIT) compilers, which convert applets into native-machine code. Third, applets generally are not persistent, so an applet has to be downloaded each time you return the Web site that uses it. This really is only a problem with slow Internet connections because it causes the user to stare at a white screen until the applet is loaded. With a fast connection, the wait time usually is minimal.

So, you might be wondering, why aren't applets everywhere? And why are many sites that used to have applets removing them? Applets seem like such a godsend.

There are two reasons:

- *Applets in most cases are overkill:* After all the hoopla about them settled, developers realized that almost everything applets are used for already has a technology to handle it, without the overhead of having to do complex Java coding. Plug-ins and ActiveX already handled multimedia, and client-side scripting handled most of the GUI-related development.

- *Usually only programmers can develop applets:* Programmers (I am a programmer so I can say this) are the worst GUI designers. Yes, programmers can do wonders with code, but when asked which shade of blue to use in an interface, most programmers will have no clue. With applets, there is no good way to separate logic from presentation. Add to this the fact that it takes a lot longer to create a Web interface in Java than in HTML, and you can see why applets are losing their appeal.

Server-Side Technologies

Client-side technologies may have the advantage of *possibly* running local to the user's computer, but with server-side technologies, you know they will run, and you have complete control of how they will run.

There is no guessing which types of computers and O/Ss the server-side technologies are being run on because you know exactly what they are. You probably bought them yourself or, at the very least, determined their specifications.

Even though there is a lot of hype about client-side technologies, you will find that most large-scale Web sites use primarily server-side technologies to provide their dynamic content to users. The main reason is that all browsers support HTML, and it is easy to determine which version of HTML the browser supports. With this information, a server-side technology can create HTML, which it knows without a doubt will run on the client machine. By the way, the server-side technology will also know which client-side script the browser supports, so it can generate the appropriate script, too.

Basically, all server-side technologies do the same thing. They dynamically generate HTML and possibly client-side scripts to run on users' browsers. The only real difference is the approach they take to do this.

All server-side technologies suffer from the same major drawback. All processing of the information on the page is on the server-side, and thus, whenever a user needs some type of response from the Web page, a transaction must be sent to the server side, processed there, and sent back. On a slow network connection, the responsiveness could be horrendous. In addition, a server is simultaneously handling many users, thus there is the potential of causing two more problems: The network may get congested because of the amount of data passing through it, and the server may get overwhelmed by the number of calculations it might have to do at the same time.

There are ways to mitigate all of these problems, but currently there really are no solutions. To handle the round-trip problem, you can use client-side scripting. For the congestion of the network, larger bandwidths must be used. To alleviate the possibility of overwhelming a Web server, Web server farms can be used.

Common Gateway Interface (CGI)

Common Gateway Interface (CGI) is the oldest of all the server-side technologies. It is hardly rocket science. Basically, it consists of programs that run on the server machine that handle HTTP requests—in particular, GET and POST—and generate HTTP responses. (Isn't it fortunate that we explored those earlier?)

Usually, CGI programs are written in Perl, a very powerful language when it comes to strings, but any language can be used to write CGI programs. Because most CGI programs are written in Perl, a relatively slow, interpreted language, CGIs have the stigma of being slow. In actuality, if a CGI program is written in C or C++, it can be extremely fast.

The real problem with CGIs is that they are memory hogs. Whenever a CGI program is called, a new instance of it is created with its own memory space. If multiple concurrent users are accessing the Web site, it is possible to exhaust the available memory on the server running CGIs.

CGIs also can be a security risk if not handled properly. Because they are little programs, it is possible for a hacker to create one, load it onto a server, and then run it. To stop just such an event, permit the running of CGI programs only from one protected directory (usually named cgi-bin), which you control.

Server Application Programming Interfaces (APIs)

To try to alleviate the memory problem of CGIs, many Web servers have made APIs available to add functionality to the Web server. For example, Netscape servers offer NSAPI, Microsoft servers have ISAPI, and Apache servers provide Apache modules. You can think of the added server API functionality as server-side plug-ins.

Basically, APIs provide a way for a programmer to write some additional functionality that a Web server lacks and then add it to the Web server. Because the code is loaded only once in the same memory space as the Web server itself, it is possible to create multiple instances of the same piece of functionality without incurring the overhead of loading the code space over and over again.

The major gotcha of server APIs is that developing additional functionality is usually quite complex and prone to being buggy. Also, if the added functionality crashes on a production server, it brings the entire Web server down, which terminates all active users and disallows any new users until the server is rebooted and purged of the problem created by the added functionality. This is because the added functionality shares the same space as the Web server. Hmm . . . it's sad that its strength is also its greatest weakness.

Server-Side Scripting

Server-side scripting is very similar to client-side scripting in many respects. It is simply adding scripted logic to HTML, which is parsed prior to being sent to the user's computer. The code generated and sent to the user's computer by the server-side script interpreter is usually straight HTML or possibly HTML and client-side scripts.

Many server-side scripting languages exist, and all claim to be the best. The most common top performers are Active Server Pages (msdn.microsoft.com/asp), ColdFusion (www.macromedia.com), server-side JavaScript (www.netscape.com), and PHP (www.php.net).

Server-side scripting is fairly powerful and is usually easy to work with. The logic provided by server-side scripting is all the standard syntax found in any programming language, such as variables, calculations, if-else conditions, and loops.

Unfortunately, server-side scripting executes slowly because all scripts are implemented using interpreted languages. To alleviate this slowness, many Web sites implement some type of caching system that allows the more common Web pages to be stored in memory and then, when requested, sent immediately to the client without running the server-side script interpreter.

JavaServer Pages (JSP) and Servlets

Here come JavaServer Pages (JSP) and servlets to the rescue. This one-two punch seems to provide an elegant solution to the server-side Web development problems previously mentioned.

JSP is a server-side scripting language based on the Java language. It allows a programmer to combine Java statements with HTML. So, you might be thinking, how does this differ from a server-side JavaScript? A JSP script is compiled into a Java class, which can then be executed using a JIT compiler. In other words, it will be far faster to execute.

Servlets are small Java programs that run off a Web server in a manner very similar to server-side APIs, except that all the execution of the programs occurs within the memory space of the JRE and not the Web server. Servlets are loaded once and execute many times, just like server-side APIs. The JRE is far more robust than a Web server when it comes to running programs, and it is designed to handle memory recovery and program crashes. This means that a servlet can crash and not bring down the Web server.

Another bonus is that JSP combined with servlets also allows for the separation of HTML and programming code. It is possible to build user-defined tags that encompass all the programming code and then embed them in the HTML, just like any other HTML tag. Now all an HTML developer needs to learn is the new tags instead of how to program in Java, and a Java programmer only has to learn how to create tags and doesn't have to mess with HTML.

The JSP and servlet combination sounds like a winner. This is probably why it is rapidly becoming one of the most used server-side technologies. It is also the only true competition to Microsoft's .NET as a complete solution.

Web Programming Using .NET

I bet you were wondering if I would ever start covering .NET. Well, from here on, as a basketball announcer would say, it's " . . . nothing but .NET."

The .NET Framework encompasses much more than Web development, but for the sake of simplicity, this book only explores the Web development portion. The .NET Framework covers all layers of software development, from the operating system all the way up to Web-page generation. When you look at the .NET Framework from a Web architecture point of view, you will see that it provides coverage for all three standard layers of the architecture as well as the means of communicating between them.

Microsoft has taken some of the best ideas from the industry, combined them with a few ideas of its own, and built a solid and complete development platform. Overall, the .NET Framework simplifies the whole infrastructure on which all Microsoft Windows programming is based.

Boy, that sounded like a Microsoft ad.

Let's break the .NET Framework down into its parts and see how each part affects Web programming.

What Is the .NET Framework?

Simply put, the .NET Framework is Microsoft's next generation for software development. It encompasses all aspects of software development, from accessing the operating system right up to handling things such as Web controls.

As you can see in Figure 5-5, the .NET Framework consists of three simple layers, each building on the previous one.

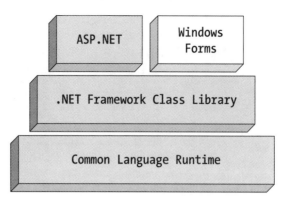

Figure 5-5. The .NET Framework for Web development

The basis of the .NET Framework is the common language runtime or, as it is commonly known, the CLR. The CLR provides memory management and garbage collection. The most notable feature of this layer is that it provides the facility to allow language-independent development.

The second layer, known as the .NET Framework class library, is a huge library of classes that any programming language can use to develop software. In this layer are classes to support things such as database, I/O, and network access.

The top layer, known as ASP.NET and Windows Forms, provides the capability to generate Web and desktop applications. This book will not cover desktop applications, but it is included in this explanation to give the full picture of the Framework. Web pages are developed in the ASP.NET layer.

Common Language Runtime (CLR)

The CLR has many similarities to Java's JRE. It is obvious where Microsoft got a lot of its ideas when it came to creating the CLR. Just like the JRE, the CLR handles the loading of programs, manages memory, and does garbage collection.

Another striking similarity between the JRE and the CLR is that executables are compiled to a machine-independent language called Microsoft Intermediate Language (MSIL), which is very much like Java's Bytecodes. Microsoft is not harping on this currently, but I am sure once .NET stabilizes, Microsoft will start an effort to port MSIL to other platforms just as Java does now. When this occurs, Microsoft will also have a "write once, execute anywhere" platform-independent software like Java. This obviously is a powerful feature when it comes to Web development.

When the code is about to run on a computer, the MSIL is run through one of two JIT compilers in a way that's similar to Java. The first JIT compiler, known as the Econo-JIT, compiles the MSIL very fast with no optimizations. The second JIT, known as the standard JIT, generates optimized code and obviously is a little slower. Both JITs are designed to generate machine code specific to the processor on which they are running.

As you will see shortly, ASP.NET programs are precompiled before they are put into production. Then they are JIT-compiled when first accessed. Once compiled, they stay cached in memory so that they don't need to be compiled again. This makes the first call to an ASP.NET program somewhat slow, but any subsequent calls are extremely fast.

It no longer matters which language you develop in when it comes to .NET because all languages ultimately generate MSIL. In fact, objects created in one language have absolutely no problem being linked and run with objects of another language. No longer is there a need for variant data types because all data types from one language map directly to the data types of another language.

Now Web developers can develop ASP.NET programs in the language of their choice. They also no longer have to worry about whether their program will work with someone else's program, even if it was written in a different language.

.NET Framework Class Library

This layer is nothing more than a set of language-independent classes that provide the programmer with a vast array of prepackaged functionality. In this layer, you will find classes that handle database access, I/O, mathematical calculation, security, threads, network access, and much more.

It is here that a Web programmer will find many of the standard system and utility functions that will make her development a lot easier and faster.

ASP.NET

ASP.NET is the next generation of server-side Web technology. When written correctly, it is considerably different from its predecessor, ASP. In fact, you can't even code ASP.NET using ASP's default language, VBScript, because VBScript is no longer supported.

ASP.NET programs are now compiled like any other program before they move to production, thus giving a major speed boost to the old interpreted ASP. To call an ASP.NET program in a browser, you use a file ending in .aspx instead of .asp. There is still support for the old ASP files, but files ending with .asp are run through a different interpreter when requested by a user.

ASP.NET programs are written in standard languages such as Visual Basic (VB), managed C++, or the new C#. All ASP.NET programs in this book will be written in C#, but they could have just as easily been written in VB or managed C++.

A very powerful feature of ASP.NET that is used extensively throughout this book is the Codebehind feature. This feature allows for the complete separation of HTML and logic code into different files, thus letting HTML experts and software developers specialize in what they do best.

State can now be maintained without any special coding on the part of the developer between form submittals because all the logic to handle this is automatically generated when the ASP.NET program is compiled.

Validations are now very simple to do because ASP.NET will generate the appropriate client-side JavaScript to handle the validation on the client machine and will also validate for correctness on the server-side. This is just in case hackers try to cause problems by overriding the generated JavaScript.

ASP.NET provides many other features, and this book will show them to you when they are needed. This short list shows you that ASP.NET and JSP/servlets will have quite a battle for supremacy for the server-side technology market.

Summary

This chapter covered Web architecture in great detail. It started by describing Web architectures in general and their three layers: database, application, and presentation. It then moved on to explore the presentation layer in more detail, showing how it is divided into a client side and a server side and that communication between them takes place using HTTP. From there, this chapter covered several of the more common client- and server-side technologies on the market. Finally, this chapter made the book's first foray into the world of .NET by showing, at a high level, what the .NET Framework is.

The next chapter leaves the general theory behind. You'll start getting your hands dirty, refreshing your knowledge of C#, ASP.NET, and Visual Studio .NET by taking a step-by-step journey through the development of some rudimentary Web page code.

CHAPTER 6

ASP.NET, C#, and Visual Studio .NET

What do you think, enough theory already? Let's have some fun and get our hands dirty!

This book assumes you already have a decent degree of understanding about ASP.NET, C#, and Visual Studio .NET. Nevertheless, to get everybody on a level playing field, this chapter will walk through one step-by-step example covering many of the features you should already know. If you have difficulty following this chapter, it would probably be a good idea to buy a book or two on ASP.NET and C#, read them first, and then come back when you feel more comfortable.

This chapter really isn't a tutorial for .NET coding. It is more like a quick walk-through to get your bearings if you've been away from .NET for a while. It is also a chance to point out a few helpful tidbits of information of which you may not be aware.

So, sit back and code along. This chapter should be enough to get the rust out and get you back into the groove of thinking like an ASP.NET and C# developer.

The Simple Dynamic Content Viewer

We will start with a simple ASP.NET Web page to view dynamic content. The final Web page should end up looking like Figure 6-1.

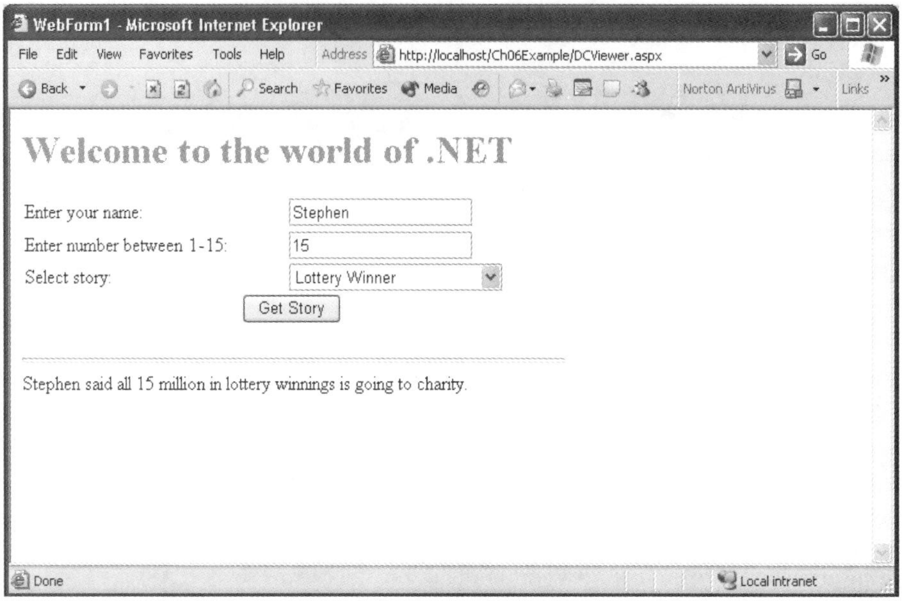

Figure 6-1. The simple Dynamic Content Viewer

The Web page contains a simple, dynamically loaded, drop-down list of stories available for reading. After a user selects a story, he clicks the Get Story button, at which point a transaction is sent to the Web server to retrieve the story. Then, once the story is loaded on the user's machine, it is displayed below the story selector area.

I thought the program was a little boring, so I livened it up with a little personalization. I added two additional boxes: one to get the user's name and the other to get a magical number. Both of these input text fields are validated on the client using JavaScript and are verified on the server. Each field is mandatory, and the number must be between 1 and 15.

Now when the user clicks the Get Story button, he is the subject of the story.

A Summary of the Steps

In this chapter, you will follow these steps to build the simple Dynamic Content Viewer:

1. Create a new project using Visual Studio .NET.

2. Rename WebForm1.aspx.

3. Design the Dynamic Content Viewer.

    a. Create a title.

    b. Create a table to lay out the Web page design.

    c. Add Web controls to the table.

    d. Add validation to the Web controls.

    e. Add a label to display the selected story.

4. Create a Content class.

5. Add properties and a constructor to the Content class.

6. Declare and load the content repository.

7. Fill the drop-down list from the content repository.

8. Manipulate and load the story for viewing.

Creating a New Project Using Visual Studio .NET

To get the ball rolling, you have to create a new project to store all the files that make up the Web page. You will be creating a C#-based Web page, but you just as easily could generate a Visual Basic–based Web page instead. The process is very straightforward. You just need to start the process and select the appropriate template. If the template needs any additional information, it will ask you for it.

1. Click the New Project button from the Start Page. (This should open the New Project dialog box, as shown in Figure 6-2.)

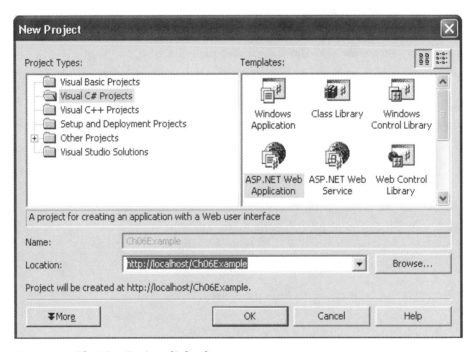

Figure 6-2. The New Project dialog box

2. Click the Visual C# Projects folder in the Project Types window. This will display all available C# project templates in the Templates window.

3. Click the ASP.NET Web Application icon in the Templates window.

4. Replace WebApplication1 with **Ch06Example** in the Location field. Notice that the grayed-out Name field is automatically updated with Ch06Example.

5. Click OK.

After 30 seconds or so, depending on the speed of your computer, you should have a project to start developing. When Visual Studio is finished doing its stuff, you should be presented with a screen similar to the one shown in Figure 6-3.

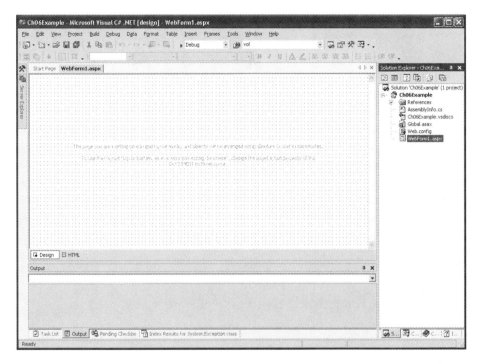

Figure 6-3. An empty project

Renaming WebForm1.aspx

The first thing you may notice is that the default name for the Web page, to put it nicely, stinks. The first thing you should do is rename it. Follow these steps:

1. Right-click the WebForm1.aspx file in the Solution Explorer.

2. Select Rename from the menu presented.

3. Enter **DCViewer.aspx** in the edit field that appears in the
    Solution Explorer.

4. Press the Enter key. Now you are ready to design your Web page.

Designing the Dynamic Content Viewer

You have the option to place all your components at exact x and y coordinates.
I've never had to use this option because what is provided by standard HTML is
quite sufficient. Using standard HTML tables should be good enough for laying
out a Web page. Web pages should be simple and easy to use.

Changing to FlowLayout

The default layout mode is GridLayout, so now that the newly named Web page is
available, let's change the layout to FlowLayout.

1. Select PageLayout in the Properties dialog box. If the Properties dialog
    box is not visible, select Properties Window from the View menu.

2. Select FlowLayout from the drop-down list box. The grid should disap-
    pear from the Web design editor.

 NOTE   *This book uses FlowLayout exclusively, and it is
assumed that you will do the preceding two steps for every
page designed with this book.*

Now design your Web page so that it looks like Figure 6-4. You will be amazed
at the amount of functionality your Web page will have after you complete these
simple steps.

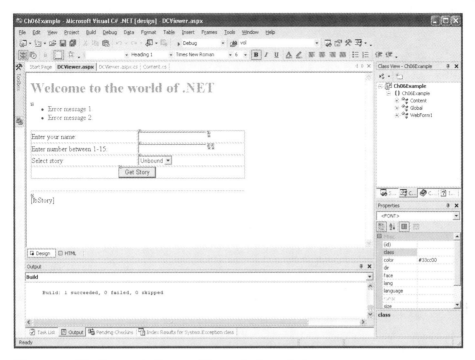

Figure 6-4. The Dynamic Content Viewer design window

Creating a Title

Let's add a cheery title to the Web page. It is usually a good idea to add a title or company logo near the top of your Web page so that a user will know where she is. To do this, you should follow these steps:

1. In the main edit window, type **Welcome to the world of .NET**. Notice that an asterisk has been added to the filename in the edit window tabs. This is a simple reminder that the file is "dirty" and needs saving.

2. Highlight the text you entered with the mouse.

3. Click the Block Format drop-down list box on the main toolbar.

4. Select Heading 1.

5. Click the Foreground Color button on the main toolbar.

6. On the presented dialog box, select a color of your liking. I selected green (#33cc00).

Creating a Table to Lay Out the Web Page Design

As I mentioned previously, you could have selected the X and Y layout option, but using a table is just as good in this case. Once you have a table, you will be able to fill it in with all the edit fields of the entry portion of the Web page. Follow these steps:

1. Select Insert Table from the Table menu.

2. In the Insert Table dialog box, set the following:

   - Rows: 4

   - Columns: 2

   - Width: 65 percent

   - Border Size: 0

3. Click OK.

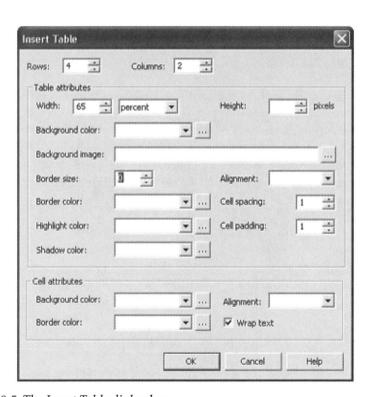

Figure 6-5. The Insert Table dialog box

4. Select the bottom row of the created table.

5. Select Merge Cells from the Table menu.

Adding Web Controls to the Table

Now you are ready to design the data entry part of the Web page, or what is better known as a Web form. The Web form is the part of a Web page used to communicate with the Web server. Information entered into it is packaged up in an HTTP request and sent to the server when the Submit button is clicked. The server then sends back an HTTP response. Chapters 10 and 11 cover Web forms in great detail.

1. In the first column of the first three rows, type the following:

    - Enter your name:

    - Enter number between 1–15:

    - Select story:

> **NOTE**   *Don't worry that the second column collapsed to nothing; this will correct itself with the next step.*

2. Click and drag a TextBox from the Toolbox on the left border (see Figure 6-6) into the second column of the first and second rows.

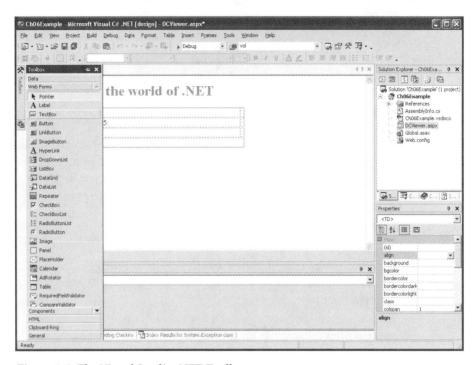

Figure 6-6. The Visual Studio .NET Toolbox

3. Select TextBox1 and enter **tbUserName** in the (ID) field of the Properties dialog box on the right side of the screen.

4. Select TextBox2 and enter **tbNumber** in the (ID) field of the Properties dialog box.

5. Click and drag a DropDownList from the Toolbox into the second column of the third row.

6. Select the DropDownList and enter **ddlStories** in the (ID) field of the Properties dialog box.

7. Place the cursor in the fourth row and click the Center button in the main toolbar. This will cause all things added to the row to be centered.

8. Click and drag a Button from the Toolbox into the fourth row.

9. Select the Button and enter **bnGetStory** in the (ID) field of the Properties dialog box.

10. Enter **Get Story** in the Text field of the Properties dialog box.

Okay, I'm sure you're dying to give the Web page a try. So, let's give it a go. Save DCViewer.aspx and then select Build from the Build menu. You now have two options for viewing your Web page. You can use the slow-to-start Debug button on the main toolbar, or to start quickly you can right-click the DCViewer.aspx file in the Solution Explorer and then select View in Browser.

Now, play around a bit. Notice that the button you added has defaulted to a Submit button. Also notice this very important fact: The session state of the form is retained after it returns from the Web server without any special coding of your own. In other words, the name and number fields retain their values after the round-trip from the server. Pretty spiffy, no?

Okay, let's get back to work.

Adding Validation to the Web Controls

As you were playing with the Web page, I'm sure you noticed that it didn't matter what you typed into the text boxes. Fixing this is almost too easy. All you have to do is add four more Web controls, adjust some properties, and you're done.

I didn't tell you the best part. ASP.NET provides both client-side and server-side validation without any effort on your side. The default is to provide both, but if you don't want client-side validation, just turn it off. You can do this by adding to the top of your Web page file the following directive:

```
<%@ Page ClientTarget="DownLevel" %>
```

By the way, you can force client-side validation even if the browser doesn't support it. Use the following directive:

```
<%@ Page ClientTarget="UpLevel" %>
```

Why you would want to do the UpLevel attribute, though, escapes me.

There are two types of validation: static and dynamic. When an error occurs, *static* validation places the error message exactly at the place where the validation control is located in the HTML. *Dynamic* validation, on the other hand, lets you group all the errors at one place on the page, plus you can place some type of marker next to the edit field to flag it in the case of an error. Follow these steps:

1. Click and drag a RequiredFieldValidator control from the Toolbox into the first and second rows right after each TextBox.

2. Select the RequiredFieldValidator control for the tbUserName control and, in the Properties dialog box, set the following:

   - Display: Dynamic

   - Error Message: You must enter a user name

   - Text: *

   - Control To Validate: tbUserName

   - (ID): rfvUserName

3. Select the RequiredFieldValidator control for the tbNumber control and, in the Properties dialog box, set the following:

   - Display: Dynamic

   - Error Message: You must enter a number

   - Text: *

   - Control To Validate: tbNumber

   - (ID): **rfvNumber**

4. Click and drag a RangeValidator control from the Toolbox into the second row right after the RequiredFieldValidator control.

5. Select the RangeValidator control for the tbNumber control and, in the Properties dialog box, set the following:

- Display: Dynamic

- Error Message: Enter a number between 1–15

- Text: *

- Control To Validate: tbNumber

- Maximum Value: 15

- Minimum Value: 1

- Type: Integer

- (ID): **rvNumber**

6. Click and drag a ValidationSummary control from the Toolbox onto a line of its own just after the title and before the table.

Now, if you compile and run the Web page, you will find that the Web page will only complete successfully if there is a name and a number between 1 and 15.

Adding a Label to Display the Selected Story

You need to include only two more pieces, and then your Web page design is complete: first, a horizontal line to separate the two parts of the page; second, a label to display the story. Believe it or not, you are not going to need to embed any code or create any special tags or what have you. Just a Label will do. By the way, the Label supports full HTML formatting as well. Follow these steps:

1. Click and drag a Label control from the Toolbox and place it after the table.

2. Select the Label control and enter **lbStory** in the (ID) field of the Properties dialog box.

3. Delete everything from the Text field of the Properties dialog box.

4. Select the Toolbox on the left side of the screen.

5. Select the HTML button near the bottom of the Toolbox.

6. Click and drag a HorizontalRule control from the Toolbox and place it after the table and before the Label control.

7. Select the HorizontalRule control and, in the Properties dialog box, set the following:

   - Align: Left

   - Size: **4**

   - Width: **65%**

Okay, you are done with the design of the Web page and with the file DCViewer.aspx. Save, compile, and run the Web page. Still doesn't do much, does it? That is what the C# code is for. So, let's take a quick look at Listing 6-1, which shows the entire DCViewer.aspx file generated by the visual design tool provided by Visual Studio .NET. Then we'll move on to the world of C#.

Listing 6-1. DCViewer.aspx

```
<%@ Page language="c#" Codebehind="DCViewer.aspx.cs"
                       AutoEventWireup="false"
                       Inherits="Ch06Example.WebForm1" %>
<!DOCTYPE HTML PUBLIC "-//W3C//DTD HTML 4.0 Transitional//EN" >
<HTML>
  <HEAD>
    <meta name="GENERATOR" Content="Microsoft Visual Studio 7.0">
    <meta name="CODE_LANGUAGE" Content="C#">
    <meta name="vs_defaultClientScript" content="JavaScript">
    <meta name="vs_targetSchema"
          content="http://schemas.microsoft.com/intellisense/ie5">
  </HEAD>
  <body >
    <form id="Form1" method="post" runat="server">
      <H1>
        <FONT color=#33cc00>Welcome to the world of .NET</FONT>
      </H1>
      <P>
        <asp:ValidationSummary id=ValidationSummary1 runat="server">
        </asp:ValidationSummary>
      </P>
```

```
<P>
  <TABLE id="Table1" cellSpacing="1" cellPadding="1"
        width="65%" border="0">
    <TR>
      <TD>Enter your name:</TD>
      <TD>
        <asp:TextBox id=tbUserName runat="server">
        </asp:TextBox>
        <asp:RequiredFieldValidator id=rfvUserName
            runat="server"
            ErrorMessage="You must enter a user name"
            Display="Dynamic"
            ControlToValidate="tbUserName">*
        </asp:RequiredFieldValidator>
      </TD>
    </TR>
    <TR>
      <TD>Enter number between 1-15</TD>
      <TD>
        <asp:TextBox id=tbNumber runat="server"></asp:TextBox>
        <asp:RequiredFieldValidator id=rfvNumber
            runat="server"
            ErrorMessage="You must enter a number"
            Display="Dynamic"
            ControlToValidate="tbNumber">*
        </asp:RequiredFieldValidator>
        <asp:RangeValidator id=rvNumber
            runat="server"
            ErrorMessage="Enter a number between 1 and 15"
            Display="Dynamic"
            ControlToValidate="tbNumber"
            MaximumValue="15"
            MinimumValue="1"
            Type="Integer">*
        </asp:RangeValidator>
      </TD>
    </TR>
    <TR>
      <TD>Select Story</TD>
      <TD>
        <asp:DropDownList id=ddlStories runat="server">
        </asp:DropDownList>
      </TD>
    </TR>
```

113

```
            <TR>
              <TD colSpan=2>
                <P align=center>
                  <asp:Button id=bnGetStory runat="server" Text="Get Story">
                  </asp:Button>
                </P>
              </TD>
            </TR>
          </TABLE>
      </P>
      <P>
        <HR align=left width="65%" SIZE="4">
      <P></P>
      <P>
        <asp:Label id=lbStory runat="server"></asp:Label>
      </P>
    </form>
  </body>
</HTML>
```

Wait a minute. This isn't HTML. What are all these `<asp:xxx runat="server">` things? The first thing you should know is that you can still use plain old HTML, but then you lose the capability to completely separate HTML and code logic. This will be covered in more detail shortly.

Starting backward, the `runat="server"` is an attribute to tell the ASP.NET compiler that it is a server control, thus allowing the compiler to process it. Without `runat="server"`, the compiler will ignore it because it will believe it is a client-only control. You see this happening with the `<table></table>`, `<tr></tr>`, and `<td></td>` controls.

ASP.NET has taken every HTML form element and replaced it with an intrinsic control. Table 6-1 is a list of all the intrinsic controls used in Listing 6-1. If you want, you can put them in Listing 6-1 to give you a better understanding of what the code is doing.

Table 6-1. Intrinsic Controls in Listing 6-1

Intrinsic Control	HTML Form Element
`<asp:TextBox>`	`<input type="text" value="...">`
`<asp:DropDownList>`	`<select>...</select>`
`<asp:Button>`	`<input type="submit">`
`<asp:Label>`	`<span>...</span>`

Intrinsic controls are more consistent because they provide a common set of properties to work with. Because they are written using C#, they have been implemented using the common language runtime (CLR) and thus can be used with any language that supports the .NET Framework. You will find out shortly that, if you provide a name=xxx attribute in the controls, you can access the control using that name like any other object.

You may have noticed that there is not a single line of C# code in the DCViewer.aspx file. Believe it or not, because of intrinsic controls, you don't need C# here.

What? Didn't I just say earlier that you need C# to make this Web page do its stuff? Yes, you need C# code, but it isn't going to go into the ASPX file.

ASP.NET has gone the extra mile and provided the capability to completely separate the HTML from code logic. You will see that you can create almost any Web page without mixing HTML and code. Unfortunately, many examples on the Internet don't have this separation, probably for one of three reasons:

- The developer is used to doing it the old way and is unwilling to do it—or figure out how to do it—the new proper way.

- The developer is too lazy to make the effort to separate them.

- The developer doesn't know that he can.

Let's see how you achieve this separation of HTML and code. How observant are you? Notice at the top of DCViewer.aspx the following directive:

```
<%@ Page language="c#" Codebehind="DCViewer.cs"
                       AutoEventWireup="false"
                       Inherits="Ch06Example.WebForm1" %>
```

The Codebehind and Inherits attributes in this directive allow the ASPX Web page to link itself with C# code. The Codebehind attribute tells the ASPX Web page where its code logic is, and the Inherits attribute tells from which class in the Codebehind to inherit logic.

Now, if you use intrinsic controls with their capability to become objects, you can access the controls inside the C# code and change their properties at will, thus giving you complete control to change what you want about the control and not actually have to be in the HTML to do it. You will see that this is exactly what you are going to do to load the drop-down list ddlStories, which you may have noticed is empty. You will also display the story using the label lbStory.

You've spent enough time with HTML for now. Let's move on to some C# coding. Listing 6-2 shows what the DCViewer.cs file has in it now before you make any changes.

Wait a second, what DCViewer.cs file? It's not in the Solution Explorer. Well, actually it is, but it's hidden. There are three easy ways to view it:

- The first way is to click the Show All Files button in the Solution Explorer and then click the plus (+) symbol next to DCViewer.aspx. This method clutters up your Solution Explorer with a bunch of files that you care little about.

- The second method is to simply right-click the file DCViewer.aspx and then select View Code from the menu options.

- The third option is to select Code from the View menu or press F7 when DCViewer.aspx is the current file being edited.

Listing 6-2. The Default DCViewer.cs

```
using System;
using System.Collections;
using System.ComponentModel;
using System.Data;
using System.Drawing;
using System.Web;
using System.Web.SessionState;
using System.Web.UI;
using System.Web.UI.WebControls;
using System.Web.UI.HtmlControls;

namespace Ch06Example
{
    /// <summary>
    ///     Summary description for WebForm1.
    /// </summary>
    public class WebForm1 : System.Web.UI.Page
    {
        protected System.Web.UI.WebControls.Label lbStory;
        protected System.Web.UI.WebControls.Button bnGetStory;
        protected System.Web.UI.WebControls.DropDownList ddlStories;
        protected System.Web.UI.WebControls.RangeValidator rvNumber;
        protected System.Web.UI.WebControls.RequiredFieldValidator
                    rfvNumber;
        protected System.Web.UI.WebControls.TextBox tbNumber;
        protected System.Web.UI.WebControls.RequiredFieldValidator
                    rfvUserName;
        protected System.Web.UI.WebControls.TextBox tbUserName;
```

```
    protected System.Web.UI.WebControls.ValidationSummary
            ValidationSummary1;
    protected System.Web.UI.WebControls.TextBox tbName;
    protected System.Web.UI.WebControls.RequiredFieldValidator rfvName;

    private void Page_Load(object sender, System.EventArgs e)
    {
        // Put user code to initialize the page here
    }

#region Web Form Designer generated code
    override protected void OnInit(EventArgs e)
    {
        //
        // CODEGEN: This call is required by the ASP.NET Web Form Designer.
        //
        InitializeComponent();
        base.OnInit(e);
    }

    /// <summary>
    ///     Required method for Designer support - do not modify
    ///     the contents of this method with the code editor.
    /// </summary>
    private void InitializeComponent()
    {
        this.Load += new System.EventHandler (this.Page_Load);
    }
    #endregion
    }
}
```

The code is very simple. The first time that the WebForm1 is accessed, the
OnInit event is triggered. This causes the OnInit() method to be called. This, in
turn, calls the InitializeComponent() method, which adds Page_Load() as the
Load event so that every time the page is loaded it will be able to run. In some
ASP.NET programs, the InitializeComponent() method will add Page_Unload() as
the Unload event so that every time the page is unloaded it will be run.

In the Page_Load() method, you will notice the IsPostBack variable. This
handy variable enables the Page_Load() method to do something special the first
time it is called (for example, load some intrinsic control with some information).

All ASP.NET Web pages have this basic shell (shown in Listing 6-2), except for the declarations of the intrinsic controls, of course, which are specific to each Web page:

```
protected System.Web.UI.WebControls.Label lbStory;
protected System.Web.UI.WebControls.Button bnGetStory;
protected System.Web.UI.WebControls.DropDownList ddlStories;
protected System.Web.UI.WebControls.TextBox tbNumber;
protected System.Web.UI.WebControls.TextBox tbUserName;
protected System.Web.UI.WebControls.TextBox tbName;
protected System.Web.UI.WebControls.RequiredFieldValidator rfvUserName;
```

You should know these controls because you created them when you changed their (ID) property. (For clarity, I took the liberty of removing the controls you didn't change.) Now that they are declared, you have complete control to do with them what you want, and you will do just that in a second.

Creating a Content Class

First, you need to create a helper class to store the vast amount of content that this viewer will provide (all three stories). The class is simple. It will store the headline and the story and will provide a constructor to load itself and two properties to extract the information.

1. Click Ch06Example in the Solution Explorer.

2. Select Add Class from the Project menu. This will create a dialog box similar to the one you see in Figure 6-7.

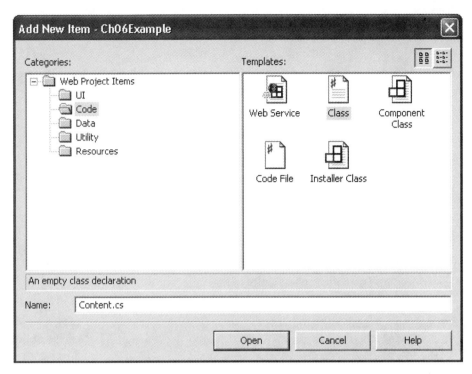

Figure 6-7. The Add New Item dialog box

3.   Click the Web Project Items folder in the Categories window.

4.   Click the Code folder under the Web Project Items folder.

5.   Click the C# Class icon.

6.   Enter **Content.cs** in the Name field.

7.   Click Open.

Adding Properties and a Constructor to the Content Class

Normally, I would just go ahead and code the statements to add the property to the class, but this is a good opportunity to examine the Class View dialog box. You will use the dialog box to create the properties, but then you'll just go ahead and create the constructor the old-fashioned way, by typing three whole lines of code.

1. Select Class View from the View menu.

2. Click Ch06Example in the Class View dialog box.

3. Right-click the Content class.

4. Select Add Property from the Add menu item. This will create a dialog box similar to the one in Figure 6-8.

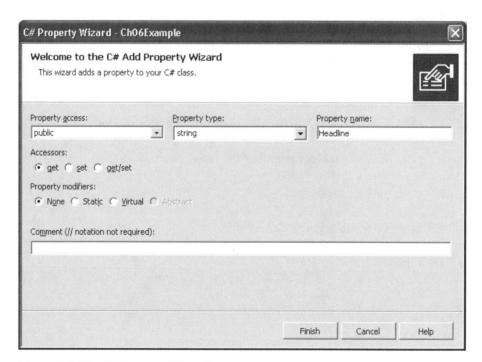

Figure 6-8. The C# Property Wizard

5. On the presented dialog box, set the following:

- Property Access: Public

- Property Type: String

- Property Name: **Headline**

- Accessors: get

- Property Modifiers: None

6. Click Finish.

7. Change the null in the Headline get statement to **headline** and add the headline variable, as shown in Listing 6-3 in the Content.cs file.

Listing 6-3. Fix the Headline get Statement in Content.cs

```
protected string headline;

public string Headline
{
    get
    {
        return headline;
    }
}
```

8. Right-click the Content class.

9. Select Add Property from the Add menu item.

10. On the presented dialog box, set the following:

- Property Access: Public

- Property Type: String

- Property Name: **Story**

- Accessors: get

- Property Modifiers: None

11. Click Finish.

12. Change the null in the Story get statement to **story** and add the story variable, as shown in Listing 6-4 in the Content.cs file.

Listing 6-4. Fix the Story get Statement in Content.cs

```
protected string story;

public string Story
{
    get
    {
        return story;
    }
}
```

13. Update the Content class constructor to initialize the headline and story, as shown in Listing 6-5.

Listing 6-5. Update the Content Constructor in Content.cs

```
public Content(string h, string s)
{
    headline = h;
    story = s;
}
```

When you have finished updating Content.cs, you should have a Content class that looks like Listing 6-6.

Listing 6-6. Content.cs

```
using System;

namespace Ch06Example
{
    public class Content
    {
```

```
    protected string headline;
    protected string story;

    public Content (string h, string s)
    {
        headline = h;
        story = s;
    }

    public string Headline
    {
        get
        {
            return headline;
        }
    }

    public string Story
    {
        get
        {
            return story;
        }
    }
    }
    }
}
```

Declaring and Loading the Content Repository

Now that you have a class to store your content, albeit a very simple one, you can create an instance of it in WebForm1 in DCViewer.cs and then load it.

This example obviously is very simplified. I really don't recommend loading all of your stories in a huge array on your Web server as you are with the Dynamic Content Viewer. In fact, a simple array is not a good choice because normally the number of pieces of content in your system is a running target. It grows or shrinks based on what is created or removed by the content management application (CMA). A simple array works best when you know the number of elements that will make up the array and the number does not change too often.

An ArrayList might be a better choice because it can grow and shrink dynamically. More likely, you will store your content in a database (Chapter 7 covers this) or in an XML file or set of XML files (which Chapter 8 covers) and then retrieve them on demand. You will see in Chapter 13 that ASP.NET can cache the most common Web pages for you. Therefore, you don't have to worry about wasting time retrieving the same pages repeatedly from the database or XML file(s).

1. Create a variable to store all of the stories by entering the highlighted text in Listing 6-7 into DCViewer.cs using the main edit window.

Listing 6-7. Declaring an Array of Stories

```
public class WebForm1 : System.Web.UI.Page
{
    protected Content[] Stories = new Content[3];
    protected System.Web.UI.WebControls.Label lbStory;
```

2. Load the stories into the Content array by entering the highlighted text in Listing 6-8 into DCViewer.cs using the main edit window.

Listing 6-8. Loading the Array of Stories

```
override protected void OnInit(EventArgs e)
{
    //
    // CODEGEN: This call is required by the ASP+ Windows Form Designer.
    //
    InitializeComponent();
    Base.OnInit(e);

    Stories[0] = new Content("New Hall of Fame Member",
        "{0} joined the hockey hall of fame due to {1} MVP trophies.");
    Stories[1] = new Content("Hacker Located",
        "{0} has been arrested on {1} accounts of bad coding.");
    Stories[2] = new Content("Lottery Winner",
        "{0} said all {1} million in lottery winnings is going to charity.");
}
```

Filling the Drop-Down List from the Content Repository

It is time to fill in the drop-down list because you now have the headlines of the stories available. You can load a drop-down list in three different ways.

The first way is to use the intrinsic control <asp:ListItem>. This control is very similar to the <OPTION> element of the <SELECT> list found in HTML. You could have hard-coded them directly into the ASPX file, as you did in Listing 6-8, but then the content viewer would not be very dynamic because the only way to change the drop-down list would be to go into the ASPX file and change the hard-coded <asp:ListItem> values. Not that it is dynamic now—because you have hard-coded the content in the code logic—but changing the logic to load in the stories from a file is much easier than continually changing the HTML.

Listing 6-9. Loading a Drop-Down List Using <asp:ListItem>

```
<tr>
  <td>Select story:</td>
  <td>
    <asp:DropDownList id=ddlStories runat="server">
      <asp:ListItem Value="1">New Hall of Fame Member</asp:ListItem>
      <asp:ListItem Value="2">Hacker Located</asp:ListItem>
      <asp:ListItem Value="3">Lottery Winner</asp:ListItem>
    </asp:DropDownList>
  </td>
</tr>
```

The second way to load a drop-down list is to use the DataSource property of the intrinsic control <asp:DropDownList>. It is fairly easy to implement; all you need to do is assign a class that implements the IEnumerable interface to the DataSource property. Sound tough? Ever heard of an array? An array implements the IEnumerable interface (arrays are actually an alias for System.Array classes), so all you have to do is assign an array to the DataSource and then call the DataBind() method of the drop-down list. Listing 6-10 shows how this can be done.

> **WARNING**   *If you forget to call the DataBind() method, your array is not bound to the drop-down list and thus your drop-down list will still be empty. (I know because I pulled my hair out on this one.)*

Listing 6-10. Loading a Drop-Down List Using the DataSource Property

```
protected string[] hlines = new string[]
{
    "New Hall of Fame Member",
    "Hacker Located",
    "Lottery Winner"
};

private void Page_Load(object sender, System.EventArgs e)
{
```

```
if (!IsPostBack)
{
    ddlStories.DataSource = hlines;
    ddlStories.DataBind();
}
}
```

The third way to load the drop-down list is the hardest way (which doesn't say much), and it is how I implemented it in the Dynamic Content Viewer. The technique is to enter one entry at a time using the Items property of the intrinsic control <asp:DropDownList>.

This technique is the most powerful because it provides you the ability to do things such as add, remove, insert, and count the number of entries programmatically, thus providing the functionality needed to be dynamic. And, as you see in Listing 6-11, it is actually very easy to implement.

1. Select the View Class from View menu.

2. Expand the Ch06Example folder.

3. Expand the WebForm1 object.

4. Double-click the Page_Load() method.

5. Enter the highlighted text in Listing 6-11 using the edit window, which should now be positioned at the Page_Load() method.

Listing 6-11. Loading a Drop-Down List Using the Items Property

```
private void Page_Load(object sender, System.EventArgs e)
{
    if (!IsPostBack)
    {
        for (int i = 0; i < Stories.Length; i++)
        {
            ddlStories.Items.Add(Stories[i].Headline);
        }
    }
}
```

Manipulating and Loading the Story for Viewing

You are almost done. All you need is a way to display the actual story selected. Because this is beyond easy, I decided to spice things up a bit and add a little fun personalization.

You probably noticed the {0} and {1} in the stories loaded into the `Stories` array. If these don't mean anything to you, a little refresher course on string formatting using the `String.Format()` static method is in order.

The `String.Format()` method has the following basic format:

```
String.Format([format string], [substitute for marker {0}],
                               [substitute for marker {1}],
                               ...,
                               [substitute for marker {n}]);
```

Formatting strings are made up of two parts: the constant string to be displayed and markers to display dynamic content. Any time you see a number surrounded by curly brackets, you have encountered a marker; anything else is the constant text. The number in the curly brackets specifies which parameter following the format string to insert.

There is a lot more functionality available, but this is all you need to know for the current example. If you want to learn more about formatting, the online help is quite detailed.

Now that you know how formatting of strings is done, I'm sure you can guess now that {0} is a marker for `tbUserName` and {1} is for `tbNumber`.

All that's left to do to complete the Dynamic Content Viewer are the following two steps:

1. Position the cursor in the main edit window.

2. Enter the highlighted text in Listing 6-12.

Listing 6-12. Displaying the Selected Story Using a Label

```csharp
private void Page_Load(object sender, System.EventArgs e)
{
    if (!IsPostBack)
    {
        ...
    }
    else
    {
        lbStory.Text = String.Format(Stories[ddlStories.SelectedIndex].Story,
                                     tbUserName.Text, tbNumber.Text);
    }
}
```

I used a little trick to figure out which story to display. It just so happens that the SelectedIndex property of the ddlStories drop-down list is also zero-based like the Stories array. When I loaded the ddlStories drop-down list, I had to make sure I retained the same index order as the Stories array.

A safer way would be to store, in the ddlStories drop-down list, the value of the index to the Stories array corresponding to the Headline loaded. Listing 6-13 shows how it would look if you were to do it this way.

Listing 6-13. Displaying the Selected Story Using a Label

```
private void Page_Load(object sender, System.EventArgs e)
{
    if (!IsPostBack)
    {
        for (int i = 0; i < Stories.Length; i++)
        {
            ddlStories.Items.Add(new ListItem(Stories[i].Headline,
                                              i.ToString()));
        }
    }
    else
    {
        lbStory.Text =
            String.Format(
                Stories[Convert.ToInt16(ddlStories.SelectedItem.Value)].Story,
                tbUserName.Text, tbNumber.Text);
    }
}
```

Just to make sure you didn't miss anything when you were following along, Listing 6-14 is the complete DCViewer.cs.

Listing 6-14. DCViewer.cs

```
using System;
using System.Collections;
using System.ComponentModel;
using System.Data;
using System.Drawing;
using System.Web;
using System.Web.SessionState;
using System.Web.UI;
using System.Web.UI.WebControls;
using System.Web.UI.HtmlControls;
```

```
namespace Ch06Example
{
    public class WebForm1 : System.Web.UI.Page
    {
        protected System.Web.UI.WebControls.Label lbStory;
        protected System.Web.UI.WebControls.Button bnGetStory;
        protected System.Web.UI.WebControls.DropDownList ddlStories;
        protected System.Web.UI.WebControls.RangeValidator rvNumber;
        protected System.Web.UI.WebControls.RequiredFieldValidator
                    rfvNumber;
        protected System.Web.UI.WebControls.TextBox tbNumber;
        protected System.Web.UI.WebControls.RequiredFieldValidator
                    rfvUserName;
        protected System.Web.UI.WebControls.TextBox tbUserName;
        protected System.Web.UI.WebControls.ValidationSummary
                    ValidationSummary1;

        protected Content[] Stories = new Content[3];

        private void Page_Load(object sender, System.EventArgs e)
        {
            if (!IsPostBack)
            {
                for (int i = 0; i < Stories.Length; i++)
                {
                    ddlStories.Items.Add(new ListItem(Stories[i].Headline,
                                                      i.ToString()));
                }
            }
            else
            {
                lbStory.Text =
                  String.Format
                  (
                        Stories[
                        Convert.ToInt16(ddlStories.SelectedItem.Value)
                        ].Story,
                        tbUserName.Text, tbNumber.Text
                  );
            }
        }
```

```
#region Web Form Designer generated code
override protected void OnInit(EventArgs e)
{
    InitializeComponent();
    base.OnInit(e);
```

```
Stories[0] = new Content("New Hall of Fame Member",
  "{0} was added to the hockey hall of fame due to the {1} MVP trophies.");
Stories[1] = new Content("Hacker Located",
  "{0} has been arrested on {1} accounts of bad coding.");
Stories[2] = new Content("Lottery Winner",
  "{0} said all {1} million in lottery winnings is going to charity.");
```

```
}

    private void InitializeComponent()
    {
        this.Load += new System.EventHandler (this.Page_Load);
    }
    #endregion
}
}
```

Now you're finished. Go ahead and compile and run it from within Visual Studio .NET. Even better, run it from your browser. Go load up your browser and type the following in the Address field:

```
http://localhost/Ch06Example/DCViewer.aspx
```

Hey, doesn't that look like Figure 6-1?

Summary

This chapter completed a little refresher on ASP.NET, C#, and Visual Studio .NET by developing the Dynamic Content Viewer. Pat yourself on the back for a job well done.

I bet you're saying that the Viewer doesn't do much. All you did was drag 15 objects in a designer and code 33 lines, 21 of them a helper class. Yes, this doesn't seem like much, but let's see what you got:

- A compiled Web page

- Retained session state

- A colored title

- Two fully client-side and server-side validated input fields

- A dynamic drop-down box

- A personalized dynamic content message

- The HTML and code logic completely separated into two different files

- A helper class to hold your headlines and stories

- Full HTML content formatting (entering **your name** in the user-name field)

Not too bad if you ask me. Once you get comfortable with the Visual Studio .NET, it might take all of an hour's worth of work to complete. Try getting this much functionality with as little work from any of the other client- or server-side technologies.

The next chapter tackles the topic of ADO.NET.

Database Development and ADO.NET

AN AMAZING AMOUNT OF FUNCTIONALITY is built into Visual Studio .NET when it comes to Microsoft SQL Server database development. If you combine it with ADO.NET, you don't ever have to leave Visual Studio .NET when it comes to your database efforts.

Visual Studio .NET does not leave you in the cold when it comes to database-development utilities. It provides you with a way to create a database, table, view, and stored procedure. When combined, these cover almost everything you need to build your database.

ADO.NET takes over where the utilities leave off and enables you to seamlessly join your databases to your Web page code. With little effort, you can connect, extract data, and then load the data into your Web pages.

You don't have to take my word for it. Take a look for yourself.

Visual Studio .NET's Database Utilities

Visual Studio .NET is well equipped when it comes to the design and development of Microsoft SQL Server databases. It provides the functionality to create databases, tables, views, stored procedures, and many other features. This book will cover only these four features, however, because they are all you need to create the content management system that this book is building.

The starting point of all database utilities is the Server Explorer. Select Server Explorer from the View menu to open it; it looks similar to Figure 7-1. You will find your database in one of two places. If the database is Microsoft SQL Server 7.0 or higher, it will be located in the SQL Servers database folder inside your Servers folder. If a supported OLE DB connects the database, it will be found in the Data Connections folder just above the Servers folder.

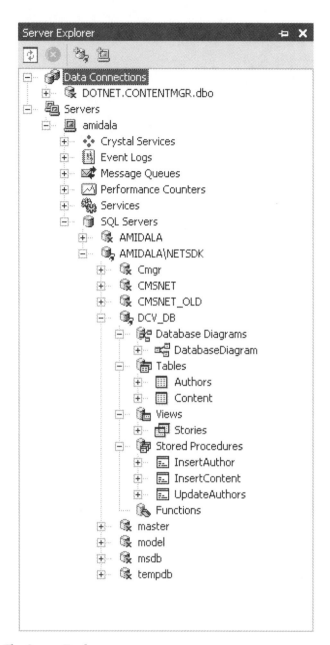

Figure 7-1. The Server Explorer

The functionality provided to OLE DB–connected databases is mostly restricted to viewing and editing records. On the other hand, Visual Studio .NET provides Microsoft SQL Server databases with much of the functionality that comes with SQL Enterprise Manager. This book focuses on Microsoft SQL Server and will cover the functionality provided by Visual Studio .NET. If you are developing using an OLE DB–connected database, much of the first part of this chapter will not help you because you will have to use the database maintenance tools provided by your database.

> **TIP**   *I recommend that you install the MSDE 2000 database server provided with the .NET Framework samples to get a feel for the functionality provided by Visual Studio .NET. You can always uninstall it later.*

There is nothing stopping you from building your Microsoft SQL Server databases outside of Visual Studio .NET and then adding the database to the Server Explorer. I will show you how to do this later when you walk through the process of adding the CMSNET database in Chapter 9. First, let's do it the hard way and build a simple content management database that you can integrate into the Dynamic Content Viewer you built in Chapter 6.

Creating a New Database

The first step in database development is not creating one. Obviously, creating the data model, designing the logic database, and designing the physical database should come first. But hey, I'm a programmer. I'll code first and then go ask questions. (I'm joking—really!)

Visual Studio .NET makes creating databases so easy that it's almost not worth explaining how to do it.

> **WARNING**   *Be sure you really want the database you are creating because there is no way to delete it once it's created in Visual Studio .NET. I had to go to the Microsoft SQL Enterprise Manager to delete my test databases. It is also possible to execute the* DROP DATABASE *command to remove the database.*

The following steps will create the database DCV_DB, which you will use throughout the chapter.

1. Select Server Explorer from the View menu.

2. Expand the SQL Servers database folder from within your Servers folder.

3. Right-click the database folder.

4. Select the New Database menu item, which will display the Create Database dialog box shown in Figure 7-2.

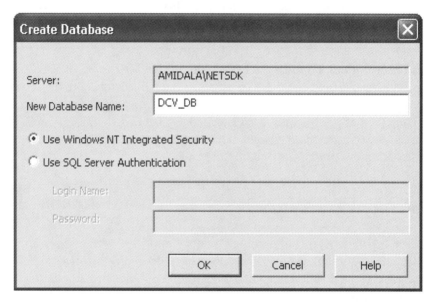

Figure 7-2. The Create Database dialog box

5. Enter **DCV_DB** in the New Database Name field.

6. Click OK.

Now you should have a new database called DCV_DB in your database folder. You can expand it and see all the default folders built. If you click these folders, however, you will see that there is nothing in them. That's your next job.

Adding and Loading Tables and Views to a Database

An empty database is really quite useless, so let's add a couple of tables to the database to provide a place to store your content.

 NOTE *The tables and views you are using in this chapter are purposely very simple (you might even call them minimal) and are not the best schema around. I did this so that you don't get bogged down with the details of the database and so it doesn't take much effort or time for you to build them yourself.*

The first table is for storing authors and information about them, and the second table is for storing headlines and stories. The two databases are linked together by a common AuthorID key. Figure 7-3 presents a data diagram of the database.

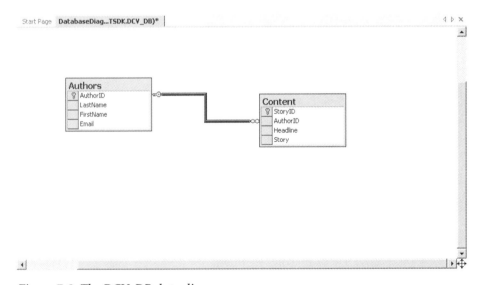

Figure 7-3. The DCV_DB data diagram

Having this separation means you only have to store one copy of the author information, even though the author may have written many stories. If you had created only one table to contain all the information, a lot of duplicated author information would have to be rekeyed each time a story is added to maintain the database. It also, conveniently, enables me to show you how to create a relationship between tables.

The process of building a new table is only slightly more difficult than creating a database. The hard part is figuring out what columns are needed and the format for each table in the database. It's nice to know you can spend most of your time designing the ultimate database schema instead of figuring out how to implement it.

Creating Tables

To create the first table, follow these steps:

1. Navigate down to the database folder as you did in the previous section.

2. Expand the database folder.

3. Expand the DCV_DB folder.

4. Right-click the Tables folder.

5. Select the New Table menu item. You should now have an entry form in which to enter the database columns found in Table 7-1.

Table 7-1. Authors Database Column Descriptions

COLUMN NAME	DATA TYPE	LENGTH	DESCRIPTION	IDENTITY	KEY
AuthorID	int	4	Autogenerated ID number for author	Yes	Yes
LastName	char	32	Last name of the author	No	No
FirstName	char	32	First name of the author	No	No
Email	char	64	E-mail address of the author	No	No

6. Select Save Table1 from the File menu.

7. Enter **Authors** into the edit field in the dialog box.

8. Click OK.

Go ahead and repeat this for the second table, but use the information in Table 7-2 and save the table as **Content**.

Table 7-2. Content Database Column Descriptions

COLUMN NAME	DATA TYPE	LENGTH	DESCRIPTION	IDENTITY	KEY
StoryID	int	4	Autogenerated ID number for author	Yes	Yes
AuthorID	int	4	Foreign key to author database	No	No
Headline	char	64	Headline for the content	No	No
Story	text	16	Story portion of the content	No	No

This book will not go into what all the data types mean, but if you are interested, many good books on Microsoft SQL Server and SQL cover this topic in great detail.

The Identity field, when set to Yes, will turn on autonumber generation for the column. Why you call the field Identity (instead of Autonumber) is a mystery to me. I'm an application programmer, though, and not a database person. It's probably some special database term.

Okay, you now have your tables. The next step is to build a relationship between them. In this database, it is fairly obvious—AuthorID is the column that should link these two tables.

Creating a Relationship

To create a relationship between your tables, follow these steps:

1. Right-click the Content table in the Server Explorer.

2. Select Design Table from the menu items.

3. Right-click anywhere on the Table Designer.

4. Select Relationships from the menu items. This will bring up a Relationships property page similar to Figure 7-4.

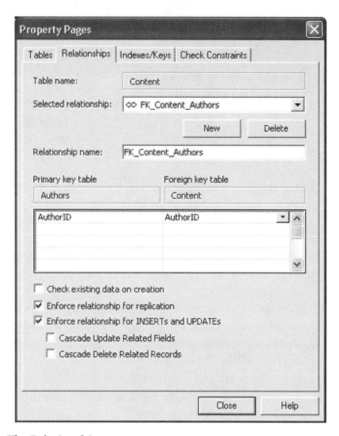

Figure 7-4. The Relationships property page

5. Click the New button.

6. Select Authors as the primary key side of the relationship from the Primary Key Table drop-down list.

7. Select AuthorID as the primary key in the grid beneath the Primary Key Table drop-down list.

8. Select Content as the foreign key side of the relationship from the Foreign Key Table drop-down list.

9. Select AuthorID as the foreign key in the grid beneath the Foreign Key Table drop-down list.

10. Click Close.

Now you have two tables and a relationship between them. Quite often, when you want to get data from a database, you need information from multiple tables. For example, in this case, you want to get all stories with each author's first and last name. As mentioned previously, you could have created the Content table that way, but then you would have a lot of duplicate data floating around. There is nothing stopping you from executing a SQL statement that gets this information, as shown in Listing 7-1.

Listing 7-1. Getting Data from Two Tables

```
SELECT      FirstName,
            LastName,
            Headline,
            Story
FROM        Authors,
            Content
WHERE       Authors.AuthorID = Content.AuthorID
ORDER BY    StoryID ASC
```

Personally, I prefer to be able to write something like this instead:

```
SELECT * FROM Stories
```

This is exactly what you can do with database views. Basically, you might think of a view as a virtual table without any data of its own, based on a predefined query. If you know you are going to use the same set of data based on a query, you might consider using the view instead of coding.

NOTE *Those of you who are knowledgeable about SQL and views might have noticed the* ORDER BY *clause. Microsoft SQL Server supports the* ORDER BY *clause in its views, unlike some other database systems.*

Creating a View

Follow these steps to create a view:

1. Right-click the Views table from within the DCV_DB folder in the Server Explorer.

2. Select New View from the menu items. This will bring up an Add Table dialog box similar to Figure 7-5.

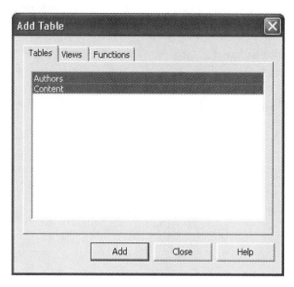

Figure 7-5. The Add Table dialog box

3. Select both Authors and Content and click the Add button.

4. Click Close. This should generate a window similar to Figure 7-6.

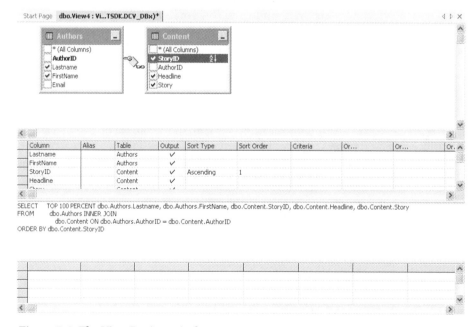

Figure 7-6. The View Design window

5. Click the check boxes for FirstName and LastName in the Authors table.

6. Click the check boxes for StoryID, Headline, and Story in the Content table.

7. Right-click StoryID and select Sort Ascending from the menu items.

8. Select Save View1 from the File menu.

9. Enter **Stories** into edit field.

10. Click OK.

Pretty painless, don't you think? You have the option of testing your view right there, too. Click the Run Query button on the main toolbar. (It is the button that has an exclamation point on it.) The View Design window is pretty powerful. If you play with it for a while, you will see what I mean.

Did you try the Run Query button and get nothing? Oops . . . I forgot to tell you to load some data into the database. You can do this with Visual Studio .NET as well. Simply double-click either of the tables you created, and an editable table will appear.

First enter the data for the authors. If you don't, you will not have an Author ID to enter into the AuthorID column in the Content view. Enter the data found in Table 7-3. Notice that there are no Author IDs to enter; this field is automatically created. In fact, Visual Studio .NET will yell at you if you try to enter something in the AuthorID column.

Table 7-3. Author Data

LASTNAME	FIRSTNAME	EMAIL
Doors	Bill	bill@contentmgr.com
Ellidaughter	Larry	larry@contentmgr.com
Fraser	Stephen	stephen@contentmgr.com

Now enter the data found in Table 7-4. Notice that StoryID cannot be entered. It, too, is an autogenerated number. You do have to enter AuthorID, though, because it is not automatically generated in this table.

Table 7-4. Content Data

AUTHORID	HEADLINE	STORY
1	.NET Is the Best	According to my research, the .NET product has no competition, though I am a little biased.
2	Oracle Is #1	Research suggests that it is the best database on the market, not that I have any biases in that conclusion.
3	Content Management Is Expensive	Not anymore. It now costs the price of a book and a little work.
1	SQL Server Will Be #1	This database has no real competition. But then again, I am a little biased.

Building Stored Procedures

It is important to cover this one last utility because you will use it quite frequently throughout the rest of this book. Truthfully, you don't have to use stored procedures because anything you can run using stored procedures you can run using standard SQL. So, why cover this utility at all?

There are two main reasons: First, stored procedures let a software developer call database code using function calls with parameters. Second, and more important, the utility is compiled before it gets loaded. This makes the calls to the database faster and more efficient because it has already been optimized.

Because you haven't covered ADO.NET yet, you will not be able to do much with the stored procedure you will create. Fortunately, Visual Studio .NET provides an option so that it can be tested.

Unlike the previous utilities, you have to actually code stored procedures. If you don't know SQL, don't worry because the coding is short and, I think, pretty self-explanatory. As always, there are many good books you can read to get a better understanding of it.

You will create a stored procedure to insert data into the Authors table. You already did this process manually, so you should have a good idea of what the stored procedure needs to do.

Creating a Stored Procedure

To create a stored procedure, follow these steps:

1. Right-click the Stored Procedures table from within the DCV_DB folder in the Server Explorer.

2. Select New Stored Procedure from the menu items. This will bring up an editing session with the default code shown in Listing 7-2.

Listing 7-2. Default Stored Procedure Code

```
CREATE PROCEDURE dbo.StoredProcedure1
/*
    (
        @parameter1 datatype = default value,
        @parameter2 datatype OUTPUT
    )
*/
AS
    /* SET NOCOUNT ON */
    RETURN
```

First you have to set up the parameters that will be passed from the program. Obviously, you need to receive all the mandatory columns that make up the row. In the Authors table's case, that's the entire column except AuthorID, which is autogenerated. Listing 7-3 shows the changes that need to be made to the default code provided in order to add parameters. Note that the comments /* . . . */ are removed.

Listing 7-3. Setting the Parameters

```
CREATE PROCEDURE dbo.StoredProcedure1

    (
        @LastName  NVARCHAR(32) = NULL,
        @FirstName NVARCHAR(32) = NULL,
        @Email     NVARCHAR(64)  = NULL
    )

AS
```

Next, you turn on the SET NOCOUNT. This option prevents the message about the number of rows affected by the stored procedure from being returned to the calling program every time it is called.

```
SET NOCOUNT ON
```

Finally, you code the actual insert command. The key to this stored procedure is that instead of hard-coding the values to be inserted, you use the parameters you previously declared. Listing 7-4 is the final version of the stored procedure. Note that you rename the stored procedure to InsertAuthor.

Listing 7-4. InsertAuthor Stored Procedure

```
CREATE PROCEDURE dbo.InsertAuthor

    (
        @LastName NVARCHAR(32) = NULL,
        @FirstName NVARCHAR(32) = NULL,
        @Email NVARCHAR(64)    = NULL
    )
AS
    SET NOCOUNT ON

    INSERT INTO   Authors ( LastName,  FirstName,  Email)
    VALUES               (@LastName, @FirstName, @Email)

    RETURN
```

All that's left is to save the stored procedure. If you made a mistake while coding, the save will fail and an error message will tell you where the error is.

To run or debug the stored procedure, just right-click the newly created stored procedure and select Run Stored Procedure or Debug.

What Is ADO.NET?

You have tables, views, relationships, and stored procedures, so what's the big deal? The answer is one word: ADO.NET (or is that two words?). Gone are things that have been plaguing developers for some time now such as the variant, firewalls, and COM marshalling. If you don't know what these things are or why they were a problem, don't worry about it; just be glad they are gone.

ADO.NET is a set of classes that encompasses all aspects of accessing data sources within the .NET architecture. It is designed to provide full support for disconnected data access, while using an Extensible Markup Language (XML) format for transmitting data when data transfer is required. Chapter 8 contains more details about XML, so let's not worry about it for now. Just think of ADO.NET as a programmer's window into a data source, in our case the DCV_DB database.

The Benefits of Disconnected Data Access

Disconnected data access is a key feature of ADO.NET. Basically, it means that most of the time when you are accessing a database, you aren't getting the data from the database at all. Instead, you are accessing a copy of the data that was moved earlier to your client computer. Don't worry about all the technical issues surrounding this; just be glad that it works because it provides two major benefits:

- Less congestion on the database server because users are spending less time connected to it

- Faster access to the data because the data is already on the client

It also offers one benefit (associated with a disconnect access) that is less obvious: Data does not have to be stored in a databaselike format. Realizing this, Microsoft decided to implement ADO.NET using a strong typed XML format. A bonus that comes along with this is that data can be transmitted by means of XML and standard HTTP. This causes a further benefit: Firewall problems disappear. An HTTP response within the body of XML flows freely through a firewall (see Chapter 5 for information about HTTP), unlike the pre-ADO.NET technology's system-level COM marshalling requests.

Strong Data Types

Strong typed data saves the programmer the headache of having to use the variant data type and continually having to convert it to the data type desired. With ADO.NET, if a column in a database is an integer, you work, store, and retrieve it as an integer. The only time you have to do a data conversion is when you don't want it to be an integer.

Not having to do the type conversion will speed things up. It seems that speeding things up is a very common theme with ADO.NET.

Most Common ADO.NET Classes

If you spend a lot of time working with ADO.NET, you may have an opportunity to work with almost all of ADO.NET's classes. For the purpose of this book, however, I've trimmed these classes down to the following:

- Two managed providers

- DataSet

- TablesCollection

- DataTable

- DataRow

- DataColumn

- RelationsCollection

- DataRelation

All of these classes interact with each other in some way. Figure 7-7 shows the flow of the interaction. Essentially, the managed provider connects the data store to the DataSet. The DataSet stores the data in a TablesCollection made up of one or more DataTables. Each DataTable is made up of DataRows and DataColumns. All of the DataTables store their relationships in a RelationsCollection made up of DataRelations. Finally, all these classes can be affected by constraints. Simple, no?

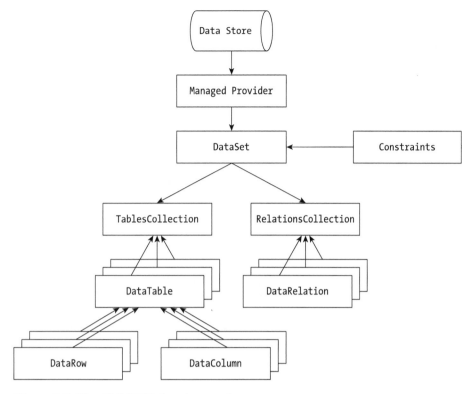

Figure 7-7. The ADO.NET class interaction

Managed Providers

Managed providers provide ADO.NET with the capability to connect and access data sources. Their main purpose, as far as most developers are concerned, is to provide support for the DataAdapter class. This class is essentially for mapping between the data store and the DataSet.

Currently only two managed providers exist for ADO.NET:

- *SQL managed provider:* Connects to Microsoft SQL Server version 7.0 or higher

- *OLE DB managed provider:* Connects to several supported OLE DB data sources

The managed provider you use determines which namespace you need to use. If you are using the SQL managed provider, you will need to use the System.Data.SqlClient namespace, which will include classes such as SqlDataAdapter, SqlConnection, and SqlCommand. On the other hand, if you are using the OLE DB managed provider, you will need to use the `System.Data.OleDb` namespace, which will include classes such as `OleDbDataAdapter`, `OleDbConnection`, and `OleDbCommand`.

Once you have learned one managed provider, you have pretty much learned both because they are nearly the same, except for the `Sql` and `OleDb` prefixes and a few other small differences.

The most noticeable difference is that the OLE DB managed provider is slower than the SQL managed provider. This is mainly because the SQL managed provider accesses the Microsoft SQL Server directly, whereas the OLE DB managed provider must go through OLE DB first. As time goes on, Microsoft hopes that more database providers will create a managed provider for its database, thus removing the issue of slow access.

Because this book uses Microsoft SQL Server 2000, you will use the SQL managed provider and thus the namespace associated with it.

DataSet

The `DataSet` is the major controlling class of ADO.NET. A `DataSet` is a memory cache used to store all data retrieved from a data source, in most cases a database or XML file. The data source is connected to the `DataSet` using a managed provider. It also stores the format information about the data of which it is made up.

A `DataSet` consists of a `TablesCollection`, a `RelationsCollection`, and constraints. I will not use constraints in this book, but for the curious, two examples would be the `UniqueConstraint` and `ForeignKeyConstraint`, which ensure that the primary key value and foreign keys are unique.

A `DataSet` is data source independent. All it understands is XML. In fact, all data sent or received by the `DataSet` is in the form of an XML document. The `DataSet` has methods for reading and writing XML, and these are covered in Chapter 8.

TablesCollection

A `TablesCollection` is a standard collection class made up of one or more `DataTables`. Like any other collection class, it has methods such as `Add()`, `Remove()`, and `Clear()`. Usually, you will not use any of this functionality. Instead, you will use it to get access to the `DataTables` it stores. The method of choice in doing this will probably be to access the `TablesCollection` like an array.

DataTable

Put simply, a DataTable is one table of data stored in memory. A DataTable will also contain constraints, which help ensure the integrity of the data it is storing.

A DataTable is made up of zero or more DataRows because it is possible to have an empty table.

DataRow

The DataRow is where the data is actually stored. You will frequently access the data from the database using the DataRow as an array of columns.

DataColumn

The DataColumn is used to define the columns in a DataTable. Each DataColumn has a data type that determines the kind of data it can hold. A DataColumn also has properties similar to a database, such as AllowNull and Unique. If the DataColumn autoincrements, the AutoIncrement property is set. (Now, that makes more sense than Identity.)

RelationsCollection

A RelationsCollection is a standard collection class made up of one or more DataRelations. Like any other collection class, it has methods such as Add(), Remove(), and Clear(). Usually, as with the TablesCollection, you will not use any of this functionality. Instead, you will simply use it to get access to the DataRelations it stores.

DataRelation

A DataRelation is used to relate two DataTables together. It does this by matching DataColumns between two tables. You can almost think of it as the ADO.NET equivalent of the foreign-key relationship in a relational database (like you previously set).

One important thing you have to keep in mind is that the DataColumns must be the same data type. Remember that ADO.NET has strong data types, and when comparing different data types, one data type must be converted to the other. This conversion is not done automatically, thus the restriction of common data types.

If you are like me, you are probably saying, "Enough with theory, how do I code it?" Okay, let's have some more fun and play with the database you previously built.

Examples of ADO.NET Development

Two of the most common things you will do with ADO.NET are read data out of a database and insert data back into a database. Reading data out is so common that a special ASP.NET intrinsic control has been created to help display the data.

This section first shows how to read data out of a database the old-fashioned way and into a list. Then it shows how to read data from a database and into a DataGrid, the special ASP.NET intrinsic control. The next example shows how to load data into a database using stored procedures. Finally, you will finish by updating the Dynamic Content Viewer to get its data from a database.

Reading Data from a Database Using ADO.NET

Let's start pretty simple by getting some data out of the database and displaying it in a list. This will not look fancy, as you can see in Figure 7-8, but it will show you the basics of accessing data out of a database.

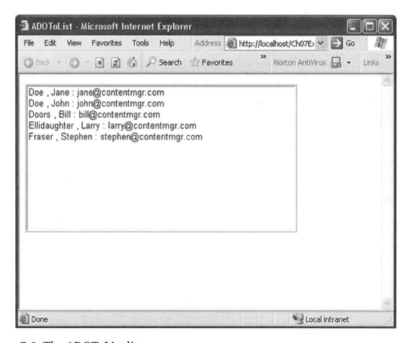

Figure 7-8. The ADOToList list

The first thing you are going to need is a new project in which to create your sample Web pages. If you need help doing this, Chapter 6 covers the process in detail. Name the project **Ch07Examples**. Then rename WebForm1.aspx to **ADOToList.aspx**.

Something you might have noticed is that the name of the class in the new ADOToList.aspx remains WebForm1. I recommend changing this to ADOToList to be consistent with the name of the ADOToList.cs file. The procedure is very simple.

Renaming WebForm1 to ADOToList

Follow these steps to rename WebForm1 to ADOToList:

1. Change the edit window of ADOToList.aspx to HTML mode.

2. Find all occurrences of WebForm1 and change them to ADOToList. There should be two. The first will be in the Inherits attribute in the first line of the HTML and the second will be within the <title></title> tag.

3. Select Save All from the main toolbar.

4. Open up the code for ADOToList in the edit window.

5. Find the occurrence (the name of the class) of WebForm1 and change it to ADOToList.

6. Select Save All from the main toolbar to complete the procedure.

Now that you have a clean place to start your development from, the first thing you need to do is design your Web page. By the way, designing the Web page will almost always be the first thing you do in creating ASP.NET Web pages using Visual Studio .NET.

You should know how to drag controls from the Toolbox because this was covered in Chapter 6. For this example, all you need is to drag over a list box and resize it to be a little bigger. That's it for the design. (I'm sure you broke out in a sweat with that design effort.)

Now that you have someplace to put your data, let's go get some. Change the edit window to ADOToList.cs and let's proceed.

Coding the Reading of Data from a Database

The first thing you need to add is the namespace for the managed provider you will be using to access the data. This will give you access to all the classes needed to access the database using ADO.NET.

This book uses Microsoft SQL Server, so you'll use the SQLClient provider. If you are using a different database, just replace the prefix of every method starting with Sql with OleDb, and of course, you will have to change the connection string, but I'll get to that in a second.

When I add a namespace, I try to keep common namespaces together. In the case of ADOToList, add the highlighted code near the top of this listing:

```
using System.Data;
using System.Data.SqlClient;
using System.Drawing;
```

For those of you using a database different than Microsoft SQL Server, use this highlighted code instead:

```
using System.Data;
using System.Data.OleDb;
using System.Drawing;
```

If you recall from Figure 7-7, the first piece in the puzzle of accessing a database using ADO.NET is the managed provider. You need to initialize your managed provider so that it can figure out where the database is and the privileges needed to access it. Then you tell it what SQL command to execute.

ADO.NET simplifies the process by allowing you to code this in one method. It is possible and necessary to break this method into its two parts, and this is shown in the section "Inserting Data Using a Stored Procedure" later in this chapter.

The hardest part of this piece of the coding (unless you don't know SQL) is figuring out what is the connection string. For SQL managed providers, this is fairly easy because it is made up of four parts:

- The location of the server: server=localhost;

- *The user ID:* uid=sa; (Note: This may vary with how you configured your database server.)

- *The user password:* pwd=; (In my case this is empty, but again this will depend on how you configured your database server.)

- The name of the database: database=DCV_DB;

It will look like this in the code:

```
"server=localhost;uid=sa;pwd=;database=DCV_DB"
```

The options are more varied for ADO managed providers, but it will probably look something like this:

```
"Provider=SQLOLEDB; Data Source=(local); Initial Catalog=DCV_DB; User ID=sa"
```

You will not be too elaborate when it comes to coding the SQL for this example because all you are doing is getting all the data out of the Authors table and sorting it by last name. If you are not happy with this simple SQL, you are welcome to experiment with it to your heart's content.

Here is my simple SQL:

```
"SELECT * FROM Authors ORDER BY LastName"
```

The only thing left to do now is call the managed provider's constructor with the SQL command and the connection string. Here is how the code looks:

```
protected void Page_Load(object sender, EventArgs e)
{
    if (!IsPostBack)
    {
        string ConnectStr = "server=localhost;uid=sa;pwd=;database=DCV_DB";
        string Cmd = "SELECT * FROM Authors ORDER BY LastName";

        SqlDataAdapter DAdpt = new SqlDataAdapter(Cmd, ConnectStr);
```

The next piece of the puzzle is to create the DataSet and fill it with the data collected by the managed provider. You can do this simply by creating an instance of a DataSet and then letting the managed provider fill it in by calling its method Fill(), which takes two parameters. The first parameter is the newly created DataSet, and the second is the name of the table you want to extract from the managed provider. Here is how it should look:

```
DataSet ds = new DataSet();
        DAdpt.Fill(ds, "Authors");
```

The last piece of the puzzle is to simply take the table out of the `DataSet` and add the data from the table row by row into the list box designed earlier. I think the code is pretty self-explanatory, so I'll just list it now:

```
DataTable dt = ds.Tables["Authors"];

        foreach (DataRow dr in dt.Rows)
        {
            ListBox1.Items.Add(dr["LastName"] + ", " +
                                dr["FirstName"] + ": " +
                                dr["Email"]);
        }
```

The only thing of note in the preceding code—if you come from the C++ and Java world as I do—is what appears to be a string inside of an array. This handy syntax makes arrays in ADO.NET much more understandable than the equivalent:

```
        DataTable dt = ds.Tables[0];

        foreach (DataRow dr in dt.Rows)
        {
            ListBox1.Items.Add(dr[1] + ", " +
                                dr[2] + ": " +
                                dr[3]);
```

You also have to know the order of the columns in the array. As you might have noticed, `LastName` is the second element in the array, not the first. The first is `AuthorID`, something you are not adding to the list box. Also, note that the array starts at zero, but of course, you already knew that.

Okay, you are done. Listing 7-5 shows ADOToList.cs in its entirety so that you can check to make sure you coded everything correctly. Go ahead and save it and execute it. You should see something like Figure 7-8, which was shown at the beginning of this example.

Listing 7-5. ADOToList.cs

```
using System;
using System.Collections;
using System.ComponentModel;
using System.Data;
using System.Data.SqlClient;
using System.Drawing;
using System.Web;
using System.Web.SessionState;
```

```
using System.Web.UI;
using System.Web.UI.WebControls;
using System.Web.UI.HtmlControls;

namespace Ch07Examples
{
    public class ADOToList : System.Web.UI.Page
    {
        protected System.Web.UI.WebControls.ListBox ListBox1;

        private void Page_Load(object sender, System.EventArgs e)
        {
            if (!IsPostBack)
            {
                string ConnectStr =
                        "server=localhost;uid=sa;pwd=;database=DCV_DB";
                string Cmd = "SELECT * FROM Authors ORDER BY LastName";

                SqlDataAdapter DAdpt = new SqlDataAdapter(Cmd, ConnectStr);

                DataSet ds = new DataSet();
                DAdpt.Fill (ds, "Authors");

                DataTable dt = ds.Tables["Authors"];

                foreach (DataRow dr in dt.Rows)
                {
                    ListBox1.Items.Add(dr["LastName"] + ", " +
                                    dr["FirstName"] + ": " +
                                    dr["Email"]);
                }
            }
        }

        #region Web Form Designer generated code
        override protected void OnInit(EventArgs e)
        {
            InitializeComponent();
            base.OnInit(e);
        }
```

```
        private void InitializeComponent()
        {
            this.Load += new System.EventHandler (this.Page_Load);
        }
        #endregion
    }
}
```

Okay, let's move on to the next example.

Building an ASP.NET DataGrid

The previous example had a pretty boring display, don't you think? I think the authors of ADO.NET thought so, too, and decided to provide a standard intrinsic control called the DataGrid to provide a simple and elegant way of displaying data on a Web page. When you are finished, you will have a Web page that looks similar to Figure 7-9.

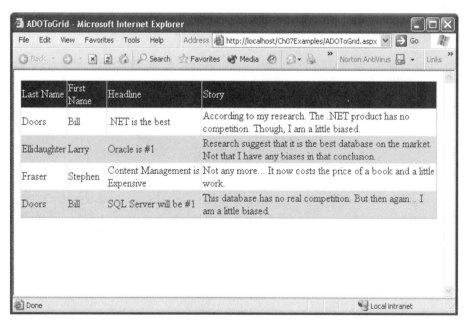

Figure 7-9. The ADOToGrid DataGrid

This example is actually simpler than the previous one when it comes to the code. The design is more difficult, but hey, it's an intrinsic control, how hard can that be?

Take my word for it, an intrinsic control can be tough, especially the DataGrid because it has quite a few different options available. In fact, this example will not even skim the surface. If you want more information about the DataGrid, you might want to check out the Microsoft documentation.

Let's not create a new project. Instead, you will add a new Web page to the existing project.

Adding a Web Page to a Project

Follow these steps to add a Web page to your project:

1. Right-click Ch07Examples.

2. Select Add Web Form from the Add submenu item. This will display a dialog box similar to the one shown in Figure 7-10.

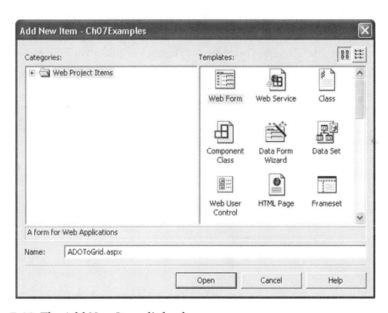

Figure 7-10. The Add New Item dialog box

3. Enter **ADOToGrid.aspx** in the Name field.

4. Click Open.

The best part is that everything has the name ADOToGrid, so now you don't have to do any renaming.

Coding the Connection of a Database to a DataGrid

Now that you have your new Web page, drag a DataGrid from the Toolbox to it. Leave it in its default state to start with and then come back and fix it up slightly after you have finished connecting it to the database. Save the design and then change the edit window to the Web page code ADOToGrid.cs.

First, remember to add the namespace of the managed provider you are using. As before, this book will use the SqlClient namespace, so the code should look like this:

```
using System.Data;
using System.Data.SqlClient;
using System.Drawing;
```

As in the previous example, the next thing you have to do is connect to the managed provider. Note that once you know the connection string for the database to which you are connecting, you will be able to continually use it without having to do a single change ever again (unless you change your database server configuration).

Just for grins and giggles, you are going to get your data out of the database using the Stories view previously created. So, with this minor change, the code will look like this:

```
protected void Page_Load(object sender, EventArgs e)
{

    if (!IsPostBack)
    {
        string ConnectStr = "server=localhost;uid=sa;pwd=;database=DCV_DB";
        string Cmd = "SELECT * FROM Stories";


        SqlDataAdapter DAdpt = new SqlDataAdapter(Cmd, ConnectStr);
```

Next, you create a DataSet and fill it with the data gathered by the managed provider. The only difference between this example and the previous one is that the second parameter of the Fill() method will change to the Stories view.

```
        DataSet ds = new DataSet();
        DAdpt.Fill (ds, "Stories");
```

The last thing you need to do is place the data from the DataSet into the DataGrid designed earlier. Do you remember from Chapter 6 that you can load a drop-down list using its DataSource property? You can do the exact same thing with a DataGrid. All you need to find is an object that implements the IEnumerable interface. Fortunately, the DataTable has a property called DefaultView that provides a (what a coincidence!) default view of the table. This property also happens to implement the IEnumerable interface. After you load the DataSource, you must DataBind() it to the DataGrid, as shown in the following code:

```
DataGrid1.DataSource = ds.Tables["Stories"].DefaultView;
DataGrid1.DataBind();
```

Just to make sure you coded correctly, Listing 7-6 shows the entire ADOToGrid.cs.

Listing 7-6. ADOToGrid.cs

```
using System;
using System.Collections;
using System.ComponentModel;
using System.Data;
using System.Data.SqlClient;
using System.Drawing;
using System.Web;
using System.Web.SessionState;
using System.Web.UI;
using System.Web.UI.WebControls;
using System.Web.UI.HtmlControls;

namespace Ch07Examples
{
    public class ADOToGrid : System.Web.UI.Page
    {
        protected System.Web.UI.WebControls.DataGrid DataGrid1;

        private void Page_Load(object sender, System.EventArgs e)
        {
            if (!IsPostBack)
            {
                string ConnectStr =
                    "server=localhost;uid=sa;pwd=;database=DCV_DB";
                string Cmd = "SELECT * FROM Stories";

                SqlDataAdapter DAdpt = new SqlDataAdapter(Cmd, ConnectStr);

                DataSet ds = new DataSet();
                DAdpt.Fill(ds, "Stories");
```

```
                DataGrid1.DataSource = ds.Tables["Stories"].DefaultView;
                DataGrid1.DataBind();
            }
        }

        #region Web Form Designer generated code
        override protected void OnInit(EventArgs e)
        {
            InitializeComponent();
            base.OnInit(e);
        }

        private void InitializeComponent()
        {
            this.Load += new System.EventHandler (this.Page_Load);
        }
        #endregion
    }
}
```

Now you can save, compile, and execute it. Notice in Figure 7-11 that the headings used by the DataGrid are the actual column names from the database and that the grid is quite boring. Let's change it to something more pleasant.

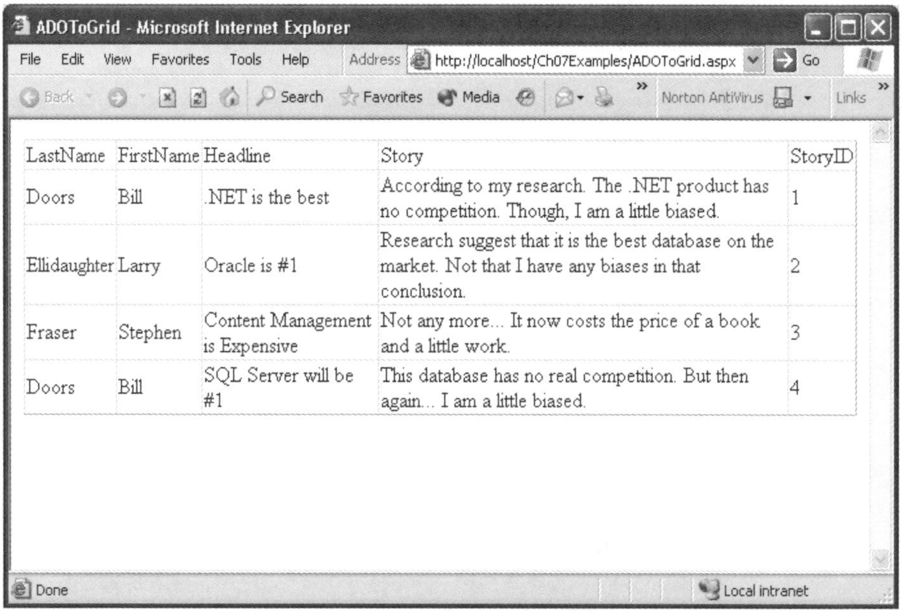

LastName	FirstName	Headline	Story	StoryID
Doors	Bill	.NET is the best	According to my research. The .NET product has no competition. Though, I am a little biased.	1
Ellidaughter	Larry	Oracle is #1	Research suggest that it is the best database on the market. Not that I have any biases in that conclusion.	2
Fraser	Stephen	Content Management is Expensive	Not any more... It now costs the price of a book and a little work.	3
Doors	Bill	SQL Server will be #1	This database has no real competition. But then again... I am a little biased.	4

Figure 7-11. The ADOToGrid DataGrid before facelift

Change the edit window back to the Web page ADOToGrid.aspx and select the HTML view.

Changing DataGrid Layout

Perform the following steps to change the DataGrid layout:

1. Select the DataGrid control in Design editor.

2. Select False in the AutoGenerateColumns property.

3. Click the ellipsis in the Columns property. This will display a DataGrid Properties dialog box, as shown in Figure 7-12.

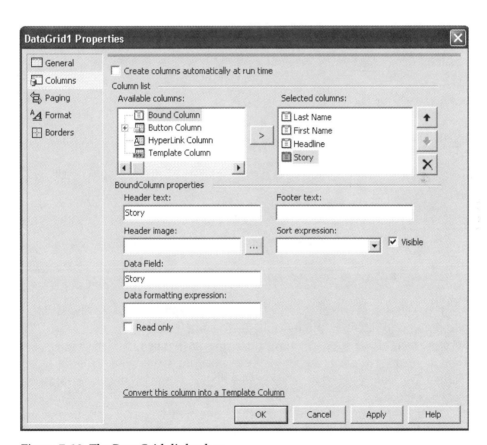

Figure 7-12. The DataGrid dialog box

4. Click Columns in left selection list.

5. Select Bound Column in the Available Columns list.

6. Click the Add arrow button to add a bound column to selected columns list.

7. Enter **Last Name** in the Header Text box.

8. Enter **LastName** in the Data Field box.

9. Repeat steps 5 through 8 for the following three columns:

HEADER TEXT	DATA FIELD
First Name	FirstName
Headline	Headline
Story	Story

10. Click the OK button.

11. Expand the AlternatingItemStyle property.

12. Enter **Gainsboro** in the BackColor property of AlternatingItemStyle.

13. Expand the HeaderStyle property.

14. Enter **Navy** in the BackColor property of HeaderStyle.

15. Enter **White** in the ForeColor property of HeaderStyle.

If you get sets of columns in the DataGrid—the first with the new heading and the second with the default heading—you forgot to set the AutoGenerateColumns property to False. (It took me a while to find it. Guess I should read the manual first before I use something.) After you do this, be warned: The DataGrid no longer generates all the columns in the table, only the ones you specify.

Listing 7-7 presents the finished HTML code of ADOToGrid.aspx, just in case you missed something when entering your own code.

Listing 7-7. ADOToGrid.aspx

```
<%@ Page language="c#" Codebehind="ADOToGrid.aspx.cs"
                       AutoEventWireup="false"
                       Inherits="Ch07Examples.ADOToGrid" %>
<!DOCTYPE HTML PUBLIC "-//W3C//DTD HTML 4.0 Transitional//EN" >
<HTML>
  <HEAD>
    <title>ADOToGrid</title>
    <meta name="GENERATOR" Content="Microsoft Visual Studio 7.0">
    <meta name="CODE_LANGUAGE" Content="C#">
    <meta name=vs_defaultClientScript content="JavaScript">
    <meta name=vs_targetSchema
          content="http://schemas.microsoft.com/intellisense/ie5">
  </HEAD>
  <body >
    <form id="ADOToGrid" method="post" runat="server">
      <asp:DataGrid id=DataGrid1 runat="server" AutoGenerateColumns="False">
        <HeaderStyle ForeColor="White" BackColor="Navy">
        </HeaderStyle>
        <AlternatingItemStyle BackColor="Gainsboro">
        </AlternatingItemStyle>
        <Columns>
          <asp:BoundColumn DataField="LastName" HeaderText="Last Name">
          </asp:BoundColumn>
          <asp:BoundColumn DataField="FirstName" HeaderText="First Name">
          </asp:BoundColumn>
          <asp:BoundColumn DataField="Headline" HeaderText="Head Line">
          </asp:BoundColumn>
          <asp:BoundColumn DataField="Story" HeaderText="Story">
          </asp:BoundColumn>
        </Columns>
      </asp:DataGrid>
    </form>
  </body>
</HTML>
```

Inserting Data Using a Stored Procedure

Do you remember from Chapter 1 the term "content management application (CMA)"? Figure 7-13 shows the building of a (very) rudimentary one for the Dynamic Content Viewer that you started in Chapter 6.

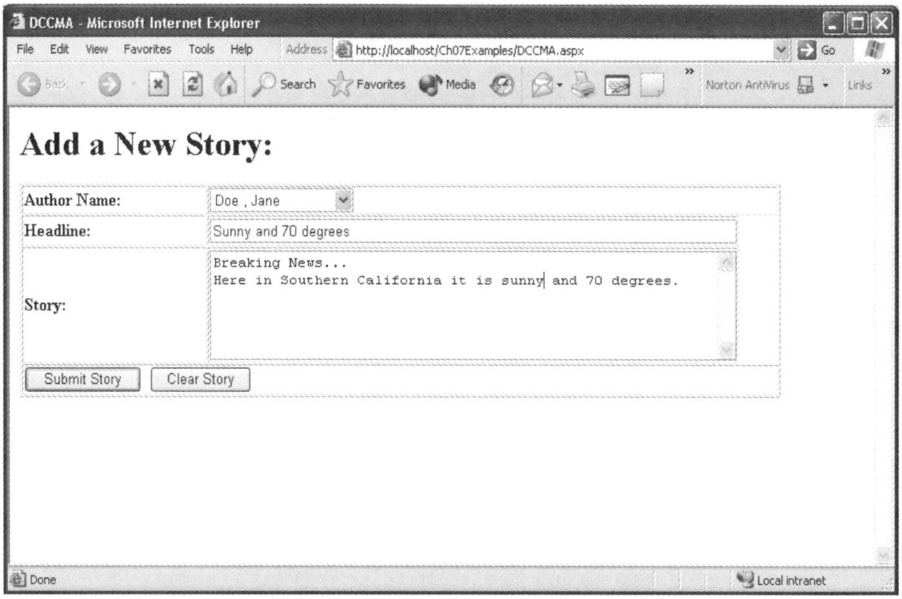

Figure 7-13. A Dynamic Content CMA

When I developed the Dynamic Content CMA Web page (which I shortened to DCCMA.aspx), I created it within the CH07Examples project. You can do this as well, or you can separate it out into its own project.

The first thing, as always, is to design your Web page. Figure 7-14 shows what I came up with as a simple design. Table 7-5 describes all the intrinsic controls so that you can build a similar Web page.

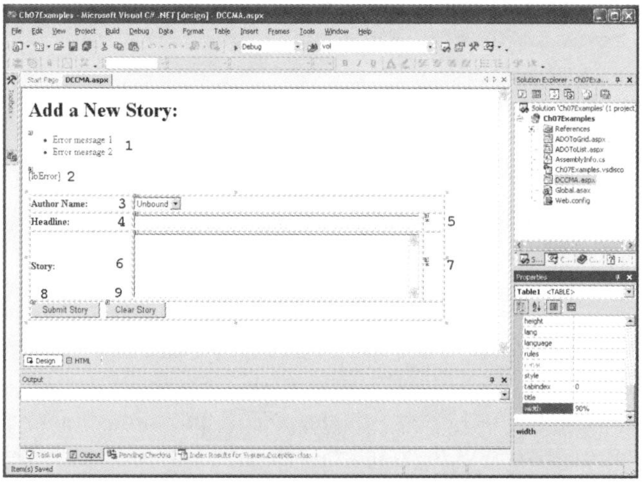

Figure 7-14. A Dynamic Content CMA design

Table 7-5. Dynamic Content CMA Design

NUMBER	CONTROL TYPE	ID	OTHER DETAILS
1	ValidationSummary	ValSum	Default values.
2	Label	lbError	Set ForeColor to Red and blank out all text.
3	DropDownList	ddlAuthor	Default values.
4	TextBox	tbHeadline	Set Width to 100%.
5	RequiredFieldValidator	rfvHeadline	Set Display to Dynamic, Error Message to **You must enter a Headline**, Text to *****, and Control To Validate to tbHeadline.
6	TextBox	tbStory	Set Rows to 6, Text Mode to MultiLine, and Width to 100%.
7	RequiredFieldValidator	rfvStory	Set Display to Dynamic, Error Message to **You must enter a Story**, Text to *****, and Control To Validate to tbStory.
8	Button	bnSubmit	Set Text to **Submit Story**.
9	Button	bnClear	Set Text to **Clear Story**.

Listing 7-8 shows the finished HTML code of DCCMA.aspx, just in case you missed something when entering your own code.

Listing 7-8. DCCMA.aspx

```
<%@ Page language="c#" Codebehind="DCCMA.cs"
                    AutoEventWireup="false"
                    Inherits="Ch07Examples.DCCMA" %>
<html>
  <head>
    <meta name="GENERATOR" Content="Microsoft Visual Studio 7.0">
    <meta name="CODE_LANGUAGE" Content="C#">
    <meta name="vs_defaultClientScript" content="JavaScript">
    <meta name="vs_targetSchema"
          content="http://schemas.microsoft.com/intellisense/ie5">
  </head>
```

```
<body>
  <form id="DCCMA" method="post" runat="server">
    <h1>Add a new story:</h1>
    <p>
      <asp:ValidationSummary id=ValSum runat="server">
      </asp:ValidationSummary>
    </p>
    <p>
      <asp:Label id=lbError runat="server" ForeColor="Red">
      </asp:Label>
    </p>
    <table cellspacing=1 cellpadding=1 width="90%" border=1>
      <tr>
        <td width="25%"><strong>Author Name:</strong></td>
        <td width="70%" colspan="2">
          <asp:DropDownList id=ddlAuthor runat="server">
          </asp:DropDownList>
        </td>
      </tr>
      <tr>
        <td width="25%"><strong>Headline:</strong></td>
        <td width="70%">
          <asp:TextBox id=tbHeadline width="100%" runat="server">
          </asp:TextBox>
        </td>
        <td width="5%">
          <asp:RequiredFieldValidator id=rfvHeadline
                                      runat="server"
                                      ErrorMessage="You must enter a Headline"
                                      Display="Dynamic"
                                      ControlToValidate="tbHeadline">
            *
          </asp:RequiredFieldValidator>
        </td>
      </tr>
      <tr>
        <td width="25%"><strong>Story:</strong></td>
        <td width="70%">
          <asp:TextBox id=tbStory runat="server" Rows="6"
                       TextMode="MultiLine" width="100%">
          </asp:TextBox>
        </td>
```

```
        <td width="5%">
          <asp:RequiredFieldValidator id=RequiredFieldValidator2
                                      runat="server"
                                      ErrorMessage="You must enter a story"
                                      Display="Dynamic"
                                      ControlToValidate="tbStory">
            *
          </asp:RequiredFieldValidator>
        </td>
      </tr>
      <tr>
        <td colspan="3">
          <asp:Button id=bnSubmit runat="server" Text="Submit Story">
          </asp:Button>
           
          <asp:Button id=bnClear runat="server" Text="Clear Story">
          </asp:Button>
        </td>
      </tr>
    </table>
  </form>
  </body>
</html>
```

Alarms should be going off right now in your head. There are two buttons; how does the Web page differentiate between the two? Taking a look at the HTML source doesn't help either:

```
<tr>
  <td colspan="3">
    <asp:Button id=bnSubmit runat="server" Text="Submit Story">
    </asp:Button>
     
    <asp:Button id=bnClear runat="server" Text="Clear Story">
    </asp:Button>
  </td>
</tr>
```

Other than the id, there is no difference as far as the HTML is concerned. Believe it or not, this is a good thing. Remember that you are trying to keep HTML and code logic separate. Because this is logic you are dealing with, it only seems appropriate that all the code that handles logic would handle this. Guess what? It does.

Adding Code Specific to a Button

To add code specific to a button, perform these steps:

1. Select the Clear Story button.

2. Click the Events button in the toolbar of the Properties dialog box.

3. Enter **bnClear_Click** in the Click entry field.

4. Change the edit window to DCCMA.cs.

You should notice that the highlighted code automatically gets added:

```
private void InitializeComponent()
{
    this.bnClear.Click += new System.EventHandler (this.bnClear_Click);
    this.Load += new System.EventHandler (this.Page_Load);
}

private void bnClear_Click (object sender, System.EventArgs e)
{

}
```

By the way, you could also double-click the button instead of doing the preceding four steps, but then you can't give the button a custom name without additional effort. Personally, I prefer to double-click and use the method name provided.

Basically, the added code adds an event handler to watch for events received by the bnClear button. When the event occurs, the bnClear_Click() method is executed after the Page_Load() method. Read that again: The Page_Load() method is always run first.

So, how do you use these two buttons? First, you have to create events for all buttons by double-clicking them, and then you place the logic specific to each in its respective event handler methods. If you have any generic code, which all methods need to execute, put that in the Page_Load() method. You will see this in action in a second when you examine the Web page logic code.

The Dynamic Content CMA Code Logic

As always, the first thing you add is the namespace to the managed provider you are using. For the SQL managed provider, the code is as follows:

```
using System.Data;
using System.Data.SqlClient;
using System.Drawing;
```

With the SqlClient namespace ready, you can now tackle the coding of the Web page. The first thing you need to do is populate the author drop-down list. There is nothing new here, as you can see in Listing 7-9.

Listing 7-9. Populating the Author Drop-Down List in DCCMA

```
private void Page_Load(object sender, System.EventArgs e)
{
    if (!IsPostBack)
    {
        string ConnectStr = "server=localhost;uid=sa;pwd=;database=DCV_DB";
        string Cmd =
        "SELECT AuthorID, LastName, FirstName FROM Authors ORDER BY LastName";

        SqlDataAdapter DAdpt = new SqlDataAdapter(Cmd, ConnectStr);

        DataSet ds = new DataSet();
        DAdpt.Fill(ds, "Authors");

        DataTable dt = ds.Tables["Authors"];

        foreach (DataRow dr in dt.Rows)
        {
            ddlAuthor.Items.Add(new ListItem(dr["LastName"] + ", " +
                                            dr["FirstName"],
                                            dr["AuthorID"].ToString()));
        }
    }
}
```

Clearing the form is very straightforward. You need to set the text properties of both text boxes to an empty string in the new event method created by double-clicking the Clear Story button. Listing 7-10 shows the story clearing method.

Listing 7-10. Clearing a Web Form

```
private void bnClear_Click (object sender, System.EventArgs e)
{
    tbHeadline.Text = "";
    tbStory.Text = "";
}
```

Now, let's move on to the meat of this example: the inserting of data using a stored procedure.

The first thing you need is the stored procedure. I already covered building a stored procedure, and there is nothing new about this one, as you can see in Listing 7-11.

Listing 7-11. The InsertContent Stored Procedure

```
CREATE PROCEDURE dbo.InsertContent
    (
        @AuthorID INT      = NULL,
        @Headline CHAR(64) = NULL,
        @Story    TEXT     = NULL
    )
AS
    SET NOCOUNT ON

    INSERT INTO   Content ( AuthorID,  Headline,  Story)
    VALUES                 (@AuthorID, @Headline, @Story)

    RETURN
```

The approach I use to execute a stored procedure is two-pronged. The first prong is located in the code portion of the Web page, and the second is located in a helper class. Both of these contain new code, so you will break them down to make following it easier.

All the code is located in the event method of the bnSubmit button. You put it there instead of in the Load_Page() method because, if you didn't, the Clear Story button would also run it. Thus, it would cause the headline and story to be stored in the database even though you just want it cleared. Putting it into its own method means it will only be called when the Submit Story button is clicked.

The first thing in the bnSubmit_Click method is a second way to set up the managed provider. As hinted before, you can set up a connection to the database without submitting a SQL command. Obviously, you don't want to send one because you will be using a stored procedure.

The code is easy to follow. All you need to do is create an instance of a SqlConnection and then set its ConnectionString property with a merged data source, user ID, password, and database name string, just like the connection string you used with a `SqlDataAdapter`. Once you have the connection prepared, you create an instance of the helper class, content, passing it the `SqlConnection` in a parameter to its constructor.

```
private void bnSubmit_Click (object sender, System.EventArgs e)
{
    if (Page.IsValid)
    {
        SqlConnection myConnection = new SqlConnection();

        myConnection.ConnectionString =
            "server=localhost;uid=sa;pwd=;database=DCV_DB";

        Content content = new Content(myConnection);
```

A neat feature of ASP.NET is that exception handling works fine, no matter which language you are implementing it in. You use this to your advantage here because you call the `Insert()` method of the helper class, confident that if something goes wrong, the exception handling routine will catch it. The `Insert()` method takes three parameters: `AuthorID`, `Headline`, and `Story`. This is not coincidental because it corresponds directly to the parameters of the stored procedure created previously. Because ADO.NET is strong typed, you convert the Author drop-down list value to an integer type. After it is inserted, you clear the headline and story, so it is ready for the next entries.

```
    try
    {
        content.Insert(Convert.ToInt16(ddlAuthor.SelectedItem.Value),
                            tbHeadline.Text,
                            tbStory.Text);

        tbHeadline.Text = "";
        tbStory.Text = "";
    }
    catch (SqlException err)
    {
        lbError.Text = "Sorry, the following error occured: " + err.Message;
    }
```

Just to make sure you didn't miss anything, Listing 7-12 shows DCCMA.cs in its entirety.

Listing 7-12. DCCMA.cs

```csharp
using System;
using System.Collections;
using System.ComponentModel;
using System.Data;
using System.Data.SqlClient;
using System.Drawing;
using System.Web;
using System.Web.SessionState;
using System.Web.UI;
using System.Web.UI.WebControls;
using System.Web.UI.HtmlControls;

namespace Ch07Examples
{
    public class DCCMA : System.Web.UI.Page
    {
        protected System.Web.UI.WebControls.Button bnClear;
        protected System.Web.UI.WebControls.Button bnSubmit;
        protected System.Web.UI.WebControls.RequiredFieldValidator
                    RequiredFieldValidator2;
        protected System.Web.UI.WebControls.TextBox tbStory;
        protected System.Web.UI.WebControls.RequiredFieldValidator
                    rfvHeadline;
        protected System.Web.UI.WebControls.TextBox tbHeadline;
        protected System.Web.UI.WebControls.DropDownList ddlAuthor;
        protected System.Web.UI.WebControls.Label lbError;
        protected System.Web.UI.WebControls.ValidationSummary ValSum;

        private void Page_Load(object sender, System.EventArgs e)
        {
            if (!IsPostBack)
            {
                string ConnectStr =
                        "server=localhost;uid=sa;pwd=;database=DCV_DB";
                string Cmd =
        "SELECT AuthorID, LastName, FirstName FROM Authors ORDER BY LastName";

                SqlDataAdapter DAdpt = new SqlDataAdapter(Cmd, ConnectStr);

                DataSet ds = new DataSet();
                DAdpt.Fill(ds, "Authors");
```

```
            DataTable dt = ds.Tables["Authors"];

            foreach (DataRow dr in dt.Rows)
            {
                ddlAuthor.Items.Add(new ListItem(dr["LastName"] + ", " +
                                        dr["FirstName"],
                                        dr["AuthorID"].ToString()));
            }
        }
    }
}


#region Web Form Designer generated code
override protected void OnInit(EventArgs e)
{
    InitializeComponent();
    base.OnInit(e);
}

private void InitializeComponent()
{
    bnClear.Click += new System.EventHandler (this.bnClear_Click);
    bnSubmit.Click += new System.EventHandler (this.bnSubmit_Click);
    this.Load += new System.EventHandler (this.Page_Load);
}
#endregion

private void bnSubmit_Click (object sender, System.EventArgs e)
{
    if (Page.IsValid)
    {
        SqlConnection myConnection = new SqlConnection();

        myConnection.ConnectionString =
            "server=localhost;uid=sa;pwd=;database=DCV_DB";

        Content content = new Content(myConnection);

        try
        {
            content.Insert(Convert.ToInt16(
                            ddlAuthor.SelectedItem.Value),
                        tbHeadline.Text,
                        tbStory.Text);
```

```
                        tbHeadline.Text = "";
                        tbStory.Text = "";
                }
                catch (SqlException err)
                {
                        lbError.Text =
                            "Sorry, the following error occured: " + err.Message;
                }
            }
        }

        private void bnClear_Click (object sender, System.EventArgs e)
        {
            tbHeadline.Text = "";
            tbStory.Text = "";
        }
    }
}
```

All that is left for this Web page is the helper class. This class is actually derived from a helper class used by the CMS system that this book will develop, so it is a little more feature-rich than it needs to be.

After creating the new class, you need to add the necessary namespaces to access the SQL managed provider and a couple of member variables. The first variable will hold the SqlConnection passed by the constructor. The second is a copy of the SqlCommand you will be building. This is so that after it has been built once, it doesn't have to be built again.

After the variables is the constructor, which only initializes the SqlConnection member variable.

```
using System;
using System.Data;
using System.Data.SqlClient;

namespace Ch07Examples
{
    public class Content
    {
        private SqlConnection m_Connection;
        private SqlCommand    m_InsertCommand;
```

```
        public Content(SqlConnection Connection)
    {
        m_Connection = Connection;
    }
    . . .
  }
}
```

Now you come to the Insert() method. The method looks complex but it's not. First, you check whether the Insert() method has been run before. If it has, you can bypass the command-building code because you stored it off the first time you accessed the method.

You call a managed provider method, called SqlCommand, to set up the command to call the stored procedure InsertContent using the connection passed by the constructor. You set the CommandType property to StoredProcedure. Finally, you add parameter definitions to SqlCommand so that it can pass data to the stored procedure.

```
    public void Insert(int AuthorID, string Headline, string Story)
    {
        SqlParameterCollection Params;

        if ( m_InsertCommand == null )
        {
            // Only create Insert command the first time
            m_InsertCommand = new SqlCommand("InsertContent",
                                            m_Connection);
            m_InsertCommand.CommandType = CommandType.StoredProcedure;
            Params = m_InsertCommand.Parameters;

            Params.Add(new SqlParameter("@AuthorID", SqlDbType.Int));
            Params.Add(new SqlParameter("@Headline", SqlDbType.Char, 64));
            Params.Add(new SqlParameter("@Story",    SqlDbType.Text));
        }
```

Next, you load the SqlCommand's parameters with the values passed in through the method's parameters.

```
        Params = m_InsertCommand.Parameters;

        Params["@AuthorID"].Value = AuthorID;
        Params["@Headline"].Value = Headline;
        Params["@Story"].Value    = Story;
```

You use a little trick of exception handling. By including the `finally` clause of the exception, you are guaranteed that the connection will be closed, even on error. The actual exception is caught in the method that calls this one.

Finally, you open a connection to the database and execute the stored procedure using the `ExecuteNonQuery()` method.

```
try
{
    m_Connection.Open();
    m_InsertCommand.ExecuteNonQuery();
}
finally
{
    m_Connection.Close();
}
}
```

Not that bad, was it? Save, compile, and execute it. Try entering some HTML formatting into the stories. You will see in the next example that they come out formatted as you specified.

Now let's move on to the last example: revisiting the Dynamic Content Viewer.

Updating the Dynamic Content Viewer with ADO.NET

Let's finish off the chapter by revisiting the Dynamic Content Viewer you created in Chapter 6. As you can see in Figure 7-15, the Web page has become much simpler because all the personalization code was removed, thus removing all the validation intrinsic controls because they were no longer needed. A label called `lbAuthor` was also added in a smaller font so that you can see who wrote the story. All the code needed to create the design is in Listing 7-13.

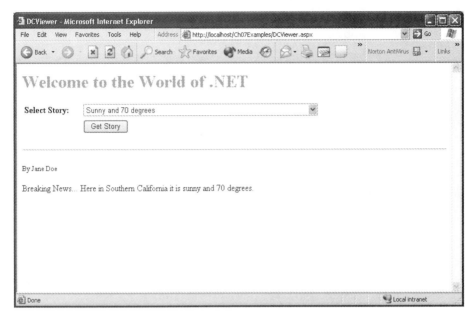

Figure 7-15. The updated Dynamic Content Viewer

Listing 7-13. DCViewer.aspx

```
<%@ Page language="c#" Codebehind="DCViewer.aspx.cs"
                       AutoEventWireup="false"
                       Inherits="Ch07Examples.DCViewer" %>
<!DOCTYPE HTML PUBLIC "-//W3C//DTD HTML 4.0 Transitional//EN" >
<HTML>
  <HEAD>
    <title>DCViewer</title>
    <meta name="GENERATOR" Content="Microsoft Visual Studio 7.0">
    <meta name="CODE_LANGUAGE" Content="C#">
    <meta name=vs_defaultClientScript content="JavaScript">
    <meta name=vs_targetSchema
          content="http://schemas.microsoft.com/intellisense/ie5">
  </HEAD>
  <body >
    <form id="DCViewer" method="post" runat="server">
      <H1> <FONT color="#66cc00">Welcome to the world of .NET </FONT></H1>
      <P>
        <TABLE id="Table1" cellSpacing=1 cellPadding=3 width="100%" border=0>
          <TR>
            <TD width="20%"><STRONG>Select Story:</STRONG></TD>
            <TD width ="80%">
```

```
                    <asp:DropDownList id=ddlStories runat="server">
                    </asp:DropDownList>
                </TD>
            </TR>
            <TR>
                <TD width ="20%"> </TD>
                <TD width ="80%">
                    <asp:Button id=bnGetStory runat="server" Text="Get Story">
                    </asp:Button>
                </TD>
            </TR>
        </TABLE>
    </P>
    <P>
        <HR width="100%" SIZE="1">
    <P>
        <asp:Label id=lbAuthor runat="server" Font-Size="X-Small">
        </asp:Label>
    </P>
    <P>
        <asp:Label id=lbStory runat="server">
        </asp:Label>
    </P>
    </form>
  </body>
</HTML>
```

As you can see in Listing 7-14, there is really nothing new when it comes to coding the functionality of the Web page. You load the drop-down list from the Content table the first time the page is loaded, and all subsequent times you check which value has been selected in the drop-down list and do a SQL select on the Stories view to find it. Then you display the author and story using their respective labels.

Listing 7-14. DCViewer.cs

```
using System;
using System.Collections;
using System.ComponentModel;
using System.Data;
using System.Data.SqlClient;
using System.Drawing;
using System.Web;
using System.Web.SessionState;
```

```
using System.Web.UI;
using System.Web.UI.WebControls;
using System.Web.UI.HtmlControls;

namespace Ch07Examples
{
    public class DCViewer : System.Web.UI.Page
    {
        protected System.Web.UI.WebControls.Label lbStory;
        protected System.Web.UI.WebControls.Label lbAuthor;
        protected System.Web.UI.WebControls.Button bnGetStory;
        protected System.Web.UI.WebControls.DropDownList ddlStories;

        private void Page_Load(object sender, System.EventArgs e)
        {
            if (!IsPostBack)
            {
                string ConnectStr =
                        "server=localhost;uid=sa;pwd=;database=DCV_DB";
                string Cmd = "SELECT StoryID, Headline FROM Content";

                SqlDataAdapter DAdpt = new SqlDataAdapter(Cmd, ConnectStr);

                DataSet ds = new DataSet();
                DAdpt.Fill(ds, "Content");

                DataTable dt = ds.Tables["Content"];

                foreach (DataRow dr in dt.Rows)
                {
                    ddlStories.Items.Add(
                        new ListItem(dr["Headline"].ToString(),
                                    dr["StoryID"].ToString()));
                }
            }
        }

        #region Web Form Designer generated code
        override protected void OnInit(EventArgs e)
        {
            InitializeComponent();
            base.OnInit(e);
        }
```

```
private void InitializeComponent()
{
    bnGetStory.Click += new System.EventHandler(this.bnGetStory_Click);
    this.Load += new System.EventHandler (this.Page_Load);
}
#endregion

private void bnGetStory_Click(object sender, System.EventArgs e)
{
    if (Page.IsValid)
    {
        string ConnectStr =
            "server=localhost;uid=sa;pwd=;database=DCV_DB";
        string Cmd = "SELECT * FROM Stories WHERE StoryID = "
            + ddlStories.SelectedItem.Value.ToString();

        SqlDataAdapter DAdpt =
            new SqlDataAdapter(Cmd, ConnectStr);

        DataSet ds = new DataSet();
        DAdpt.Fill (ds, "Stories");

        DataRow dr = ds.Tables["Stories"].Rows[0];

        lbAuthor.Text = "By " + dr["FirstName"] + " " + dr["LastName"];
        lbStory.Text = dr["Story"].ToString();
    }
}
}
```

There are only two things of note in Listing 7-14. The first is how you populate the DataRow:

```
DataRow dr = ds.Tables["Stories"].Rows[0];
```

What is interesting is that because you know that only one row will be retrieved, you can directly populate the DataRow with the first row of the table. Remember that the Rows collection starts with zero.

The second thing is that you need to be careful about the use of the Page.IsValid variable. I had originally coded this example with the retrieving of the stories from the database within the Page_Load() method. Unfortunately, this causes an error because when the page is run an exception is thrown due to

`Page.IsValid` not being set. To fix this problem, `Page.IsValid` needs to be coded within an event handler with the control property `CausesValidation` set to its default `true` (as we have done previously) or the Web page code must call `Page.Validate` itself.

All that is left to do is save, compile, and execute. All the stories you entered in the previous example show up, and if you formatted them using HTML, the formatting appears as expected.

Summary

This chapter covered in detail the database utilities provided by Visual Studio .NET and ADO.NET.

It started by covering four common database utilities:

- Creating databases

- Adding tables

- Adding views

- Building stored procedures

Next, it discussed ADO.NET and explored some of its common classes. It finished with four example programs:

- Reading data from a database using ADO.NET

- Building an ASP.NET DataGrid

- Inserting data using a stored procedure

- Updating the Dynamic Content Viewer with ADO.NET

In the next chapter, you are going to have some fun with XML.

CHAPTER 8

XML

EXTENSIBLE MARKUP LANGUAGE (XML) is the final piece of background information needed before you can delve into building a fully functional content management system (CMS) called CMS.NET. Even though I cover it last, it is hardly unimportant. In fact, depending on how you implement your CMS repository, it could be one of the most important areas I cover.

This chapter is not designed to explore XML in great detail, though like all the previous chapters, it will provide a brief explanation. It is instead focused on how to implement XML in a .NET environment. In particular, this chapter covers how a developer would go about reading, writing, inserting, updating, and navigating XML using C# code.

Microsoft has gone to a lot of effort to simplify XML development. If you have written any XML code using the Microsoft XML Parser (MSXML) or Java, you will see that it has a lot of similarities to the .NET implementation.

This chapter provides all the XML coding knowledge you will need for the rest of the book, but it hardly scratches the surface of what can be done with XML. This chapter does not even cover XSLT or XML Schemas, which are other related XML technologies.

The best way to get a grip on XML coding is to walk through sample programs that show you how to do it instead of just explaining it. This chapter has three simple examples (reading, writing, and updating and inserting XML) and one complex example (showing how to build a NavBar using XML).

What Is XML?

Veteran developers like to make XML sound mysterious when it is anything but. It was designed to be easy: Ease of use was one of the original requirements when XML was being developed.

The first hurdle that a newbie developer must cross is to understand that XML is not a computer language. Rather, it is a metalanguage for defining or specifying how to mark up a document in such a way as to identify its structure.

Okay, one more time in English. . . .

XML is a method for someone to arrange a document so that it is broken up into parts. For example, in the case of a CMS, a document could be broken up by author name, headline, and story. Each of these parts is surrounded by a tag that describes what content is contained within. Listing 8-1 is a very simple example of XML, and it is the one you will use for the first sample program in this chapter.

Listing 8-1. Content.xml

```xml
<?xml version="1.0" encoding="utf-8"?>
<Content>
  <ContentForAuthor>
      <Author>
        <FirstName>
          Bill
        </FirstName>
        <LastName>
          Doors
        </LastName>
      </Author>
      <Articles>
        <Headline>
          .NET is the best
        </Headline>
        <Story>
          According to my research. The .NET product has no competition.
Though, I am a little biased.
        </Story>
        <Headline>
          SQL Server will be #1
        </Headline>
        <Story>
          This database has no real competition. But then again ... I am a
little biased.
        </Story>
      </Articles>
  </ContentForAuthor>
  <ContentForAuthor>
      <Author>
        <FirstName>
          Larry
        </FirstName>
        <LastName>
          Ellidaughter
        </LastName>
      </Author>
```

```
    <Articles>
      <Headline>
        Oracle is #1
      </Headline>
      <Story>
        Research suggests that it is the best database on the market. Not
that I have any biases in that conclusion.
      </Story>
    </Articles>
  </ContentForAuthor>
  <ContentForAuthor>
      <Author>
        <FirstName>
          Stephen
        </FirstName>
        <LastName>
          Fraser
        </LastName>
      </Author>
      <Articles>
        <Headline>
          Content Management is expensive
        </Headline>
        <Story>
          Not any more ... It now costs the price of a book and a little
work.
        </Story>
      </Articles>
  </ContentForAuthor>
</Content>
```

Why would you ever want to add so much overhead to a document? Why not just write the document like this:

```
Bill
Doors
.NET is the best
According to my research. The .NET product has no competition. Though, I am a
little biased.
SQL Server will be #1
This database has no real competition. But then again ... I am a little biased.
```

```
Larry
Ellidaughter
Oracle is #1
Research suggests that it is the best database on the market. Not that I have
any biases in that conclusion.
Stephen
Fraser
Content Management is expensive
Not any more . . . It now costs the price of a book and a little work.
```

Can you find all the authors' names in the document? How about the headlines? Sure, finding that type of stuff is easy for a human, but the same cannot be said for a computer. This example is simple and fairly straightforward. It is possible for XML to get extremely complex, though.

Look at Listing 8-1 again. With XML, a computer can look for tags and then, based on the logic of the XML program parsing the document, it can break up the document into its parts. It is now possible to ask a computer to provide all the first names in the documents. Hey, doesn't that sound a lot like the following SQL statement?

```
Select LastName From Authors
```

Just think, you can store all your data in XML format and not in database tables and rows. (By the way, that is exactly what an ADO.NET DataSet does.)

If a computer can now parse a document with 100 percent reliability, it can be used to transfer data from one application or part of an application or to another. Each of the applications participating in the transaction will be secure in knowing that the other will understand what it is trying to send. Guess what? .NET uses this, too.

XML is extremely powerful. If you don't know XML at least at a basic level, you need to take a brief detour. I recommend spending some quality time learning XML, especially if you want to tackle .NET. As you have briefly just seen and will be seeing in more detail in the next section, XML permeates the .NET architecture. In fact, XML is the underlying core of .NET.

Where Is XML Used in Web Architecture?

Don't be fooled by the simplicity of XML. It has a lot of power under the hood, and Microsoft's .NET taps into this power full-throttle. Almost all parts of the .NET architecture use XML. I will cover only the Web-related elements of .NET, but XML is just as well represented in all the other areas of .NET.

ASP.NET

Taking a quick look around the Inetpub directory structure, you will find many XML files. The following are the two most common:

- *Global.asax:* Used to set application-level event and state settings for when the application starts and ends.

- *Config.web:* Contains configuration information about the Web application being developed. Chapter 10 discusses Config.web in more detail.

You also may have noticed that ASPX files have a very strong XML flavor to them, especially intrinsic controls. Truthfully, though, they are still HTML files with some new tags. Even these tags get interpreted into HTML later downstream.

ADO.NET

As discussed in Chapter 7, ADO.NET has XML as its heart. Data flows back and forth from the database and the DataSet formatted as XML. ADO.NET even stores its data in an XML format instead of in the row/column format of the databases from which it most likely derived.

Looking at the DataSet class, you will find many XML-related read and write methods. Using these methods, you can load a DataSet directly with an XML file instead of a database.

C#

Like all common language runtime (CLR) programming languages, C# provides full support for XML programming through the .NET Framework class library. All supporting methods for XML programming can be found in the namespace System.XML and (as previously mentioned) System.Data's DataSet class.

Content Files

Though not essential or even necessary, content files can be stored using XML rather than databases. This might be a valid solution for a simple CMS, but as the size of a Web site's content starts to grow, it is probably better to migrate to a database solution because maintainability, reliability, and scalability become major factors to which databases are better suited.

XmlReader, XmlWriter, and XPathNavigator

The .Net Framework class library provides two ways of processing XML data. The first way is by a fast, noncached, forward-only stream, and the second way is random access via an in-memory Document Object Model (DOM) tree. DOM trees are stored in memory using an XmlDocument.

XmlReader and XmlWriter are abstract classes that define the base functionality for handling fast, noncached, forward-only streams of XML data. XPathNavigator provides an implementation for randomly accessing an in-memory DOM tree (obviously, or I wouldn't have made it part of this section).

Both methods of accessing XML data are equally valid. In certain situations, it is better to use one method over the other. At other times, both will work equally well, and it is up to the developer's taste.

The major deciding factors for choosing one method over the other are whether all data needs to be in memory at one time (especially if the XML file is large) and whether random access to the data is needed. When either of these factors occurs, XmlDocument, using XPathNavigator, should probably be used because reading forward sequentially through a document stream to read, update, or write the needed random data could get time-consuming.

On the other hand, if the data can be processed sequentially, XmlReader and XmlWriter are probably better because they are easier to develop and use resources more efficiently than XmlDocument using XPathNavigator. There is nothing stopping you from using XmlDocument in this scenario; in fact, there is an implementation of XmlReader and XmlWriter that does this. Programmers from Java and MSXML backgrounds will probably continue to use XmlDocument, more for its similarity to what they know than for any other reason.

XmlReader

This abstract class provides the base functionality to read XML data in a forward-only, noncached fashion. It currently has two implementations.

- XmlTextReader: Processes an XML document by tokenizing a text-based stream

- XmlNodeReader: Reads sequentially an in-memory DOM using XmlNodes

XmlReader, when you first look at it, seems a lot like the Simple API for XML (SAX), but actually they are fundamentally different. Whereas SAX uses a more complex push model, XmlReader uses a simple pull model. This means that a developer requests or pulls data one record at a time instead of having to capture the data using event handlers.

Coding using XmlReader seems, to me, more intuitive because you can handle the processing of an XML document as you would a simple file, using a good old-fashioned while loop. There is no need to learn about event handlers or SAX's complex state machine.

XmlWriter

XmlWriter is an abstract class that provides the base functionality to write XML data in a forward-only, noncached fashion. It currently has two implementations.

- XmlTextWriter: Processes an XML document by writing out a text-based stream

- XmlNodeWriter: Writes sequentially into an in-memory DOM using XmlNodes

People who use SAX to write out their XML documents will find XmlWriter to be quite similar.

XPathNavigator

An XmlDocument is an in-memory copy of an entire document's XML. As you saw previously, an XmlDocument can be accessed by the XmlNodeReader and XmlNodeWriter classes, but to get the full benefit of having the entire XML document in memory, it is better to use the XPathNavigator class instead.

XPathNavigator provides much of the same functionality as XmlReader and XmlWriter. In addition, XPathNavigator has the following features:

- It provides random access to the DOM tree.

- It allows the selection of a subset of nodes within the DOM tree for processing.

For those of you coming from Java or MSXML, XPathNavigator should feel very similar.

XML Examples

You keep hearing how good and easy XML is. After the initial learning bump (there is no real curve), it is actually easy to work with. In the examples that follow, you will explore multiple ways of doing the exact same thing. When you continue and develop your own code, choose the method with which you feel most comfortable because, in most cases, it really doesn't matter which method you use.

Let's see XML coding in action. You will start with three simple examples showing the basics of XML code development: reading, writing, and updating. Then you will launch into a more complex example that involves implementing a NavBar using an XML document to store the NavBar's navigational structure.

Reading from an XML File

I'll start first with something easy, yet it's probably the most important process in XML coding: the reading of an XML document.

In this example, you will use XmlTextReader to read through the XML document you saw earlier (in Listing 8-1). The remaining examples show three other ways of reading through an XML file.

The first thing you are going to do is create a new project to develop the new Web page. You can use any name you want for your project. I used Ch08Example just to be consistent.

Until now, you have been using only default .NET components to develop your code. For some unknown reason, XML is not a default component. This seems a little weird to me because XML is such an integral part of .NET. Anyway, you now have to add a reference to System.XML.dll to your newly created project because all XML-related code you will need is bundled into it.

Adding an External Reference to a Project

To add an external reference to your project, follow these steps:

1. Select Add Reference from the Project menu. This will display the Add Reference dialog box, as shown in Figure 8-1.

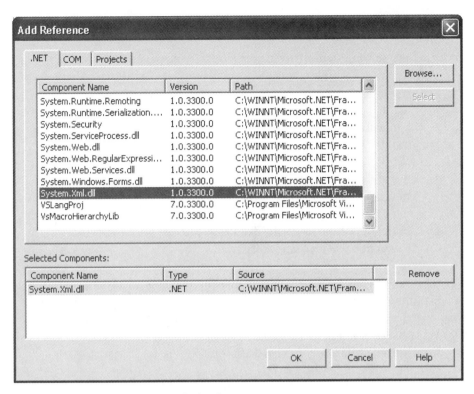

Figure 8-1. The Add Reference dialog box

2. Select System.XML.dll from the component list box.

3. Click the Select button.

4. Click the OK button.

Once you have added a reference to System.XML.dll to your project, you are ready to create the first example. As always, I recommend that you rename the ASPX file and class called WebForm1 to something more meaningful, in this case ReadXML.

The ReadXML Web Page Design

Perform the following steps to design the ReadXML Web page:

1. Give the Web page the title **ReadXML**.

2. Change the title's format so that it stands out. I changed it to the block format of Heading 3 and changed its color to green.

3. Click and drag a ListBox from the Toolbox onto the Web page and give it a new (ID) of **lbReadXML**.

4. You might want to resize the list box so you can see more of the XML document it will ultimately display.

Now that you have a display, you might want to create an XML file to display. The first thing I recommend, though it is not essential, is to put your XML files in their own directory. That way, your ASPX files don't get cluttered up with XML files, and it's also easier to locate them.

To create a new directory in Visual Studio .NET:

1. Right-click Ch08Examples in the Solution Explorer.

2. Select New Folder from the Add menu item.

3. Enter **XMLFiles** into the displayed edit box.

To create a new XML file in Visual Studio .NET:

1. Right-click the XMLFiles folder in the Solution Explorer.

2. Select New Item from the Add menu item. This will display the Add New Item dialog box, as shown in Figure 8-2.

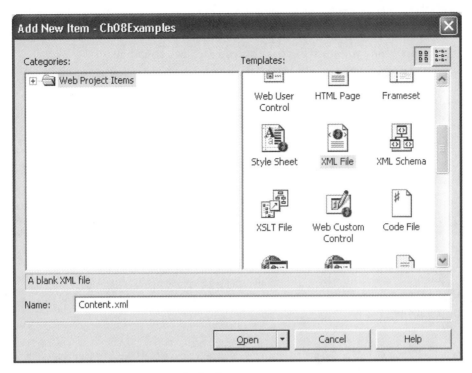

Figure 8-2. The Add New Item dialog box

3. Click the XML File icon in the Templates window.

4. Enter **Content.xml** in the Name box.

5. Click the Open button.

6. Enter in the edit window an XML document found in Listing 8-1.

All the preliminary stuff is done. Let's have some fun and do some coding.

Reading an XML File Using XmlTextReader

Open the code for ReadXML in the edit window. Nothing should be new to you. For ReadXML, you need to add the XML namespace. The code is just like adding any other namespace:

```
using System.Web.UI.HtmlControls;
using System.Xml;
...
```

From here on, all the code you are going to add will be found within the `IsPostBack` if statement in the `Page_Load()` method.

The first thing you need to do is open up the XML stream in an `XmlTextReader` so that it can be read. The method is quite straightforward. Basically, pass the constructor a stream as a parameter. The code should look like this:

```
private void Page_Load(object sender, System.EventArgs e)
{
    if (!IsPostBack)
    {
        XmlTextReader reader = new
            XmlTextReader("http://localhost/Ch08Examples/XMLFiles/Content.xml");
        ...
```

Remember a time when you used to read your files using plain old `while` statements? You probably wrote one of your first programs using logic like the following:

```
        while (reader.Read())
        {
            ...
        }
```

The `Read()` method of `XmlTextReader` parses the XML document into small XML nodes. You should only care about three types of nodes in this example:

- *Element:* An element of the document. You might also think of this as a tag.

- *Text:* The text information found between tags.

- *EndElement:* The closing of an element.

The code in this example is simple. Check the type of node and, if it is one of the types you are interested in, add it to the list box. The following code shows how easy this is:

```
        while (reader.Read())
        {
            if (reader.NodeType == XmlNodeType.Element)
            {
                lbReadXML.Items.Add("<" + reader.LocalName + ">");
            }
```

```
        else if (reader.NodeType == XmlNodeType.Text)
        {
            lbReadXML.Items.Add("->" + reader.Value);
        }
        else if (reader.NodeType == XmlNodeType.EndElement)
        {
            lbReadXML.Items.Add("</" + reader.LocalName + ">");
        }
    }
}
```

Note that I added some simple formatting in the code to make the list box look more like XML. The `Read()` method actually strips off all the angle brackets. I also added the arrow to help the text stand out a little more. The final outcome of this example should be a Web page that looks similar to the one shown in Figure 8-3.

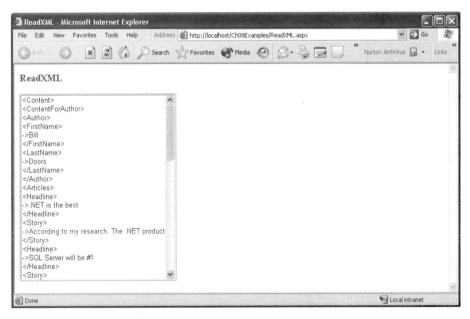

Figure 8-3. The ReadXML Web page

Just to make sure that you don't miss anything when you enter this code, Listing 8-2 shows the entire source code for ReadXML.cs.

Listing 8-2. ReadXML.cs

```csharp
using System;
using System.Collections;
using System.ComponentModel;
using System.Data;
using System.Drawing;
using System.Web;
using System.Web.SessionState;
using System.Web.UI;
using System.Web.UI.WebControls;
using System.Web.UI.HtmlControls;
using System.Xml;

namespace Ch08Examples
{
    public class ReadXML : System.Web.UI.Page
    {
        protected System.Web.UI.WebControls.ListBox lbReadXML;

        private void Page_Load(object sender, System.EventArgs e)
        {
            if (!IsPostBack)
            {
                // Read using XmlReader

                XmlTextReader reader = new XmlTextReader(
                    "http://localhost/Ch08Examples/XMLFiles/Content.xml");

                while (reader.Read())
                {
                    if (reader.NodeType == XmlNodeType.Element)
                    {
                        lbReadXML.Items.Add("<" + reader.LocalName + ">");
                    }
                    else if (reader.NodeType == XmlNodeType.Text)
                    {
                        lbReadXML.Items.Add("->" + reader.Value);
                    }
                    else if (reader.NodeType == XmlNodeType.EndElement)
                    {
                        lbReadXML.Items.Add("</" + reader.LocalName + ">");
                    }
                }
```

```
            }
        }

        #region Web Form Designer generated code
        override protected void OnInit(EventArgs e)
        {
            InitializeComponent();
            base.OnInit(e);
        }

        private void InitializeComponent()
        {
            this.Load += new System.EventHandler (this.Page_Load);
        }
        #endregion
    }
}
```

Writing to an XML File

Great, you can read an XML file. Now, how do you get a program to write one?
The process is so simple that I decided to also provide you with another way of
reading XML files.

Using the same project, create a new Web form and call it WriteXML.aspx.
Keep all the examples in the same project because you will be using them again
in the final example of the chapter.

Design your Web page exactly the same way you did in the first example. The
only differences should be the Web page title (for obvious reasons) and the (ID) of
the list box, which you should change to **lbXPath**.

Now bring up the code for WriteXML in the main edit window and you can
get started.

The first thing you have to do is add the namespace for XML, as you would
for any XML coding endeavor. You will also have to add the XPath namespace so
that you can access the XPathNavigator. The code should look like this:

```
using System.Web.UI.HtmlControls;
using System.Xml;
using System.Xml.XPath;
...
```

The next step is to open up an XML stream in an `XmlTextWriter` so that it can be (you guessed it) written to. The constructor is pretty simple. All you need to provide it is the stream where you want the XML document to be written and the encoding you want the stream to have. Use `null` because it writes out UTF-8, which is sufficient in most cases.

To add a little excitement to this method, I decided to implement it using the `Server.MapPath()` method. This helpful little method will convert the virtual path of the Web page's directory and replace it with the physical location. For example:

```
http://localhost/Ch08Examples/XMLFiles/MyContent.xml
```

gets converted to the following (on my computer):

```
C:\Inetpub\wwwroot\Ch08Examples\XMLFiles\MyContent.xml
```

This method is not really needed, but I threw it in for grins and giggles. Here is the constructor code:

```
if (!IsPostBack)
{
    XmlTextWriter writer = new XmlTextWriter(
                              Server.MapPath("XMLFiles/MyContent.xml"),
                              null);
    ...
```

The first thing you will note when `XmlTextWriter` writes out the XML document is that it is unformatted. In fact, it comes out as one long line with no breaks. This is fine for a computer, but for a human, it is not the most pleasant format. To fix this, `XmlTextWriter` provides a few formatting properties. You can look them up in the .NET documentation provided by Visual Studio .NET. This example, to make the XML document more human-friendly, adds the following formatting code:

```
writer.Formatting = Formatting.Indented;
writer.Indentation = 2;
```

Okay, now let's get down to writing the XML. The first thing you need to do is start the document using the `WriteStartDocument()` method. This method adds the following standard XML header to the XML document:

```
<?xml version="1.0" encoding="utf-8"?>
```

Next, you simply write the XML document. The only real difference (at least with a simple XML document) between real XML and the code is that the `WriteStartElement` and `WriteEndElement` method calls replace the angle brackets. Once you have finished adding the XML document, you finish off with a `WriteEndDocument()` method. The following code snippet shows how easy writing XML really is:

```
// start XML document
writer.WriteStartDocument();

// Write XML document
writer.WriteStartElement("", "Content", "");
writer.WriteStartElement("", "ContentForAuthor", "");
writer.WriteStartElement("", "Author", "");
writer.WriteStartElement("", "FirstName", "");
writer.WriteString("John");
writer.WriteEndElement();
writer.WriteStartElement("", "LastName", "");
writer.WriteString("Doe");
writer.WriteEndElement();
writer.WriteEndElement();
writer.WriteStartElement("", "Articles", "");
writer.WriteStartElement("", "Headline", "");
writer.WriteString("This is the Headline");
writer.WriteEndElement();
writer.WriteStartElement("", "Story", "");
writer.WriteString("The story is entered here.");

// not needed as XmlTextWrite closes all open elements
// with WriteEndDocument

// writer.WriteEndElement();
// writer.WriteEndElement();
// writer.WriteEndElement();
// writer.WriteEndElement();

// End XML document
writer.WriteEndDocument();
```

Now that you have a new XML document, you must close up the stream so that some other process can access it (in this case, so that the document can be read into the list box using XPathNavigator). The Close() method should not surprise anyone:

```
writer.Close();
```

Because that was too easy, let's explore another way to read XML files. This method loads the entire document into memory and then uses a random access navigator to move through the document. This process is a little more complex because you have to be aware of the recursive structure of an XML file and you must navigate using it. On the other hand, this method is very powerful because you can access a node randomly, unlike with XmlTextReader, which only works in a forward direction.

First, open up an XPathDocument, load it into memory, create an XPathNavigator to the in-memory document, move the navigation point to the root of the document, and display the XML document as shown in this code:

```
XPathDocument doc = new XPathDocument(
    new XmlTextReader(
        "http://localhost/Ch08Examples/XMLFiles/MyContent.xml"));

XPathNavigator nav = doc.CreateNavigator();

nav.MoveToRoot();

DisplayXMLTree(nav);
```

Now comes the fun part. You need to write a recursive method if you want to completely navigate the document tree. The following code snippet shows the recursive method that simply checks for child nodes and, if it finds one, calls itself to see whether the child has children, and so on. Once there are no more children, it finds its way back up to the parent and then looks for a parent's sibling. If it finds one, it calls itself so that it can process the sibling's children.

```
private void DisplayXMLTree (XPathNavigator nav)
{
    if (nav.HasChildren)
    {
        nav.MoveToFirstChild();
        FormatXML (nav);
        DisplayXMLTree (nav);
        nav.MoveToParent();
```

```
            lbXPath.Items.Add("</" + nav.Name + ">");
        }
        while (nav.MoveToNext())
        {
            FormatXML (nav);
            DisplayXMLTree (nav);
        }
    }
```

The FormatXML() method simply adds the node information to the list box so that you can see that it works. If it doesn't have children, the navigation point points to some text; otherwise, it points to an element. The code formats the node to look like XML. As with XmlTextReader, the angle brackets are not stored.

```
private void FormatXML (XPathNavigator nav)
{
    if (!nav.HasChildren)
    {
        lbXPath.Items.Add("->" + nav.Value);
    }
    else
    {
        lbXPath.Items.Add("<" + nav.Name + ">");
    }
}
```

Listing 8-3 shows the entire WriteXML.cs.

Listing 8-3. WriteXML.cs

```
using System;
using System.Collections;
using System.ComponentModel;
using System.Data;
using System.Drawing;
using System.Web;
using System.Web.SessionState;
using System.Web.UI;
using System.Web.UI.WebControls;
using System.Web.UI.HtmlControls;
using System.Xml;
using System.Xml.XPath;
```

```csharp
namespace Ch08Examples
{
    public class WriteXML : System.Web.UI.Page
    {
        protected System.Web.UI.WebControls.ListBox lbXPath;

        private void DisplayXMLTree (XPathNavigator nav)
        {
            if (nav.HasChildren)
            {
                nav.MoveToFirstChild();
                FormatXML (nav);
                DisplayXMLTree (nav);
                nav.MoveToParent();
                lbXPath.Items.Add("</" + nav.Name + ">");
            }
            while (nav.MoveToNext())
            {
                FormatXML (nav);
                DisplayXMLTree (nav);
            }
        }

        private void FormatXML (XPathNavigator nav)
        {
            if (!nav.HasChildren)
            {
                lbXPath.Items.Add("->" + nav.Value);
            }
            else
            {
                lbXPath.Items.Add("<" + nav.Name + ">");
            }
        }

        private void Page_Load(object sender, System.EventArgs e)
        {
            if (!IsPostBack)
            {
                XmlTextWriter writer = new XmlTextWriter(
                        Server.MapPath("XMLFiles/MyContent.xml"),
                        null);
```

```
                    // set up indenting format
                    writer.Formatting = Formatting.Indented;
                    writer.Indentation = 2;

                    // start XML document
                    writer.WriteStartDocument();

                    // Write XML document
                    writer.WriteStartElement("", "Content", "");
                    writer.WriteStartElement("", "ContentForAuthor", "");
                    writer.WriteStartElement("", "Author", "");
                    writer.WriteStartElement("", "FirstName", "");
                    writer.WriteString("John");
                    writer.WriteEndElement();
                    writer.WriteStartElement("", "LastName", "");
                    writer.WriteString("Doe");
                    writer.WriteEndElement();
                    writer.WriteEndElement();
                    writer.WriteStartElement("", "Articles", "");
                    writer.WriteStartElement("", "Headline", "");
                    writer.WriteString("This is the Headline");
                    writer.WriteEndElement();
                    writer.WriteStartElement("", "Story", "");
                    writer.WriteString("The story is entered here.");

                    // not needed as XmlTextWrite closes all open elements
                    // with WriteEndDocument

                    // writer.WriteEndElement();
                    // writer.WriteEndElement();
                    // writer.WriteEndElement();
                    // writer.WriteEndElement();

                    // End XML document
                    writer.WriteEndDocument();

                    // Close document so that it can be opened again
                    // from the XPathNavigator process of document
                    writer.Close();

                    // Read created file using XPathNavigator
                    XPathDocument doc = new XPathDocument(
                    new XmlTextReader(
                        "http://localhost/Ch08Examples/XMLFiles/MyContent.xml"));
```

```
                    XPathNavigator nav = doc.CreateNavigator();

                    nav.MoveToRoot();

                    // Recursive navigation of the DOM tree
                    DisplayXMLTree(nav);
                }
        }

        #region Web Form Designer generated code
        override protected void OnInit(EventArgs e)
        {
            InitializeComponent();
            base.OnInit(e);
        }

        private void InitializeComponent()
        {
            this.Load += new System.EventHandler (this.Page_Load);
        }
        #endregion
    }
}
```

After you have entered, compiled, and run this example, you will probably get an error. Normally, you don't want just anyone writing to your hard drive. But, in this case, you want ASP.NET to be able to write the XML file. To allow this, you need to change the security setting of the directory where the file is going to be written to, as follows:

1. Open Windows Explorer and navigate to directory where file is to be written to—in this case, C:\Inetpub\wwwroot\Ch08Examples.

2. Right-click the directory folder XMLFiles.

3. Select the Properties menu item.

4. Click the Security tab.

5. Click the Add button. This will display the dialog box shown in Figure 8-4.

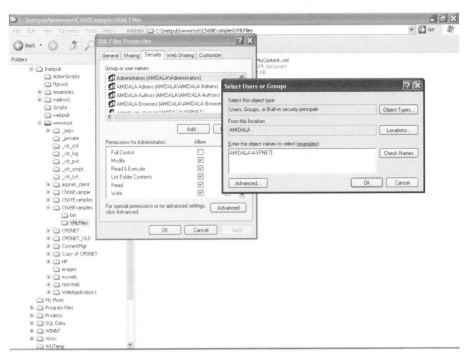

Figure 8-4. The Select User or Groups dialog box

6. Enter *{Machine Name}***ASPNET** into the text box. For me this is **AMIDALA\\ASPNET**.

7. Click the OK button.

8. Click the OK button.

When you run this example, you should get a Web page that looks like the one shown in Figure 8-5. Exciting, don't you think?

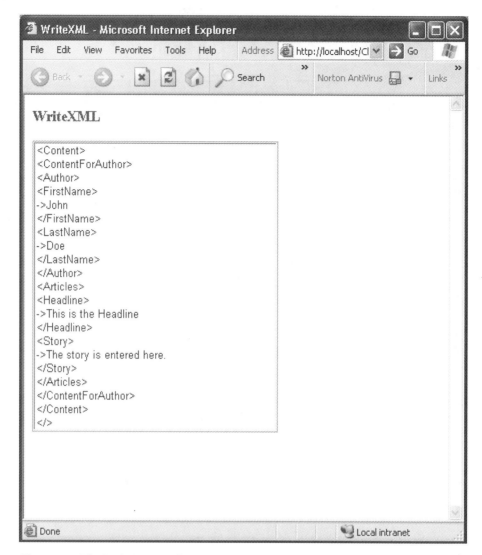

Figure 8-5. The WriteXML Web page

Inserting and Updating an XML File

You can now read and write an XML document, so let's take the final plunge and go ahead and complete the ways of working with XML documents. All that's left to cover is inserting and updating.

Just to simplify things, you will work with the minimal XML file shown in Listing 8-4. Basically, I removed the Articles elements from the original Content.xml. You should put the XML document in the XMLFiles directory that you created earlier in the Solution Explorer.

Listing 8-4. Authors.xml

```xml
<?xml version="1.0" encoding="utf-8"?>
<Authors>
  <Author>
    <FirstName>Bill</FirstName>
    <LastName>Doors</LastName>
  </Author>
  <Author>
    <FirstName>Larry</FirstName>
    <LastName>Ellidaughter</LastName>
  </Author>
  <Author>
    <FirstName>Stephen</FirstName>
    <LastName>Fraser</LastName>
  </Author>
</Authors>
```

The goal of this example is to insert a new author after Ellidaughter. You will follow that with updating my last name. For more grins and giggles, I will show a third way of reading an XML file.

First, you will add a new Web form to your project. Name the Web form UpdateXML.aspx. Then design a Web page consisting of titles and two list boxes, changing the (ID) of these list boxes to **lbBefore** and **lbAfter**. Finally, bring up the code for UpdateXML in the main edit window.

As always, the first thing you need to do is add namespaces. In this example, you will need two. You are obviously going to need the XML namespace, but to implement the third method of how to read an XML document, you need the IO namespace as well. The code, as you can see, is nothing you shouldn't already know.

```csharp
using System.Web.UI.HtmlControls;
using System.IO;
using System.Xml;
...
```

With the namespaces squared away, let's open up the authors.xml file and assign an XmlTextReader to it. Next, create a new XmlDocument and load it with XmlTextReader. Finally, close the authors.xml file so that it can be opened later with the inserted and updated authors.xml file.

```
if (!IsPostBack)
{
    XmlReader reader = new XmlTextReader(
        File.OpenRead(Server.MapPath("XMLFiles\\Authors.xml")));

    XmlDocument doc = new XmlDocument();
    doc.Load(reader);
    reader.Close();
    ...
```

Before I get to inserting and updating, you are going to look at a third way of reading an XML file. This method only needs the functionality provided by the XmlDocument and XmlNodeList classes.

This method provides the capability to do simple searches in tag names and then load an array with the retrieved values. In this example, I note that there is a first name for every last name, so you can do a search on both and then concatenate the retrieved values into the list box, displaying the author's full name.

```
XmlNodeList fnames = doc.GetElementsByTagName("FirstName");
XmlNodeList lnames = doc.GetElementsByTagName("LastName");

for (int i = 0; i < lnames.Count; i++)
{
    lbBefore.Items.Add(fnames[i].InnerText + " " + lnames[i].InnerText);
}
```

You will use this same code after you do your inserts and updates. The only difference will be the name of the list box you will populate.

```
fnames = doc.GetElementsByTagName("FirstName");
lnames = doc.GetElementsByTagName("LastName");

for (int i = 0; i < lnames.Count; i++)
{
    lbAfter.Items.Add(fnames[i].InnerText + " " + lnames[i].InnerText);
}
```

The steps for inserting a piece of XML into another piece of XML are hardly difficult. The following method of inserting XML after a sibling is one way, but there are many others. Some of the other, more common methods of inserting XML are before another sibling, after all children, and before all children.

The first thing you need to do is create the XML you want to insert. The easiest way to do so is simply to create the entire piece as a string and insert it into an XmlDocumentFragment, as you see in this piece of code:

```
XmlDocumentFragment newAuthor = doc.CreateDocumentFragment();
newAuthor.InnerXml=("\n    <Author>\n" +
                "        <FirstName>John</FirstName>\n" +
                "        <LastName>Doe</LastName>\n" +
            "    </Author>\n");
```

You might notice that you can embed new line characters using the escape code "/n". If you don't add new line characters of your own, the fragment inserted will end up as one long line of XML. This is not a problem for a computer, but humans like nice formatting. Go figure.

Admittedly, the following code is a bit of a hack, but it does show the basics of how to insert XML. First, you locate the sibling node after which you want to insert. Then you use the InsertAfter() method to squeeze it in. In the example, you are placing the new XML fragment after the second Author element.

```
XmlElement  root  = doc.DocumentElement;
XmlNodeList nodes = root.GetElementsByTagName("Author");
root.InsertAfter(newAuthor,nodes.Item(1));
```

To insert the fragment before the second Author, you would simply change the last line as follows:

```
root.InsertBefore(newAuthor,nodes.Item(1));
```

The process to update an XML file is only slightly trickier. You must navigate to the node you want to change and then replace the old values in the node with the new. In the example, I get an array of all Authors, and then I navigate through all of them, getting all of the LastName elements. There is only one, but this shows how you can find a node if there were more. Finally, I check if the LastName contains my last name: Fraser. If it does, I replace it with TheAuthor. As you can see, the code is quite easy:

```
nodes = root.GetElementsByTagName("Author");

for (int i = 0; i < nodes.Count; i++)
{
    XmlNodeList authornodes =
            ((XmlElement)(nodes.Item(i))).GetElementsByTagName("LastName");
```

```
    for (int j = 0; j < authornodes.Count; j++)
    {
        if (authornodes[j].InnerText.Equals("Fraser"))
        {
            authornodes[j].InnerText = "TheAuthor";
        }
    }
}
```

The last thing you need to do is save the XML document to disk. If you don't, all the changes you made will disappear when you exit the program. I do this purposely in this example, as you may note in the final version. This code is commented out in the final version.

```
StreamWriter writer = new StreamWriter(
    File.OpenWrite(Server.MapPath("XMLFiles\\Authors.xml")));
doc.Save(writer);
writer.Close();
```

Listing 8-5 shows the entire UpdateXML.cs so that you can make sure you entered it correctly.

Listing 8-5. The UpdateXML Codebehind

```
using System;
using System.Collections;
using System.ComponentModel;
using System.Data;
using System.Drawing;
using System.IO;
using System.Web;
using System.Web.SessionState;
using System.Web.UI;
using System.Web.UI.WebControls;
using System.Web.UI.HtmlControls;
using System.Xml;

namespace Ch08Examples
{
    public class UpdateXML : System.Web.UI.Page
    {
        protected System.Web.UI.WebControls.ListBox lbAfter;
        protected System.Web.UI.WebControls.ListBox lbBefore;
```

```
private void Page_Load(object sender, System.EventArgs e)
{
    if (!IsPostBack)
    {
        XmlReader reader = new XmlTextReader(
        File.OpenRead(Server.MapPath("XMLFiles\\Authors.xml")));

        XmlDocument doc = new XmlDocument();
        doc.Load(reader);
        reader.Close();

        // Displaying XML Document before insert & update
        XmlNodeList fnames = doc.GetElementsByTagName("FirstName");
        XmlNodeList lnames = doc.GetElementsByTagName("LastName");

        for (int i = 0; i < lnames.Count; i++)
        {
            lbBefore.Items.Add(fnames[i].InnerText + " " +
                                lnames[i].InnerText);
        }

        // Inserting

        XmlDocumentFragment newAuthor = doc.CreateDocumentFragment();
        newAuthor.InnerXml=("\n   <Author>\n" +
                            "      <FirstName>John</FirstName>\n" +
                            "      <LastName>Doe</LastName>\n" +
                            "   </Author>\n");

        //insert the new author after 2nd author
        XmlElement  root  = doc.DocumentElement;
        XmlNodeList nodes = root.GetElementsByTagName("Author");
        root.InsertAfter(newAuthor,nodes.Item(1));

        // Updating

        // Get New node list with inserted author
        nodes = root.GetElementsByTagName("Author");

        for (int i=0; i < nodes.Count; i++)
        {
            XmlNodeList authornodes =
                ((XmlElement)(nodes.Item(i))).
                GetElementsByTagName("LastName");
```

```
                    for (int j=0; j < authornodes.Count; j++)
                    {
                            if (authornodes[j].InnerText.Equals("Fraser"))
                            {
                                    authornodes[j].InnerText = "TheAuthor";
                            }
                    }
            }


            // Normally you would save the document but we want to
            // be able to re-run this

            // StreamWriter writer = new StreamWriter(
    // File.OpenWrite(Server.MapPath("XMLFiles\\Authors.xml")));
            // doc.Save(writer);
            // writer.Close();

            // Reading XML Document after insert & update

            fnames = doc.GetElementsByTagName("FirstName");
            lnames = doc.GetElementsByTagName("LastName");

            for (int i = 0; i < lnames.Count; i++)
            {
                lbAfter.Items.Add(fnames[i].InnerText + " " +
                                    lnames[i].InnerText);
            }
        }
    }
}

#region Web Form Designer generated code
override protected void OnInit(EventArgs e)
{
    InitializeComponent();
    base.OnInit(e);
}

private void InitializeComponent()
{
    this.Load += new System.EventHandler (this.Page_Load);
}
```

```
        #endregion
    }
}
```

After you enter, compile, and run this program, you should get a Web page that looks similar to the one shown in Figure 8-6.

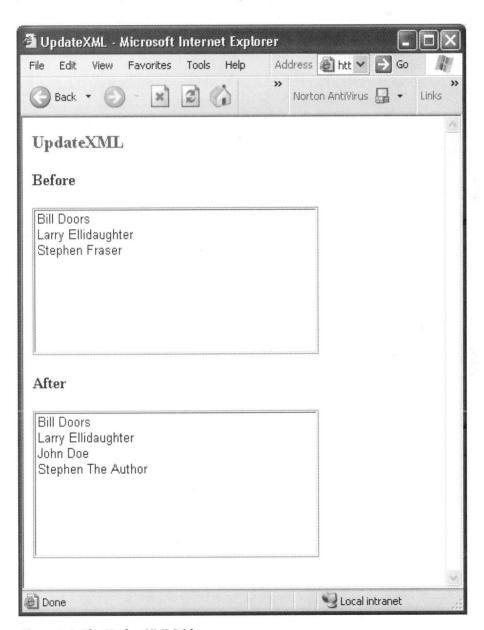

Figure 8-6. The UpdateXML Web page

Creating a NavBar Using XML

Let's finish off all the background material needed to build a CMS with an example you can actually use. Almost all Web sites have a NavBar, and implementing one (using XML to store the navigation structure) is really quite easy.

Actually, the hard part of implementing an XML NavBar is not the XML code at all. It is the intrinsic Table control code that complicates things. It would be a simple thing to write the `<table>` HTML in the CodeBehind C# file, but then you would not be separating the code and HTML as I promised in the beginning of the book.

Before you get to the coding of the NavBar, let's take a quick look at the XML file that stores the Web site navigation. As you can see in Listing 8-6, the structure is very simple.

Listing 8-6. The XML Menu Structure

```
Menu 1
    Menu Name
    Menu Item 1
        Name
        Link
    Menu Item 2
        . . .
    Menu Item n
    . . .
Menu 2
    . . .
Menu n
. . .
```

The structure is a list of menus. Each menu has a menu name followed by a list of menu items. Each menu item has a name and a link. Listing 8-7 shows the navigation structure of the example. Note that the first two menus contain nonexistent Web pages, and the final menu has menu items pointing to the Web pages developed in this chapter. As with all the other examples, you should place this XML file in the XMLFiles directory in the Solution Explorer.

Listing 8-7. MainMenu.xml

```xml
<?xml version="1.0" encoding="utf-8" ?>
<MainMenu>
  <Menu>
    <MenuName>Users</MenuName>
    <MenuItem>
      <Name>User Summary</Name>
```

```
    <Link>Users.aspx</Link>
  </MenuItem>
  <MenuItem>
    <Name>Create User</Name>
    <Link>CreateUser.aspx</Link>
  </MenuItem>
  <MenuItem>
    <Name>Edit User</Name>
    <Link>EditUser.aspx</Link>
  </MenuItem>
  <MenuItem>
    <Name>Remove User</Name>
    <Link>RemoveUser.aspx</Link>
  </MenuItem>
</Menu>
<Menu>
  <MenuName>Groups</MenuName>
  <MenuItem>
    <Name>Group Summary</Name>
    <Link>Groups.aspx</Link>
  </MenuItem>
  <MenuItem>
    <Name>Create Group</Name>
    <Link>CreateGroup.aspx</Link>
  </MenuItem>
  <MenuItem>
    <Name>Edit Group</Name>
    <Link>EditGroup.aspx</Link>
  </MenuItem>
  <MenuItem>
    <Name>Group Members</Name>
    <Link>MemberGroup.aspx</Link>
  </MenuItem>
  <MenuItem>
    <Name>Remove Group</Name>
    <Link>RemoveGroup.aspx</Link>
  </MenuItem>
</Menu>
<Menu>
<MenuName>Test Items</MenuName>
  <MenuItem>
    <Name>Read XML</Name>
    <Link>ReadXML.aspx</Link>
```

```
    </MenuItem>
    <MenuItem>
      <Name>Write XML</Name>
      <Link>WriteXML.aspx</Link>
    </MenuItem>
    <MenuItem>
      <Name>Update XML</Name>
      <Link>UpdateXML.aspx</Link>
    </MenuItem>
  </Menu>
</MainMenu>
```

To pretty up the NavBar, I decided to add three images:

- *Minus.gif:* Showing that the menu is expanded

- *Plus.gif:* Showing that the menu is contracted

- *Blank.gif:* Showing that the menu item doesn't expand or contract

For this example, all the images were put into their own directory called Images, oddly enough, which we created in the Solution Explorer. You can find a copy of the images I used on the Apress Web site in the Downloads section (www.apress.com/downloads/downloadPrompt.html). Alternatively, you can use almost any small image you like.

The design of the NavBar Web page, which I call Menu.aspx, is easy enough. All it contains is one intrinsic Table control from the Toolbox, with an (ID) of tblMenu. It is livened up a bit by changing the background color to tan and the font to bold.

The first thing you do in the code is the same as always: You add the namespaces needed. In this case, you need to add both the XML and IO namespaces, as shown in the following code:

```
using System.Web.UI.HtmlControls;
using System.IO;
using System.Xml;
...
```

Loading the XML file into an XMLDocument was covered in the third example. The only thing worth noting is that this code is run every time the page is loaded. This is because session state is not preserved between calls. It is easier to simply rebuild the menu from scratch and expand on the clicked menu item. Instead of remembering what was expanded, contract it and then expand the clicked menu item.

```
private void Page_Load(object sender, System.EventArgs e)
{
XmlReader reader = new XmlTextReader(
    File.OpenRead(Server.MapPath("XMLFiles\\MainMenu.xml")));

    XmlDocument doc = new XmlDocument();
    doc.Load(reader);
    reader.Close();

    ...
```

Next, you use a little trick by having prior knowledge of the possible return values of `Request.QueryString`. Whenever you click an expanding menu item, Menu.aspx is recalled with the number of the menu selected as an `Expand=n` parameter. You will later take that number and expand all its menu items. The trick is that the `Request.QueryString` property, if accessed with an unknown or missing parameter, returns `null`. Because this is the case, you can check the return value for `null` and, if found, initialize the number of the menu to expand to a nonvalid menu value: –1. If you have a valid `Expand=n` parameter, use it. The code snippet showing this follows:

```
string expand = Request.QueryString["Expand"];

int ExpandWhich;
if (expand == null)
    ExpandWhich = -1;
else
    ExpandWhich = Convert.ToInt16(expand);
```

The code that builds the menu, at first glance, seems quite complex, but actually it is fairly simple. First, you declare a couple of variables that you will use repeatedly, so you just declare them here once. Then you create an array of all the menu XmlNodes.

```
TableCell    cell;
HyperLink    link;

XmlNodeList Menus = doc.GetElementsByTagName("Menu");
```

Next, you cycle through all the menus found in the XML file.

```
for (int i = 0; i < Menus.Count; i++)
{
```

For each menu, you are going to need to add a new row in your Table control. You do this by creating a new empty row and then adding it to the tblMenu.

```
TableRow row = new TableRow();
tblMenu.Rows.Add(row);
```

When you come to the menu item that needs to be expanded, which can be easily determined by comparing the current row number with the value passed in the Expand=n parameter, you branch to the code to handle it.

```
if (ExpandWhich == i)
{
```

Because you know that this menu item is to be expanded, you can put the minus.gif into the first column of the row. You do this by creating an empty cell and then creating an image control. You then place the image in the cell, which is in turn placed in the row.

Because the creation of images is done three times in the code, you probably want to make it a method of its own.

```
cell = new TableCell();
cell.Width = Unit.Percentage(1.0);

System.Web.UI.WebControls.Image image =
    new System.Web.UI.WebControls.Image();
image.ImageUrl = "Images/minus.gif";
image.Width = Unit.Pixel(11);
image.Height = Unit.Pixel(11);
image.BorderWidth = Unit.Pixel(0);
cell.Controls.Add(image);

row.Cells.Add(cell);
```

Next, you create a literal control with the name of the menu that has been expanded. This is pretty simple. Create the literal control, place it in a new cell, and place the cell in the row.

```
LiteralControl lit =
    new LiteralControl(Menus[i].FirstChild.InnerText);

cell = new TableCell();
cell.Width = Unit.Percentage(99.0);
```

```
        cell.Controls.Add(lit);

        row.Cells.Add(cell);
```

Because this is the expanded row, you now fetch all the menu items out of the MainMenu.xml. Then for each menu item, you create a row and place a blank.gif image in the first cell.

```
        XmlNodeList MenuNodes = Menus[i].ChildNodes;

        // start at 1 since 0 is the Menu Name
        for (int j = 1; j < MenuNodes.Count; j++)
        {
            row = new TableRow();
            tblMenu.Rows.Add(row);

            cell = new TableCell();
            cell.Width = Unit.Percentage(1.0);

            image = new System.Web.UI.WebControls.Image();
            image.ImageUrl = "Images/blank.gif";
            image.Width = Unit.Pixel(11);
            image.Height = Unit.Pixel(11);
            image.BorderWidth = Unit.Pixel(0);
            cell.Controls.Add(image);

            row.Cells.Add(cell);
```

Each menu item needs to be associated with a hyperlink to the page to which it will be jumping. Simply build a new HyperLink and place in it the name you assigned to it and its hyperlink as specified in the MainMenu.xml. Then create a new cell, place the hyperlink in the cell, and place the cell in the row.

```
            link = new HyperLink();
            link.Text = MenuNodes[j].ChildNodes[0].InnerText;
            link.NavigateUrl = MenuNodes[j].ChildNodes[1].InnerText;

            cell = new TableCell();
            cell.Width = Unit.Percentage(99.0);
            cell.Controls.Add(link);

            row.Cells.Add(cell);
        }
    }
```

If this menu is not expanded, you execute this branch. First, you create a new row and then place a plus.gif in the first column.

```
    else
    {
        cell = new TableCell();
        cell.Width = Unit.Percentage(1.0);

        System.Web.UI.WebControls.Image image =
            new System.Web.UI.WebControls.Image();
        image.ImageUrl = "Images/plus.gif";
        image.Width = Unit.Pixel(11);
        image.Height = Unit.Pixel(11);
        image.BorderWidth = Unit.Pixel(0);
        cell.Controls.Add(image);


        row.Cells.Add(cell);
```

Finally, you come to the magic of this NavBar. You create a hyperlink back to itself (Menu.aspx) with an Expand=n parameter, assigning the value of the current menu to n . What this does, when selected, is cause the Expand=n parameter to be passed to the next execution of the Menu.aspx so that it can be expanded.

```
        link = new HyperLink();
        link.Text = Menus[i].FirstChild.InnerText;
        link.NavigateUrl = "Menu.aspx?Expand=" + i;

        cell = new TableCell();
        cell.Width = Unit.Percentage(99.0);
        cell.Controls.Add(link);


        row.Cells.Add(cell);
    }
}
```

So you can check to make sure you didn't miss anything, Listing 8-8 shows the entire code for Menu.cs.

Listing 8-8. Menu.cs

```
using System;
using System.Collections;
using System.ComponentModel;
using System.Data;
```

```csharp
using System.Drawing;
using System.IO;
using System.Web;
using System.Web.SessionState;
using System.Web.UI;
using System.Web.UI.WebControls;
using System.Web.UI.HtmlControls;
using System.Xml;

namespace Ch08Examples
{
    public class Menu : System.Web.UI.Page
    {
        protected System.Web.UI.WebControls.Table tblMenu;

        private void Page_Load(object sender, System.EventArgs e)
        {
            XmlReader reader = new XmlTextReader(
                File.OpenRead(Server.MapPath("XMLFiles\\MainMenu.xml")));

            XmlDocument doc = new XmlDocument();
            doc.Load(reader);
            reader.Close();

            int ExpandWhich;

            try
            {
                ExpandWhich = Convert.ToInt16(Request.QueryString["Expand"]);
            }
            catch (Exception)
            {
                // First time there is no "Expand" parameter
                ExpandWhich = -1;
            }

            TableCell   cell;
            HyperLink   link;

            XmlNodeList Menus = doc.GetElementsByTagName("Menu");

            for (int i = 0; i < Menus.Count; i++)
            {
```

```
            TableRow row = new TableRow();
            tblMenu.Rows.Add(row);

            if (ExpandWhich == i)
            {
                cell = new TableCell();
                cell.Width = Unit.Percentage(1.0);

                System.Web.UI.WebControls.Image image =
                    new System.Web.UI.WebControls.Image();
                image.ImageUrl = "Images/minus.gif";
                image.Width = Unit.Pixel(11);
                image.Height = Unit.Pixel(11);
                image.BorderWidth = Unit.Pixel(0);
                cell.Controls.Add(image);

                row.Cells.Add(cell);

                LiteralControl lit =
                    new LiteralControl(Menus[i].FirstChild.InnerText);

                cell = new TableCell();
                cell.Width = Unit.Percentage(99.0);
                cell.Controls.Add(lit);

                row.Cells.Add(cell);

                XmlNodeList MenuNodes = Menus[i].ChildNodes;

                // start at 1 since 0 is the Menu Name
                for (int j = 1; j < MenuNodes.Count; j++)
                {
                    row = new TableRow();
                    tblMenu.Rows.Add(row);

                    cell = new TableCell();
                    cell.Width = Unit.Percentage(1.0);

                    image = new System.Web.UI.WebControls.Image();
                    image.ImageUrl = "Images/blank.gif";
                    image.Width = Unit.Pixel(11);
                    image.Height = Unit.Pixel(11);
                    image.BorderWidth = Unit.Pixel(0);
                    cell.Controls.Add(image);
```

```
                        row.Cells.Add(cell);

                link = new HyperLink();
                link.Text = MenuNodes[j].ChildNodes[0].InnerText;
                link.NavigateUrl =
                    MenuNodes[j].ChildNodes[1].InnerText;

                cell = new TableCell();
                cell.Width = Unit.Percentage(99.0);
                cell.Controls.Add(link);

                row.Cells.Add(cell);
            }
        }
        else
        {
            cell = new TableCell();
            cell.Width = Unit.Percentage(1.0);

            System.Web.UI.WebControls.Image image =
                new System.Web.UI.WebControls.Image();
            image.ImageUrl = "Images/plus.gif";
            image.Width = Unit.Pixel(11);
            image.Height = Unit.Pixel(11);
            image.BorderWidth = Unit.Pixel(0);
            cell.Controls.Add(image);

            row.Cells.Add(cell);

            link = new HyperLink();
            link.Text = Menus[i].FirstChild.InnerText;
            link.NavigateUrl = "Menu.aspx?Expand=" + i;

            cell = new TableCell();
            cell.Width = Unit.Percentage(99.0);
            cell.Controls.Add(link);

            row.Cells.Add(cell);
        }
    }
}
```

```
#region Web Form Designer generated code
override protected void OnInit(EventArgs e)
{
    InitializeComponent();
    base.OnInit(e);
}

private void InitializeComponent()
{
    this.Load += new System.EventHandler (this.Page_Load);
}
#endregion
    }
}
```

Enter, compile, and execute Menu.aspx. You should get a Web page similar to the one shown in Figure 8-7. Try clicking some of the links in the third menu. They should call up the three examples you created earlier in the chapter. The hyperlinks in the first two menus will generate errors. You haven't created those pages yet.

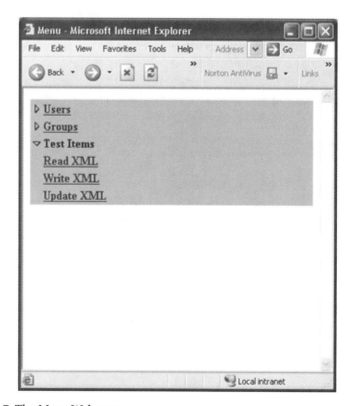

Figure 8-7. The Menu Web page

Summary

This chapter covered XML coding in a .NET architecture in detail.

First, it explained the basics of XML and showed an example. Then it explored where XML is used in a .NET Web architecture and examined some of its more common classes. It finished with four sample programs:

- Reading from an XML file

- Writing to an XML file

- Inserting and updating an XML file

- Creating a NavBar using XML

Enough background, don't you think? The next chapter provides a brief overview of CMS.NET—the real reason you are reading this book. Then, in the chapter after that, you will start to build your own CMS, which you will call CMS.NET.

A Quick Overview of CMS.NET

ARE YOU READY FOR SOME FUN? I know that I am. All this background information can start to get pretty dull unless you finally get to play with it. That's why I developed CMS.NET, a fully functional content management system, although it's a little thin when it comes to the fancy functionality you'd find on (much) more expensive commercial CMS software.

So, what are you getting with CMS.NET? Here is a high-level list of CMS.NET's features, which the remainder of this book covers:

- Initialization system

- Fully remote administration system

- Role-based, workflow-controlled content management application

- Full authentication and role-based authorization using encrypted passwords

- Fully ASP.NET-controlled metacontent management application

- Three-level dynamic content delivery application

- User profile collection system

- Restricted content

Also hidden in the code are many coding hints and tips that will save you hours of research and experimentation when it comes to your own endeavors in building a CMS (or any other ASP.NET application, for that matter).

What Is CMS.NET?

Simply put, CMS.NET is a content management system written from scratch in ASP.NET, ADO.NET, and C#, and it uses Microsoft SQL Server to store its content.

It was designed from the ground up to support remote Internet maintainability. It uses the power of Microsoft's .NET to handle most of its dirty work. CMS.NET uses many of the most common ASP.NET features used by Web developers and should provide a leg up for new ASP.NET developers, even if they have no interest in developing a content management system.

CMS.NET is a complete content management system, but more than likely, you will want to add a few features. Thus, it will most likely be the starting point for a CMS more suited to your needs. With some customization, CMS.NET can provide much of the functionality needed to maintain and display content on the average Web site.

Installing CMS.NET

Normally, when installing software, you use a setup program of some type. This book is not going to make it that easy for you. I will show you how to install CMS.NET manually, just to show you how easy it is to install a .NET Web application.

As you will see shortly, all the difficult parts of installing CMS.NET are in creating and loading the database. Because there are many ways to do this, I will show you a couple of different ways.

Installing CMS.NET Application Code

Now (insert drum roll) here is how you install all the code of CMS.NET:

Go to the Apress Web site (`www.apress.com`), click the Downloads link, select this book's title and click the Submit button, and then copy the entire CMSNET directory structure in the Final directory to C:\Inetpub\wwwroot.

Yep, that's it! No registering DLLs and no copying code to special locations. Heck, you don't even have to copy the code to the directory stated here. You can copy it almost anywhere because next you will be creating a virtual directory to it in Internet Information Services (IIS).

Configuring IIS

When you have the CMS.NET code where you want it, the next step is to let IIS know where it is. To do this, use the Internet Information Services program found in the Administrative Tools folder.

1. Start up the Internet Information Services program.

2. Navigate to and then right-click the Default Web Site folder.

3. Select Virtual Directory from New menu item (see Figure 9-1).

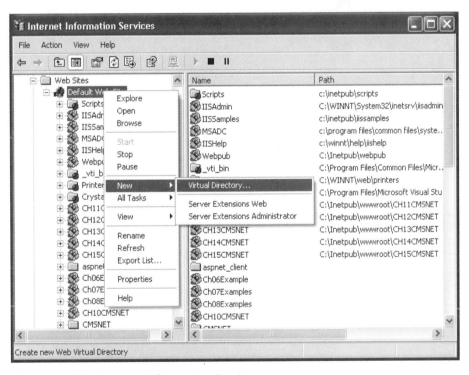

Figure 9-1. The Internet Information Services program

4. Click the Next button on the Virtual Directory Creation Wizard welcome screen (see Figure 9-2).

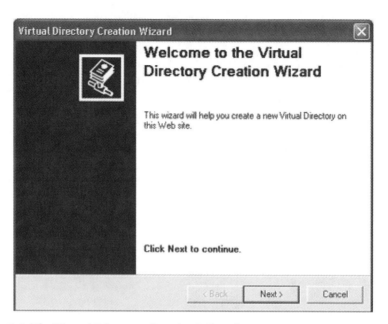

Figure 9-2. The Virtual Directory Creation Wizard

5. Enter **CMSNET** in the Alias edit field.

6. Click the Next button (see Figure 9-3).

7. Use the Browse button and navigate to the location where you copied the CMSNET directory earlier. Or, if you used the defaults during IIS installation, enter **C:\Inetpub\wwwroot\CMSNET** in the Directory field.

8. Click the Next button (see Figure 9-4).

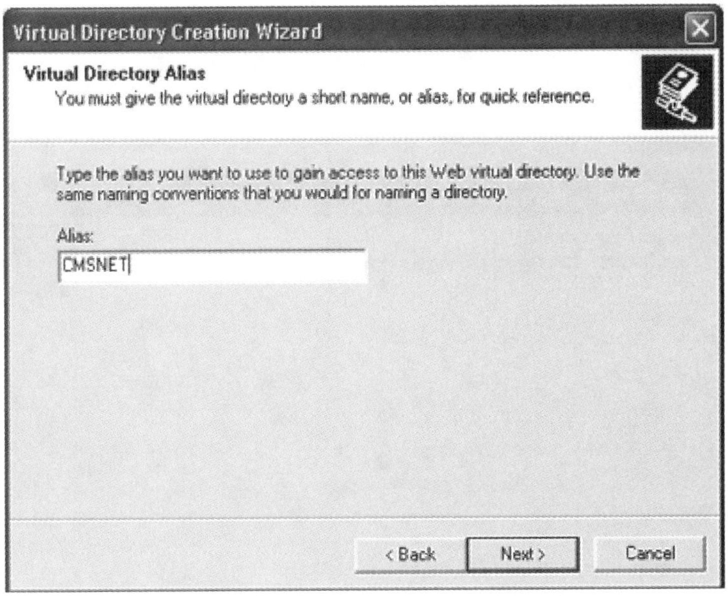

Figure 9-3. Setting the virtual directory alias

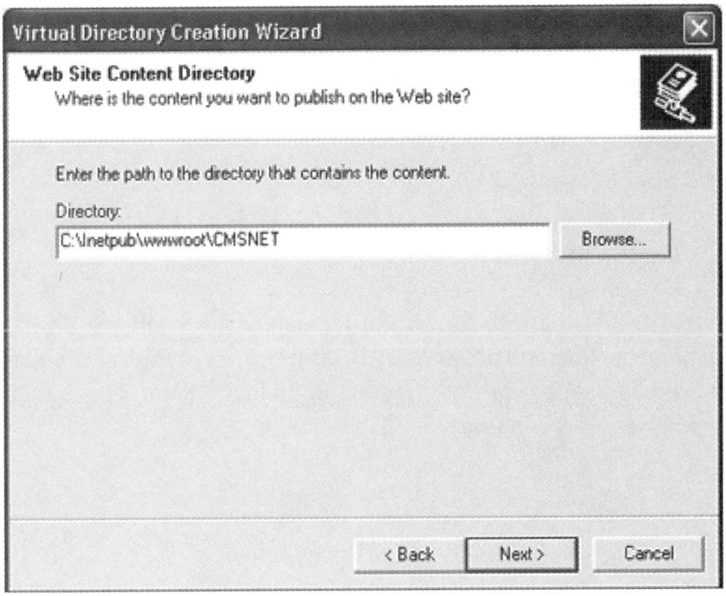

Figure 9-4. Setting the virtual directory

9. Use the default check boxes.

10. Click the Next button (see Figure 9-5).

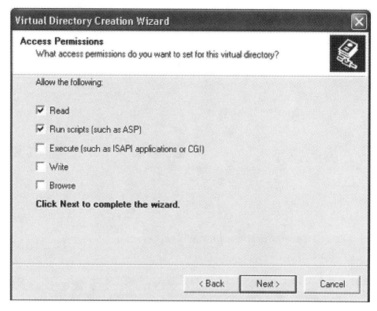

Figure 9-5. Setting the virtual directory access permissions

11. Click the Finish button.

12. Exit the IIS program.

CMS.NET is now ready to run (without a database, of course). If you want, you can type **http://localhost/CMSNET** in your browser's Address field and get your first CMS.NET Web page (see Figure 9-6). In fact, it's the "I'm changing" Web page that will be covered in Chapter 13.

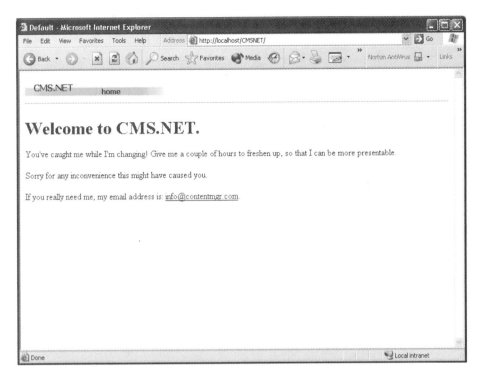

Figure 9-6. The "I'm changing" Web page

Creating and Loading the CMSNET Database

You can create and load the CMSNET database in numerous ways. You can, of course, do it the long way and enter everything by hand. But because I've already done that, let's do it three easier ways.

Using Visual Studio .NET

I am aware that not everyone has Microsoft SQL Server 2000 available, so first I will show you how to install CMSNET into the Microsoft SQL Server Desktop Engine (MSDE), which comes free with Visual Studio .NET. I happened upon this method by luck. There probably is a correct way of doing it, but the following method works and it is very easy:

1. Copy only the CMSNET.mdf file from the Final\MS SQL Database directory on the Apress Web site to the C:\Program Files\Microsoft SQL Server\MSSQL\Data directory. This file makes up an empty copy of the CMS.NET database.

2. Load Visual Studio .NET.

3. Using the Server Explorer, right-click the Data Connections folder.

4. Select the Add Connection menu item (see Figure 9-7).

Figure 9-7. Using the Server Explorer to add a database connection

5. In the Data Link Properties dialog box, select the Connection tab.

6. Enter your server name or enter **local** into the Select or Enter a Server Name field.

7. Select the Use a Specific User Name and Password radio button.

8. Enter **sa** into the User Name field.

9. Select the Blank Password check box.

10. Select the Attach a Database File as a Database Name radio button.

11. Enter **CMSNET** in the field below the radio button.

12. Using the button with the ellipses, navigate to where you placed the CMSNET.mdf file.

13. Click the Open button.

14. Click the OK button (see Figure 9-8).

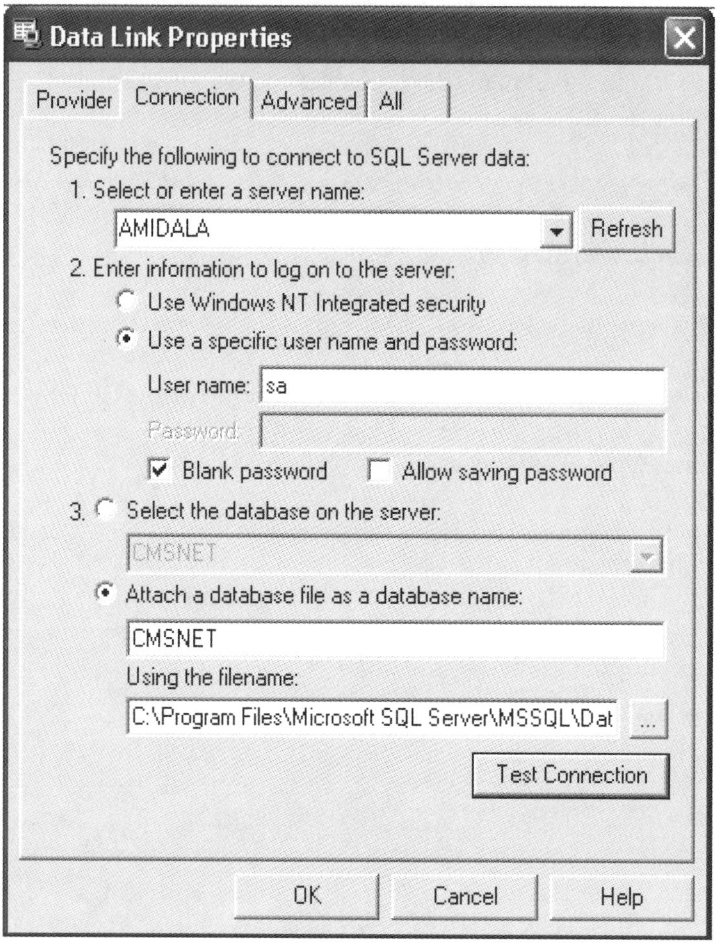

Figure 9-8. The Data Link Properties dialog box

Now, believe it or not, delete the newly created data connection. Yes, you read that right! You do this because you now have two copies of the connection: the one you just deleted and the one in the SQL Servers section, where it is supposed to be (see Figure 9-9).

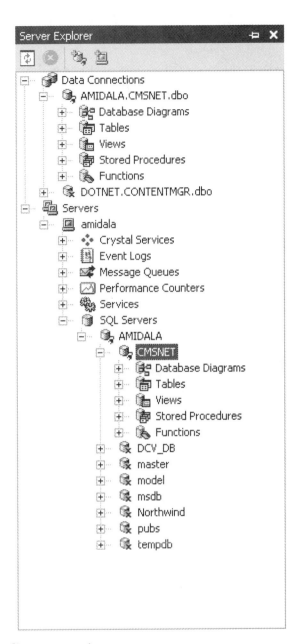

Figure 9-9. Duplicate connections

Exit Visual Studio .NET. Now you are all set to play with CMS.NET.

Using Microsoft SQL Server Enterprise Manager

For those of you who are lucky enough to have Microsoft SQL Server available to you, I will now show you how to do virtually the same thing you did with Visual Studio .NET but this time with Enterprise Manager.

1. Copy the CMSNET.mdf and CMSNET_Log.ldf files from the Final\MS SQL Database directory on the Apress Web site to the C:\Program Files\Microsoft SQL Server\MSSQL\Data directory.

2. Load Enterprise Manager.

3. Navigate down to your Server Group and right-click the Databases folder.

4. Select the Attach Database submenu item from the All Tasks menu item (see Figure 9-10).

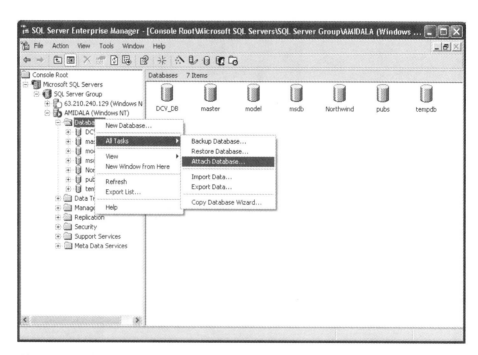

Figure 9-10. Using Enterprise Manager to attach a database

5. Using the button with the ellipses, navigate to where you placed the CMSNET.mdf file.

6. Click the OK button to close the Navigation dialog box.

7. Enter **CMSNET** in the Attach As field.

8. Enter **sa** in the Specific Database Owner field.

9. Click the OK button (see Figure 9-11).

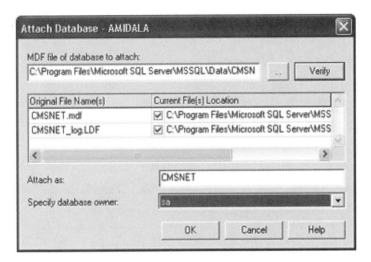

Figure 9-11. The Attach Database dialog box

Exit Enterprise Manager. Now you are all set to play with CMS.NET.

Using Microsoft Query Analyzer

Just for grins and giggles, I will show you a third way to create and load the CMSNET database. This time, you will execute a SQL script that defines the database. You will find the SQL script, CMSNET.sql, in the same directory on the Apress Web site as the .mdf and .ldf database files: Final\MS SQL Database.

This procedure is a lot easier to execute than the previous two. (It was also a lot harder to build the SQL script, but that is a story for another time.) First, make sure you connect to the SQL Server using SQL Server Authentication and use the login name sa without a password. Then, simply load the Query Analyzer, open the CMSNET.sql file in the script editor, and execute the script. It couldn't be any easier (see Figure 9-12).

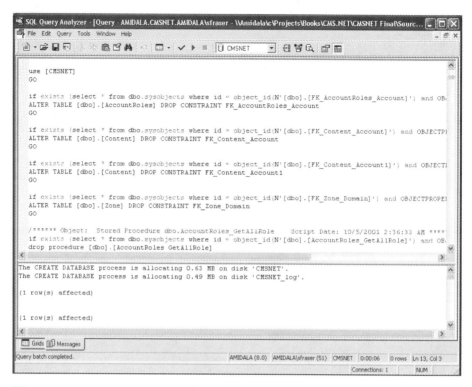

Figure 9-12. Running CMSNET.sql in the Query Analyzer

Exit the Query Analyzer. Now you are all set to play with CMS.NET.

Running CMS.NET Setup

The first thing you need to do to get CMS.NET up and running is to let CMS.NET know where its database is. After that is established, CMS.NET needs to know who its administrator is. Chapter 10 covers the actual coding of the setup procedure, so for now, let's pretend you are just an administrator.

You don't have to do anything special to run the setup procedure—just access CMS.NET's administration Web site. You can do this in one of two ways. If CMS.NET is on your own machine, enter **http://localhost/CMSNET/admin.aspx** in your browser's Address field. If, on the other hand, you are accessing CMS.NET remotely, enter the host address instead of "localhost." In my case, I entered **www.contentmgr.com/CMSNET/admin.aspx**.

The first time the administration Web site is run, CMS.NET intercepts the request and runs the setup routine. The first Web page you will see is the "Welcome to the CMS.NET Setup" Web page (see Figure 9-13). Read it and then click the Continue button.

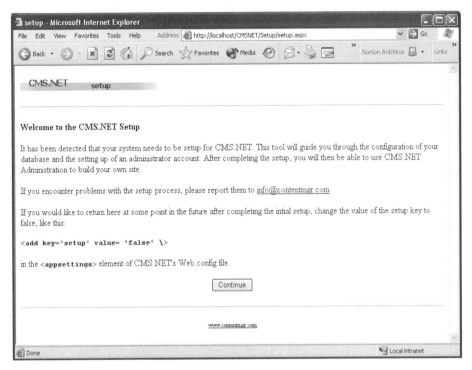

Figure 9-13. The "Welcome to the CMS.NET Setup" Web page

The next setup Web page requests where to find its database (see Figure 9-14). On this Web form, you will enter the following:

- *Database:* The name you gave the database. It defaults to CMSNET.

- *Data Source:* The server where the database is housed. If it is on your local machine, enter **localhost**. On the other hand, if it is remote, enter the server name or the IP address of the database server.

- *User ID:* The user ID needed to connect to the database. I used the default **sa**, but your database administrator could use just about anything.

- *Password:* The password needed to connect to the database. I left this blank, but again, you might want to consult with your database administrator because she might have assigned a password.

- *Connection Timeout:* The length of time in seconds that the system will wait before timing out due to connection problems.

- *SMTP Server:* The name of the SMTP server to be used to send e-mail alerts. If this field is left blank, no e-mail alerts will be sent.

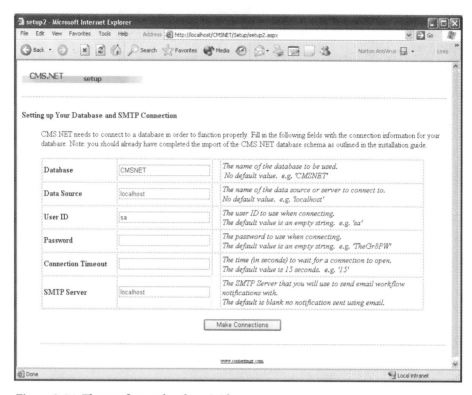

Figure 9-14. The configure database Web page

After you have entered the appropriate data, click the Make Connection button. If CMS.NET can connect to the database you provided, you will be presented with the next Web page. If not, you will be presented with an error message that should point you in the right direction to fix the problem.

If you get this error:

```
Access to the path "C:\Inetpub\wwwroot\CMSNET\web.config.001" is denied.
```

you have to provide write privileges to the CMSNET directory for the user group *{Machine}*\ASPNET. To do this, perform the following steps:

1. Using Windows Explorer, right-click the
    C:\Inetpub\wwwroot\CMSNET directory.

2. Select Properties. This will bring up the dialog box shown in Figure 9-15.

Figure 9-15. The CMSNET Properties dialog box

3. Select the Security tab.

4. Click the Add button.

5. Enter *{Machine}***ASPNET** in the presented dialog box. For my computer I entered **AMIDALA\ASPNET**.

6. Click the OK button.

7. Click the Modify or Write check box.

8. Click the OK button.

With the database connection out of the way, the setup process next needs to find out who is the primary administrator (see Figure 9-16). There is really nothing difficult about this Web page; just enter the appropriate information. You have probably entered this same information a hundred times or more elsewhere.

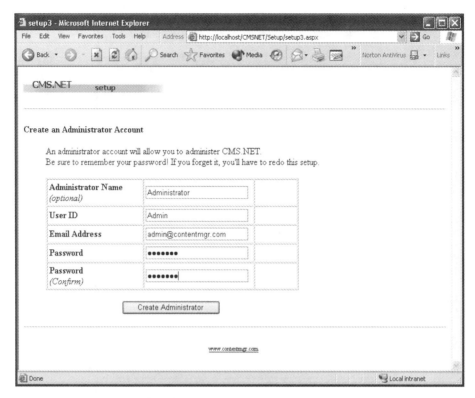

Figure 9-16. Setting up the administrator account

That's all there is to setting up CMS.NET. Your CMS might need more configuration, but this is all that CMS.NET needs to work. The setup procedure presents one more Web page that tells you of your success (see Figure 9-17), and then it offers you a button to start administrating the Web site.

Click Login to CMS.NET Administration, and I will meet you in the next section.

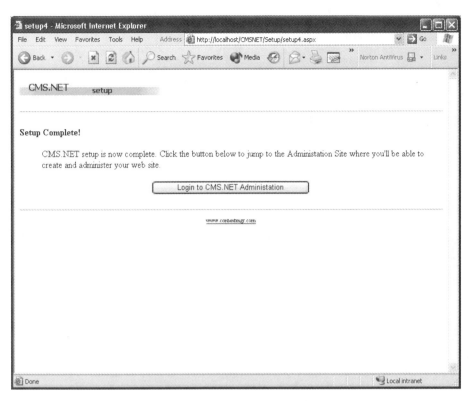

Figure 9-17. Successful completion of the setup procedure

A Brief Tutorial

Before I get to coding CMS.NET, let's take a quick trip through the features of the CMS.NET administration system. If you are like me, seeing things in action before getting into the details provides a frame of reference and makes it easier to understand. This book will not provide a tutorial of the Internet Web site because that should be self-explanatory or the site is not going to be successful.

Logging In

Obviously, the first thing you are going to do before you enter the administration Web site is enter your username and password (see Figure 9-18). If you are the primary administrator, you need to enter the username and password you created during the setup procedure. If you don't want to have to re-enter your password every time you enter the system, you can click the Remember Login check box.

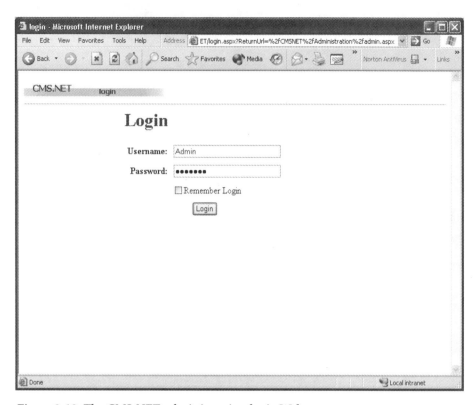

Figure 9-18. The CMS.NET administration login Web page

Adding Users

Most likely, you will be developing the Web site with the help of others, and each of these people will have a different role to play. CMS.NET provides a role-based approach to developing content. Chapter 3 covers some of the roles that might make up CMS administration, and Chapter 14 goes over the roles used by CMS.NET. So, for now, let's just create a user that does everything on the system. By the way, you already have someone who has that capability. He is called the administrator, but let's create another one. As time progresses, your user will start to have smaller or more specific roles, but for now let him have the world.

1. Select Account Maint from the NavBar.

2. Select Create Account. This will display a Web form to create a new user (see Figure 9-19).

3. Enter the data that is requested in the top half of the form.

4. In the bottom half, Ctrl-click all the roles.

5. Click the Create Account button.

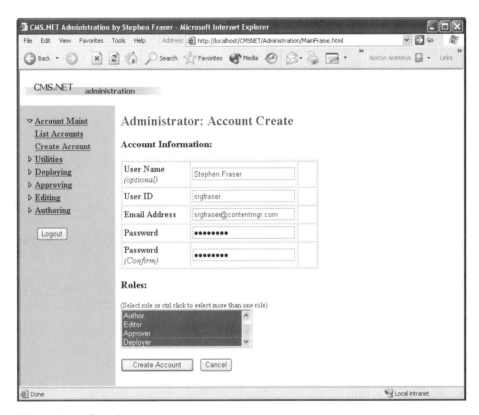

Figure 9-19. Creating a power user

You now have a user that can do anything on the system—a very dangerous person, indeed. Log out and then log back in as this new power user.

Creating a Story

Without content, there is no purpose for the CMS, so let's create our first story and walk it through to deployment. The process of entering the story is very simple.

1. Select Authoring from the NavBar.

2. Select the Create Content menu item. This will display a Web form to create a story (see Figure 9-20).

3. Enter the data that is requested.

4. Click the Create Content button.

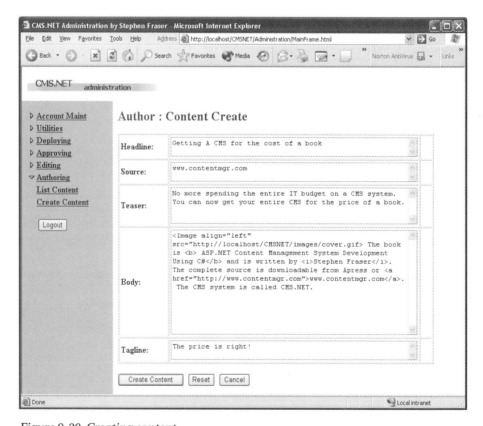

Figure 9-20. Creating content

You now have your first story in CMS.NET. I'm sure you want to see if you typed in all that HTML right.

Viewing a Story

Let's take a look at what you entered. When you finished creating your story, you then jumped to the Content List Web page. This Web page gives an author a snapshot of everything she is currently working on. From here, the author can view, update, submit, and delete the content, and create a note (see Figure 9-21).

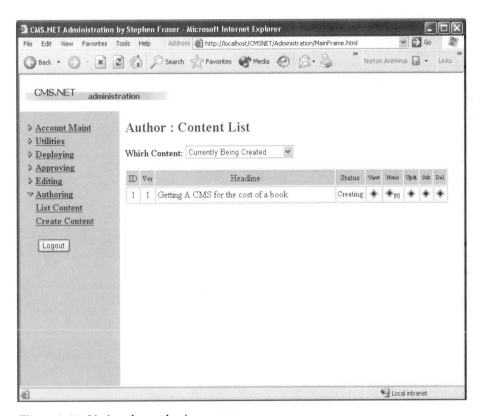

Figure 9-21. Listing the author's content

Okay, let's view the story you entered. Click the button that looks like a diamond under the View heading for the story you want to view. You will be presented with an author's view of the story. This is nothing like the view that will be presented to the Internet users. It shows all the content components as separate entities on the Internet site; these components will be merged seamlessly.

Figure 9-22 shows what you wrote. Not what you were expecting! This shows the danger of giving an author the capability to enter HTML code; if HTML is used incorrectly, complete garbage can be the result, as you can see.

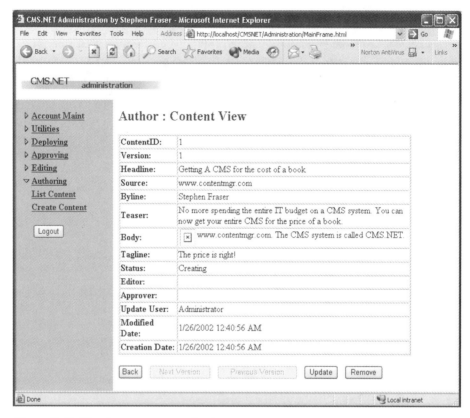

Figure 9-22. Viewing a content mistake

Updating a Story

The Web page for updating is very similar to the Web page for creating. The big difference is that it shows more information about the content, such as who was the original author and when she wrote this story.

To update content, simply click the diamond button under the Update column for the story you want to update. This will open the Update content Web form.

The problem with the page is actually a simple and very common mistake in HTML. I forgot a quote after the address of the image. After fixing this, all is well with the story.

Take a look at the options at the bottom of the Update Web page (see Figure 9-23). CMS.NET provides simple content versioning. It is possible to create a new version of the content with each update or to fix the current version. It is up to the author whether she wants to use versioning or not. Let's make the change and create a new version.

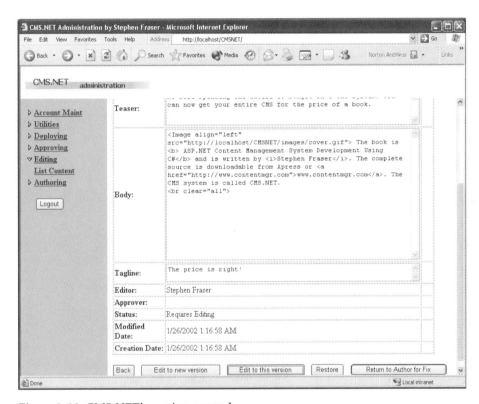

Figure 9-23. CMS.NET's version control

When you view the content now, you notice that it says it is version 2, just as expected (see Figure 9-24). You might also notice that at the bottom of the View Web page, you can view previous versions of the content.

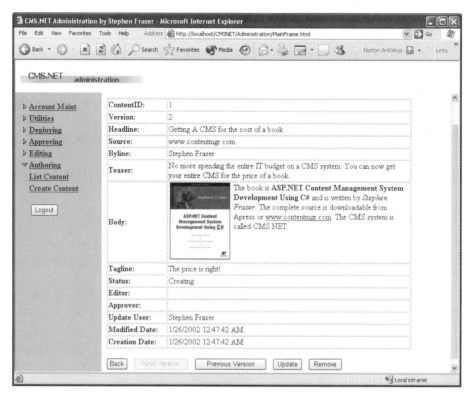

Figure 9-24. Viewing the corrected content

Creating a Note

Even though the note facility is very simple in CMS.NET, it provides a lot of functionality if used correctly. It can be used as a means of passing information between roles as the content progresses through its life cycle. It also can be a simple notepad to jot down ideas about a story. Because it is a free format of almost unlimited size, you can put nearly anything you want in it.

Creating a note is simple. Click the diamond Note button, click the Create A Note button, and then type to your heart's content. Finally, just click the Create Note button (see Figure 9-25) to save the note and have it associated with a specific piece of content.

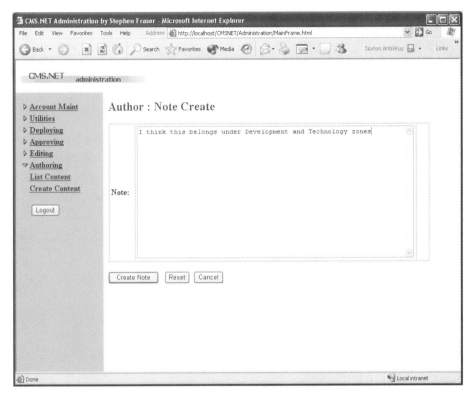

Figure 9-25. The Note Web page

Submitting Content to Editors

You've finished your masterpiece, and you're ready for the editors to rip it to shreds. It's time to submit the content back into the workflow. The process barely needs explanation. Just click the diamond Submit button and then click the Submit Content button (see Figure 9-26). At this point, the story is no longer under your control. In fact, you now only have read access to the story. You still have the ability to create notes for the story, and using this method, you can request it back for any changes you think you need to make.

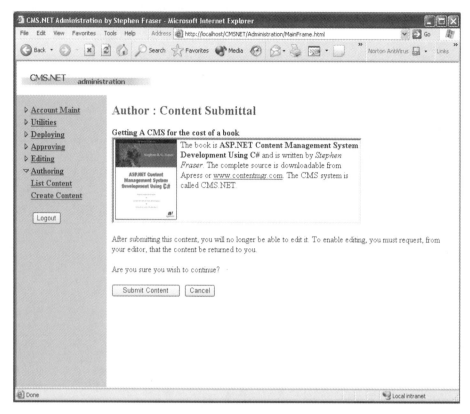

Figure 9-26. Submitting content

That's it from the author's point of view. There are a few other features, and I recommend that you play around with the content development Web pages. But it's now time to move on to the editor's role.

Editing Content

The editing process is very similar to the authoring process. The big difference is that a piece of content does not originate with an editor. Thus, there is no menu item to create content. An editor has the ability to create notes and view, edit, withdraw, submit, and return content back to the author (see Figure 9-27). I have already covered viewing content, creating notes, and submitting content during the discussion of the author's functionality.

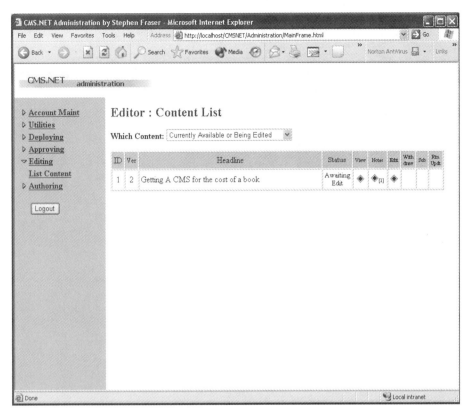

Figure 9-27. Listing the editor's content

In fact, I have already covered editing as well because it is nearly identical to the author's updating process. The only difference is that when an editor first selects a piece of content to edit, it gets assigned to him and no one else can edit it. Before this time, the content was available to all editors for editing.

Withdrawing

Because the editor has exclusive rights to the content, CMS.NET needed to add a way for the editor to give up his lock on the content so that another editor could work on it. Why do you need to be able to do this? Editors get sick and go on vacations, so if the content is important enough, withdrawing and allowing another editor to finish the work might enable the content to get through the system faster.

The withdrawing process is nearly the same as the submitting process. Click the diamond Withdraw button and then click the Withdraw As Editor button (see Figure 9-28). By the way, there is nothing stopping an editor from reselecting a piece of content at a later date.

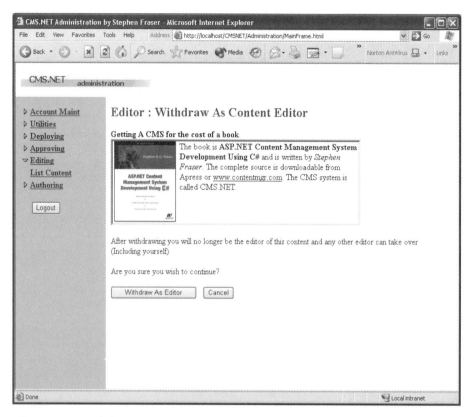

Figure 9-28. Withdrawing as the editor

Returning Content to the Author

If the editor feels that the author needs to do more work on the content, he can return it. When the author finishes with her updates to the story and resubmits it, this time the story is routed directly to the editor who returned it to the author. This author-to-editor cycle can be repeated as many times as necessary to complete an acceptable story for the Web site.

The returning process is the same as all role-transition processes. Click the diamond Return button and then click the Return Content button (see Figure 9-29).

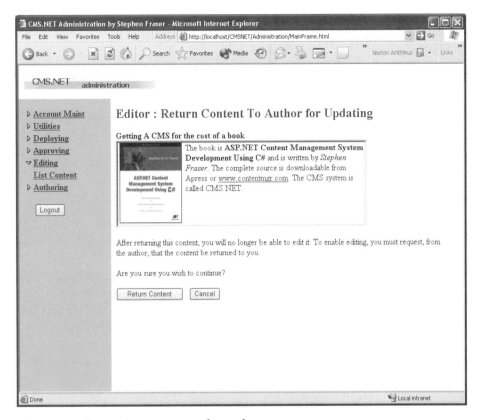

Figure 9-29. Returning content to the author

That's it for the new functionality provided to the editor. Now let's move on to the approver, who has the ultimate say on whether the story is acceptable for the Web site.

Approving Content

CMS.NET requires only one person with approval status to approve content. After an approver approves content, it will be eligible to be placed on the Web site. Approvers cannot change the content they are approving in any way. If changes need to be made, the content must be returned to the editor, usually accompanied by a note discussing what needs to be fixed.

The role of the approver is very simple. She can view, create notes, approve, return, or cancel content (see Figure 9-30). I have covered almost every one of these functions in the previous roles. The only one that needs some clarification is canceling content.

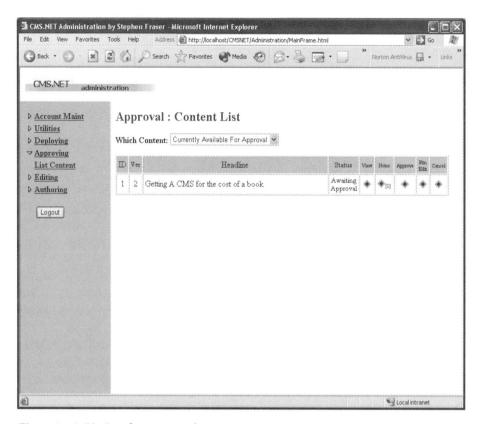

Figure 9-30. Listing the approver's content

Canceling Content

The workflow of CMS.NET is modeled after the simple workflow presented in Chapter 3, and as was pointed out there, the approver has the ability to stop midstream the development of a piece of content. This obviously means that if the approval staff is not kept in the loop as to what is in the content pipeline, it is possible that time could be wasted by authoring and editing an unwanted piece of content.

The process of canceling is very similar to any of the other role-transition processes. The big difference is that the author and editor of the content are e-mailed and told the reason why the content was canceled (see Figure 9-31).

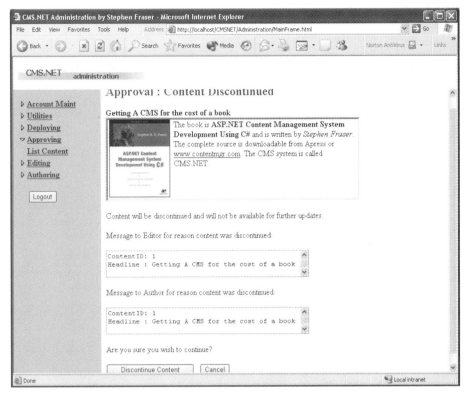

Figure 9-31. Canceling content

All that is left after approval is deploying the content to the Web site. Once deployed, it will be visible to the Internet world (if, of course, the Web site is visible to the Web).

Deploying Content

The role of a deployer is very simple and is broken into two parts: routing and prioritizing. *Routing* is the process of placing the content into the appropriate zone or zones. *Prioritizing* is the process of ranking content to determine in what order the content is displayed.

The deployment process starts by receiving content in the Deploy List (see Figure 9-32). All content that is approved is routed to this list. From here, the deployer views the content and determines which zone to place it in. If notes have been used, the job of the deployer may be simplified because the author, editor, and approver might also provide suggestions as to where to deploy the content.

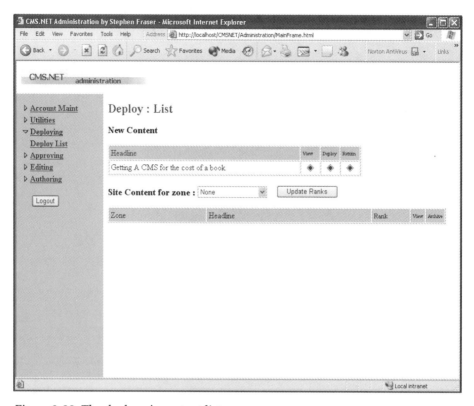

Figure 9-32. The deployer's content list

After the deployer decides where the content is to be placed, he then clicks the diamond Deploy button. This will bring up the Content Deployment Web page (see Figure 9-33). This page simply displays the content and asks the deployer to Ctrl-click any zones in which the content should be deployed. After all the zones have been selected, click the Deploy Content button.

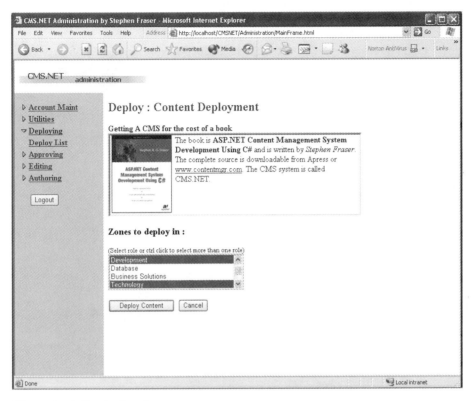

Figure 9-33. Deploying the content

Prioritizing Content

The final step before the content is displayed is prioritizing the content. Each piece of content can have a different priority in each zone in which it appears. There are four priorities in CMS.NET:

- *Low:* This content will be displayed last, sorted by date last modified.

- *Average:* This content will be displayed before the Low setting but after the High setting. It is also sorted by date last modified.

- *High:* This content will be displayed first, sorted by date last modified. The exception is if there is a lead.

- *Lead:* This is the top story, and there is only one per zone. It will always be displayed first.

All content is deployed with a default value of Average. To change the default, select the zone in which the content resides from the Site Content For Zone drop-down box. Then, after all the content is displayed for that zone (see Figure 9-34), update the ranking in the drop-down box for the content. Finally, click the Update Ranks button. (If you forget to do this, no ranking changes will be saved.)

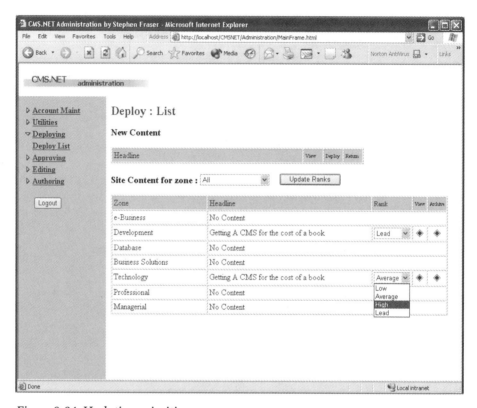

Figure 9-34. Updating priorities

You now have a piece of content that you can view from your Web site—congratulations! Okay, log onto the Web site and take a peek.

Oops, the "I'm changing" Web page is still there. Not a big deal. Let's fix that.

Starting and Stopping the Web Site

I ramble on about my pet peeve, page-not-found errors, in Chapter 13, so I'll save you from it here. All you need to know now is how to start up the site. This procedure, incidentally, is also how you shut down the Web site.

First, click the Utilities and Site Start/Stop menu items on the NavBar and then simply click the Bring Site Up? button (see Figure 9-35). The button will then change to Bring Site Down?, which you click to shut the Web site down. Pretty easy, don't you think?

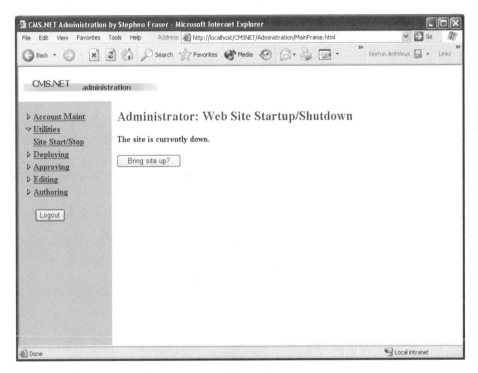

Figure 9-35. Starting and stopping the Web site

Okay, now log in and see your story. You will find it in the zone into which you deployed it. Here it is in Figure 9-36. Not too bad, if you ask me.

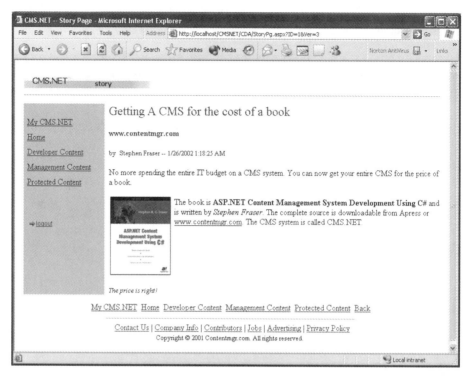

Figure 9-36. Your first CMS.NET story

Summary

This chapter provided an overview of CMS.NET. It started with a brief description of CMS.NET and then covered how to install it. The chapter ended with a quick tutorial.

The next chapter will start the long road of building CMS.NET, which in turn will be the start of building your own CMS (I hope).

CHAPTER 10

Initializing CMS.NET

NOW YOU GET TO THE GOOD STUFF: building CMS.NET. Well, maybe not just yet. First, you have to build the setup procedure for CMS.NET so that you don't have to worry about hard-coding the system configuration. This enables you to move CMS.NET to different hardware configurations while developing, testing, and deploying it to production—without having to change any code within the system. It also enables you to give CMS.NET to someone else without worrying how his system is configured.

The first thing this setup procedure will do is allow the system installer to specify the correct link to the Microsoft SQL Server that CMS.NET will be using. All computer systems are different. Each has its own IP addresses, server names, directory structure, and administrator names and passwords. With a setup procedure, you don't have to worry about any of these things.

The second thing this setup procedure will do is set up an administrator account so you can limit access to that account for now. Chapter 12 covers authentication, authorization, and encryption, so for now, don't worry about the complete lack of security in CMS.NET. A system will be of little use if the same administrator username and password are used for all implementations. This setup procedure enables you to provide a unique administration account and password.

Along the way, this chapter looks at web.config and how to programmatically update it. You will start building CMSNET—CMS.NET's database. You also will learn how to navigate from page to page in ASP.NET. This is all fun stuff, so let's get started.

NOTE *Unlike in previous chapters, from here on, the code presented in this book will only be the directly relevant parts. For a complete listing, you need to see the source code, which you can find by going to the Apress Web site (*www.apress.com*) and clicking the Downloads link.*

The code presented on the Apress Web site is continually being extended from previous chapters. In other words, it contains all the code to execute CMS.NET, up to and including that chapter. Thus, there is a lot of recurring code from previous chapters, not just code from the current chapter.

It should also be noted that as the code progresses, portions of code from previous chapters may be updated, replaced, or even deleted as they are improved, enhanced, or expanded upon.

All code for CMS.NET is located in one project called CMSNET. Most of the code is in directories of the main CMSNET project. When I cover a code snippet from CMS.NET, I will note its name as directory/codename.ext. When you are looking for the code on the Apress site, make sure you look in the specified directory because code names may repeat themselves.

To Set Up or Not to Set Up?

To ensure that the setup procedure is run, CMS.NET checks every time. This approach is overkill, but the cost is so minimal and easy to implement that I thought it an acceptable solution. In your implementation, you might want to have a separate admin and setup Web page.

The Admin.aspx Web Page

Admin.aspx (see Listing 10-1) is one of the few Web pages in CMS.NET that is not found in a subdirectory off of CMSNET. In fact, it is not much of a Web page at all. It is actually a blank jump page that merely makes a simple check to see whether the system has been set up and then routes to the appropriate Web page.

Listing 10-1. Admin.aspx

```
<%@ Page language="c#" Codebehind="Admin.cs"
                       AutoEventWireup="false"
                       Inherits="CMSNET.Admin" %>
<html>
  <head>
    <meta name="GENERATOR" Content="Microsoft Visual Studio 7.0">
    <meta name="CODE_LANGUAGE" Content="C#">
  </head>
  <body>
    <form method="post" runat="server">
    </form>
  </body>
</html>
```

The Admin.cs Codebehind

Pretty barren, don't you think? Something that people who are used to HTML navigation might find weird is that the form has no action attribute. This Web page, when submitted, will return back to itself. So, you might be wondering, how does it jump to the correct Web page? The magic happens in the Codebehind.

The Admin Page_Load() method (see Listing 10-2) is extremely simple. The AppEnv class, which is covered a little later in this chapter, checks the web.config to see whether the setup value is set to true. This will mean more as you get further into the chapter.

If the setup variable is equal to true, the Web page jumps happily to the administration system and, for now, will jump to a Web page stub that looks like the one shown in Figure 10-1. If the setup variable has some other value or is empty, it jumps to the setup system, which is what I cover in the rest of this chapter.

Listing 10-2. The Admin.Page_Load Method

```
private void Page_Load(object sender, System.EventArgs e)
{
    string setup = new AppEnv(Context).GetAppSetting("setup");

    if(setup.Equals("true"))
    {
        Response.Redirect("Administration/admin.aspx");
    }
    else
    {
        Response.Redirect("Setup/setup.aspx");
    }
}
```

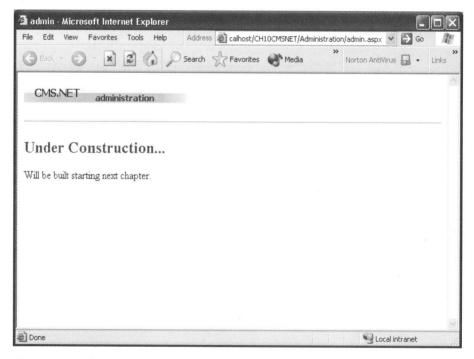

Figure 10-1. The administration Web page stub

For those of you coming from the old ASP world, you should be familiar with using Response.Redirect(URL) to cause a page to jump to another URL. During Beta1, a new option was introduced—the cleaner Navigate() method—that was inherited from System.Web.UI.Page to handle navigation. Unfortunately, the Navigate() method disappeared in Beta2 for some reason.

All navigation is relative to the current Web page. If you are navigating to an external URL, you must prefix the URL with `http://`. For example, to jump to Microsoft's .NET development home page, you would use the following:

```
Response.Redirect("http://msdn.microsoft.com/net");
```

First, Describe the Process

It is always a good idea to give the user some idea of where she is and what she is about to do, especially if you are about to do something as important as setting up the system. Providing information such as whom to contact if something goes wrong and how to restart the process if you make a mistake are nice touches and can help increase the user's comfort level.

The Setup/setup.aspx Web Page

The first Web page that is actually displayed during the setup process is Setup/setup.aspx. This page is simply an informational page that looks like Figure 10-2. It indicates what is about to happen, whom to contact if something goes wrong, and how to repeat the process if you want to change something. It also includes a button to continue to the next Web page, where the real work of the setup process begins.

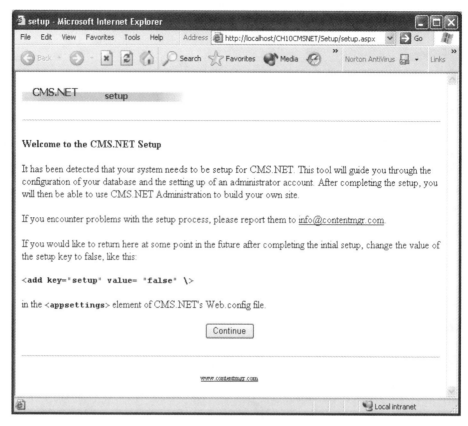

Figure 10-2. Setup/setup.aspx

The Setup/setup.cs Codebehind

There really isn't anything special about the code for setup. In fact, everything is the default except the bnContinue_Click() method (see Listing 10-3), which does a simple jump to setup2.aspx.

Listing 10-3. The setup.bnContinue_Click Method

```
private void bnContinue_Click (object sender, System.EventArgs e)
{
    Response.Redirect("setup2.aspx");
}
```

Using `web.config` to Save the Database Connection String

You have several options when it comes to storing the database connection string. Before ASP.NET, a file with a hard-coded location, the INI file, the Registry, and the IIS metabase were some of the most frequently used locations for storing the database connection string. These solutions are no longer needed because ASP.NET provides a more elegant solution: web.config.

Basically, the web.config file is an XML file that stores all the configuration information for an ASP.NET Web application. It's only appropriate to add the database connection string here because it is a piece of configuration information. In fact, the web.config file has an optional predefined element, `<appSettings>`, to address such user-defined configuration information.

`<appSettings>` is made up of one or more `<add>` elements containing key/value attribute pairs. These elements are perfect for CMS.NET to store database connection information, and they look like Listing 10-4 when finally implemented by the setup procedure.

Listing 10-4. CMS.NET's web.config <appSettings>

```
<!--APPSETTINGS
        This section sets all the custom application settings
    -->
<appSettings>
  <add key="setup" value="true"/>
  <add key="database" value="CMSNET"/>
  <add key="datasource" value="localhost"/>
  <add key="userid" value="sa"/>
  <add key="password" value=""/>
  <add key="timeout" value=""/>
</appSettings>
```

Adding the `<appSettings>` element to the web.config XML file is the purpose of Setup/setup2.aspx.

The `Setup/setup2.aspx` Web Page

Setup/setup2.aspx is a Web form designed to capture all the information needed to determine where CMS.NET's database is located as well as the username and password needed to get access. It is a very simple form that looks like Figure 10-3. As you can see, there is not much to the form except that it validates that `Database` and `Data Source` both have values and that the optional `Connection Timeout` is numeric if entered.

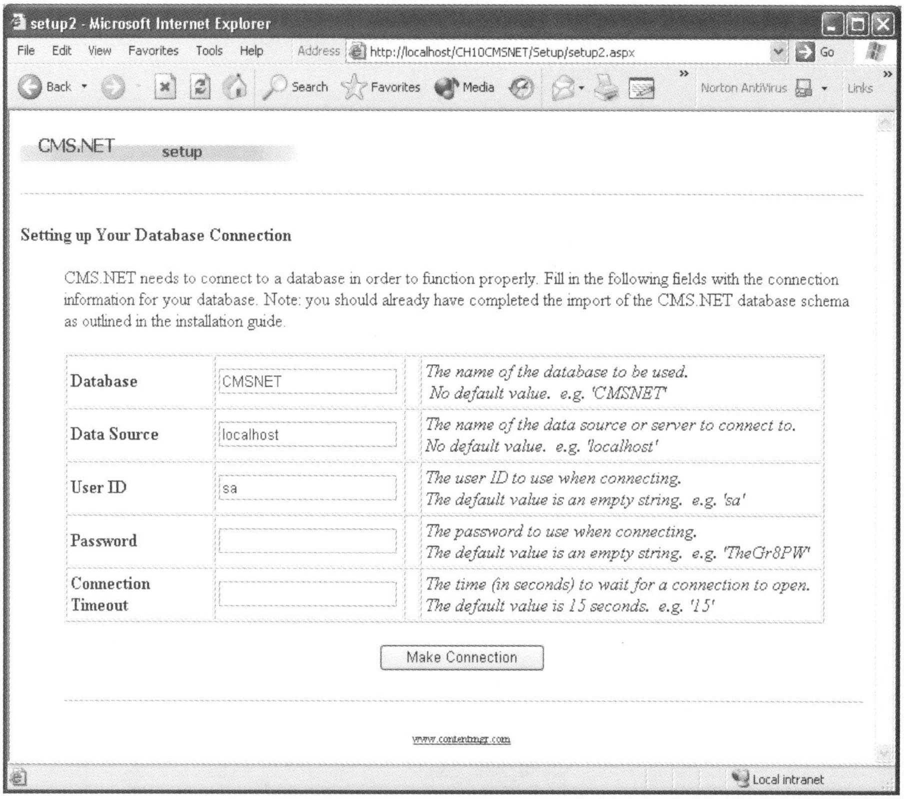

Figure 10-3. Setup/setup2.aspx

Processing a Web Form—Setup/setup2.cs

What is really interesting about this Web page is what happens behind the scenes in the Codebehind.

The first thing the Codebehind for setup2 does is repopulate the values in the edit fields of the form (if this is a return visit to the setup procedure) or, more likely, set the edit fields to their default value.

```
private void Page_Load(object sender, System.EventArgs e)
{
    if (!IsPostBack)
    {
        AppEnv appEnv = new AppEnv(Context);

        txtDatabase.Text   = appEnv.GetAppSetting("database");
        if (txtDatabase.Text.Length <= 0)
```

```
    {
        txtDatabase.Text = "CMSNET";
    }
    txtDataSource.Text = appEnv.GetAppSetting("datasource");
    txtUserID.Text     = appEnv.GetAppSetting("userid");
    txtPassword.Text   = appEnv.GetAppSetting("password");
    txtTimeout.Text    = appEnv.GetAppSetting("timeout");
}
```

The user first enters the appropriate values into the edit fields and clicks the Make Connection button. The Codebehind then does a page validation checking to see whether the information is valid for connecting to the database by actually attempting to connect using the entered values. By using exception handling, the code is able to catch any errors that occur and present them back to the user for correction.

If all is well, the values are added to the web.config XML file, and you then navigate to the next step in the setup process.

```
else
{
    Page.Validate();

    lblConnectError.Text = "";

    if (Page.IsValid)
    {
        try
        {
            SqlConnection myConnection = new SqlConnection();

            myConnection.ConnectionString =
                "server=" + txtDataSource.Text +
                ";database=" + txtDatabase.Text +
                ";uid=" + txtUserID.Text +
                ";pwd=" + txtPassword.Text +
                ((txtTimeout.Text.Length > 0) ?
                ";Connection Timeout=" + txtTimeout.Text :
                "");

            SqlDataAdapter myCommand =
                new SqlDataAdapter("select * from Account", myConnection);
```

```
                    // Can we get to the database?
                    DataSet ds = new DataSet();
                    myCommand.Fill(ds, "Account");

                    UpdateConfigWeb(txtDatabase.Text, txtDataSource.Text,
                                    txtUserID.Text, txtPassword.Text,
                                    txtTimeout.Text);

                    Response.Redirect("setup3.aspx");
                    return;
                }
                catch (Exception err)
                {
                    lblConnectError.Text = err.Message;
                }
            }
            lblErrorHeader.Text =
            "Sorry, cannot connect to your database the following errors occurred:";
        }
```

Programmatically Updating a web.config File– Setup/setup2.cs

The UpdateConfigWeb() method handles all the gory details of updating the web.config file. It takes as parameters all the values that will be placed in the web.config file.

```
public void UpdateConfigWeb(String database, String datasource, String userid,
                            String password, String timeout)
{
```

It then opens the web.config file, loads it into an XmlDocument for processing, and closes it so that it may be opened later for writing.

```
XmlReader xtr = new
            XmlTextReader(File.OpenRead(Server.MapPath("..\\web.config")));

XmlDocument doc = new XmlDocument();
doc.Load(xtr);
xtr.Close();
```

The first thing it does is look for the `<appSettings>` tag. If it doesn't find it, the method dumps the key/values into the web.config file wholesale.

```
XmlElement  root  = doc.DocumentElement;
XmlNodeList nodes = root.GetElementsByTagName("appSettings");

if (nodes.Count <= 0)
{
    // place in complete appSettings section
    XmlDocumentFragment newAppSettings = doc.CreateDocumentFragment();
    newAppSettings.InnerXml=
        ("<!-- APPSETTINGS\n              " +
        "This section sets all the custom application settings\n    -->" +
        "<appSettings>\n" +
        "    <add key=\"setup\" value=\"false\" />\n" +
        "    <add key=\"database\" value=\"" + database + "\" />\n" +
        "    <add key=\"datasource\" value=\"" + datasource + "\" />\n" +
        "    <add key=\"userid\" value=\"" + userid + "\" />\n" +
        "    <add key=\"password\" value=\"" + password + "\" />\n" +
        "    <add key=\"timeout\" value=\"" + timeout + "\" />\n" +
        "   </appSettings>");

    //add the new appSettings to the doc            .
    root.AppendChild(newAppSettings);
}
```

On the other hand, if there is an `<appSettings>` tag, the method has the arduous task of going through all the key/value pairs one by one, looking for the values it needs to update while noting the ones that are missing.

You might note that this code shows how to update attributes in an element. The process is simple because each element gets all its attributes in a collection using the `Attributes` property. Get the specific attributes you want by name using the `GetNamedItem()` method, in this case the key and value attributes. Finally, check which key you have and update its value appropriately.

```
else
{
    bool issetup      = false;
    bool isdatabase   = false;
    bool isdatasource = false;
    bool isuserid     = false;
    bool ispassword   = false;
    bool istimeout    = false;
```

```csharp
for (int i=0; i < nodes.Count; i++)
{
    XmlNodeList appnodes =
        ((XmlElement)(nodes.Item(i))).GetElementsByTagName("add");

    for (int j=0; j < appnodes.Count; j++)
    {
        // replace with new values
        // record to make sure none are missing
        XmlAttributeCollection attrColl = appnodes.Item(j).Attributes;
        XmlAttribute tmpNode =
            (XmlAttribute)attrColl.GetNamedItem("key");
        XmlAttribute tmpNodeValue =
            (XmlAttribute)attrColl.GetNamedItem("value");
        if (tmpNode.Value.Equals("setup"))
        {
            // will be set to true later
            tmpNodeValue.Value = "false";
            issetup = true;
        }
        else if (tmpNode.Value.Equals("database"))
        {
            tmpNodeValue.Value = database;
            isdatabase = true;
        }
        else if (tmpNode.Value.Equals("datasource"))
        {
            tmpNodeValue.Value = datasource;
            isdatasource = true;
        }
        else if (tmpNode.Value.Equals("userid"))
        {
            tmpNodeValue.Value = userid;
            isuserid = true;
        }
        else if (tmpNode.Value.Equals("password"))
        {
            tmpNodeValue.Value = password;
            ispassword = true;
        }
        else if (tmpNode.Value.Equals("timeout"))
        {
            tmpNodeValue.Value = timeout;
```

```
            istimeout = true;
        }
    }
```

After you have updated all the values, go through and append any missing key/value attribute pairs.

```
        XmlDocumentFragment newAppSetting = doc.CreateDocumentFragment();

        if (!issetup)
        {
            // will be set to true later
            newAppSetting.InnerXml =
            ("\n    <add key=\"setup\" value=\"false\" />");
            ((XmlElement)(nodes.Item(i))).AppendChild(newAppSetting);
        }
        if (!isdatabase)
        {

            newAppSetting.InnerXml =
            ("\n    <add key=\"database\" value=\"" + database + "\" />");
            ((XmlElement)(nodes.Item(i))).AppendChild(newAppSetting);
        }
        if (!isdatasource)
        {

            newAppSetting.InnerXml =
            ("\n    <add key=\"datasource\" value=\"" +
              datasource + "\" />");
            ((XmlElement)(nodes.Item(i))).AppendChild(newAppSetting);
        }
        if (!isuserid)
        {

            newAppSetting.InnerXml =
            ("\n    <add key=\"userid\" value=\"" + userid + "\" />");
            ((XmlElement)(nodes.Item(i))).AppendChild(newAppSetting);
        }
        if (!ispassword)
        {

            newAppSetting.InnerXml =
            ("\n    <add key=\"password\" value=\"" + password + "\" />");
            ((XmlElement)(nodes.Item(i))).AppendChild(newAppSetting);
        }
        if (!istimeout)
        {
```

```
        newAppSetting.InnerXml =
        ("\n    <add key=\"timeout\" value=\"" + timeout + "\" />");
        ((XmlElement)(nodes.Item(i))).AppendChild(newAppSetting);
    }
  }
}
```

The final steps are to save a copy of the previous version of web.config, delete the original, open the web.config file for writing, and then save it.

```
File.Copy(Server.MapPath("..\\web.config"),
        Server.MapPath("..\\web.config.001"),
        true);
File.Delete(Server.MapPath("..\\web.config"));

StreamWriter sr = new
    StreamWriter(File.OpenWrite(Server.MapPath("..\\web.config")));
doc.Save(sr);
sr.Close();
}
```

It's all fine and dandy to store it in the web.config file, but how do you get it out when you need it? Funny you should ask, because ASP.NET provides a simple solution. Let's say you want to find out the value for the `setup` key in Listing 10-4. All you need to code is the following:

```
string setup = (string)
    ((NameValueCollection)Context.GetConfig("appSettings"))["setup"];
```

After this line is executed, the string `setup` contains the value `true`. It's pretty easy, if you ask me.

`Context` is a copy of the `HttpContext` provided by `System.Web.UI.Page`, from which your Web form is derived. `HttpContext` encapsulates all HTTP-specific context used to process Web requests, including the web.config file. By using the simple `GetConfig()` method, you now have access to your user-defined application information.

The Common/AppEnv.cs Helper Class

One of the most important and most used classes in CMS.NET is Common/AppEnv.cs. This class is a common helper class to much of the CMS.NET application. Not only does this class provide access to web.config, but it also generates an `SqlConnection`, which you will always use to connect to the CMSNET database.

The AppEnv constructor (see Listing 10-5) is simple enough and just takes in a copy of HttpContext (easily provided by the inherited Context member variable found in every Web page) so that it can be used later in the GetAppSetting() method. The only unusual namespace to be added is System.Collections.Specialized. This namespace will be used by the NameValueCollection typecast in the GetAppSetting() method.

Listing 10-5. The Namespaces and AppEnv Constructor Method

```
using System;
using System.Collections.Specialized;
using System.Web;
using System.Data.SqlClient;


...


public AppEnv(HttpContext Context)
{
    context = Context;
}
```

The GetAppSetting() method (see Listing 10-6) provides a simplified inter-face to the Context.GetConfig() method. Now you don't have to worry about all the type casting from the NameValueCollection to string, nor the weird string inside of an array—syntax, for you C++ and Java developers.

Listing 10-6. The AppEnv.GetAppSetting Method

```
public string GetAppSetting (string setting)
{
    string val;
    try
    {
        val =
        (string)((NameValueCollection)context.GetConfig("appSettings"))[setting];
    }
    catch (NullReferenceException)
    {
        val = "";
    }

    if (val == null)
        val = "";

    return val;
}
```

The real star of this class is the GetConnection() method (see Listing 10-7). This method returns an SqlConnection, which you will use to connect to the database from now on. No more hard-coding of the database connection string. The beauty of this method is that after you run the setup procedure, you never have to worry about where your database is again.

Listing 10-7. The AppEnv.GetConnection Method

```
public SqlConnection GetConnection()
{
    SqlConnection myConnection = new SqlConnection();

    myConnection.ConnectionString =
        "server=" + GetAppSetting("datasource") +
        ";database=" + GetAppSetting("database") +
        ";uid=" + GetAppSetting("userid") +
        ";pwd=" + GetAppSetting("password") +
        ((GetAppSetting("timeout").Length > 0) ?
            ";Connection Timeout=" + GetAppSetting("timeout") :
            "");

    return myConnection;
}
```

Setting Up the All-Powerful Administrator

Now that you have your database connection string conveniently available, the next Web page in the setup procedure doesn't waste any time using it as it sets up a unique administrator account into the CMSNET database.

The Setup/setup3.aspx Web Page

Setup/setup3.aspx is a very simple Web form (see Figure 10-4) designed to capture all the information needed for the administrative account. All the edit fields except the optional Administrator Name are validated to make sure they exist before being submitted. Also, the Email Address edit field is validated to make sure it contains a valid e-mail-formatted entry, and the Password Confirm edit field is validated to make sure it contains the same value as the Password edit field.

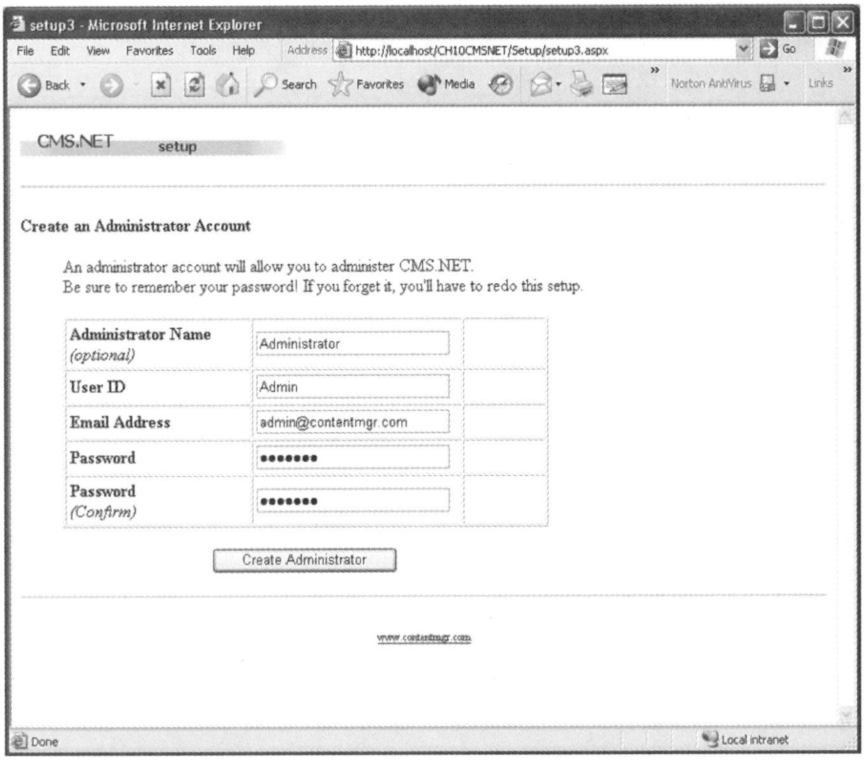

Figure 10-4. Setup/setup3.aspx

The Setup/setup3.cs Codebehind

Just like the previous Web page in the setup procedure, all the interesting things happen in the Codebehind file.

As you see in Figure 10-4, CMS.NET does not require much information about the administrator, but your implementation can be as detailed as you want. Believe it or not, you will not have to change the database schema to store any additional information about the administrator.

How is this done? Basically, the account where all user accounts are stored is actually split into two tables. The first, called the Account table (see Figure 10-5), holds the information needed by CMS.NET to function. The second, called the AccountProperty table (see Figure 10-6), stores information in key/value pairs, very similar to <appSettings> in the web.config. Now, if you want to add the administrator name as you do in setup3, just add the key of AdministratorName and its value. When you want to retrieve it back, just select the AccountProperty table with AccountID and Key. The neat thing about this is that if a user doesn't enter optional information about herself, no wasted space is placed in the database. This can be a good thing if you have a lot of optional information that you are requesting from your users.

Column Name	Data Type	Length	Allow Nulls
AccountID	int	4	
UserName	char	32	
Password	char	40	
Email	char	64	✓
ModifiedDate	datetime	8	
CreationDate	datetime	8	

Figure 10-5. The CMSNET Account table

Column Name	Data Type	Length	Allow Nulls
AccountID	int	4	
Property	char	32	
Value	text	16	
ModifiedDate	datetime	8	
CreationDate	datetime	8	

Figure 10-6. The CMSNET AccountProperty table

The process that setup3 follows is fairly easy because all the details are hidden in database helper classes. In fact, the first thing setup3 does in its Page_Init() method (see Listing 10-8) is create an instance of an Account and AccountProperty database helper class.

Listing 10-8. The Setup3.Page_Init Method

```
override protected void OnInit(EventArgs e)
{
    InitializeComponent();
    base.OnInit(e);

    SqlConnection connection = new AppEnv(Context).GetConnection();
    account  = new Account(connection);
    property = new AccountProperty(connection);
}
```

After the Page_Load() method (see Listing 10-9) receives a valid Web form, it uses the Account helper class created in the Page_Init() method to check whether the Administrator account already exists. The Administrator account always has an AccountID of 1. When the Administrator account does not exist, you insert a new account with the information provided by the Web form. When the account does exist, you update it again with the information provided by the Web page. You then call the ProcessAdministratorName() method to add or update the optional administrator name to the AccountProperty table. Finally, you call the last Web page in the setup process: Setup/setup4.aspx.

Setup3 relies on exception handling to handle all errors created by the Account database helper and ProcessAdminstratorName() method. When an error occurs, it is captured and then placed on the Web form in intrinsic label control lblError.

Listing 10-9. The Setup3.Page_Load Method

```
private void Page_Load(object sender, System.EventArgs e)
{
    if (IsPostBack)
    {
        Page.Validate();

        if (Page.IsValid)
        {
            try
            {
                if (!account.Exist(1))
                {
                    account.Insert(txtUserName.Text, txtPassword.Text,
                                    txtEmail.Text);
                }
                else
                {
                    account.Update(1, txtUserName.Text, txtPassword.Text,
                                    txtEmail.Text);
                }
                ProcessAdministratorName();

                Response.Redirect("setup4.aspx");
            }
            catch (Exception err)
            {
                lblError.Text = "Sorry, the following error occurred: " +
                                err.Message;
            }
        }
    }
}
```

The ProcessAdministratorName() method (see Listing 10-10) handles the insertion of AccountProperty rows differently than Load Page() does Accounts. The reason is that there is no autogenerated key in AccountProperty as there is in Account. Because there is no key, the method can try to insert an AccountProperty row every time, and when a duplicate key exception occurs, it knows that the key is already present. Thus, the method can go ahead and update the row instead.

Listing 10-10. The Setup3 ProcessAdministratorName Method

```
private void ProcessAdministratorName()
{
    if (txtAdministratorName.Text.Length > 0)
    {
        try
        {
            property.Insert(1, "AdministratorName",
                                txtAdministratorName.Text);
        }
        catch (SqlException sqlerr)
        {
            if (sqlerr.Message.IndexOf("duplicate key") >= 0)
            {
                property.Update(1, "AdministratorName",
                                txtAdministratorName.Text);
            }
            else
                throw sqlerr;
        }
    }
}
```

Database Helper Classes and Stored Procedures

Let's take a look at these database helper classes. By the time you finish building CMS.NET, every table in CMSNET will have a helper class. The purpose of these classes is to provide a simple, consistent interface to the database table they are supporting. They also allow developers for the rest of the application to not worry about SQL because these should be the only classes for which someone with SQL knowledge is needed.

DataAccess/Account.cs

The first helper class is DataAccess/Account.cs (see Listing 10-11), which handles all transactions in the Account table of the CMSNET database. As you progress through this book more methods will be added, but for now, these four are all that are needed:

- Constructor

- Insert()

- Update()

- Exist()

This class has a simple constructor that stores the SqlConnection passed to it.

Listing 10-11. The Account Constructor Method

```
public class Account
{
    private SqlConnection m_Connection;
    private SqlCommand    m_InsertCommand;
    private SqlCommand    m_UpdateCommand;

    public Account(SqlConnection Connection)
    {
        m_Connection = Connection;
    }
```

The Account class has an Insert() method (see Listing 10-12) that configures the parameters for the Account_Insert stored procedure. The configuration is stored in a member variable so that, the next time it is called, it doesn't have to repeat the process. It then places the values to be inserted into the stored procedure parameters. Finally, it opens a connection to the database, calls the stored procedure, and then closes the connection. To guarantee the closing of the database connection, the call to the close method is placed inside a finally clause of an exception handler.

Listing 10-12. The Account.Insert() Method

```
public void Insert(string UserName, string Password, string Email)
{
    SqlParameterCollection Params;

    if ( m_InsertCommand == null )
    {
        m_InsertCommand = new SqlCommand("Account_Insert", m_Connection);
        m_InsertCommand.CommandType = CommandType.StoredProcedure;
        Params = m_InsertCommand.Parameters;

        Params.Add(new SqlParameter("@UserName",     SqlDbType.Char, 32));
        Params.Add(new SqlParameter("@Password",     SqlDbType.Char, 40));
        Params.Add(new SqlParameter("@Email",        SqlDbType.Char, 64));
        Params.Add(new SqlParameter("@ModifiedDate", SqlDbType.DateTime));
        Params.Add(new SqlParameter("@CreationDate", SqlDbType.DateTime));
    }

    Params = m_InsertCommand.Parameters;

    Params["@UserName"].Value     = UserName;
    Params["@Password"].Value     = Password;
    Params["@Email"].Value        = Email;
    Params["@ModifiedDate"].Value = DateTime.Now;
    Params["@CreationDate"].Value = DateTime.Now;

    try
    {
        m_Connection.Open();
        m_InsertCommand.ExecuteNonQuery();
    }
    finally
    {
        m_Connection.Close();
    }
}
```

The Update() method (see Listing 10-13) is virtually the same as the Insert()
method, except that it calls the UpdateAccount stored procedure and passes
slightly different parameters.

Listing 10-13. The Account.Update() Method

```
public void Update(int AccountID, string UserName, string Password,
                   string Email)
{
    SqlParameterCollection Params;

    if ( m_UpdateCommand == null )
    {
        m_UpdateCommand = new SqlCommand("Account_Update", m_Connection);
        m_UpdateCommand.CommandType  = CommandType.StoredProcedure;
        Params = m_UpdateCommand.Parameters;

        Params.Add(new SqlParameter("@AccountID",    SqlDbType.Int));
        Params.Add(new SqlParameter("@UserName",     SqlDbType.Char, 32));
        Params.Add(new SqlParameter("@Password",     SqlDbType.Char, 40));
        Params.Add(new SqlParameter("@Email",        SqlDbType.Char, 64));
        Params.Add(new SqlParameter("@ModifiedDate", SqlDbType.DateTime));
    }

    Params = m_UpdateCommand.Parameters;

    Params["@AccountID"].Value    = AccountID;
    Params["@UserName"].Value     = UserName;
    Params["@Password"].Value     = Password;
    Params["@Email"].Value        = Email;
    Params["@ModifiedDate"].Value = DateTime.Now;

    try
    {
        m_Connection.Open();
        m_UpdateCommand.ExecuteNonQuery();
    }
    finally
    {
        m_Connection.Close();
    }
}
```

The Exist() method (see Listing 10-14) is a simple select on the Account table, seeing if the AccountID parameter passed exists. For a change—and to show how to create an SqlDataAdapter using an SqlConnection (I should probably be using a stored procedure here as well)—the method uses a DataSet to capture all AccountIDs that match the method's parameter. There should always be only one.

Listing 10-14. The Account.Exist() Method

```
public bool Exist(int AccountID)
{

    string Command = "Select * from Account WHERE AccountID="+AccountID;
    SqlDataAdapter DSCmd = new SqlDataAdapter(Command, m_Connection);

    DataSet ds = new DataSet();
    DSCmd.Fill(ds, "Account");

    return (ds.Tables["Account"].Rows.Count > 0);
}
```

The two stored procedures for the Account table are pretty standard fare and, for someone with SQL knowledge, should be trivial. The first is simply a standard SQL insert (see Listing 10-15).

Listing 10-15. The Account_Insert Stored Procedure

```
CREATE PROCEDURE dbo.Account_Insert
    (
        @UserName NVARCHAR(32) = NULL,
        @Password NVARCHAR(40) = NULL,
        @Email NVARCHAR(64)    = NULL,
        @ModifiedDate DATETIME = NULL,
        @CreationDate DATETIME = NULL
    )
AS

    SET NOCOUNT ON

    INSERT INTO Account (UserName, Password, Email, ModifiedDate,
                         CreationDate)

        VALUES      (@UserName, @Password, @Email, @ModifiedDate,
                     @CreationDate)

    RETURN
```

The second stored procedure is a standard update. It uses AccountID as the key to determine where to insert (see Listing 10-16).

Listing 10-16. The UpdateAccount Stored Procedure

```
CREATE PROCEDURE dbo.Account_Update
    (
        @AccountID INT         = NULL,
        @UserName NVARCHAR(32) = NULL,
        @Password NVARCHAR(40) = NULL,
        @Email NVARCHAR(64)    = NULL,
        @ModifiedDate DATETIME = NULL
    )
AS
    SET NOCOUNT ON

    UPDATE Account

    SET    UserName = @UserName,
           Password = @Password,
           Email    = @Email,
           ModifiedDate = @ModifiedDate

    WHERE  AccountID = @AccountID

    RETURN
```

DataAccess/AccountProperty.cs

The second half of the two parts of a user account is stored in the
`AccountProperty` table. As previously described, `AccountProperty` holds all user
information that is not essential for CMS.NET to function. This database helper
function aids in the storing and retrieving of data into and out of the
`AccountProperty` database table.

For the setup process, you only have to worry about the storing of data. This
means you only need the `Insert()` and `Update()` methods. In later chapters, we
will add some methods to retrieve data out of the table.

The constructor (see Listing 10-17) is identical to all database helper classes
and requires an `SqlConnection` passed as a parameter. The `SqlConnection` is then
used later to open a connection to the CMSNET database.

Listing 10-17. The AccountProperty Constructor Method

```
public class AccountProperty
{

    private SqlConnection m_Connection;
    private SqlCommand     m_InsertCommand;
    private SqlCommand     m_UpdateCommand;

    public AccountProperty(SqlConnection Connection)
    {
        m_Connection = Connection;
    }
}
```

As you saw in the Account database helper class, the AccountProperty's Insert() method (see Listing 10-18) is coded to simply set up the call to the AccountProperty_Insert stored procedure, store the setup for later calls to insert, initialize all the parameters, and then make the call to the stored procedure. You will see virtually the same thing in all database helper classes.

Listing 10-18. The AccountProperty.Insert() Method

```
public void Insert(int AccountID, string Property, string Value)
{
    SqlParameterCollection Params;

    if ( m_InsertCommand == null )
    {
        m_InsertCommand = new SqlCommand("AccountProperty_Insert",
                                            m_Connection);
        m_InsertCommand.CommandType  = CommandType.StoredProcedure;
        Params = m_InsertCommand.Parameters;

        Params.Add(new SqlParameter("@AccountID",    SqlDbType.Int));
        Params.Add(new SqlParameter("@Property",     SqlDbType.Char, 32));
        Params.Add(new SqlParameter("@Value",        SqlDbType.Text));
        Params.Add(new SqlParameter("@ModifiedDate", SqlDbType.DateTime));
        Params.Add(new SqlParameter("@CreationDate", SqlDbType.DateTime));
    }

    Params = m_InsertCommand.Parameters;

    Params["@AccountID"].Value    = AccountID;
    Params["@Property"].Value     = Property;
    Params["@Value"].Value        = Value;
    Params["@ModifiedDate"].Value = DateTime.Now;
    Params["@CreationDate"].Value = DateTime.Now;
```

```
try
{
    m_Connection.Open();
    m_InsertCommand.ExecuteNonQuery();
}
finally
{
    m_Connection.Close();
}
}
```

AccountProperty's Update() method (see Listing 10-19) is virtually the same as the Insert() method. The only differences are that the UpdateAccountProperty stored procedure is called and the CreationDate is not set up as a parameter. This is because it will not be updated because, obviously, you are not creating the record now.

Listing 10-19. The AccountProperty.Update() Method

```
public void Update(int AccountID, string Property, string Value)
{
    SqlParameterCollection Params;

    if ( m_UpdateCommand == null )
    {
        m_UpdateCommand = new SqlCommand("AccountProperty_Update",
                                          m_Connection);
        m_UpdateCommand.CommandType = CommandType.StoredProcedure;
        Params = m_UpdateCommand.Parameters;

        Params.Add(new SqlParameter("@AccountID",    SqlDbType.Int));
        Params.Add(new SqlParameter("@Property",     SqlDbType.Char, 32));
        Params.Add(new SqlParameter("@Value",        SqlDbType.Text));
        Params.Add(new SqlParameter("@ModifiedDate", SqlDbType.DateTime));
    }

    Params = m_UpdateCommand.Parameters;

    Params["@AccountID"].Value    = AccountID;
    Params["@Property"].Value     = Property;
    Params["@Value"].Value        = Value;
    Params["@ModifiedDate"].Value = DateTime.Now;
```

```
    try
    {
        m_Connection.Open();
        m_UpdateCommand.ExecuteNonQuery();
    }
    finally
    {
        m_Connection.Close();
    }
}
```

The real difference in the Insert() and Update() methods occurs in their stored procedures. In the case of the AccountProperty_Insert stored procedure (see Listing 10-20), it is simply a standard SQL insert. This is hardly rocket science when it comes to SQL.

Listing 10-20. The AccountProperty_Insert Stored Procedure

```
CREATE PROCEDURE dbo.AccountProperty_Insert
    (
        @AccountID INT         = NULL,
        @Property NVARCHAR(32) = NULL,
        @Value TEXT            = NULL,
        @ModifiedDate DATETIME = NULL,
        @CreationDate DATETIME = NULL
    )
AS

    SET NOCOUNT ON

    INSERT INTO AccountProperty (AccountID, Property, Value, ModifiedDate,
                                    CreationDate)

    VALUES      (@AccountID, @Property, @Value, @ModifiedDate, @CreationDate)

    RETURN
```

The UpdateAccountProperty stored procedure (see Listing 10-21) is simply a standard SQL update. In this case, the insertion uses a key of both the AccountID and the Property (the key of the key/value pair).

Listing 10-21. The UpdateAccountProperty Stored Procedure

```
CREATE PROCEDURE dbo.AccountProperty_Update

    (
        @AccountID INT         = NULL,
        @Property NVARCHAR(32) = NULL,
        @Value TEXT            = NULL,
        @ModifiedDate DATETIME = NULL
    )
AS

    SET NOCOUNT ON

    UPDATE AccountProperty

    SET     Value = @Value,
            ModifiedDate = @ModifiedDate

    WHERE   (AccountID = @AccountID AND Property = @Property)

    RETURN
```

Finally, Wrap Up the Installation

It is always a good idea to let users know that they are finished and that they completed successfully. I hate getting statements at the end of setup such as "Successfully completed but some nonfatal errors occurred during setup." Believe it or not, these types of messages actually appear quite frequently at the end of software setup procedures. I always wonder what is going to happen if I try to access a program in which a nonfatal error occurred. Will my software work properly? As far as I am concerned, a setup was successful or it was not. A "but" clause has no place at the end of a setup procedure. Okay, I'll get off my soapbox—for now.

The Setup/setup4.aspx Web Page

Setup4 is designed to tell the user that everything is fine, now go ahead and play. As you see in Figure 10-7, there is no guesswork on the part of the user. The process has ended, and it completed successfully. It even provides a button so that the user can go and have fun immediately.

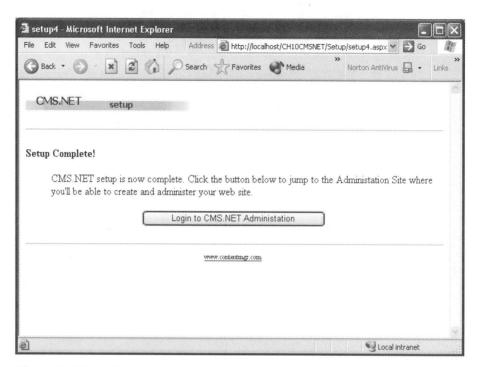

Figure 10-7. Setup/setup4.aspx

The Setup/setup4.cs Codebehind

Setup4 still requires a little bit of work before it is free to display the cheery message of successful completion. It needs to set the <appSettings> add setup attribute value in the web.config file to true. By setting it to true, the admin.aspx (which was discussed at the beginning of the chapter) knows that it can now run CMS.NET's administration system.

The code for the Page_Load() method (see Listing 10-22) is virtually the same as the UpdateConfigWeb() method found in setup2.cs. First, you open the web.config. Then, navigate to the <appSettings> add setup attribute. Next, you set the value to true. Finally, you update web.config to disk.

Listing 10-22. The setup4.Page_load Method

```
private void Page_Load(object sender, System.EventArgs e)
{
    if (!IsPostBack)
    {
        XmlReader xtr = new
            XmlTextReader(File.OpenRead(Server.MapPath("..\\web.config")));
```

```
XmlDocument doc = new XmlDocument();
doc.Load(xtr);
xtr.Close();

XmlNodeList nodes =
    doc.DocumentElement.GetElementsByTagName("appSettings");

for (int i = 0; i < nodes.Count; i++)
{
    XmlNodeList appnodes =
        ((XmlElement)(nodes.Item(i))).GetElementsByTagName("add");

    for (int j = 0; j < appnodes.Count; j++)
    {
        XmlAttributeCollection attrColl = appnodes.Item(j).Attributes;
        XmlAttribute tmpNode =
            (XmlAttribute)attrColl.GetNamedItem("key");
        if (tmpNode.Value.Equals("setup"))
        {
            ((XmlAttribute)attrColl.GetNamedItem("value")).Value =
                "true";
        }
    }
}

File.Copy(Server.MapPath("..\\web.config"),
                          Server.MapPath("..\\web.config.002"),
                          true);
File.Delete(Server.MapPath("..\\web.config"));

StreamWriter sr = new
    StreamWriter(File.OpenWrite(Server.MapPath("..\\web.config")));
doc.Save(sr);
sr.Close();
    }
}
```

The final method I need to cover is the btnLogin_Click() method (see Listing 10-23). This method enables the happy event of leaving the setup process and starting the administration process of the Web site.

There is not much to it, just a simple redirect to the same Web page that started this whole process. This time, though, because the setup flag is true, the Admin.aspx will jump to Administration/admin.aspx instead of Setup/setup.aspx.

Listing 10-23. The setup4.btnLogin_Click Method

```
private void btnLogin_Click (object sender, System.EventArgs e)
{
    Response.Redirect("../admin.aspx");
}
```

Summary

This chapter covered the building of a setup process for CMS.NET.

First, it explained how to navigate from Web page to Web page. Then, it covered the web.config file, how to programmatically update it, and how to extract information out of it. Next, it showed how to create an administrator account, and it described how to allow the adding of user-defined information to the Account/AccountProperty databases without having to change their schemas. It covered database helper classes and stored procedures, and it ended by describing the proper way to end the setup procedure.

In the next chapter, you get to start developing CMS.NET itself. In particular, this chapter will be your first cut at the content management application (CMA).

CHAPTER 11

Getting Content into the System

BEFORE YOU CAN DISPLAY CONTENT on a Web site, you need a way to get the content into the system. As you learned in Chapter 1, this is the job of the content management application (CMA). The CMA is the core of any CMS and is thus a good place to start truly developing a CMS or, in this case, CMS.NET.

Before you run, you need to learn how to crawl. This first cut at the CMA is without many bells and whistles. It lacks security (covered in Chapter 12), workflow (covered in Chapter 14), personalization preparation, and importing and exporting. In all of these chapters, you will come back and fix, or even replace, some of the code you develop in this chapter.

Some developers call what you are developing in this chapter the CRUD (create, read, update, and delete) of the system. This is not an acronym that I particularly like, but because it appears in so many programs, it seems almost appropriate. In the case of CMS.NET, this chapter covers the CURVeS (create, update, remove, view, and submit) of the system. I don't think anybody else uses this acronym, but I like it better.

 NOTE *In preparation for future changes, all Web pages are prefixed with Aut for "author" because the code you are developing is mostly for the author role of a CMS.*

Let's get started with the CMS proper with our first stab at CMS.NET's CMA.

Breaking a Page into Frames

It was once a very common practice to divide up a Web page into its parts, or sections, using frames and framesets (see Figure 11-1). It seems logical to break up a page in a consistent way so that a user will know where everything is without having to figure it out.

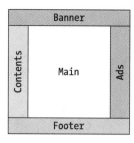

Figure 11-1. Standard Web page frames

- *Banner frame:* This section frequently holds the Web page logo and banner ads. It also sometimes holds links to major sections, zones, or areas of the site.

- *Contents frame:* This is the home of most NavBars. You might think of it as the table of contents frame. If the banner frame has links to sections or zones, the contents frame would then have links to content within only the current section.

- *Main frame:* This is where the content of the site is placed.

- *Ads frame:* Targeted ads associated with the content or other referenced story links are found here. This frame is less common than the previous three.

- *Footer frame:* Company copyrights and a simplified site map are often found here. This frame is seldom used.

As sites became larger, they started to outgrow the Web page real estate limitations imposed by frames. Also, Web users have become more sophisticated and don't need all the coddling and hand-holding. Thus, Web sites have now moved toward a better use of the entire browser screen area. Instead of forcing particular areas of the browser screen to hold certain types of content, now the Web page itself is broken up into these sections, and the browser is allowed to scroll over to these sections.

The Web browser is now a window looking at a section of the whole page. Users know that at the top will be the company logo and probably some form of advertisement, the left side will have a NavBar, the right side will contain additional relevant material, and the bottom will have a high-level site map and the company copyright notices. Some sites deviate from this, but most now use this layout.

CMS.NET's CMA uses a frame layout because Web page real estate is not an issue and a frame layout is much easier to understand. Chapter 12 covers the more prevalent approach of Web page design when you look at displaying Web page content.

Creating a Frame

After you create a new directory called CMA, off of the Administration directory, you need to add a good old-fashioned HTML page to house your frame. Frames use standard HTML and actually have nothing to do with ASP.NET or .NET. Even so, Visual Studio .NET provides a miniwizard to handle the building of them.

1. Right-click the new CMA directory in the Solution Explorer.

2. Select the Add HTML Page menu item from the Add menu. This will bring up the standard Add New Item dialog box.

3. Select the Frameset icon in the Templates window.

4. Type **CMA.html** in the Name edit box. (I prefer the suffix .html, but you can leave it as .htm, which is the default.)

5. Click the Open button. This will bring up the Select a Frameset Template dialog box, as shown in Figure 11-2.

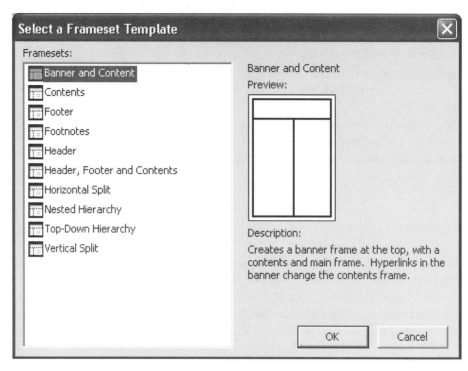

Figure 11-2. The Select a Frameset Template dialog box

6. Select the Banner and Content template.

7. Click the OK button.

You should now have a frameset in your main Web page designer. The design tool is pretty easy to use. The only thing you have to realize is that this is just a Web page holder. You have to build other Web pages separately and then insert them into the frame in which you want to view them.

Inserting a Page into a Frame

Follow these steps to insert a page into a frame:

1. Create a new Web page and then, when you've finished, come back to the frameset you built.

2. Right-click the frame you want to fill.

3. Select the Set Page for Frame menu item. This will bring up the Select Page dialog box shown in Figure 11-3.

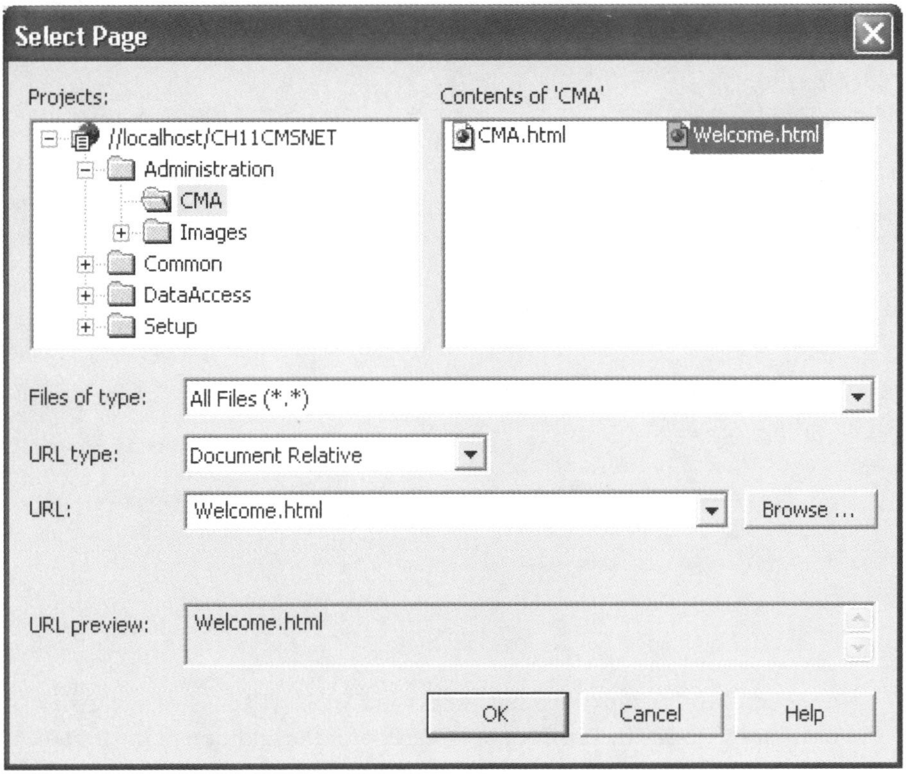

Figure 11-3. The Select Page dialog box

4. Navigate to the page you want placed in the frame.

5. Click the OK button.

You can get pretty elaborate with your frame layout, but personally, I think the simpler the better. By right-clicking anywhere in a frame, you can select how you want it to be split.

It is also possible to fix the width of the frame and seamlessly join two frames together so that there isn't a gray splitter bar for the user to play with. Just right-click anywhere on the Frameset edit window and select the Seamless Join Between Frames menu item.

The XML-Driven NavBar

The NavBar is extremely simple at this point. All it does is provide a drop-down menu with two menu items for authors. Later, when you add security in Chapter 13 and roles in Chapter 14, it will become much more elaborate.

The last example in Chapter 8 covered the XML NavBar. Listing 11-1 is the XML menu file, which is located in the XMLFiles directory found off the CMSNET root directory.

Listing 11-1. CMAMenu.xml

```xml
<?xml version="1.0" encoding="utf-8" ?>
<MainMenu>
  <Menu>
    <MenuName>Author</MenuName>
    <MenuItem>
      <Name>List Content</Name>
      <Link>AutList.aspx</Link>
    </MenuItem>
    <MenuItem>
      <Name>Create Content</Name>
      <Link>AutCreate.aspx</Link>
    </MenuItem>
  </Menu>
</MainMenu>
```

The code—NavBar.aspx, which handles the XML NavBar—is virtually the same as what was described in Chapter 8, except for the addition of the frame page target to the Hyperlink menu item. Listing 11-2 shows the additional code.

Listing 11-2. Adding Target to the Hyperlink

```
    row.Cells.Add(cell);

    link = new HyperLink();
    link.Text = MenuNodes[j].ChildNodes[0].InnerText;
    link.NavigateUrl = MenuNodes[j].ChildNodes[1].InnerText;
    link.Target = "main";

    cell = new TableCell();
```

You need to add this statement because the browser needs to know where to place the page it is linking to. Without the statement, the browser will place the selected Web page in the same frame as the hyperlink, thus overwriting the NavBar.

First CMS.NET Administration Page

All you need is a logo (one is provided in the Downloads section of the Apress Web site at www.apress.com) to place in the header frame of the CMA.html frameset page. Then you will have all the components that make up the first and most basic CMS.NET Web page. As you progress through the book, this simple page will expand considerably into something you will be truly proud of. Figure 11-4 shows your first masterpiece.

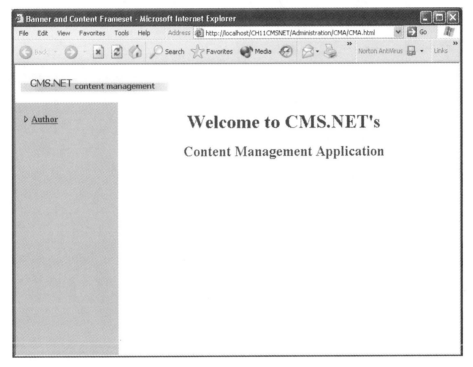

Figure 11-4. Your CMS.NET Administration Web page

As you can see, CMS.NET doesn't use ads or footer frames, as shown in Figure 11-1, but that doesn't mean your administration site can't. Changing your frameset to support this is as simple as selecting a different frameset icon when creating your initial Web page.

Content Database Table

Two major approaches exist for storing content for a CMS: an XML file or a database. For a small CMS, storing data in an XML file is fine because its biggest benefit is that it doesn't cost anything. As the system gets larger, however, you should definitely consider a database because it allows for better performance, concurrent users, and a myriad of other features that a straight XML file does not.

Microsoft has merged the two, and with Microsoft SQL Server 2000, you now have a database that can act like an XML file. CMS.NET uses any database you configured using the setup procedure, which was covered in Chapter 10. This book uses the MSDE provided with Visual Studio .NET samples for developing CMS.NET.

The Content database table (see Table 11-1) is designed to be simple and requires just the columns needed to support CMS.NET. Like the Account database table, optional data should be stored in a key/value property table called ContentProperty.

Table 11-1. Content Database Table Design

COLUMN NAME	DATA TYPE	LENGTH	KEY	DESCRIPTION
ContentID	int	4	true	ID of the content
Version	int	4	true	Version of the content
Headline	text	16	false	Headline
Byline	int	4	false	Author
Teaser	text	16	false	Summary to attract reader's interest
Body	text	16	false	Main text
TagLine	text	16	false	Tagline
Status	int	4	false	Current status of content
UpdateUserID	int	4	false	Last person to update in this version
ModifiedDate	datetime	8	false	Date last modified
CreationDate	datetime	8	false	Date content was created

There is nothing new about the database table except that the key is made up of two columns: `ContentID` and `Version`. Multiple versions of the same piece of content can be created; thus to make a unique key, we need to combine the ID with the version.

Another thing you should note is that the database stores each new version of the content in its entirety as opposed to using deltas. The code to create deltas is not simple and is not important to understanding CMS development. If you want to implement delta version control, the source code for GNU CVS (`www.gnu.org/software/cvs/cvs.html`) and RCS (`ftp://prep.ai.mit.edu/gnu/rcs`) is available for exploration.

Listing Site Content

Off the NavBar, two options are available to the author of content. The first is to bring up a list of content in the system. Normally, this would only bring up the content available to the logged-in author, but logging in isn't covered until Chapter 12, so for now, the list will display all content. The second option available on the NavBar is to bring up a Web form to create new content, which is covered shortly.

The AutList Web Page

When designing the AutList.aspx page, I had the option of creating the entire list and headings in C# code. Instead, I decided to use the design tool to create the static table headers and then have the code append all the content list information. This approach not only simplifies the code, but it also allows a graphic designer to decide on colors and fonts for the headers, as well as the image for the function buttons found in the right four columns. Listing 11-3 shows the design code used to create the headers.

Listing 11-3. The AutList.aspx Header Design

```
<form id=AutList method=post runat="server">
  <H2>
    <FONT color=darkslategray>Author : Content List</FONT>
  </H2>
  <P>
    <asp:table id=tblView runat="server" GridLines="Both" CellPadding="3"
        CellSpacing="1">
      <asp:TableRow BackColor="#8CD3EF">
        <asp:TableCell Width="10%" HorizontalAlign="Center" Text="ID">
        </asp:TableCell>
        <asp:TableCell Width="6%" Font-Size="XX-Small" HorizontalAlign="Center"
            Text="Last Version">
        </asp:TableCell>
        <asp:TableCell Width="76%" HorizontalAlign="Center" Text="Headline">
        </asp:TableCell>
        <asp:TableCell Width="2%" Font-Size="XX-Small" HorizontalAlign="Center"
            Text="View">
        </asp:TableCell>
        <asp:TableCell Width="2%" Font-Size="XX-Small" HorizontalAlign="Center"
            Text="Updt">
        </asp:TableCell>
        <asp:TableCell Width="2%" Font-Size="XX-Small" HorizontalAlign="Center"
            Text="Sub">
        </asp:TableCell>
        <asp:TableCell Width="2%" Font-Size="XX-Small" HorizontalAlign="Center"
            Text="Del">
        </asp:TableCell>
      </asp:TableRow>
    </asp:table>
  </P>
</form>
```

The AutList.aspx Web form has two distinct states.

The first state is when there is no content available to be seen. When this occurs, a Web page similar to Figure 11-5 is displayed. I decided to give the user the option of clicking a hyperlink within the empty table to generate a new piece of content. I could have just as easily stated that it was empty and forced the user to click the NavBar to create new content.

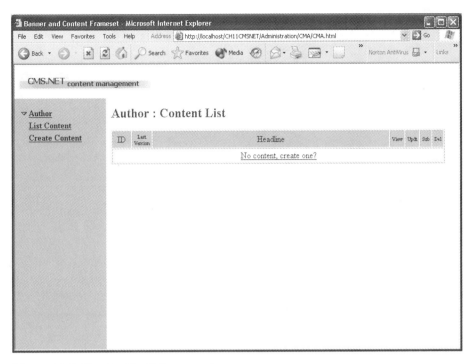

Figure 11-5. The AutList Web page when empty

The second state is obviously when there is content. As you can see in
Figure 11-6, there are four options that a user might choose for each piece
of content:

- *View:* Allows the viewing of the entire piece of content.

- *Update:* Allows the author to update his content.

- *Submit:* Allows the author to submit his work to the next stage in the workflow. Because workflow isn't covered until Chapter 14, it will simply be
  a toggle from a creation state to a submitting state.

- *Delete/Remove:* Allows the author to delete his content. For now, the code
  actually deletes the content. Later, the code will simply change the status
  of the content to "removed." This way, content can be retrieved at a later
  date if needed.

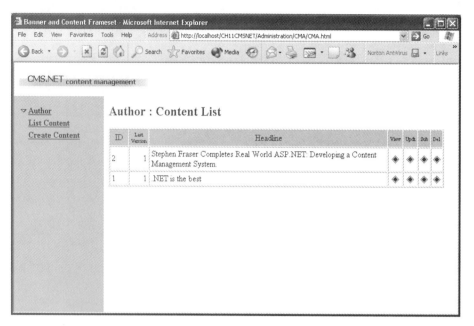

Figure 11-6. The AutList Web page with content

The AutList Codebehind

Okay, let's look at some code. Listing 11-4 shows all the code needed to handle the first state (no content). All the code can be found in the Page_Load() method and contains pretty standard table control code. The only things new are TableCell's ColumnSpan and HorizontalAlign properties, though, as you can see, there is nothing tricky about them. All you have to do with the ColumnSpan property is set it to the number of columns you want it to span. For the HorizontalAlign property, just assign it HorizontalAlign's static value of Left, Right, Center, or Justify.

Listing 11-4. The AutList.cs Empty Content Code

```
private void Page_Load(object sender, System.EventArgs e)
{
    content  = new Content(new AppEnv(Context).GetConnection());
    DataTable dt = content.GetHeadlines();

    if (dt.Rows.Count > 0)
    {
        ...
    }
    else
```

```
{
    TableRow row = new TableRow();
    tblView.Rows.Add(row);

    HyperLink link = new HyperLink();
    link.Text = "No content, create one?";
    link.NavigateUrl = "AutCreate.aspx";

    TableCell cell = new TableCell();
    cell.ColumnSpan = 7;
    cell.HorizontalAlign = HorizontalAlign.Center;
    cell.Controls.Add(link);

    row.Cells.Add(cell);
}
}
```

The code for handling the state when content exists (see Listing 11-5) is a little more complex, but the complexities are hidden in another submethod. The code in the Page_Load() method is fairly easy to follow. For each row of content, display the ID, version, and headline as well as the setup buttons to functions that the table can call. When setting up the buttons, check to see if the status of the content is "creating." If so, allow the updating and deleting functions.

Listing 11-5. The AutList.cs Content List Code

```
private void Page_Load(object sender, System.EventArgs e)
{
    content  = new Content(new AppEnv(Context).GetConnection());
    DataTable dt = content.GetHeadlines();

    if (dt.Rows.Count > 0)
    {
        LiteralControl lit;
        TableCell       cell;
        int prv = -1;
        int cur;

        foreach (DataRow dr in dt.Rows)
        {
            cur = Convert.ToInt32(dr["ContentID"]);

            if (cur != prv)
            {
```

```
          prv = cur;
          TableRow row = new TableRow();
          tblView.Rows.Add(row);

          lit = new LiteralControl(dr["ContentID"].ToString());
          cell = new TableCell();
          cell.Controls.Add(lit);
          row.Cells.Add(cell);

          lit = new LiteralControl(dr["Version"].ToString());
          cell = new TableCell();
          cell.Controls.Add(lit);
          cell.HorizontalAlign = HorizontalAlign.Right;
          row.Cells.Add(cell);

          lit = new LiteralControl(dr["Headline"].ToString());
          cell = new TableCell();
          cell.Controls.Add(lit);
          row.Cells.Add(cell);

          BuildImageButton(row, "AutView.aspx?ContentID=" +
                               dr["ContentID"].ToString());

          if (Convert.ToInt32(dr["Status"]) == StatusCodes.Creating)
              BuildImageButton(row, "AutUpdate.aspx?ContentID=" +
                                   dr["ContentID"].ToString());
          else
              BuildImageButton(row, null);

          BuildImageButton(row, "AutSubmit.aspx?ContentID=" +
                               dr["ContentID"].ToString());

          if (Convert.ToInt32(dr["Status"]) == StatusCodes.Creating)
              BuildImageButton(row, "AutRemove.aspx?ContentID=" +
                                   dr["ContentID"].ToString());
          else
              BuildImageButton(row, null);
      }
   }
}
```

Commands and CommandArguments

The tricky part of the code falls in the BuildImageButton() method (see Listing 11-6). Originally, I wrote a command event for each of the view, update, submit, and remove functions, but then it became obvious that they were in fact the same command event but with different arguments. The arguments were simply the parameter to the Redirect() method, which each of these methods calls.

To create a Command with a CommandArgument, simply assign a CommandEventHandler, of the method you want to execute, to the image button's Command property. Then assign a string argument to the CommandArgument property.

Listing 11-6. The AutList.cs BuildImageButton Code

```
private void BuildImageButton(TableRow row, string cArg)
{

    ImageButton ibn = new ImageButton();

    if (cArg != null)
    {
        ibn.Command += new CommandEventHandler(this.btn_Click);
        ibn.ImageUrl = "Images/btnSelect.gif";
        ibn.CommandArgument = cArg;
    }
    else
        ibn.ImageUrl = "Images/blank.gif";

    TableCell cell = new TableCell();
    cell.Controls.Add(ibn);
    cell.HorizontalAlign = HorizontalAlign.Center;
    cell.VerticalAlign   = VerticalAlign.Middle;

    row.Cells.Add(cell);
}
```

When the user eventually clicks any of the Image buttons, the btn_Click() command is triggered. As you can see in Listing 11-7, all you need to do is get the CommandArgument you stuffed in earlier from the CommandEventArgs parameter passed by the method.

Listing 11-7. The AutList.cs btn_Click Code

```
private void btn_Click(object sender, CommandEventArgs e)
{
    Response.Redirect(e.CommandArgument.ToString());
}
```

Creating New Content

You can list all the content in the system. It's kind of boring, however, if you don't have any way of getting content into the CMS. Let's fix that.

The AutCreate Web Page

Figure 11-7 shows CMS.NET's simple content-creation Web page. The CMS you plan to develop will probably be a little more detailed, but this is what is needed for this CMS.NET system.

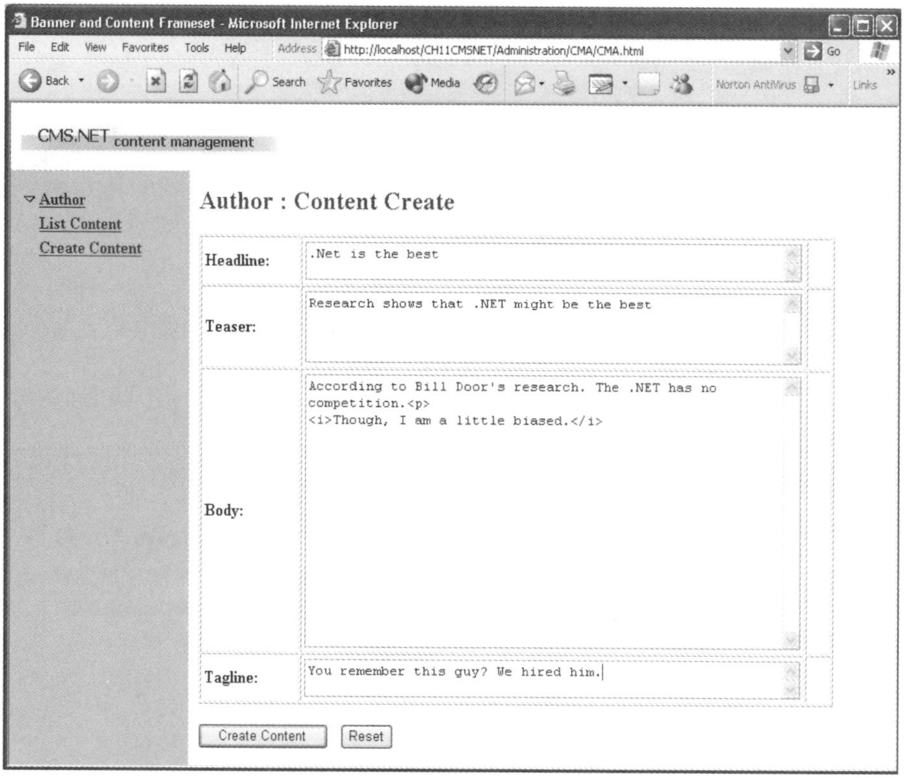

Figure 11-7. The AutCreate Web page

Creating AutCreate.aspx is pretty straightforward. As you can see in Listing 11-8, the form is simply four text boxes, `RequiredFieldValidator` on the headline and body, a button to create the content, and another button to reset the form back to empty.

Listing 11-8. The AutCreate Web Form

```
<FORM id=AutCreate method=post runat="server">
  <H2>
    <FONT color=darkslategray>Author : Content Create</FONT>
  </H2>
  <P>
    <asp:ValidationSummary id=ValidationSummary1 runat="server"
        HeaderText="Error(s) occurred while creating content">
    </asp:ValidationSummary>
    <TABLE cellSpacing=1 cellPadding=3 width="95%" border=1>
      <TR>
        <TD style="WIDTH: 16%"><STRONG>Headline:</STRONG></TD>
        <TD style="WIDTH: 80%">
          <asp:TextBox id=tbHeadline runat="server" Width="100%"
              TextMode="MultiLine">
          </asp:TextBox>
        </TD>
        <TD>
           
          <asp:RequiredFieldValidator id=RequiredFieldValidator1 runat="server"
              ErrorMessage="A Headline must be entered." Display="Dynamic"
              ControlToValidate="tbHeadline" EnableClientScript="False">*
          </asp:RequiredFieldValidator>
        </TD>
      </TR>
      <TR>
        <TD style="WIDTH: 16%"><STRONG>Teaser:</STRONG></TD>
        <TD style="WIDTH: 80%">
          <asp:TextBox id=tbTeaser runat="server" Width="100%"
              TextMode="MultiLine" Rows="4">
          </asp:TextBox>
        </TD>
        <TD> </TD>
      </TR>
      <TR>
        <TD style="WIDTH: 16%"><STRONG>Body:</STRONG></TD>
        <TD style="WIDTH: 80%">
          <asp:TextBox id=tbBody runat="server" Width="100%"
```

```
                         TextMode="MultiLine" Rows="16">
                 </asp:TextBox>
             </TD>
             <TD>
                  
                 <asp:RequiredFieldValidator id=RequiredFieldValidator2 runat="server"
                     ErrorMessage="A body must be entered." Display="Dynamic"
                     ControlToValidate="tbBody" EnableClientScript="False">*
                 </asp:RequiredFieldValidator>
             </TD>
         </TR>
         <TR>
             <TD style="WIDTH: 16%"><STRONG>Tagline:</STRONG></TD>
             <TD style="WIDTH: 80%">
                 <asp:TextBox id=tbTagline runat="server" Width="100%"
                     TextMode="MultiLine">
                 </asp:TextBox>
             </TD>
             <TD> </TD>
         </TR>
     </TABLE>
 </P>
 <asp:Button id=bnNext runat="server" Text="Create Content">
 </asp:Button>
  
 <INPUT type=reset value=Reset>
</FORM>
```

A simple little trick I found while designing this Web form is that you can use the plain old HTML Reset button to blank out the page. This will save you from having to do any coding in the Codebehind, which would be required if you were to use the intrinsic button control.

The AutCreate Codebehind

The code to handle the creation of a piece of content is beyond easy (see Listing 11-9). Get a Content table helper class. (Remember the helper classes from Chapter 10?) Then, insert the content you gathered using the helper class' Insert() method. Finally, go back to the content list Web page.

NOTE *The byline is hard-coded to "1" because at this point there is only one user: the administrator. This code will be updated later to use the current logged-in Account ID.*

Listing 11-9. The AutCreate Page_Load Method

```
private void Page_Load(object sender, System.EventArgs e)
{
    if (IsPostBack)
    {
        Page.Validate();

        if (Page.IsValid)
        {
            Content content = new Content(new AppEnv(Context).GetConnection());

            content.Insert(tbHeadline.Text, 1, tbTeaser.Text,
                        tbBody.Text, tbTagline.Text);

            Response.Redirect("AutList.aspx");
        }
    }
}
```

It is true that the Content.cs helper class method Insert() (see Listing 11-10) is a little more complex, but you have already seen this almost exact code twice before in the Account and AccountProperty table helper classes.

To simplify the call made to the Insert() method in AutCreate.cs, I created an overloaded version of it. You should already know that overloaded methods are two or more methods within a class that use the same name but different parameters. Usually each method has very similar functionality, but this is not a requirement.

The overloaded method includes the NextContentID() method (see Listing 11-10), which determines the next ContentID. It also hard-codes the version number to "1" because it is always the first version. You also know that the user to last touch the content is the same person who is creating it, so you can set that parameter to the same as the Byline.

Listing 11-10. The Content Database Helper Insert and NextContentID Methods

```
public void Insert(string Headline, int Byline, string Teaser, string Body,
                   string Tagline)
{
    Insert(NextContentID(), 1, Headline, Byline, Teaser, Body,
           Tagline, Byline);
}

public void Insert(int ContentID, int Version, string Headline, int Byline,
                   string Teaser, string Body, string Tagline, int UpdUserID)
{
    // INSERT INTO Content (ContentID, Version, Headline, Byline,
    //                      Teaser, Body, Tagline, Status, UpdateUserID,
    //                      ModifiedDate, CreationDate)
    // VALUES (@ContentID, @Version, @Headline, @Byline, @Teaser, @Body,
    //         @Tagline, @Status, @UpdateUserID, @ModifiedDate, @CreationDate)

    SqlCommand Command = new SqlCommand("Content_Insert", m_Connection);
    Command.CommandType = CommandType.StoredProcedure;

    Command.Parameters.Add(new SqlParameter("@ContentID", SqlDbType.Int));
    Command.Parameters.Add(new SqlParameter("@Version", SqlDbType.Int));
    Command.Parameters.Add(new SqlParameter("@Headline", SqlDbType.Text));
    Command.Parameters.Add(new SqlParameter("@Byline", SqlDbType.Int));
    Command.Parameters.Add(new SqlParameter("@Teaser", SqlDbType.Text));
    Command.Parameters.Add(new SqlParameter("@Body", SqlDbType.Text));
    Command.Parameters.Add(new SqlParameter("@Tagline", SqlDbType.Text));
    Command.Parameters.Add(new SqlParameter("@Status", SqlDbType.Int));
    Command.Parameters.Add(new SqlParameter("@UpdateUserID", SqlDbType.Int));
    Command.Parameters.Add(new SqlParameter("@ModifiedDate",
                                            SqlDbType.DateTime));
    Command.Parameters.Add(new SqlParameter("@CreationDate",
                                            SqlDbType.DateTime));

    Command.Parameters["@ContentID"].Value    = ContentID;
    Command.Parameters["@Version"].Value       = Version;
    Command.Parameters["@Headline"].Value      = Headline;
    Command.Parameters["@Byline"].Value        = Byline;
    Command.Parameters["@Teaser"].Value        = Teaser;
    Command.Parameters["@Body"].Value          = Body;
    Command.Parameters["@Tagline"].Value       = Tagline;
    Command.Parameters["@Status"].Value        = StatusCodes.Creating;
    Command.Parameters["@UpdateUserID"].Value = UpdUserID;
```

```
        Command.Parameters["@ModifiedDate"].Value = DateTime.Now;
        Command.Parameters["@CreationDate"].Value = DateTime.Now;

        try
        {
            m_Connection.Open();
            Command.ExecuteNonQuery();
        }
        finally
        {
            m_Connection.Close();
        }
    }

    public int NextContentID()
    {
        // SELECT DISTINCT ContentID
        // FROM     Content
        // ORDER BY ContentID DESC

        SqlCommand Command = new SqlCommand("Content_NextContentID", m_Connection);
        Command.CommandType = CommandType.StoredProcedure;

        SqlDataAdapter DAdpt = new SqlDataAdapter(Command);

        DataSet ds = new DataSet();
        DAdpt.Fill(ds, "Content");

        if (ds.Tables["Content"].Rows.Count <= 0)
            return 1;

        return Convert.ToInt32(ds.Tables["Content"].Rows[0]["ContentID"]) + 1;
    }
```

Error Handling

Okay, what happens if you get an unexpected database error during the insertion of the content? I bet you've seen Figure 11-8—the error page of shame. Is there a better page you can show the user or at least a page that is less embarrassing? Thank goodness, there is. In fact, there are several options.

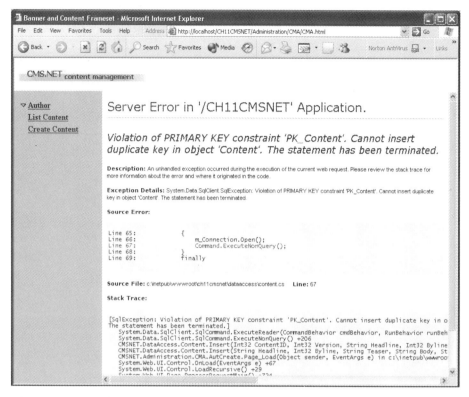

Figure 11-8. .NET's error page of shame

The easiest way to replace the .NET error page is to replace it with a generic one of your own. It's very simple to do this. You just make the following change to the root directory version of your web.config file:

```
<configuration>
  <system.web>

    ...

    <customErrors defaultRedirect="http://localhost/CMSNET/ErrorPage.aspx"
                  mode="On"/>

    ...

  </system.web>
</configuration>
```

Obviously, the location of the ErrorPage.aspx can be anywhere you want and, of course, you have to create the ErrorPage.aspx.

If you want a user to see your generic message, on the other hand, but you also want the developers on the local host to see the more informative error message, you simply change the mode to remoteOnly.

The `<customErrors>` element has one more trick up its sleeve. It is possible to redirect error messages based on the status code of the Web page error, as shown here:

```
<customErrors defaultRedirect="http://localhost/CMSNET/ErrorPage.aspx
              mode="remoteOnly">
  <error statuscode="403" redirect="NoAccess.aspx" />
  <error statuscode="404" redirect="NotFound.aspx" />
</customErrors>
```

As long as you have set the mode to on or redirect, it is also possible to redirect the error page based specifically on the Web page where the error occurred. This is done in the @page directive at the top of each ASPX file, as shown here:

```
< @page ... ErrorPage="thispages_errorpage.aspx" />
```

Note that only one @page directive is allowed per Web page; therefore, you must tack it onto the end of the autogenerated one.

Each of the preceding handles errors generically. If the Web page errors out, this error page will intercept the error before the .NET error page appears. But what if you know that an error happens periodically and you want to capture it in a more exacting fashion?

Of course, this is a job for the exception handler. All you have to do is catch the exception yourself and process or redirect the error as you see fit. Listing 11-11 shows AutCreate's `Page_Load()` method using exception handling. As you can see, when an error occurs, the Web page redirects the user to another custom error page. This time, you can pass almost any information you like to the error page. Here, I'm passing the exception error message.

Wait a second, what is this `HttpUtility.UrlEncode()` method? As you probably know, certain characters should not appear in an http address, most notably the space character. To overcome this, .NET provides a method that encodes the URL so that it is valid for redirecting. There is also a `HttpUtility.UrlDecode()` method, but I am sure you figured that out already.

Listing 11-11. The Revised AutCreate's Page_Load Method
```
private void Page_Load(object sender, System.EventArgs e)
{
    if (IsPostBack)
    {
        if (Page.IsValid)
        {
            try
            {
```

```
            Content content =
                new Content(new AppEnv(Context).GetConnection());

            content.Insert(tbHeadline.Text, 1, tbTeaser.Text,
                            tbBody.Text, tbTagline.Text);
    }
    catch (Exception err)
    {
        Response.Redirect("Error.aspx?ErrMsg=" +
            HttpUtility.UrlEncode("The following error occurred: " +
                                    err.Message));
    }

    Response.Redirect("AutList.aspx");
    }
  }
}
```

WARNING *The* Response.Redirect() *method throws a ThreadAbortException. This is because the execution is terminating the current page thread. Because this occurs, you need to place the* redirect() *method outside of the* try *block.*

Updating Content

Most authors don't get their stories perfect the first time. Thus, there will always be a need for an AutUpdate.aspx Web form.

The AutUpdate Web Page

As you see in Figure 11-9, there is nothing special about the form. In fact, it is very similar to the content-creation Web form shown earlier except that it displays a few autogenerated fields as read-only so that the author can make sure she is updating the correct version.

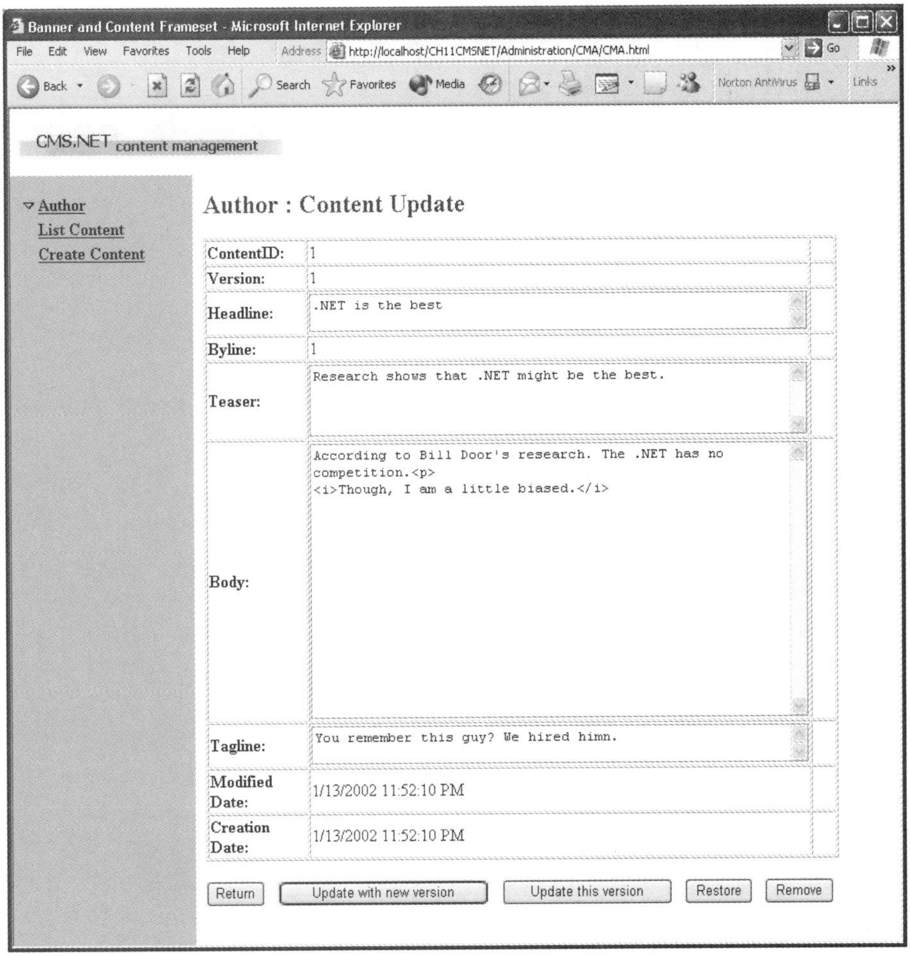

Figure 11-9. The AutUpdate Web page

There is nothing special about the code used to design the form, as
Listing 11-12 shows. It is made up of five labels, four text boxes, and five buttons,
none of which have any special features.

Listing 11-12. The AutUpdate Web Design

```
<form id="AutUpdate" method="post" runat="server">
  <H2><FONT color=darkslategray>Author : Content Update</FONT></H2>
  <P>
    <asp:ValidationSummary id=ValSum runat="server"
        HeaderText="Error(s) occurred while creating content">
    </asp:ValidationSummary>
    <TABLE cellSpacing=1 cellPadding=1 width="95%" border=1>
```

```
<TR>
  <TD style="WIDTH: 16%"><STRONG>ContentID:</STRONG></TD>
  <TD style="WIDTH: 80%">
    <asp:label id=lbContentID runat="server" Width="100%"></asp:label>
  </TD>
  <TD> </TD>
</TR>
<TR>
  <TD style="WIDTH: 16%"><STRONG>Version:</STRONG></TD>
  <TD style="WIDTH: 80%">
    <asp:Label id=lbVersion runat="server"></asp:Label>
  </TD>
  <TD> </TD>
</TR>
<TR>
  <TD style="WIDTH: 16%"><STRONG>Headline:</STRONG></TD>
  <TD style="WIDTH: 80%">
    <asp:TextBox id=tbHeadline runat="server" Width="100%"
        TextMode="MultiLine">
    </asp:TextBox>
  </TD>
  <TD>
     
    <asp:RequiredFieldValidator id=rfvHeadline runat="server"
        ErrorMessage="A Headline must be entered." Display="Dynamic"
        ControlToValidate="tbHeadline" EnableClientScript="False">*
    </asp:RequiredFieldValidator>
  </TD>
</TR>
<TR>
  <TD style="WIDTH: 16%"><STRONG>Byline:</STRONG></TD>
  <TD style="WIDTH: 80%">
    <asp:label id=lbByline runat="server" Width="100%"></asp:label>
  </TD>
  <TD width="100%"> </TD>
</TR>
<TR>
  <TD style="WIDTH: 16%"><STRONG>Teaser:</STRONG></TD>
  <TD style="WIDTH: 80%">
    <asp:TextBox id=tbTeaser runat="server" Width="100%"
        TextMode="MultiLine" Rows="4">
    </asp:TextBox>
  </TD>
```

```
        <TD> </TD>
      </TR>
      <TR>
        <TD style="WIDTH: 16%"><STRONG>Body:</STRONG></TD>
        <TD style="WIDTH: 80%">
          <asp:TextBox id=tbBody runat="server" Width="100%"
              TextMode="MultiLine" Rows="16">
          </asp:TextBox>
        </TD>
        <TD>
           
          <asp:RequiredFieldValidator id=rfvBody runat="server"
              ErrorMessage="A body must be entered." Display="Dynamic"
              ControlToValidate="tbBody" EnableClientScript="False">*
          </asp:RequiredFieldValidator>
        </TD>
      </TR>
      <TR>
        <TD style="WIDTH: 16%"><STRONG>Tagline:</STRONG></TD>
        <TD style="WIDTH: 80%">
          <asp:TextBox id=tbTagline runat="server" Width="100%"
              TextMode="MultiLine">
          </asp:TextBox>
        </TD>
        <TD> </TD>
      </TR>
      <TR>
        <TD style="WIDTH: 16%"><STRONG>Modified Date:</STRONG></TD>
        <TD style="WIDTH: 80%">
          <asp:Label id=lbModifiedDate runat="server" Width="100%"></asp:Label>
        </TD>
        <TD> </TD>
      </TR>
      <TR>
        <TD style="WIDTH: 16%"><STRONG>Creation Date:</STRONG></TD>
        <TD style="WIDTH: 80%">
          <asp:Label id=lbCreationDate runat="server" Width="100%"></asp:Label>
        </TD>
        <TD> </TD>
      </TR>
    </TABLE>
</P>
<asp:Button id=bnReturn runat="server" Text="Return"></asp:Button>
 
```

```
    <asp:Button id=bnInsert runat="server" Text="Update with new version" >
    </asp:Button>
     
    <asp:Button id=bnUpdate runat="server" Text="Update this version" >
    </asp:Button>
     
    <asp:Button id=bnRestore runat="server" Text="Restore" ></asp:Button>
     
    <asp:Button id=bnRemove runat="server" Text="Remove" ></asp:Button>
</form>
```

The AutUpdate Codebehind

The only thing special about the AutUpdate Web form is that it supports rudimentary versioning. For CMS.NET, versioning is simply saving the updated Web form into a new database record with a new version number.

Most of the code for AutUpdate class (see Listing 11-13) is pretty standard update logic:

- Get the record to update.

- Populate the update table.

- Display the Web page for updating.

- When a valid form is returned, save content to the database.

The loading of the Web table is only allowed if the ID of the content is passed to AutUpdate in the ContentID parameter. If ContentID is empty, the Web page jumps to error.aspx. The loading of the Web form table from the database is done using the Content helper class GetContentForID() method (see Listing 11-14).

Three of the buttons need a quick look over.

The Restore button, handled by the bnRestore_Click() method, is used to restore the Web page back to its original version before any edits. A simple trick is used to do this. The button simply reloads the Web page from the database.

The Update With New Version button, handled by the bnInsert_Click() method, calls the Content database help classes' Insert() method, which was covered earlier. The helper method used this time is the Insert() method with all the parameters. To figure out what the next version is, simply add one to the current version. This is possible because only the last version, the one with the highest version number, can be updated.

The Update This Version button, handled by the bnUpdate_Click() method, calls a standard update database helper method (see Listing 11-14). You've already seen a near carbon copy of this updater code before (and you will see it again).

Listing 11-13. The AutUpdate Web Page Codebehind

```
private void BuildOrigPage()
{
    DataRow dr = dt.Rows[0];

    lbContentID.Text = dr["ContentID"].ToString();
    lbVersion.Text    = dr["Version"].ToString();
    tbHeadline.Text   = dr["Headline"].ToString();
    lbByline.Text     = dr["Byline"].ToString();
    tbTeaser.Text     = dr["Teaser"].ToString();
    tbBody.Text       = dr["Body"].ToString();
    tbTagline.Text    = dr["Tagline"].ToString();
    lbModifiedDate.Text  = dr["ModifiedDate"].ToString();
    lbCreationDate.Text  = dr["CreationDate"].ToString();
}
```

```
private void Page_Load(object sender, System.EventArgs e)
{
    int cid = Convert.ToInt32(Request.QueryString["ContentID"]);

    if (cid == 0)
    {
        Response.Redirect("error.aspx?ErrMsg=" +
            HttpUtility.UrlEncode("ContentID Missing"));
    }
    dt = new Content(
        new AppEnv(Context).GetConnection()).GetContentForID(cid);

    if (!IsPostBack)
    {
        BuildOrigPage();
    }
}
...
private void bnRestore_Click(object sender, System.EventArgs e)
{
    BuildOrigPage();
}
```

```csharp
private void bnReturn_Click(object sender, System.EventArgs e)
{
    Response.Redirect("AutList.aspx");
}


private void bnRemove_Click(object sender, System.EventArgs e)
{
    Response.Redirect("AutRemove.aspx?ContentID=" + lbContentID.Text);
}


private void bnInsert_Click(object sender, System.EventArgs e)
{
    if (Page.IsValid)
    {
        try
        {
            Content content = new Content(new AppEnv(Context).GetConnection());
            content.Insert(Convert.ToInt32(lbContentID.Text),
                Convert.ToInt32(lbVersion.Text) + 1,
                tbHeadline.Text, 1, tbTeaser.Text, tbBody.Text,
                tbTagline.Text, 1);
        }
        catch (Exception err)
        {
            Response.Redirect("Error.aspx?ErrMsg=" +
                HttpUtility.UrlEncode("The following error occurred: " +
                err.Message));
        }

        Response.Redirect("AutList.aspx");
    }
}


private void bnUpdate_Click(object sender, System.EventArgs e)
{
    if (Page.IsValid)
    {
        try
        {
            Content content = new Content(new AppEnv(Context).GetConnection());
            content.Update(Convert.ToInt32(lbContentID.Text),
                Convert.ToInt32(lbVersion.Text),
                tbHeadline.Text, 1, tbTeaser.Text, tbBody.Text,
                tbTagline.Text, 1);
```

```
        }
        catch (Exception err)
        {
            Response.Redirect("Error.aspx?ErrMsg=" +
                HttpUtility.UrlEncode("The following error occurred: " +
                err.Message));
        }

        Response.Redirect("AutList.aspx");
    }
}
```

Listing 11-14. The Update and GetContentForID Content Database Helper Methods

```
public void Update(int ContentID, int Version, string Headline, int Byline,
                   string Teaser, string Body, string Tagline, int UpdUserID)
{
    // UPDATE Content
    // SET
    //        Headline    = @Headline,
    //        Byline      = @Byline,
    //        Teaser      = @Teaser,
    //        Body        = @Body,
    //        Tagline     = @Tagline,
    //        Status      = @Status,
    //        UpdateUserID = @UpdateUserID,
    //        ModifiedDate = @ModifiedDate
    // WHERE  ContentID = @ContentID
    //    AND  Version = @Version

    SqlCommand Command = new SqlCommand("Content_Update", m_Connection);
    Command.CommandType  = CommandType.StoredProcedure;

    Command.Parameters.Add(new SqlParameter("@ContentID", SqlDbType.Int));
    Command.Parameters.Add(new SqlParameter("@Version", SqlDbType.Int));
    Command.Parameters.Add(new SqlParameter("@Headline", SqlDbType.Text));
    Command.Parameters.Add(new SqlParameter("@Byline", SqlDbType.Int));
    Command.Parameters.Add(new SqlParameter("@Teaser", SqlDbType.Text));
    Command.Parameters.Add(new SqlParameter("@Body", SqlDbType.Text));
    Command.Parameters.Add(new SqlParameter("@Tagline", SqlDbType.Text));
    Command.Parameters.Add(new SqlParameter("@Status", SqlDbType.Int));
    Command.Parameters.Add(new SqlParameter("@UpdateUserID", SqlDbType.Int));
    Command.Parameters.Add(new SqlParameter("@ModifiedDate",
                                            SqlDbType.DateTime));
```

```
    Command.Parameters["@ContentID"].Value    = ContentID;
    Command.Parameters["@Version"].Value      = Version;
    Command.Parameters["@Headline"].Value     = Headline;
    Command.Parameters["@Byline"].Value       = Byline;
    Command.Parameters["@Teaser"].Value       = Teaser;
    Command.Parameters["@Body"].Value         = Body;
    Command.Parameters["@Tagline"].Value      = Tagline;
    Command.Parameters["@Status"].Value       = StatusCodes.Creating;
    Command.Parameters["@UpdateUserID"].Value = UpdUserID;
    Command.Parameters["@ModifiedDate"].Value = DateTime.Now;


    try
    {
        m_Connection.Open();
        Command.ExecuteNonQuery();
    }
    finally
    {
        m_Connection.Close();
    }
}

public DataTable GetContentForID(int cid)
{
    // SELECT *
    // FROM Content
    // WHERE ContentID=@cid
    // ORDER BY Version DESC

    SqlCommand Command =
        new SqlCommand("Content_GetContentForID", m_Connection);
    Command.CommandType = CommandType.StoredProcedure;
    Command.Parameters.Add(new SqlParameter("@cid", SqlDbType.Int));
    Command.Parameters["@cid"].Value = cid;

    SqlDataAdapter DAdpt = new SqlDataAdapter(Command);

    DataSet ds = new DataSet();
    DAdpt.Fill(ds, "Content");

    return ds.Tables["Content"];
}
```

Viewing a Piece of Content

The view form is a little terse because it only shows the content's headline, so you have to come up with another way of viewing a piece of content. Viewing content using the update function is a little risky because it runs the risk of changing the content by accident. So, to view the entire piece of content, I added the AutView.aspx Web page.

The AutView Web Page

As you can see in Figure 11-10, the Web page is just a table of all the content columns for a particular piece of content. It also has five buttons at the bottom. The first button returns to the content list. The next two buttons navigate through all the versions of the content. The next button updates the content, and the last button removes the current version.

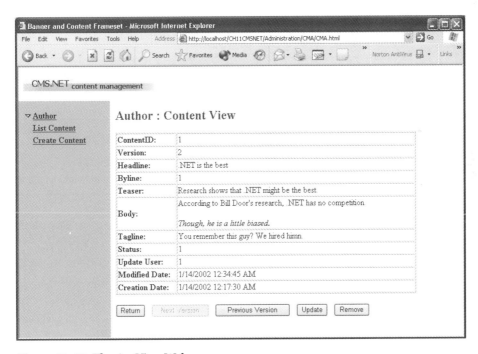

Figure 11-10. The AutView Web page

You will see as you play with AutList that the states of the buttons change depending on which version you are viewing. The most current version allows you to update, remove, and move to the previous version (if there is more than one version), but you will notice that the Next Version button is grayed out and you can't click it. When you are on a prior version, the Update and Remove buttons disappear, and the Next Version button is enabled. Depending on whether there are more versions, the Previous Version button might be grayed out or enabled. (See Figure 11-11.)

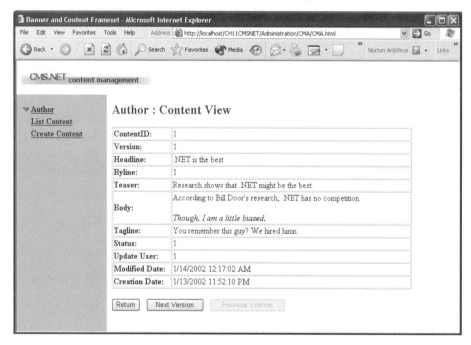

Figure 11-11. The AutView Web page

If you look at the design in Listing 11-15, you will see that it contains no code to handle any of this logic. In fact, it is simple. It is just a table with headings, labels, and five buttons.

Listing 11-15. The AutView Web Design

```
<form id=AutView method=post runat="server">
  <H2><FONT color=darkslategray>Author : Content View</FONT></H2>
  <P>
    <TABLE cellSpacing=1 cellPadding=1 width="90%" border=1>
      <TR>
        <TD style="WIDTH: 20%"><STRONG>ContentID:</STRONG></TD>
```

```
    <TD>
      <asp:label id=lbContentID runat="server" Width="100%">
      </asp:label>
    </TD>
</TR>
<TR>
  <TD style="WIDTH: 20%"><STRONG>Version:</STRONG></TD>
  <TD>
    <asp:Label id=lbVersion runat="server">
    </asp:Label>
  </TD>
</TR>
<TR>
  <TD style="WIDTH: 20%"><STRONG>Headline:</STRONG></TD>
  <TD>
    <asp:label id=lbHeadline runat="server" Width="100%">
    </asp:label>
  </TD>
</TR>
<TR>
  <TD style="WIDTH: 20%"><STRONG>Byline:</STRONG></TD>
  <TD width="100%">
    <asp:label id=lbByline runat="server" Width="100%">
    </asp:label>
  </TD>
</TR>
<TR>
  <TD style="WIDTH: 20%"><STRONG>Teaser:</STRONG></TD>
  <TD>
    <asp:label id=lbTeaser runat="server" Width="100%">
    </asp:label>
  </TD>
</TR>
<TR>
  <TD style="WIDTH: 20%"><STRONG>Body:</STRONG></TD>
  <TD>
    <asp:label id=lbBody runat="server" Width="100%">
    </asp:label>
  </TD>
</TR>
<TR>
  <TD style="WIDTH: 20%"><STRONG>Tagline:</STRONG></TD>
  <TD>
```

```
                    <asp:label id=lbTagline runat="server" Width="100%">
                    </asp:label>
                </TD>
            </TR>
            <TR>
                <TD style="WIDTH: 20%"><STRONG>Status:</STRONG></TD>
                <TD>
                    <asp:label id=lbStatus runat="server" Width="100%">
                    </asp:label>
                </TD>
            </TR>
            <TR>
                <TD style="WIDTH: 20%"><STRONG>Update User:</STRONG></TD>
                <TD>
                    <asp:Label id=lbUpdateUser runat="server" Width="100%">
                    </asp:Label>
                </TD>
            </TR>
            <TR>
                <TD style="WIDTH: 20%"><STRONG>Modified Date:</STRONG></TD>
                <TD>
                    <asp:Label id=lbModifiedDate runat="server" Width="100%">
                    </asp:Label>
                </TD>
            </TR>
            <TR>
                <TD style="WIDTH: 20%"><STRONG>Creation Date:</STRONG></TD>
                <TD>
                    <asp:Label id=lbCreationDate runat="server" Width="100%">
                    </asp:Label>
                </TD>
            </TR>
        </TABLE>
</P>
<asp:Button id=bnReturn runat="server" Text="Return">
</asp:Button>
 
<asp:Button id=bnNext runat="server" Text="Next Version">
</asp:Button>
 
<asp:Button id=bnPrevious runat="server" Text="Previous Version" >
</asp:Button>
 
```

```
<asp:Button id=bnUpdate runat="server" Text="Update" >
</asp:Button>
 
<asp:Button id=bnRemove runat="server" Text="Remove" >
</asp:Button>
</form>
```

The AutView Codebehind

The code for loading the AutView Web form (see Listing 11-16) is standard: Get the data and place labels in a table. The first time the page is loaded, the version is set to 0. Because the content is retrieved in descending order, the first row is the most recent version. Later, when a user clicks the Next Version and Previous Version buttons, which both map to the bnMove_Click() method, a different version is loaded in the table. The version loaded is determined by the argument stored in the CommandEventArgs parameter.

Listing 11-16. The AutView Loading View Table

```
private void Page_Load(object sender, System.EventArgs e)
{

    int cid = Convert.ToInt32(Request.QueryString["ContentID"]);

    if (cid == 0)
    {
        Response.Redirect("error.aspx?ErrMsg=" +
            HttpUtility.UrlEncode("ContentID Missing"));
    }
    dt = new Content(
        new AppEnv(Context).GetConnection()).GetContentForID(cid);

    if (!IsPostBack)
    {
        BuildPage(0);
    }
}

private void BuildPage(int cver)
{
    DataRow dr = dt.Rows[cver];

    lbContentID.Text = dr["ContentID"].ToString();
```

```
    lbVersion.Text     = dr["Version"].ToString();
    lbHeadline.Text    = dr["Headline"].ToString();
    lbByline.Text      = dr["Byline"].ToString();
    lbTeaser.Text      = dr["Teaser"].ToString();
    lbBody.Text        = dr["Body"].ToString();
    lbTagline.Text     = dr["Tagline"].ToString();
    lbStatus.Text      = dr["Status"].ToString();
    lbUpdateUser.Text  = dr["UpdateUserID"].ToString();
    lbModifiedDate.Text = dr["ModifiedDate"].ToString();
    lbCreationDate.Text = dr["CreationDate"].ToString();

    ...
}
```

```
private void bnMove_Click(object sender, CommandEventArgs e)
{
    BuildPage(Convert.ToInt16(e.CommandArgument));
}
```

Hiding and Enabling Buttons

The BuildPage() method (see Listing 11-17) shows how the changes in the button states occur.

Two options exist when it comes to stopping a user from using a button: Disable it (gray it out) or don't display it. In the case of the Next Version and Previous Version buttons, I decided to simply gray them out. To do this, just set the button control's Enabled property to false. For grins and giggles, in the cases of the Update and Remove buttons, I decided to not display the buttons at all. To do this, you simply set the button's Visible property to false.

The only other thing that the BuildPage() method does of note is set the Next Version and Previous Version buttons' CommandArgument to its next and previous values, which will be retrieved later (as stated previously) when the buttons are clicked.

Listing 11-17. The AutView's BuildPage Method

```
private void BuildPage(int cver)
{
...
    if (cver > 0)
    {
        bnNext.Enabled = true;
        int tmp = cver - 1;
        bnNext.CommandArgument = tmp.ToString();
```

```
    }
    else
        bnNext.Enabled = false;

    if (cver < dt.Rows.Count-1)
    {
        bnPrevious.Enabled = true;
        int tmp = cver + 1;
        bnPrevious.CommandArgument = tmp.ToString();
    }
    else
        bnPrevious.Enabled = false;

    bnUpdate.Visible =
        (cver == 0 && Convert.ToInt32(dr["Status"]) == StatusCodes.Creating);
    bnRemove.Visible =
        (cver == 0 && Convert.ToInt32(dr["Status"]) == StatusCodes.Creating);
}
```

Removing Content

Normally, you wouldn't give an author the authority to remove content from a CMS system. Most likely, you might allow him to suggest that a piece of content should be removed. Usually, to do this, the remove process would set some sort of remove flag. The status flag would do nicely for this purpose.

Usually only someone with a high level of authority should be able to remove anything from the CMS repository.

For now, because the author is also the administrator, I am allowing the remove process to actually delete the content from the database. Plus, in early stages of development, a lot of test data is added to the database, and it needs to be removed. Without this function, there is no way to delete the content within CMS.NET. And hey, it also enables me to show you how to code a database remove process.

The AutRemove Web Page

The design for AutRemove.aspx, as you can see in Figure 11-12, contains nothing you haven't already covered. Display the headline and body so that the author can verify that it is the content to be removed. Write a warning message of how dangerous this step is and then provide two buttons: Remove Content or Cancel. Listing 11-18 shows that the design to accomplish this is short and sweet.

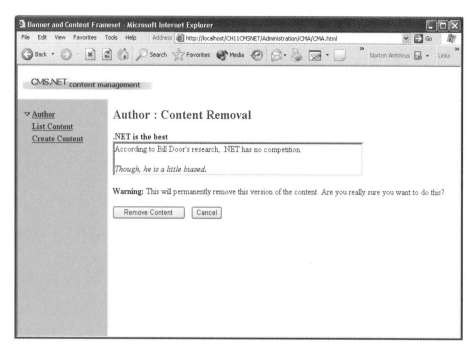

Figure 11-12. The AutRemove Web page

Listing 11-18. The AutRemove Web Design

```
<form id=AutRemove method=post runat="server">
  <H2><FONT color=darkslategray>Author : Content Removal</FONT></H2>
  <P>
    <asp:label id=lbWhichHeadline runat="server" Font-Bold="True">
    </asp:label>
    <BR>
    <asp:label id=lbWhichBody runat="server" Width="75%" BorderStyle="Inset">
    </asp:label>
  </P>
  <P>
    <B>Warning:</B>
    This will permanently remove this version of the content. Are
    you really sure you want to do this?
  </P>
  <P>
    <asp:button id=bnRemove runat="server" Text="Remove Content">
    </asp:button>
     
    <asp:button id=bnCancel runat="server" Text="Cancel">
    </asp:button>
  </P>
</form>
```

The AutRemove Codebehind

You have already seen most of AutRemove's code (see Listing 11-19) in some form or another in the preceding listing. The process is simple. It gets the ContentID passed to it. If the Web page was called without a ContentID, the error.aspx Web page is shown. Otherwise, the content is retrieved from the database, and the headline and body are placed in labels so that they can be displayed.

When the user decides to cancel and not remove the displayed content, the bnCancel_Click() method is called, redirecting the user back to the AutList Web page.

When the user decides to remove the content, the bnRemove_Click() method is called. It, in turn, calls the RemoveContent() database table help method. When the helper function returns, the user is redirected to the AutList Web page.

Listing 11-19. The AutRemove Web Page Codebehind

```
private void Page_Load(object sender, System.EventArgs e)
{
    cid = Convert.ToInt32(Request.QueryString["ContentID"]);

    if (cid == 0)
    {
        Response.Redirect("error.aspx?ErrMsg=" +
            HttpUtility.UrlEncode("ContentID Missing"));
    }

    content = new Content(new AppEnv(Context).GetConnection());
    dt = content.GetContentForID(cid);

    lbWhichHeadline.Text = dt.Rows[0]["Headline"].ToString();
    lbWhichBody.Text = dt.Rows[0]["Body"].ToString();
}

private void bnCancel_Click(object sender, System.EventArgs e)
{
    Response.Redirect("AutList.aspx");
}

private void bnRemove_Click(object sender, System.EventArgs e)
{
    content.RemoveContent(Convert.ToInt32(dt.Rows[0]["ContentID"]),
                            Convert.ToInt32(dt.Rows[0]["Version"]));

    Response.Redirect("AutList.aspx");
}
```

The RemoveContent() method (see Listing 11-20), like all helper functions that call stored procedures, is quite simple. Tell the SqlCommand which stored procedure to run, set up and populate any parameters, and then execute the stored procedure.

Listing 11-20. The Content Database Table Helper RemoveContent

```
public void RemoveContent(int cid, int ver)
{
    // DELETE FROM Content
    // WHERE ContentID=@cid
    //    AND Version=@ver

    SqlCommand Command = new SqlCommand("Content_Remove", m_Connection);
    Command.CommandType = CommandType.StoredProcedure;
    Command.Parameters.Add(new SqlParameter("@cid", SqlDbType.Int));
    Command.Parameters.Add(new SqlParameter("@ver", SqlDbType.Int));
    Command.Parameters["@cid"].Value = cid;
    Command.Parameters["@ver"].Value = ver;

    try
    {
        m_Connection.Open();
        Command.ExecuteNonQuery();
    }
    finally
    {
        m_Connection.Close();
    }
}
```

Submitting Content

The submitting process for now is just a placeholder. There is no one or no place to which to submit the content. Later, this function will send an e-mail to the next role, telling it that the content is available. For now, however, it will simply change the status from creating to submitted.

After this code is executed, you will see that you can no longer update or remove the content because all the options to do so have been disabled. To gain access again to those functions, just submit the same piece of content again. (Like I said, it is just a stub for now.)

The AutSubmit Web Page

As you can see in Figure 11-13, AutSubmit.aspx is virtually identical to AutRemove.aspx. In fact, I just copied it and changed the text and the button IDs. I am providing Listing 11-21 just so that you can see where I made the changes.

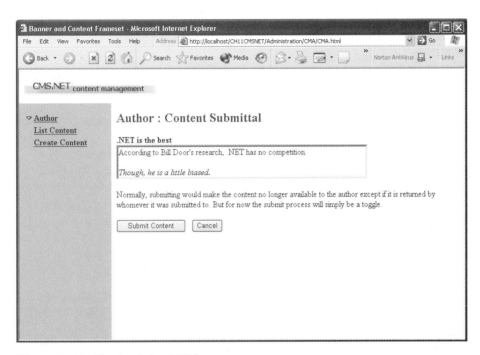

Figure 11-13. The AutSubmit Web page

Listing 11-21. The AutSubmit Web Design

```
<FORM id=AutSubmit method=post runat="server">
  <H2><FONT color=darkslategray>Author : Content Submittal</FONT></H2>
  <P>
    <asp:label id=lbWhichHeadline runat="server" Font-Bold="True">
    </asp:label>
    <BR>
    <asp:label id=lbWhichBody runat="server" Width="75%" BorderStyle="Inset">
    </asp:label>
  </P>
  <P>
    Normally, submitting would make the content no longer available to the
    author except if it is returned by whomever it was submitted to. But
    for now the submit process will simply be a toggle.
```

```
      </P>
      <P>
        <asp:button id=bnSubmit runat="server" Text="Submit Content">
        </asp:button>
         
        <asp:button id=bnCancel runat="server" Text="Cancel">
        </asp:button>
      </P>
    </FORM>
```

The AutSubmit Codebehind

AutSubmit's code for submitting is almost exactly the same as AutRemove's. The only way it differs is that it has a bnSubmit_Click() method (see Listing 11-22) instead of a bnRemove_Click() method. Also, this method gets the ContentID and the Version and then toggles the Status by calling the SetStatus() content database table helper method (see Listing 11-23).

Listing 11-22. The AutSubmit bnSubmit_Click Method

```
private void bnSubmit_Click(object sender, System.EventArgs e)
{
    content.SetStatus(Convert.ToInt32(dt.Rows[0]["ContentID"]),
        Convert.ToInt32(dt.Rows[0]["Version"]),
        (Convert.ToInt32(dt.Rows[0]["Status"]))== StatusCodes.Creating ?
            StatusCodes.Submitted : StatusCodes.Creating));

    Response.Redirect("AutList.aspx");
}
```

Listing 11-23. The Content Database Table Helper SetStatus

```
public void SetStatus(int ContentID, int Version, int Status)
{
    // UPDATE Content
    // SET
    //         Status       = @Status,
    //         ModifiedDate = @ModifiedDate
    // WHERE   ContentID = @ContentID
    //    AND  Version = @Version

    SqlCommand Command = new SqlCommand("Content_SetStatus", m_Connection);
    Command.CommandType  = CommandType.StoredProcedure;
```

```
Command.Parameters.Add(new SqlParameter("@ContentID", SqlDbType.Int));
Command.Parameters.Add(new SqlParameter("@Version", SqlDbType.Int));
Command.Parameters.Add(new SqlParameter("@Status", SqlDbType.Int));
Command.Parameters.Add(new SqlParameter("@ModifiedDate",
                                        SqlDbType.DateTime));

Command.Parameters["@ContentID"].Value    = ContentID;
Command.Parameters["@Version"].Value      = Version;
Command.Parameters["@Status"].Value       = Status;
Command.Parameters["@ModifiedDate"].Value = DateTime.Now;

try
{
    m_Connection.Open();
    Command.ExecuteNonQuery();
}
finally
{
    m_Connection.Close();
}
}
```

Summary

This chapter covered the CURVeS (create, update, remove, view, and submit) of CMS.NET's CMA.

First, it examined how to break a Web page into frames, and then it revisited the XML-driven NavBar. It also described in some detail how to handle errors. Next, it covered the Content database and then finished up by going over all the functions that make up the first cut at the CMS.NET's CMA.

The next chapter is going to take a look at cookies, authentication, authorization, encryption, and maybe some other big words.

CHAPTER 12

Cookies, Authentication, Authorization, and Encryption

IF YOU ARE LIKE ME, an author having complete control of your Web site gives you the willies. Well, after this chapter, you can rest a little more easily as you start securing CMS.NET.

The first thing you must realize is that there is no such thing as a perfectly secure site. If a computer is connected to a network, someone will eventually figure out a way into the system (if there is some reason to do so). Beating security is a game to some hackers. They have fun breaking walls of defenses that security teams spent weeks designing and implementing. And as a word to the wise, not all hacking attempts are from the outside. Internal staff members frequently are the root cause of many security breaches.

Security is like an onion. It is made up of layers upon layers. What I am covering in this book is just one layer. Some common layers that will not be covered are Windows NT or Windows 2000 and Internet Information Services (IIS) built-in security; firewalls; secured communications through SSL; and the frequently overlooked secured physical access to the system.

If the information on your site is highly classified, I strongly recommend that you hire a security expert. These people live and dream security. If your site is like many Web sites in which the information is anything but confidential, what I cover here is more than enough. By adding a firewall, implementing Windows NT or Windows 2000 and IIS built-in security, and adding SSL (https://) communications where appropriate, most Web sites should be secure enough.

This chapter does not cover all of the security features provided by .NET. Instead, it covers mostly what is used by CMS.NET.

ASP.NET Web Application Security

ASP.NET security addresses the areas of authentication, authorization, impersonation (the other big word I promised at the end of the preceding chapter), and encryption.

Authentication is the process of ensuring that a user is who he says he is. Authentication does not grant access; it just verifies the user's identity. The process of verifying authenticity usually means requesting a username and password from the user. If the username and password match a same combination stored in the system, the user is authenticated.

Authorization is the process of authorizing a user for access. Usually authorization is granted to a user having the correct username or to users who perform the correct role.

Impersonation is the process of giving an ASP.NET application the identity or authentication/authorization of a user so that it can execute on the user's behalf in a secured location. Impersonation is usually used if IIS is implemented to authenticate and authorize a user.

Encryption is the process of converting a stream of text into another stream of text that can't be read or deciphered. The most frequent usage of encryption in ASP.NET is for password storage.

CMS.NET Security Structure

Like most Web sites, CMS.NET has areas it wants to restrict from the average user. The approach CMS.NET takes in restricting access is fairly standard:

1. Authenticate the user.

2. Store the authentication so that it doesn't have to be repeated for the current session.

3. Authorize the user based on role or function.

4. Provide access.

Of authentication, authorization, impersonation, and encryption, CMS.NET only uses ASP.NET's authentication and encryption and, in the case of authentication, only partially.

It is true that ASP.NET provides a complete solution for each of these four areas, but I feel the choice of using the web.config file to store all security information is a little too dangerous, and the reliance on IIS for role-based authorization is too cumbersome. Also, CMS.NET has no need for impersonation because each task performed must have an authenticated and authorized user to carry it out.

Figure 12-1 shows CMS.NET's approach to security. A client request is first processed by IIS. How IIS is configured is really of little concern to CMS.NET. In fact, the default settings work just fine.

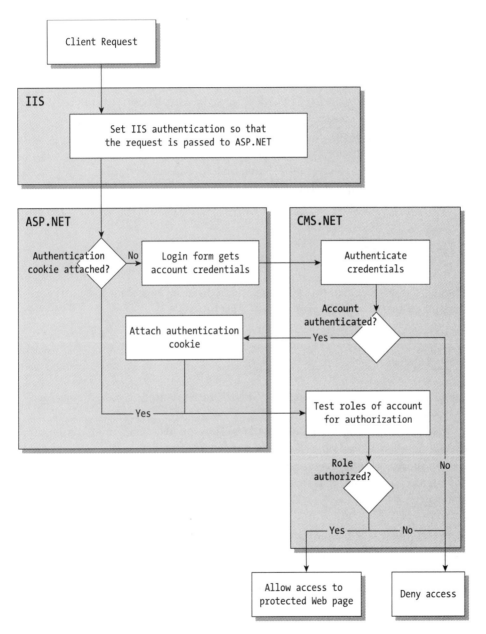

Figure 12-1. CMS.NET's security flow

After the request makes it through IIS, it is challenged by ASP.NET. If ASP.NET finds that the request has an authentication cookie attached to it—meaning that the user has already been authenticated for this session—it bypasses the next few steps and goes directly to authorization.

On the other hand, if no authentication cookie is found, the request is sent to a login form to get enough information for authentication. CMS.NET takes the authentication information and compares it to its database of password-encrypted valid users. If CMS.NET finds that the user is authentic, it then passes the request back to ASP.NET so that it can create an authentication cookie for the next request in the session. If CMS.NET fails to find an account to match the user, the user is denied access.

Because requests are authorized based on the roles of the user, ASP.NET then immediately sends the request back to CMS.NET so that it can be compared to the user's authorized roles. If a user's role matches the needed role for the request, the user's request is allowed to access the desired Web page. Of course, if CMS.NET cannot find a matching role, the user is denied access to the system.

Cookies and Session Objects

Though cookies and session objects in and of themselves are not a security feature, it is important that I cover them at least briefly.

Cookies

Cookies are the primary method for ASP.NET implementation of session state and Web site security.

There is nothing special about cookies. They are just small, often temporary text files that are stored on a client computer. The information stored in a cookie is submitted along with any requests or responses.

Though many people worry about cookies, they are not dangerous. Here's why:

- All cookies have an expiration date. Upon expiration, the browser no longer submits the cookie with the request.

- A cookie is restricted to 2KB in size.

- The browser has a set limit on how much disk space to allocate for cookies. After this allotment is exceeded, older cookies are replaced.

- The storing of cookies on the client machine is handled by the browser and is outside the control of the server from which it originated.

- A Web server can only access cookies it has created itself.

The cookie file is made up of key/value pairs. It is possible to store almost any text in these files. In the case of ASP.NET and security, they contain session state and possibly an authentication certificate.

Because HTTP is *stateless,* meaning that each transaction it sends to and receives from a Web server is independent of the others, there was a time when Web servers tried to stuff all sorts of session information into cookies. All this did was make the amount of information transferred between client and server that much larger.

ASP.NET has come up with a more elegant solution. As of now, all that needs to be sent as a cookie is an autogenerated session identifying key. All the rest of the session data is then accessed using something called a session object.

To put it bluntly, with ASP.NET, you no longer have to worry about creating session cookies. The only reason to create cookies now is if you want the data stored on the client to persist longer than the current session.

To create a cookie, you create and instance a class called the HttpCookie, containing the key and value. Optionally, you can set the expiration date. Then, you add it to the HTTP Response.

```
HttpCookie TheAnswerCookie = new HttpCookie("TheAnswer", "42");


// Expire one year from now
DateTime dt = DateTime.Now;
TimeSpan ts = new TimeSpan(365,0,0,0);
TheAnswerCookie.Expires = dt.Add(ts);


Response.Cookies.Add(TheAnswerCookie);
```

Getting the cookie key and values from a request is only slightly more difficult—as you have to deal with an array within an array—because a request can have multiple cookies and each cookie can have multiple values. The following code displays the authentication cookie, which was previously discussed, and SessionID.

```
HttpCookieCollection allCookies = Request.Cookies;


for ( int key = 0; key < allCookies.Count; key++)
{
    HttpCookie thisCookie = allCookies[key];
```

```
Response.Write("Name: " + thisCookie.Name.ToString() + "<BR>");

for ( int val = 0; val < thisCookie.Values.Count; val++)
{
    Response.Write("Value" + val + ": " + thisCookie.Values[val] + "<BR>");
}
}
```

Session Objects

Session objects are very similar in function to cookies. The big difference is that the data is stored on the server and not on the client. This means the session data doesn't have to be sent across the Internet. It also means it can be stored in its native form and doesn't have to be converted continually to text or, in some cases, encrypted text.

This is a godsend to a developer because you really don't have to worry about session state any longer. All the nitty-gritty of maintaining session state is handled behind the scenes by ASP.NET.

Session objects are probably some of the easiest things to code in ASP.NET. They are stored and retrieved using key/value pairs. To store a session object, you simply write the following:

```
Session["StringKey"] = object;
```

To retrieve a session object, use the following:

```
object = (ObjectType) Session["StringKey"];
```

If the object type is string, the type caste is not needed. The following is a simple example of placing a string and an integer on a session object and then retrieving them again:

```
int TheAnswer = 42;
Session["UltraSecretPassword"] = "password";
Session["TheAnswer"] = TheAnswer;
...
String pwd = Session["UltraSecretPassword"];
int WhatIsQuestion = (int) Session["TheAnswer"];
```

Authentication

Authentication is the process of obtaining and verifying the identity of the user requesting access to a restricted part of the Web site. .NET provides three different methods of authenticating users.

Forms Authentication

The process by which users are authenticated is by being challenged for the existence of an authentication cookie. If the cookie is available, authentication succeeds. If it's missing, the request is redirected to a custom HTML page, which requests a username and password. These are then fed back into the forms authentication process to be authenticated.

Passport Authentication

This is a centralized authentication service provided by Microsoft that allows a single logon.

Windows Authentication

This is the authentication provided by IIS. All authentications are done by IIS, which in turn passes the authenticated identity to ASP.NET for use. This method uses impersonation to allow the ASP.NET application to run.

CMS.NET Authentication Code Updates

CMS.NET uses only a portion of the forms authentication method of authenticating. Basically, it uses ASP.NET to challenge the request for an authentication cookie. If it is found, it forwards the request to CMS.NET for authorization. If it doesn't find the cookie, it forwards the request to CMS.NET to be authenticated. Once authenticated, CMS.NET sends the request back to ASP.NET, which generates an authentication cookie and then sends the request back to CMS.NET for authorization.

Updating web.config

Enabling authentication in ASP.NET requires only the updating of the web.config file. On the other hand, implementing authentication takes a little more effort, as you will find out.

The changes to web.config are quite simple (see Listing 12-1). Just change the default `<authentication>` element mode attribute of None to the desired authentication method of Windows, Passport, or Forms. In the case of CMS.NET, you changed it to Forms. Then, because you selected forms authentication, you need to add the `<forms>` element and provide two attributes: loginUrl, which is the virtual path to the login form page, and name, which is the name assigned to the cookie.

Listing 12-1. Root Directory web.config Authentication Updates

```
<!-- AUTHENTICATION This section sets the authentication policies of the
    application. Possible modes are "Windows", "Forms", "Passport" and "None"
-->
<authentication mode="Forms">
    <forms loginUrl="login.aspx" name=".CMSNETAUTH" />
</authentication>
```

There are many other options that will not be covered here.

NOTE *I recommend reading the documentation that comes with .NET. It actually provides a fairly thorough explanation of the web.config file. Just look for "ASP.NET Configuration Sections."*

Creating Directory-Specific web.config

You would think that now that you have `<authentication>` enabled, ASP.NET would start to challenge all users for authentication. Well, not quite. If everyone can access a directory, there is no need to authenticate anyone. This is the case with the root directory of CMS.NET. To have ASP.NET challenge a user, the web.config file must contain `<authorization>` elements.

Wait a minute! What happens if you want one area of the Web site to allow all users and another to allow only specific users? How can one web.config file handle this? It can't. You must include a web.config file for each directory for which you want specific user access. You don't—in fact, you can't—include all elements of the web.config file in a subdirectory. For authentication/authorization, you only need a web.config file that contains `<authorization>` elements.

In CMS.NET, you want everybody to have access to the root directory, so you don't add any <authorization> elements in the root directory copy of web.config. On the other hand, you only want specific people to access the administration directory. Listing 12-2 shows how the web.config file should look.

Listing 12-2. Subdirectory-Specific web.config

```
<?xml version="1.0" encoding="utf-8" ?>
<configuration>

  <system.web>

    <authorization>
        <allow roles="Administrator,Author,Editor,Authorizer,Deployer" />
        <deny users="?" />
    </authorization>

  </system.web>

</configuration>
```

The only element that ASP.NET cares about is the following:

```
<deny users="?" />
```

This line means that the directory denies all anonymous users. You can also think of this element as "authenticate everyone."

The element

```
        <allow roles="Administrator,Author,Editor,Authorizer,Deployer" />
```

does absolutely nothing because window authentication is not enabled. Role-based authorization is only done using Windows authentication.

So, why have it here? CMS.NET has its own version of role-based authentication, and this seems like the correct place to put this entry. Maybe, in the future, forms authentication will have role-based authorization, and you will be able to remove the role-based code from CMS.NET. CMS.NET's role-based authorization will be covered shortly.

The Login Web Page

You place the login Web page in the root directory so that you can access it without having to worry about authentication or authorization. And, as you can see in Figure 12-2, the Web page is simply two text boxes and a check box.

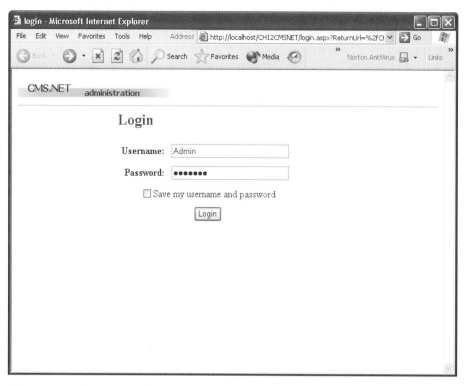

Figure 12-2. The login Web page

As you can see in Login.aspx (see Listing 12-3), nothing is new except for a check box intrinsic control that you haven't used until now.

Listing 12-3. The Login Web Page

```
<form id="login" method="post" runat="server">
  <IMG src="Administration/Images/administration.jpg">
  <HR width="100%" SIZE=1>
  <TABLE cellSpacing=1 cellPadding=1 width="95%" border=0>
    <TR>
      <TD width="25%"></TD>
      <TD>
        <H2><FONT color=darkslategray>Login</FONT></H2>
        <P>
          <asp:ValidationSummary id=ValidationSummary1 runat="server"
              HeaderText="The following error(s) occurred while login in:">
          </asp:ValidationSummary>
        </P>
```

```
<P>
  <asp:Label id=ErrorMsg runat="server" ForeColor="Red"></asp:Label>
</P>
  <TABLE cellSpacing=1 cellPadding=5 width=300 border=0>
    <TR>
      <TD width="15%">
        <P align=right><STRONG>Username:</STRONG></P>
      </TD>
      <TD width="85%">
        <asp:TextBox id=tbUsername runat="server" Width="100%">
        </asp:TextBox>
      </TD>
      <TD width="2%">
        <asp:RequiredFieldValidator id=RequiredFieldValidator1
            runat="server" ErrorMessage="You must enter a Username"
            Display="Dynamic" ControlToValidate="tbUsername">*
        </asp:RequiredFieldValidator>
      </TD>
    </TR>
    <TR>
      <TD>
        <P align=right><STRONG>Password:</STRONG></P>
      </TD>
      <TD>
        <asp:TextBox id=tbPassword runat="server" Width="100%"
            TextMode="Password">
        </asp:TextBox>
      </TD>
      <TD>
        <asp:RequiredFieldValidator id=RequiredFieldValidator2
            runat="server" ErrorMessage="You must enter a password"
            Display="Dynamic" ControlToValidate="tbPassword">*
        </asp:RequiredFieldValidator>
      </TD>
    </TR>
    <TR>
      <TD colSpan=3>
        <P align=center>
          <asp:CheckBox id=cbPersist runat="server"
              Text="Save my username and password">
          </asp:CheckBox>
        </P>
      </TD>
```

```
                </TR>
                <TR>
                  <TD colSpan=3>
                    <P align=center>
                      <asp:Button id=bnLogin runat="server" Text="Login">
                      </asp:Button>
                    </P>
                  </TD>
                </TR>
              </TABLE>
          </TD>
        </TR>
      </TABLE>
  </form>
```

The Codebehind for Login.aspx (see Listing 12-4) has some interesting code located in the Page_Load() method. First, the code verifies that the user has entered both a UserName and a Password, and then it executes a new Account database helper method Authenticate(). This code, as you will see shortly, authenticates the user against the account in the database. If the user is authentic, ASP.NET's long-winded FormsAuthentication.RedirectFromLoginPage() method is executed to create an authentication cookie using the UserName.

I originally wondered why a cookie was even needed for authentication because a session object could be used. I had forgotten that it is possible for an authentication cookie to persist after the session has ended. This is what the second Boolean parameter of RedirectFromLoginPage() is for.

Listing 12-4. The Login Codebehind Page_Load Method

```
private void Page_Load(object sender, System.EventArgs e)
{
    if (IsPostBack)
    {
        Page.Validate();

        if (Page.IsValid)
        {
            Account account = new Account(new AppEnv(Context).GetConnection());

            if (account.Authenticated(tbUsername.Text, tbPassword.Text))
```

```
        {
            FormsAuthentication.RedirectFromLoginPage(tbUsername.Text,
                cbPersist.Checked);
        }
        else
            ErrorMsg.Text = account.Message;
    }
  }
}
```

You might have noticed that nowhere in the code is the challenge for the authentication cookie. ASP.NET handles that code for you. The only way you know it is there is that you mysteriously jump to the login Web page instead of the restrict Web page you were expecting.

The Account.Authentication Method

ASP.NET provides a built-in facility to handle authentications. First, you add a <credentials> element to your web.config file, as follows:

```
<credentials passwordFormat="None">
    <user name="Admin" password="CMS.Net" />
    <user name="sfraser" password="Agr8pswd" />
</credentials>
```

Then you call the following:

```
FormsAuthentication.Authenticate(tbUsername.Text, tbPassword.Text);
```

It is even possible to encrypt the passwords in the web.config file. (Encryption is covered later in this chapter.) The problem with this method of authentication is that you have to continually update the web.config file for every new user. For some Web sites, that could be hundreds of thousands of users. This could make for a very big web.config file. Plus, having all the users in a well-known file is just begging for a hacker to figure out how to get in.

CMS.NET places all its users in a database. This method is more secure and, at the same time, easier to maintain. Listing 12-5 shows the Account database helper method Authenticate() without encryption. (You will come back to this file after I cover encryption.) It is a very simple method. Simply get the user out of the database that has the same UserName as was entered and then see if the Password matches. Nothing could be easier.

Listing 12-5. The Account.Authenticated Database Helper Method

```csharp
public bool Authenticated(string username, string password)
{
    // SELECT Password
    //   FROM Account
    //   WHERE UserName=@username

    bool ret = false;

    SqlCommand Command = new SqlCommand("Account_Authenticated", m_Connection);
    Command.CommandType = CommandType.StoredProcedure;

    Command.Parameters.Add(new SqlParameter("@username", SqlDbType.Char, 32));
    Command.Parameters["@username"].Value = username;

    try
    {
        m_Connection.Open();
        SqlDataReader dr = Command.ExecuteReader();

        if (dr.Read())
        {
            if(dr["Password"].ToString().Trim().Equals(password.Trim()))
            {
                ret = true;
            }
            else
            {
                m_ErrorMsg = "Invalid password.";
            }
        }
        else
        {
            m_ErrorMsg = "User Name not found.";
            ret = false;
        }
    }
    finally
    {
        m_Connection.Close();
    }

    return ret;
}
```

NavBar Logout

Because CMS.NET provides the capability for a user to keep an authentication cookie available indefinitely, it is a good idea to provide a way for the user to log out or, as ASP.NET puts it, SignOut(). The NavBar is always available to the user, so placing the Logout button on it only seems logical (see Figure 12-3).

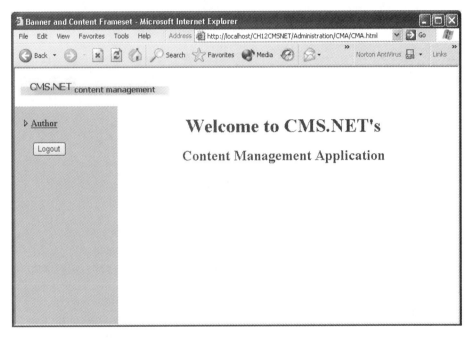

Figure 12-3. The Logout button on the NavBar

Signing out deletes the persistent authorization cookie, thus forcing the user to log in again to do anything in the administration system. You will even find that the Back history button does not access anything.

As you can see in Listing 12-6, signing out is a breeze. Getting rid of the frames of the administration system and placing the login Web page on a full screen of its own requires a little bit of magic and a whole lot of pixie dust.

I couldn't find an elegant way of doing this in C#, so I had to revert to JavaScript. When the Logout button is clicked, the Codebehind method embeds JavaScript directly into the HTML, which is then sent over to the client. When the browser interprets this HTML, the JavaScript is immediately executed because it is in the body of the HTML and is not part of a function. Thus, when the Logout button is clicked, the user is signed out and a full-screen login Web page displays. Pretty spiffy, don't you think?

Listing 12-6. The NavBar Codebehind bnLogout_Click Method

```
private void bnLogout_Click(object sender, System.EventArgs e)
{
    FormsAuthentication.SignOut();
    this.Controls.Add(new LiteralControl(
        "<script language=javascript>" +
        "    window.parent.location='../admin.aspx';" +
        "</script>")
    );
}
```

Authorization

ASP.NET provides two ways to authorize a user on the system: file authorization and URL authorization.

File authorization uses Windows itself to authorize a user's access to a particular file. The authorization process is hidden from ASP.NET because Windows has an access control list (ACL) check on the Web page to see if the user has access.

The *URL authorization* process is similar to file authorization except that the user is authorized over a URI namespace as opposed to a particular file. URL authorization uses a positive/negative approach, meaning you can both allow and deny different sets of users.

Determining which users have (or don't have) access is handled by the <authorization> element in the, you guessed it, web.config file. The elements within the <authorization> element, I feel, are quite self-evident. You can either <allow> or <deny> a role, a user, or a group of users. You can list all your roles and users individually or comma separated, as shown in Listing 12-7.

Listing 12-7. The web.config Authorization Element

```
<authorization>
    <allow roles="Administrator, Author, Editor, Authorizer, Deployer" />
    <allow user="Dick, Jane, Spot" />
    <deny users="?" />
</authorization>
```

Authorizations to a Web page can be given to individual users or to user roles. Grouping users into roles simplifies the authorization process considerably. If you authorize by user only, then any time that user's role changes, you have to find all occurrences of the user in each web.config file, delete the authorization of her old role, and then add authorizations for the new role. For large sites, this could be a long and error-prone exercise.

With roles, all you have to do is make changes in one place. You just have to delete the old role, add the new one, and you are done.

ASP.NET Role-Based Authorization

When I first heard that ASP.NET did role-based authorization, I was very excited—until I found out that the only way to implement it was using Windows authentication. This requires all users and their roles to be placed in the IIS database—not the solution I had in mind.

This solution causes a lot of duplicated effort because I already had all my users in the CMS.NET Account table. It also is not as secure and is harder to maintain because you have to maintain a separate database outside of the CMS.NET environment. The duplicated effort is the responsibility of the user administrator. The major problem is that the duplicate effort is an ongoing thing.

CMS.NET Role-Based Authorization

I decided to implement my own role-based authorization. I hope that, in the future, Microsoft will see the merits of an implementation such as this and add it to ASP.NET.

The solution is simple. Get the `<allow roles="">` elements out of the web.config file's current directory and the username from `Page.User.Identity.Name`. Check the roles allowed, as specified by the web.config file, against the roles of the user. A match allows the user access. Obviously, if no match occurs, the user gets the boot.

To be fair, the CMS.NET solution also requires a little bit of duplicate effort. Unlike ASP.NET, however, CMS.NET's duplicated effort is strictly on the part of the developer and is done once for each restricted Web page.

Role-Based Authorized Web Page Modifications

Let's take a look at an example of the authorization code you will need to add to every restricted Web page. Listing 12-8 shows all the changes needed to add authorization to Admin.aspx.

Listing 12-8. Changes to Admin.aspx to Add Authorization

```
namespace CMSNET.Administration
{
    public class admin : CMSNET.Common.AuthorizedPage
    {
    . . .
    }
}
```

Yep, that's it—one line.

All you need to do is change the base class of the Codebehind's class (in this case, admin) from System.Web.UI.Page to CMSNET.Common.AuthorizedPage. Of course, all the magic happens in the AuthorizedPage class with the help of inheritance. So, let's take a look behind the curtain.

System.Web.UI.Page Replacement—AuthorizedPage

Due to inheritance, you are able to plug in the AuthorizedPage class wherever the Page class was. AuthorizedPage is really just Page with a couple of methods and a property tacked on. Anything you can do with Page you can also do with AuthorizedPage (see Listing 12-9).

Because nearly every class in CMS.NET uses the AppEnv utility class, I decided to make it a property of AuthorizedPage so that it will be readily available. Plus, many of the Web pages redirect to an error page, so I added a simple method to handle this as well.

The Roles() method is the majority of the class. All it does is open, into an XMLDocument, the version of web.config in which the current Web page resides. Then it navigates to the <authorization> element and grabs all the <allow roles=""> elements. Finally, it places all the roles in an ArrayList to be grabbed by whoever needs them.

The last method, OnInit(), is an override method for the base class Page. First, it calls the base class' method and then it simply takes the roles and the current UserID and sends them to the AccountRoles database table helper method Authorization(). You might have noticed that this method uses all the other methods and the property in AuthorizedPage.

The key to the simplicity of this change is that the OnInit() is already called within the autogenerated code. This saves you from having to add this function call yourself.

Listing 12-9. CMSNET.Common.AuthorizedPage

```
public class AuthorizedPage : System.Web.UI.Page
{
    private AppEnv m_appenv;

    public AuthorizedPage()
    {
        m_appenv = new AppEnv(Context);
    }

    public AppEnv appEnv
    {
        get
        {
            return m_appenv;
        }
    }

    public void Page_Error(string error)
    {
        Response.Redirect("/CMSNET/Error.aspx?errmsg=" +
            HttpUtility.UrlEncode(error));
    }

    public ArrayList Roles()
    {
        ArrayList rolelist = new ArrayList();

        XmlReader xtr =
            new XmlTextReader(File.OpenRead(Server.MapPath("web.config")));

        XmlDocument doc = new XmlDocument();
        doc.Load(xtr);
        xtr.Close();

        XmlElement root = doc.DocumentElement;
        XmlNodeList nodes = root.GetElementsByTagName("authorization");

        if (nodes.Count > 0)
        {
            for (int i = 0; i < nodes.Count; i++)
            {
```

```
            XmlNodeList allowNodes =
              ((XmlElement)(nodes.Item(i))).GetElementsByTagName("allow");

            for (int j = 0; j < allowNodes.Count; j++)
            {
                XmlAttributeCollection roleColl =
                    allowNodes.Item(j).Attributes;
                XmlAttribute role =
                    (XmlAttribute)roleColl.GetNamedItem("roles");
                string[] temp = role.Value.Split(',');
                for (int k = 0; k < temp.Length; k++)
                    rolelist.Add(temp[k]);
            }
        }
    }
    return rolelist;
}

override protected void OnInit(EventArgs e)

{
    base.OnInit(e);

    AccountRoles accountRoles = new AccountRoles(appEnv.GetConnection());
    if (!accountRoles.Authorization(Roles(), User.Identity.Name))
    {
        Page_Error(accountRoles.Message);
    }
}
}
```

AccountRoles Database Table

Basically, all the AccountRoles database (see Table 12-1) does is store a list of all the roles that an account can have.

Table 12-1. AccountRoles Database Table Design

COLUMN NAME	DATA TYPE	LENGTH	KEY	DESCRIPTION
AccountID	int	4	true	The Account ID for which this role is being set
Role	char	32	true	The role that the Account ID will fulfill
CreationDate	datetime	8	false	The date that the account role was created

AccountRoles is a very simple database table. All it contains is the AccountID, the Role, and the date that the record was created. The key is both the AccountID and the Role.

AccountRoles.Authorization Method

The final piece of the actual authorization process happens within the AccountRoles database helper method authorization. Listing 12-10 shows the AccountID being selected from the Account database using the username. With the AccountID, it is now possible to select all roles out of the AccountRoles database table.

At this point, you have all the roles allowed to see the Web page and all the roles that the user performs. All it takes is a simple intersection of the two to find out whether authorization should be granted. The code does this by trying to find a strings match between the two lists. When the first equality happens, the method leaves with a true value.

The only thing that might catch a programmer's eye is that the return statement happens before the closing of the database connection. You might think that the close never occurs. This is not the case because it is within a try/finally exception clause that ensures that the statements within the finally clause are always completed (in this case, even without an exception occurring).

Listing 12-10. The AccountRoles.Authorization Method

```
public bool Authorization(ArrayList roles, string username)
{
    int AccountID;

    try
    {
        Account account = new Account(m_Connection);
        AccountID = account.GetAccountID(username);
    }
    catch (Exception e)
    {
        m_ErrorMsg = e.Message;
        return false;
    }

    // SELECT Role
    //   FROM AccountRoles
    //   WHERE AccountID=@AccountID

    SqlCommand Command = new SqlCommand("AccountRoles_GetRolesForID",
        m_Connection);
    Command.CommandType = CommandType.StoredProcedure;

    Command.Parameters.Add(new SqlParameter("@AccountID", SqlDbType.Int));
    Command.Parameters["@AccountID"].Value = AccountID;

    try
    {
        m_Connection.Open();
        SqlDataReader dr = Command.ExecuteReader();

        while (dr.Read())
        {
            foreach ( string role in roles)
            {
                if (role.Trim().Equals(dr["Role"].ToString().Trim()))
                    return true;
            }
        }
    }
```

```
    finally
    {
        m_Connection.Close();
    }


    m_ErrorMsg = "User not Authorized";
    return false;
}
```

Update Setup3 for Authorization

Now that you have a roles database, you have to go back and revisit the setup procedure covered in Chapter 10. When you wrote this initially, you did not include the setting up of the role of administrator for the Administrator account.

The Codebehind for setup3 is nothing challenging, as you can see in Listings 12-11 and 12-12.

Listing 12-11. The Setup3 Codebehind Page_Load Method Authorization Changes

```
private void Page_Load(object sender, System.EventArgs e)
{
    if (IsPostBack)
    {
        Page.Validate();

        if (Page.IsValid)
        {
            try
            {
                . . .
                ProcessAdministratorName();
                ProcessAccountRoles();

                Response.Redirect("setup4.aspx");
            }
        }
    }
}
```

Listing 12-12. The New Setup3 Codebehind ProcessAccountRoles Method

```
private void ProcessAccountRoles()
{

    try
    {

        role.Insert(1, "Administrator");

    }
    catch (SqlException)
    {

        // Duplicate key means jobs done already . . . move on.

    }

}
```

As you can see in Listing 12-13, the AccountRoles database help Insert()
method is not much different from any of the others you have previously seen.

Listing 12-13. The AccountRoles Database Helper Insert Method

```
public void Insert(int AccountID, string Role)
{
    // INSERT
    //   INTO AccountRoles ( AccountID,  Role,  ModifiedDate,  CreationDate)
    // VALUES              (@AccountID, @Role, @ModifiedDate, @CreationDate)

    SqlCommand Command = new SqlCommand("AccountRoles_Insert", m_Connection);
    Command.CommandType  = CommandType.StoredProcedure;

    Command.Parameters.Add(new SqlParameter("@AccountID", SqlDbType.Int));
    Command.Parameters.Add(new SqlParameter("@Role", SqlDbType.Char, 32));
    Command.Parameters.Add(new SqlParameter("@CreationDate",
                                            SqlDbType.DateTime));

    Command.Parameters["@AccountID"].Value    = AccountID;
    Command.Parameters["@Role"].Value         = Role;
    Command.Parameters["@CreationDate"].Value = DateTime.Now;

    try
    {
        m_Connection.Open();
        Command.ExecuteNonQuery();
    }
```

```
    finally
    {
        m_Connection.Close();
    }
}
```

Encryption

Passwords are usually stored encrypted. .NET provides two different encryption algorithms to encrypt passwords:

- *MD5:* Generates Message Digest 5 hash code. This algorithm is the faster of the two provided by .NET.

- *SHA1:* Generates a Secure Hash Algorithm 1 hash code. This algorithm is the more secure of the two.

To encrypt a password, you use a method with the overly lengthy name of `HashPasswordForStoringInConfigFile()`. Encryption is a one-way street for these two algorithms. There is no decrypting method.

web.config Credentials Element

For people who decide to use ASP.NET's method of authorization instead of the one used by CMS.NET, it is possible to store the credentials of a user using an encrypted password. Listing 12-14 shows credentials using a SHA1 encryption on the passwords. It is also possible to use MD5 encryption instead.

Listing 12-14. SHA1 Password-Encrypted Credentials

```
<credentials passwordFormat="SHA1" >
  <user name="Admin"   password="B34272C363EADA35031C69B6825C1CCF16154D67" />
  <user name="sfraser" password="5D1FF37BC03988F4A679117E75FD035759B2CBA6" />
</credentials>
```

As of this book's printing, there still is no method provided by ASP.NET (other than standard XML) to add credentials to web.config. You currently have two options: write the XML to update web.config or generate a script that dumps out the encrypted version of a password to screen or file so that you can paste it manually into the web.config file.

Updating Account Database Helper Methods for Encryption

All encryption code for CMS.NET is located in the Account helper class, so let's visit it one more time.

As you can see in Listings 12-15 and 12-16, the code updated in the Insert() and Update() methods is exactly the same. The code uses a little cheat. All SHA1 encryptions generate a hash code of exactly 40 characters. Thus, it is possible to see if the value passed into the methods contains an already-encrypted password or an unencrypted version by checking its length. Unencrypted passwords have a maximum length of 16 characters, which is enforced by the MaxLength property of the password entry fields. Therefore, whenever the password is not equal to 40, it gets encrypted before it is placed in the database.

Listing 12-15. Account Database Helper Insert Method with Encryption

```
public void Insert(string UserName, string Password, string Email)
{
    // INSERT INTO Account (UserName, Password, Email,
    //                      ModifiedDate, CreationDate)
    // VALUES (@UserName, @Password, @Email, @ModifiedDate, @CreationDate)

    SqlCommand Command = new SqlCommand("Account_Insert", m_Connection);
    Command.CommandType  = CommandType.StoredProcedure;

    Command.Parameters.Add(new SqlParameter("@UserName", SqlDbType.Char, 32));
    Command.Parameters.Add(new SqlParameter("@Password", SqlDbType.Char, 40));
    Command.Parameters.Add(new SqlParameter("@Email", SqlDbType.Char, 64));
    Command.Parameters.Add(new SqlParameter("@ModifiedDate",
                                                SqlDbType.DateTime));
    Command.Parameters.Add(new SqlParameter("@CreationDate",
                                                SqlDbType.DateTime));

    Command.Parameters["@UserName"].Value = UserName;

    if (Password.Length == 40)
    {
        Command.Parameters["@Password"].Value = Password;
    }
    else
    {
        Command.Parameters["@Password"].Value =
            FormsAuthentication.HashPasswordForStoringInConfigFile
            (Password, "SHA1");
    }
```

```
    Command.Parameters["@Email"].Value = Email;
    Command.Parameters["@ModifiedDate"].Value = DateTime.Now;
    Command.Parameters["@CreationDate"].Value = DateTime.Now;

    try
    {
        m_Connection.Open();
        Command.ExecuteNonQuery();
    }
    finally
    {
        m_Connection.Close();
    }
}
```

Listing 12-16. Account Database Helper Update Method with Encryption

```
public void Update(int AccountID, string UserName, string Password,
                   string Email)
{
    //    UPDATE Account
    //      SET UserName    = @UserName,
    //          Password    = @Password,
    //          Email       = @Email,
    //          ModifiedDate = @ModifiedDate
    //    WHERE AccountID = @AccountID

    SqlCommand Command = new SqlCommand("Account_Update", m_Connection);
    Command.CommandType   = CommandType.StoredProcedure;

    Command.Parameters.Add(new SqlParameter("@AccountID", SqlDbType.Int));
    Command.Parameters.Add(new SqlParameter("@UserName", SqlDbType.Char, 32));
    Command.Parameters.Add(new SqlParameter("@Password", SqlDbType.Char, 40));
    Command.Parameters.Add(new SqlParameter("@Email", SqlDbType.Char, 64));
    Command.Parameters.Add(new SqlParameter("@ModifiedDate",
                                            SqlDbType.DateTime));

    Command.Parameters["@AccountID"].Value = AccountID;
    Command.Parameters["@UserName"].Value = UserName;

    if (Password.Length == 40)
    {
        Command.Parameters["@Password"].Value = Password;
    }
```

```
        else
        {
            Command.Parameters["@Password"].Value =
                FormsAuthentication.HashPasswordForStoringInConfigFile
                (Password, "SHA1");
        }
```

```
    Command.Parameters["@Email"].Value = Email;
    Command.Parameters["@ModifiedDate"].Value = DateTime.Now;

    try
    {
        m_Connection.Open();
        Command.ExecuteNonQuery();
    }
    finally
    {
        m_Connection.Close();
    }
}
```

The last place that encryption is used is in the Authenticated() method (see Listing 12-17). Whenever you receive a password in the authentication form, it comes unencrypted. Therefore, to verify that the password matches the value in the database, it needs to be encrypted.

Remember, SHA1 is a one-way encryption. Therefore, the only way to see if both passwords match is to encrypt both the database password and the authentication check password.

Listing 12-17. Account Database Helper Authenticated Method with Encryption
```
public bool Authenticated(string username, string password)
{
    // SELECT Password
    //    FROM Account
    //   WHERE UserName=@username

    bool ret = false;

    SqlCommand Command = new SqlCommand("Account_Authenticated", m_Connection);
    Command.CommandType = CommandType.StoredProcedure;

    Command.Parameters.Add(new SqlParameter("@username", SqlDbType.Char, 32));
    Command.Parameters["@username"].Value = username;
```

```
try
{
    m_Connection.Open();
    SqlDataReader dr = Command.ExecuteReader();

    if (dr.Read())
    {
        if(dr["Password"].ToString().Equals(
            FormsAuthentication.HashPasswordForStoringInConfigFile
            (password, "SHA1")))
        {
            ret = true;
        }
        else
        {
            m_ErrorMsg = "Invalid password";
        }
    }
    else
    {
        m_ErrorMsg = "User Name not found.";
        ret = false;
    }
}
finally
{
    m_Connection.Close();
}

return ret;
}
```

WARNING *If you have already run the setup routine for CMS.NET, you will have to rerun it now so that your admin account will be able to log back in. The reason is that the authentication routine has been changed to look for an encrypted password but the admin password, in the databases, is readable text. Simply setting the value of the* setup *key to* false *in your root copy of web.config and then setting up CMS.NET again by executing the Web page will fix this problem.*

Restricting the CMA

Okay, you have all the code needed to support different users and roles. Let's put it into practice by restricting the CMA directory to be available only to administrators and authors. The first step is to add a web.config file that authorizes only the roles of administrator and author to the CMA directory developed in Chapter 11.

Next, change all the Aut Web page Codebehind to inherit `AuthorizedPage`. Not much of a challenge, I would say.

NavBar Update for Handling Roles

When you create a NavBar, it doesn't make sense to allow navigation to areas of the Web site for which the user does not have authorization. This will only confuse and frustrate the user. So let's give NavBar.aspx a minor facelift so that it only displays menus the user can access.

First, you need to make a small change to CMAMenu.xml (see Listing 12-18). You need to add an optional element of `<authorization>` directly after the `<Menu>` element. If this element is present, the NavBar will only present the menu if the user has authorization. To keep compatibility with the previous version, all users can see a menu if no `<authorization>` element is present.

Listing 12-18. Updated CMAMenu.xml with Authorization

```xml
<?xml version="1.0" encoding="utf-8" ?>
<MainMenu>
  <Menu>
    <authorization>Administrator</authorization>
    <MenuName>Account Admin</MenuName>
    <MenuItem>
      <Name>List Accounts</Name>
      <Link>AdmAcnt/AdmAcntList.aspx</Link>
    </MenuItem>
    <MenuItem>
      <Name>Create Account</Name>
      <Link>AdmAcnt/AdmAcntCreate.aspx</Link>
    </MenuItem>
  </Menu>
  <Menu>
    <authorization>Administrator,Author</authorization>
    <MenuName>Author</MenuName>
    <MenuItem>
      <Name>List Content</Name>
```

```
        <Link>Aut/AutList.aspx</Link>
      </MenuItem>
      <MenuItem>
        <Name>Create Content</Name>
        <Link>Aut/AutCreate.aspx</Link>
      </MenuItem>
    </Menu>
```
```
  <Menu>
    <MenuName>All</MenuName>
    <MenuItem>
      <Name>Welcome</Name>
      <Link>Welcome.html</Link>
    </MenuItem>
  </Menu>
```
```
</MainMenu>
```

The NavBar Codebehind (see Listing 12-19) to handle the updated NavBar is really quite simple. All it does is check to see if the first element in the menu is <authorization>. If it is, it grabs all the roles that the menu supports using its own Roles() method and then compares it to all the roles that the user performs. If there is a match, the menu is displayed, just like it was originally.

Listing 12-19. NavBar Updated Codebehind with Authorization
```
private void Page_Load(object sender, System.EventArgs e)
{
```
```
    bool authorized = false;
```

```
    ...
```

```
    for (int i = 0; i < Menus.Count; i++)
    {
```
```
        int currnode = 0;

        XmlNodeList MenuNodes = Menus[i].ChildNodes;

        if (MenuNodes[currnode].Name.Equals("authorization"))
        {
            AppEnv appEnv = new AppEnv(Context);
            AccountRoles accountRoles =
                new AccountRoles(appEnv.GetConnection());

            if (accountRoles.Authorization(
                Roles(MenuNodes[currnode++].InnerText),
```

```
                            User.Identity.Name))
                {
                    authorized = true;
                }
                else
                {
                    authorized = false;
                }
            }
            else
            {
                authorized = true;
            }

            if (authorized)
            {
                ...
            }
        }
    }
}

public ArrayList Roles (string role)
{
    ArrayList list = new ArrayList();

    string[] temp = role.Split(',');
    for (int k = 0; k < temp.Length; k++)
        list.Add(temp[k]);

    return list;
}
```

Account Maintenance

One of the strong points of CMS.NET's approach to role-based authentication
and authorization is that the user account and role information is stored with the
rest of the CMS.NET data. Thus, you don't have to leave the CMS.NET system for
user management. These databases were covered earlier in the chapter. It is up to
the account maintenance portion of the administration system to maintain
these databases.

The administration system handles the creating, updating, removing, and viewing (CURVe) of accounts and the roles they perform. The code to handle CURVe is almost identical to that of the authors covered in Chapter 11, so much so that I will only cover the differences. As always, the full code can be found on the Apress Web site in the Downloads section.

List

The first thing to add is the `AdmAcntList` Web page, which looks like Figure 12-4.

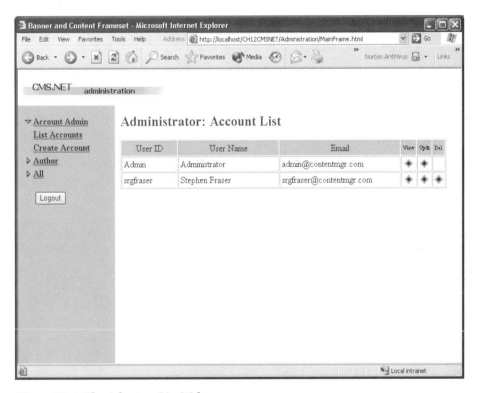

Figure 12-4. The AdmAcntList Web page

There is really no difference between the `AdmAcntList` Web page and the `AutView` Web page covered in Chapter 11, except that the `AdmAcntList` Web page does not support submit. It displays account columns (obviously), and the Administrator account can only be updated by the Administrator account itself (and it can never be deleted). Listing 12-20 shows the code that handles the special administrator scenarios.

Listing 12-20. The AdmAcntList Codebehind for Administrator Scenarios

```
private void Page_Load(object sender, System.EventArgs e)
{

    ...

    foreach (DataRow dr in dt.Rows)
    {

        ...

        if (dr["AccountID"].ToString().Trim().Equals("1"))
        {
            int i = 0;

            // is the current user the administrator
            // allow viewing and updating
            if (dr["UserName"].ToString().Trim().Equals(
                User.Identity.Name.Trim()))
            {
                BuildImageButton(row, "AdmAcntView.aspx?AccountID=" +
                                    dr["AccountID"].ToString());
                BuildImageButton(row, "AdmAcntUpdate.aspx?AccountID=" +
                                    dr["AccountID"].ToString());
                i = 2;
            }
            for ( ; i < 3; i++)
            {
                lit = new LiteralControl(" ");
                cell = new TableCell();
                cell.Controls.Add(lit);
                row.Cells.Add(cell);
            }
        }
        else
        {
            BuildImageButton(row, "AdmAcntView.aspx?AccountID=" +
                                    dr["AccountID"].ToString());
            BuildImageButton(row, "AdmAcntUpdate.aspx?AccountID=" +
                                    dr["AccountID"].ToString());
            BuildImageButton(row, "AdmAcntRemove.aspx?AccountID=" +
                                    dr["AccountID"].ToString());
        }
    }
}
```

Create

The account administration would be quite useless if you couldn't create a new account. Figure 12-5 shows the AdmAcntCreate Web page that is designed for this task.

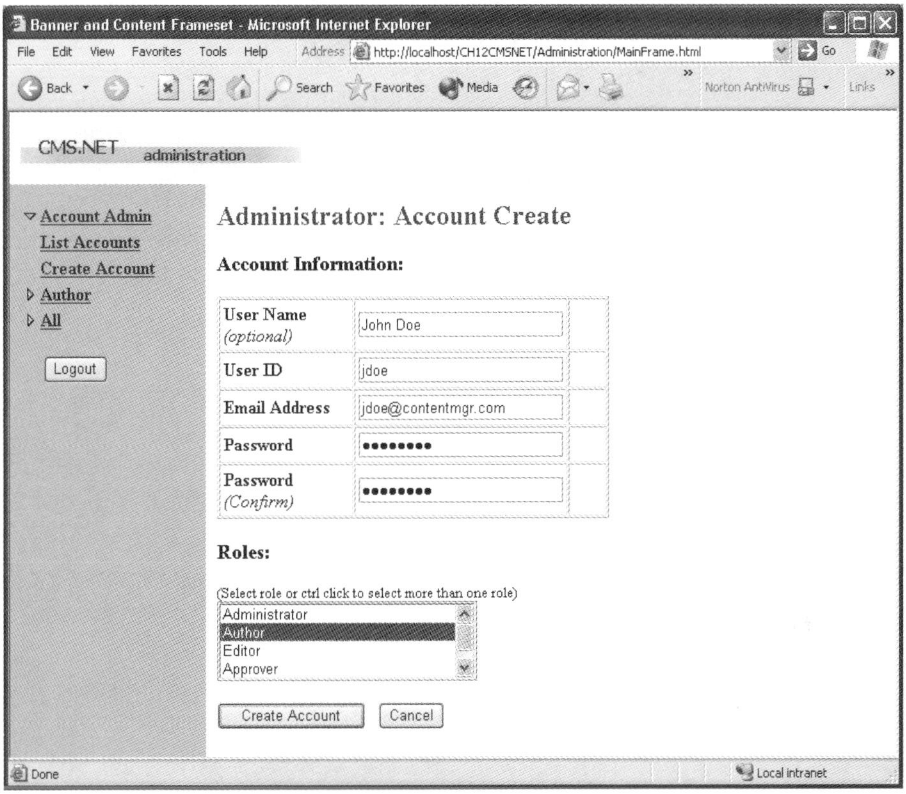

Figure 12-5. The AdmAcntCreate Web page

Looking at Figure 12-5, you should spot something you haven't used before: the multiselect list box. The list box stores all the possible roles in the system that a user can have. Listing 12-21 shows the design code specific to the list box.

Listing 12-21. The Multiselect List Box

```
<H3>Roles:</H3>
<FONT size=2>
(Select role or ctrl click to select more than one role)</FONT>
<br>
<asp:ListBox id=lbRoles runat="server" Width="40%" SelectionMode="Multiple">
</asp:ListBox>
```

The Codebehind to handle the list box (see Listing 12-22) is pretty straight-forward. The first time the page is built, the Role list box is loaded from an auxiliary database table called Roles that is made up of one column: Role. Then, when the user enters a valid page, you check to see if the username is already taken. If it is, you error out; otherwise, you insert all the information into the database.

The ProcessAccountRoles() method simply goes through the list, and if a row is selected, it is added to the AccountRoles table.

Listing 12-22. The AdmAcntCreate Codebehind

```
private void Page_Load(object sender, System.EventArgs e)
{
    if (!IsPostBack)
    {
        string Cmd = "Select * FROM Roles";
        SqlDataAdapter DAdpt = new SqlDataAdapter(Cmd, appEnv.GetConnection());

        DataSet ds = new DataSet();
        DAdpt.Fill(ds, "Roles");

        DataTable dt = ds.Tables["Roles"];

        foreach (DataRow dr in dt.Rows)
        {
            lbRoles.Items.Add(dr["Role"].ToString());
        }
    }
    else
    {
        account  = new Account(appEnv.GetConnection());
        property = new AccountProperty(appEnv.GetConnection());
        accountRoles = new AccountRoles(appEnv.GetConnection());

        Page.Validate();

        if (Page.IsValid)
        {
            try
            {
                if (account.GetAccountID(tbUserID.Text) > 0)
                    lblError.Text = "UserID already in use";
            }
            catch (Exception)
```

```
        {
            try
            {
                account.Insert(tbUserID.Text, tbPassword.Text,
                                tbEmail.Text);
                int AccountID = account.GetAccountID(tbUserID.Text);
                ProcessUserName(AccountID);
                ProcessAccountRoles(AccountID);

                Response.Redirect("AdmAcntList.aspx");
            }
            catch (Exception err)
            {
                Page_Error("The following error occurred " + err.Message);
            }
        }
    }
}

private void ProcessAccountRoles(int AccountID)
{
    for (int i = 0; i < lbRoles.Items.Count; i++)
    {
        if (lbRoles.Items[i].Selected)
        {
            accountRoles.Insert(AccountID, lbRoles.Items[i].Text);
        }
    }
}
```

Update

The AdmAcntUpdate Web page is very similar to the create Web page, as you can see in Figure 12-6. The only big difference is that it comes prepopulated with the account information that needs to be updated.

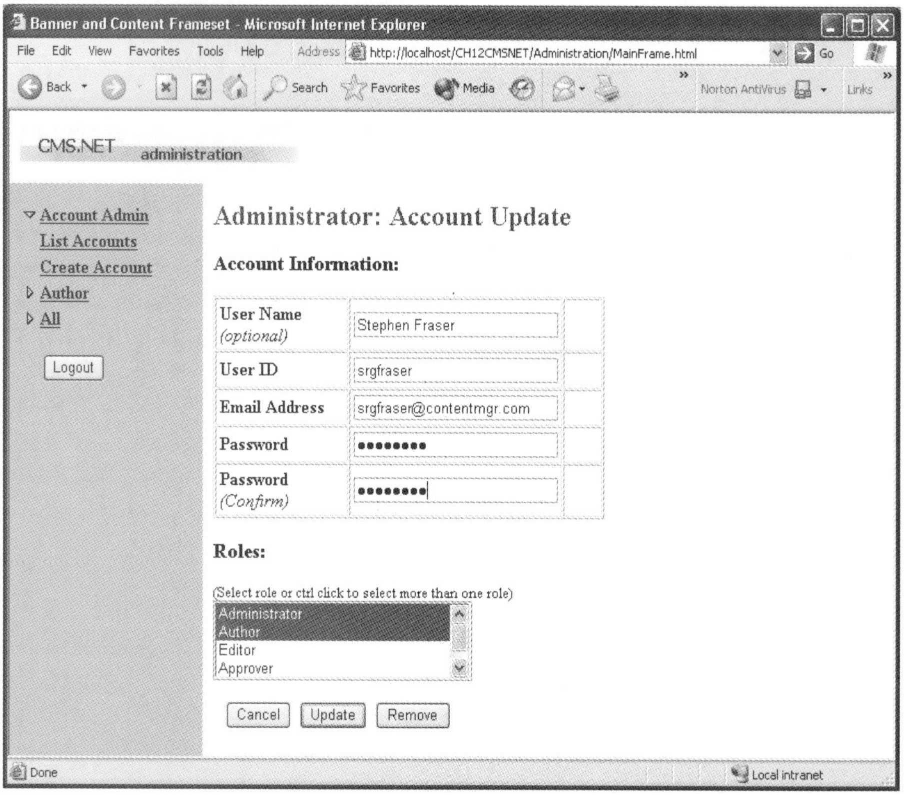

Figure 12-6. The AdmAcntUpdate Web page

The only thing of note code-wise is how the multiselect list box is built. As you can see in Listing 12-23, you build a DataSet of all the roles found in the auxiliary database Roles. Then you compare them row by row with what is in the AccountRoles database. If the row is found in both the Roles DataSet and the AccountRoles database table, the selected property is set to true. Obviously, if the reverse is true, the selected property is set to false.

Listing 12-23. The AdmAcntUpdate Codebehind

```
private void Page_Load(object sender, System.EventArgs e)
{
    . . .
    if (!IsPostBack)
    {
        . . .
        DataTable roledt = roles.GetRolesForID(aid);

        string Cmd = "Select * FROM Roles";
        SqlDataAdapter DAdpt = new SqlDataAdapter(Cmd, appEnv.GetConnection());

        DataSet ds = new DataSet();
        DAdpt.Fill(ds, "Roles");

        DataTable allRolesdt = ds.Tables["Roles"];

        foreach (DataRow dr in allRolesdt.Rows)
        {
            ListItem li = new ListItem(dr["Role"].ToString());

            foreach (DataRow adr in roledt.Rows)
            {
                if (dr["Role"].ToString().Equals(adr["Role"].ToString()))
                    li.Selected = true;
            }
            lbRoles.Items.Add(li);
        }
        if (aid == 1)
        {
            bnRemove.Visible = false;
            lbRoles.Enabled = false;
        }
    }
}
```

Remove

As you can see in Figure 12-7, there is virtually no difference between AdmAcntRemove and AutRemove except the obvious account and content differences.

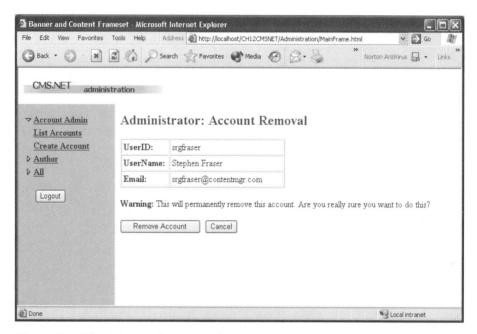

Figure 12-7. The AdmAcntRemove Web page

The only thing of interest in the code is the line to get the username:

```
lbUserName.Text =
    property.GetValue(Convert.ToInt32(dt.Rows[0]["AccountID"]), "UserName");
```

If you remember, the username is stored in the AccountProperty table, not the Account table. You might think that this overly complicates things, but as you can see in the AccountProperty database helper GetValue() method (see Listing 12-24), it is actually very easy to extract the needed information. It is just a standard select on the key fields. If the key exists, it returns the value; otherwise, it returns an empty string value.

The versatility of being able to add any information about the user you want, without having to change the database schema, quickly overshadows any complication that the AccountProperty might present.

Listing 12-24. The AccountProperty Database Table Helper GetValue Method

```
public string GetValue(int AccountID, string Property)
{
    // SELECT Value
    //   FROM AccountProperty
    //  WHERE (AccountID = @AccountID AND Property = @Property)

    SqlCommand Command = new SqlCommand("AccountProperty_GetValue",
                                        m_Connection);
    Command.CommandType  = CommandType.StoredProcedure;

    Command.Parameters.Add(new SqlParameter("@AccountID", SqlDbType.Int));
    Command.Parameters.Add(new SqlParameter("@Property", SqlDbType.Char, 32));

    Command.Parameters["@AccountID"].Value = AccountID;
    Command.Parameters["@Property"].Value = Property;

    string retval = "";

    try
    {
        m_Connection.Open();
        SqlDataReader dr = Command.ExecuteReader();

        if (dr.Read())
        {
            retval = dr["Value"].ToString();
        }
    }
    finally
    {
        m_Connection.Close();
    }

    return retval;
}
```

View

Let's finish this chapter with the AdmAcntView Web page (see Figure 12-8). There is no new code in the Web page at all, but it still is a necessary Web page because it provides a safe way to view an account. There are no fields to edit, so there is no chance that it might accidentally get updated. This Web page could be used by the administrator to see the last time the user logged on and for how long (or a myriad of other things), but for now, let's just show generic user information.

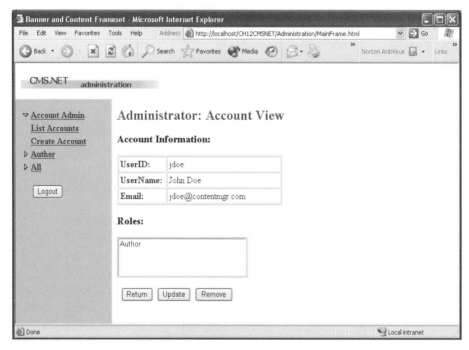

Figure 12-8. The AdmAcntView Web page

Summary

This chapter covered cookies, authentication, authorization, and encryption.

It started with a brief discussion of ASP.NET's security and then moved on to cover CMS.NET's security in a little more detail. Then it covered cookies and session objects and how to build and use them. Next, it described the method by which ASP.NET provides authentication and then went into detail on how CMS.NET does authentication. After this, it moved on to ASP.NET authorization and CMS.NET role-based authorization and why it was decided to not use ASP.NET authentication at all. This chapter briefly explored encryption and then ended by covering account management.

In the next chapter, you start to have some real fun—you get to start displaying content you have accumulated to the world.

CHAPTER 13

Displaying Dynamic Content

I'VE HAD ENOUGH OF BACK-END administrative development, how about you? All the previous chapters were fun, but there's nothing like being able to display dynamic content and show off all your hard work. The average user will never see all the work you have put into the system so far. Not so with this chapter, however, because dynamic content display is all about strutting your stuff in front of users.

You will just use a standard display template for all users visiting the site. Believe it or not, even the simple display template provides a lot to the user. But, there is nothing stopping you from creating a much more elaborate template in your implementation of CMS.NET.

CMS.NET provides a home page, a way of dividing the content into as many domains and subdomains as you think necessary, and the capability to navigate in and out of all these domains, zones, and the home page. The content is divided into a header, source, teaser, body, and tagline, of which only the header and body are mandatory. As an added bonus, you have full HTML formatting capabilities within all the aforementioned sections.

Not too bad for one chapter.

But that's not all . . . (I've always wanted to say that!) I'll throw in a content deployment system for free.

What Is Dynamic Content?

If you are like everyone else, your first attempts at building a Web site started with a tool such as Microsoft FrontPage. The first thought you probably had was "This isn't so hard." You created page after page. Soon, you began to realize all the pages were starting to look alike, except for this or that section of each page. After a while, the sheer number of pages you had to maintain became mind-boggling and you started to think "There has to be a better way." Fortunately, there is. It is called dynamic content.

As a concept, dynamic content is very easy. It is simply content created at the time it is needed rather than in advance. Basically, dynamic content is achieved by storing all the pieces of content that a user might want to view and then, when the user requests some of this content, a Web page—specific to the request of the user—is built.

Dynamic content sounds easy enough, but until the writing this book, it cost hundreds of thousands of dollars to buy a system to implement. Yes, these systems provide many bells and whistles, but I ask you, hundreds of thousands of dollars worth?

Creating a static Web site using only HTML is really a thing of the past. Even the pages you create with FrontPage enable you to throw in dynamic components and controls.

In this chapter, the designer of CMS.NET defines the dynamic nature of the Web site. That designer is, of course, yours truly. When you combine dynamic content with personalization, the design enables the user to start taking some control of the dynamic nature of the site. You will see that you can achieve a truly unique experience for each user.

Three-Level Content Navigation

CMS.NET uses the very common three-level approach to content navigation. Take a quick peek around the Internet. You will find that it usually takes about three or four levels before you get to the story you are looking for on a given Web site. Most people do not want to go much deeper than four levels into a Web site, and most Web sites hover around three levels. Personalized sites will often shave one level off your navigation.

Why Three-Level Navigation?

It seems to be an unwritten industry standard. Having three levels just feels right. I find that two-level sites require a lot of scrolling to find what you are looking for. On the other hand, with a Web site that is four levels deep or more, you start to get the feeling of "Will I ever get there?"

CMS.NET doesn't force three levels, though. If you that find the story you want pops up while navigating, there is always a quick hyperlink to it. But, of course, this is only common sense.

So What Are the Three Levels of CMS.NET?

The top level is made up of one or more subject area domains. They can be almost any high-level abstraction of your content system. As you can see in Figure 13-1, this book's implementation of CMS.NET uses Developer Content and Management Content as domains, but any high-level abstraction could be used.

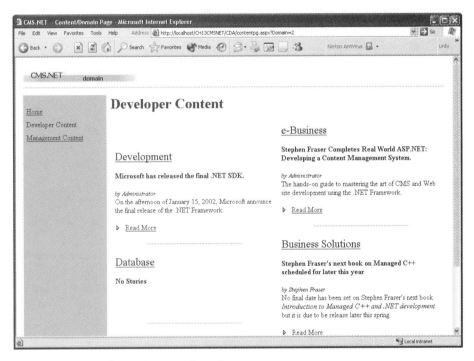

Figure 13-1. Developer Content domain zones

Inside each domain are subdomains, or what CMS.NET calls zones. Again, they could be almost any abstraction. As you can see in Figures 13-1 and 13-2, the domains are broken up as follows:

- Developer Content

  - e-Business

  - Development

  - Database

  - Business Solutions

- Management Content

  - Technology

  - Professional

  - Managerial

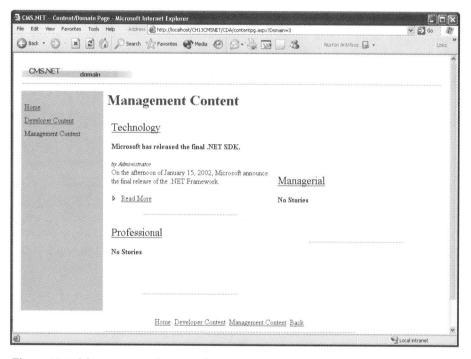

Figure 13-2. Management Content domain zones

The third and final level of CMS.NET is content grouped by story. The same piece of content can be used in different zones if it makes sense to do so. For example, if a story is about implementing a database in an e-business solution, it makes sense to include the story in both zones. As you can see in Figure 13-3, the data used is just test data, but obviously, you are going to want to implement your real content.

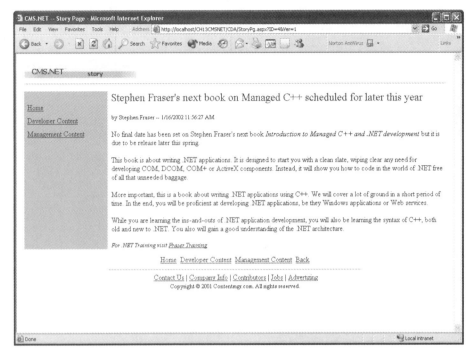

Figure 13-3. Managed C++ book story

Starting and Stopping the Web Site

There is no greater sin made by a Webmaster than allowing the "The page cannot be displayed" error (see Figure 13-4) to show up during a user's travels through the site. It is the kiss of death if it shows up just as someone is trying to access your Web site for the first time. Think of it from the perspective of the user.

The first rule to remember about users is that they think there are probably a gazillion other Web sites on the Internet with content similar to yours. If yours isn't available, the user will go elsewhere. Only by showing the user that your site is the best thing since sliced bread will he likely return.

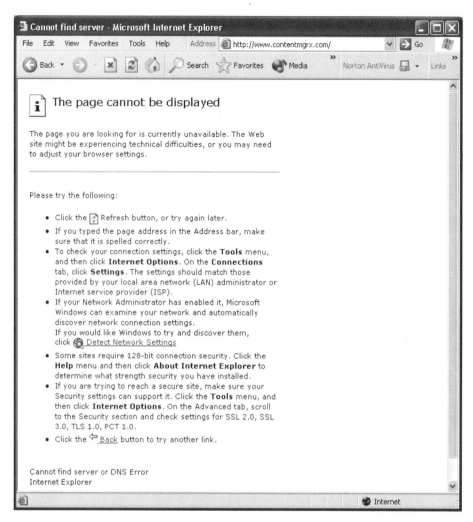

Figure 13-4. "The page cannot be found" error

If you can't have your site up for some reason (and it had better be a good one), make sure you provide a Web page that tells the user that he got the right place and to please come back later. Heck, you might get lucky and the user will try back later. If the user gets the "The page cannot be found" error page, however, the chances are nil to none that you will see either hide or hair of that user again.

There really is no excuse for the "The page cannot be found" error to show up. It is such an easy task to put up a dummy page (if the Web server is running) or to route the IP address to somewhere else while the Web server is being restarted. Figure 13-5 shows CMS.NET's friendly "I'm really here but come back later" page.

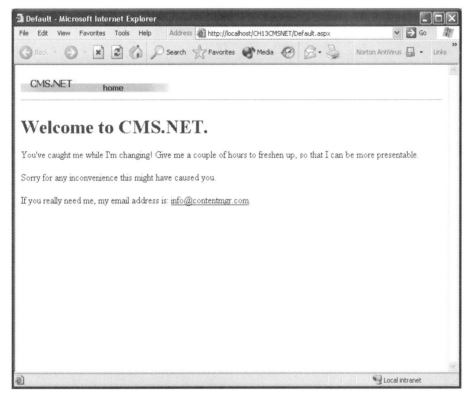

Figure 13-5. The "I'm changing" page

The Default.aspx Web Page

Chapter 10 covered all the code needed to handle shutting down and starting up the system. This time, instead of the Admin.aspx Web page checking for the setup <appSettings> element, the Default.aspx Web site is looking for the ready

<appSettings> element. If Default.aspx finds the ready <appSettings> element value set to true in the web.config file, it knows that the system is running and can continue as normal. On the other hand, if the value returned is false or does not exist, the Web site knows it is shut down and, instead of redirecting to the home page, displays it own message asking the user to come back later. Listing 13-1 shows the Default.aspx Codebehind to handle this process.

Listing 13-1. The Default.aspx Codebehind

```
private void Page_Load(object sender, System.EventArgs e)
{
    string ready = new AppEnv(Context).GetAppSetting("ready");

    if(ready.Equals("true"))
    {
        Response.Redirect("CDA/HomePg.aspx");
    }
}
```

The AdmShutdown Web Page

To give the Webmaster even less of an excuse, CMS.NET made the process of bringing the Web site up and down extremely easy. Whenever maintenance needs to be done on CMS.NET that does not require the Web server to be shut down, the Webmaster simply has to navigate to the AdmShutdown Web page and press the single button found on it. On the other hand, if you need to bring down the Web server for some reason along with the Web site, you need to reroute your host name to a new IP address. The procedure to do this differs with each host provider, but it should simply be, in most cases, a phone call telling the host provider of your intentions.

As you can see in Figure 13-6, the Web page to shut down and start the system consists of merely one heading, label, and button. If you can't create the ASP.NET design for this, you shouldn't be reading this book yet.

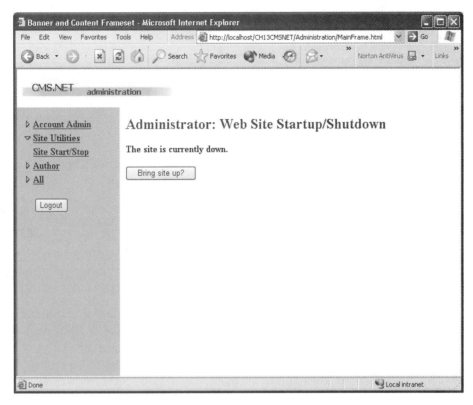

Figure 13-6. The AdmShutdown Web page

The AdmShutdown Codebehind

The Page_Load() method (see Listing 13-2) is a very simple procedure to dynamically place the appropriate label on the prompt and button. First, it gets the value of the ready <appSettings> element. Then, if the value of ready is true, meaning the site is up, it prompts the Webmaster to shut the Web site down. On the other hand, if the value is anything but true, it prompts the Webmaster to bring the Web site up.

Listing 13-2. The AdmShutdown Page_Load Method

```
private void Page_Load(object sender, System.EventArgs e)
{
    ready = appEnv.GetAppSetting("ready");

    if (ready.Equals("true"))
    {
        lbPrompt.Text = "The site is currently up.";
        bnStartStop.Text = "Bring site down?";
    }
    else
    {
        lbPrompt.Text = "The site is currently down.";
        bnStartStop.Text = "Bring site up?";
    }
}
```

The bnStartStop_Click() method (see Listing 13-3) is a little more elaborate, but you already have covered all the code in Chapter 10. All it does is simply toggle the ready <appSettings> element in the web.config file from true to false and back. The first time the Web site is ever started up, the ready <appSettings> element is added to the web.config file. Finally, the prompt and button's text gets toggled to its opposite state.

Listing 13-3. The AdmShutdown bnStartStop_Click Method

```
private void bnStartStop_Click(object sender, System.EventArgs e)
{
    bool isready = false;
    XmlReader xtr =
        new XmlTextReader(File.OpenRead(Server.MapPath("..\\..\\web.config")));

    XmlDocument doc = new XmlDocument();
    doc.Load(xtr);
    xtr.Close();

    XmlNodeList nodes =
        doc.DocumentElement.GetElementsByTagName("appSettings");

    for (int i = 0; i < nodes.Count; i++)
    {
        XmlNodeList appnodes =
            ((XmlElement)(nodes.Item(i))).GetElementsByTagName("add");
```

```
        for (int j = 0; j < appnodes.Count; j++)
        {
            XmlAttributeCollection attrColl = appnodes.Item(j).Attributes;
            XmlAttribute tmpNode = (XmlAttribute)attrColl.GetNamedItem("key");
            if (tmpNode.Value.Equals("ready"))
            {
                if (ready.Equals("true"))
                    ((XmlAttribute)attrColl.GetNamedItem("value")).Value =
                        "false";
                else
                    ((XmlAttribute)attrColl.GetNamedItem("value")).Value =
                        "true";
                isready = true;
            }
        }
        if (!isready)
        {
            // if it gets here, it's the first time the site is started up
            XmlDocumentFragment newAppSetting = doc.CreateDocumentFragment();
            newAppSetting.InnerXml=("<add key=\"ready\" value=\"true\" />\n");
            ((XmlElement)(nodes.Item(i))).AppendChild(newAppSetting);
        }
    }

    File.Delete(Server.MapPath("..\\..\\web.config"));

    StreamWriter sr =
        new StreamWriter(File.OpenWrite(Server.MapPath("..\\..\\web.config")));
    doc.Save(sr);
    sr.Close();

    // Flip prompt
    if (ready.Equals("true"))
    {
        lbPrompt.Text = "The site is currently down.";
        bnStartStop.Text = "Bring site up?";
    }
    else
    {
        lbPrompt.Text = "The site is currently up.";
        bnStartStop.Text = "Bring site down?";
    }
}
```

Navigational Database Tables

As you might think, CMS.NET's three-level navigation requires three additional database tables to be added to the repository: Domain, Zone, and Distribution. All three correspond directly to the three-level navigational scheme of CMS.NET.

The Domain database table, as the name suggests, stores all the domain information for CMS.NET. As you can see in Table 13-1, there is not much to the table. The table is primarily used to dynamically build CMS.NET's NavBar. The DomainTitle is displayed on the NavBar, whereas the DomainType is used in building the NavBar hyperlinks.

Table 13-1. Domain Database Table Design

COLUMN NAME	DATA TYPE	LENGTH	KEY	DESCRIPTION
DomainID	int	4	true	Domain ID for this domain
DomainType	char	32	false	Type of Web page associated with this domain
Title	char	32	false	Title of the domain
Description	char	64	false	Brief description of the domain
ModifiedDate	datetime	8	false	Date domain was last changed
CreationDate	datetime	8	false	Date domain was created

Figure 13-7 shows the contents of the Domain database used by CMS.NET. Each domain gets its own unique DomainID, which is used to create a one-to-many relationship with Zone. The NavBar uses DomainType to determine what type of Web page to display when a hyperlink is selected from it. In fact, we will be creating homepg.aspx and contentpg.aspx Web pages a little later on.

Start Page | dbo.Domain : ...MIDALA.CMSNET)

DomainID	DomainType	Protected	Title	Description	ModifiedDate	CreationDate
1	homepg	0	Home	The domain is the home page of the web site	1/1/2001	1/1/2001
2	contentpg	0	Developer Content	This domain handles all developer content	1/1/2001	1/1/2001
3	contentpg	0	Management Content	This domain handles all management content	1/1/2001	1/1/2001

Figure 13-7. Domain database for CMS.NET

The `Zone` database table stores all the zone information of the Web site. As you can see in Table 13-2, this table is no more difficult than the `Domain` table. ContentPg.aspx primarily uses this table. This page's role is to display the lead story for each zone within a domain.

Table 13-2. Zone Database Table Design

COLUMN NAME	DATA TYPE	LENGTH	KEY	DESCRIPTION
`ZoneID`	`int`	4	`true`	Zone ID for this domain
`Title`	`char`	32	`false`	Title of the zone
`Description`	`char`	64	`false`	Brief description of the zone
`DomainID`	`int`	4	`false`	The domain with which this zone is associated
`ModifiedDate`	`datetime`	8	`false`	Date zone was last changed
`CreationDate`	`datetime`	8	`false`	Date zone was created

Figure 13-8 shows the `Zone` database used by CMS.NET. Like the `Domain` database, each zone gets its own `ZoneID`, which is used by the `Distribution` database to distribute stories. The `DomainID` is used to create a relationship with a domain. A zone can only have a relationship with a single domain.

Start Page | dbo.Domain : T...AMIDALA.CMSNET) | dbo.Zone : Ta...MIDALA.CMSNET)

ZoneID	Protected	Title	Description	DomainID	ModifiedDate	CreationDate
1	0	Development	Zone containing Development content	2	1/1/2001	1/1/2001
2	0	Database	Zone containing Database content	2	1/1/2001	1/1/2001
3	0	e-Business	Zone containing e-Business content	2	1/1/2001	1/1/2001
4	1	Business Solutions	Zone containing Business Solutions content	2	1/1/2001	1/1/2001
5	0	Technology	Zone containing Technology content	3	1/1/2001	1/1/2001
6	0	Professional	Zone containing Professional content	3	1/1/2001	1/1/2001
7	1	Managerial	Zone containing Managerial content	3	1/1/2001	1/1/2001

Figure 13-8. Zone database for CMS.NET

It is possible to simplify CMS.NET by restricting a piece of content to only a certain zone. However, this restriction would be a mistake because many pieces of content can and should be associated with many zones. Guess what this leads to? It leads to the dreaded many-to-many relationship, and as any database developer will tell you, you are going to need an intersection entity to resolve this type of relationship.

The Distribution database table (see Table 13-3) is this intersection entity. The database table contains a list of every zone with which each piece of content is associated. The table also has a ranking or weighting factor that determines the importance of a piece of content to a particular zone. You might notice that because this ranking is in the intersection entity, you are able to have different weightings for the same piece of content in different zones.

Table 13-3. Distribution Database Table Design

COLUMN NAME	DATA TYPE	LENGTH	KEY	DESCRIPTION
ContentID	int	4	true	Content ID for this ZoneID
Version	int	4	true	Version for this ZoneID
ZoneID	int	4	true	Zone ID for this ContentID/Version pair
Ranking	int	4	false	The ranking of this content for this zone
ModifiedDate	datetime	8	false	Date distribution was last changed
CreationDate	datetime	8	false	Date distribution was created

Figure 13-9 shows the intersection data found in the Distribution database. Notice that a story with the same ContentID and Version can be related to multiple ZoneIDs. The Ranking column is used to sort content within a zone. Sorting will be done in descending order. Thus, a story with a ranking of 4 will be displayed before one with a ranking of 3.

ContentID	Version	ZoneID	Ranking	ModifiedDate	CreationDate
2	2	1	3	1/16/2002 11:57:41 AM	1/16/2002 11:54:58 AM
2	2	3	4	1/16/2002 11:57:41 AM	1/16/2002 11:54:58 AM
2	2	5	2	1/16/2002 11:54:58 AM	1/16/2002 11:54:58 AM
3	1	1	4	1/16/2002 11:41:06 AM	1/16/2002 11:38:25 AM
3	1	5	4	1/16/2002 11:41:06 AM	1/16/2002 11:38:25 AM
4	1	1	2	1/16/2002 11:56:27 AM	1/16/2002 11:56:27 AM
4	1	4	4	1/16/2002 11:57:41 AM	1/16/2002 11:56:27 AM
4	1	5	3	1/16/2002 11:57:41 AM	1/16/2002 11:56:27 AM

Figure 13-9. Distribution database for CMS.NET

User Controls

I hinted in Chapter 11 that Web frames are being replaced on the Internet by a new approach. In the ASP.NET world, this new approach is the User Control. You might think of User Control as a reusable section of code that can be inserted into a Web page. Early betas called these things *Pagelets*. Personally, I think the term "Pagelet" was a good name for them, but hey, it wasn't my call.

User Controls provide Web developers with a quick way to add the same little section of a Web page to multiple Web pages. Developers create a User Control once and then deploy it to as many Web pages as they like. Something in the User Control that gets changed immediately shows up in all Web pages that use the User Control. No longer do you have to wade through multiple pages to make the same correction to all of them.

Here are three things that a developer needs to know about User Controls:

- User Controls are basically the same thing as a Web form, except they don't have an <HTML>, <BODY>, or <FORM> tag. This obviously is because a Web page is only allowed one copy of these, and the main Web form will already have them.

- A User Control has a suffix of .acsx, enabling the compiler to differentiate between a Web form and a User Control. Also, it stops the compiler from generating an error for the missing aforementioned tags.

- A User Control cannot execute on its own. It has to be inserted into a Web form to run. Personally, I like to lay out the Web form using a table and then insert the appropriate User Control into each table cell. This is not required, though. You can use a User Control just as you do any HTML or intrinsic control. Therefore, you can place them however you like on a Web form.

Other than that, there isn't much to User Controls.

Creating a User Control in the Visual Studio .NET design tool is very similar to creating a Web form. The only differences are that you select Add Web User Control instead of Add Web Form from the Project menu and you make sure that the Web User Control icon is selected instead of the Web Form icon when opening the new item from the dialog box. Once the User Control is active in the design window, you design exactly as you do with a Web form.

Standard CMS.NET User Controls

Every Web page in CMS.NET has a header, a footer, and a NavBar. It only makes sense that these three be created as User Controls because they are nearly the same for each page, and if you change something in any of them, you are going to want to have it reflected in every Web page.

Header User Control

The design of the Header User Control only requires the dragging of an image control and a horizontal rule to the Header.ascx design window. Listing 13-4 shows the ASP.NET design code generated for this User Control.

Listing 13-4. The Header User Control Design Code

```
<%@ Control Language="c#" AutoEventWireup="false"
                        Codebehind="Header.ascx.cs"
                        Inherits="CMSNET.CDA.Header"%>


<asp:image id=imgHeader runat="server"></asp:Image><BR>
<HR width="100%" SIZE=1>
```

What do you know? It contains an image control and a horizontal rule (sarcasm intended). If you had created this as a Web form, it would also include <HTML>, <BODY>, and <FORM>, but because this is a User Control, these tags are missing.

CMS.NET provides a little navigational tip in the header because the header image is different for each zone and level. The image control in the design code in Listing 13-4 shows no reference to which image to display. You might think of the control as a placeholder for an image, which the Codebehind eventually populates.

The Header User Control Page_Load() method (see Listing 13-5) shows how the image is loaded onto the User Control by placing the image's URL in the ImageURL property. The question that needs to be asked is this: What is this level variable found in the ImageURL string?

Listing 13-5. The Header User Control Codebehind Page_Load Method

```
private void Page_Load(object sender, System.EventArgs e)
{
    imgHeader.ImageUrl = "Images/" + level + ".jpg";
}
```

The answer is in Listing 13-6. It is simply a property that you manually add to the User Control. It is up to the Web form that calls this User Control to populate the property. You will see when you develop the home page Web form how to populate the property.

Listing 13-6. The Header User Control Codebehind Level Property

```
public string Level
{
    get
    {
        return level;
    }
    set
    {
        level = value;
    }
}
```

NavBar User Control

CMS.NET could have continued to use an XML-driven NavBar, but due to the future plans for personalization and the need to dynamically change the NavBar, you now use a database-driven version.

As you can see in Listing 13-7, all that the NavBar User Control design code contains is a table control, which you will proceed to populate in the Codebehind. Again, no <HTML>, <BODY>, or <FORM> tags exist anywhere.

Listing 13-7. The NavBar User Control Design Code

```
<%@ Control Language="c#" AutoEventWireup="false"
                        Codebehind="NavBar.ascx.cs"
                        Inherits="CMSNET.CDA.NavBar"%>

<asp:Table id=tblNavBar runat="server" CellPadding="4"></asp:Table>
```

The process of building a NavBar from a database is, in this case, easier than building one using XML. All it does is simply loop through all the records in the Domain database table and build a hyperlink from the DomainType column. The code also does a comparison on the value provided by the User Control's Domain property, which contains the current active domain, to the database column. If they match, a literal text is created instead of a hyperlink. There is no reason for a page to hyperlink to itself.

Listing 13-8. The NavBar User Control Codebehind

```
private void Page_Load(object sender, System.EventArgs e)
{
    if (!IsPostBack)
    {
        Domain domain = new Domain(new AppEnv(Context).GetConnection());

        DataTable dt = domain.GetAll();
        TableCell    cell;
        HyperLink    link;
        LiteralControl lit;

        foreach (DataRow dr in dt.Rows)
        {
            TableRow row = new TableRow();
            tblNavBar.Rows.Add(row);

            cell = new TableCell();

            if (m_domain != Convert.ToInt32(dr["DomainID"]))
            {
                link = new HyperLink();
                link.Text = dr["Title"].ToString();
                link.NavigateUrl = dr["DomainType"].ToString().Trim() +
                                    ".aspx?Domain=" + dr["DomainID"];

                cell.Controls.Add(link);
            }
            else
            {
                lit = new LiteralControl(dr["Title"].ToString());

                cell.Controls.Add(lit);
            }
            row.Cells.Add(cell);
        }
    }
}


public int Domain
{
    get
    {
```

```
        return m_domain;
    }
    set
    {
        m_domain = value;
    }
}
```

Footer User Control

The footer area of CMS.NET is currently just a stub because there are no Web pages for Contact, Company, Contributors, Jobs, or Advertising. The design only makes it look like there are.

The footer does include navigational links. In fact, they are the same as the links found on the NavBar. Why the duplication? Because CMS.NET is not using frames, when a user scrolls down to read the whole story, the NavBar scrolls at the same time. Having the navigation at the bottom saves the user from having to scroll back up the page to navigate to another place.

Listing 13-9 shows the Footer User Control. The navigation links will be added to the tblFootMenu table in the Codebehind. Note that there are no hyperlinks to the other Web pages. The design is only written to look like there are.

Listing 13-9. The Footer User Control Design Code

```
<center>
  <asp:Table id=tblFootMenu runat="server" CellPadding="3"></asp:Table>
</center>
<HR width="60%" SIZE=1>
<center>
   <U><FONT color=#0a246a>Contact Us</FONT></U> |
  <U><FONT color=#0a246a>Company Info</FONT></U> |
  <U><FONT color=#0a246a>Contributors</FONT></U> |
  <U><FONT color=#0a246a>Jobs</FONT></U> |
  <U><FONT color=#0a246a>Advertising</FONT></U>
  <br>
  <FONT size=2>Copyright © 2001 Contentmgr.com. All rights reserved.</FONT>
</center>
```

As you can see in Listing 13-10, the Footer User Control's Codebehind is nearly identical to that of the NavBar User Control. There are two differences, though. This time, a hyperlink is generated even if it is to the same page. When clicked, this hyperlink jumps the user back to the top of the page.

The second difference is the use of JavaScript to navigate to previous pages. There is no elegant way of doing this in C#, so I had to revert back to my days as a JavaScript programmer to see how it was done. Lucky for me, all it takes is to place the JavaScript `history.go` function in the `NavigateURL` property.

Listing 13-10. The Footer User Control Codebehind

```
private void Page_Load(object sender, System.EventArgs e)
{
    Domain domain = new Domain(new AppEnv(Context).GetConnection());

    DataTable dt = domain.GetAll();
    TableCell    cell;
    HyperLink    link;

    TableRow row = new TableRow();
    tblFootMenu.Rows.Add(row);

    foreach (DataRow dr in dt.Rows)
    {
        cell = new TableCell();
        link = new HyperLink();
        link.Text = dr["Title"].ToString();
        link.NavigateUrl = dr["DomainType"].ToString().Trim() +
            ".aspx?Domain=" + dr["DomainID"];

        cell.Controls.Add(link);
        row.Cells.Add(cell);
    }
    cell = new TableCell();
    link = new HyperLink();
    link.Text = "Back";
    link.NavigateUrl = "javascript:history.go(-1);";
    cell.Controls.Add(link);
    row.Cells.Add(cell);
}
```

The Default Home Page Web Form

Now that you have the standard User Controls used by the home page form, let's go ahead and implement them in the default home page. You will only implement the default version of CMS.NET's Web pages in this chapter. The default pages are those pages that everyone initially sees when entering the Web site.

You might remember the standard Web page layout shown in Figure 13-10 from Chapter 11. In Chapter 11, you used this layout to break up a Web page using a frameset. In this chapter, you will use this same layout, but instead of using frames, you will use a standard HTML table. (You don't have any ads, so you won't create the ads section.)

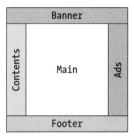

Figure 13-10. The standard Web page layout

From the developer's perspective, the process of using tables and User Controls is very similar to using framesets and Web forms. The only real difference is that you are dragging User Controls to table cells instead of dragging Web forms to frames. The biggest difference is what the user sees. Now, instead of the user having only a small frame to look at, she has the full browser window to use to see the content. When the user scrolls up, down, left, or right, the whole browser view window scrolls, not just a small frame of it. This enables the user to see more content at any one time.

CMS.NET's home page is shown in Figure 13-11. It looks like any other home page (albeit pretty empty), with its header, content navigation bar, footer, and main body. I'm sure your home page will have a little more pizzazz. In fact, it had better!

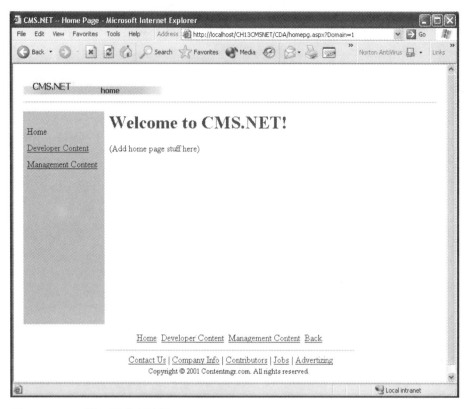

Figure 13-11. The CMS.NET home page

Home Page Web Design

Designing the home page is a snap. Simply create a table and then drag the appropriate User Controls from the Solution Explorer. Let's pretend you don't have the design tool and see what you need to design it manually.

Adding User Controls to Web Forms

Two new things have to be added to a Web form to handle User Controls. The first new thing that you see in the home page design code (see Listing 13-11) is the @Register directive at the top of the Web form. This tells the Web page about the User Control it is about to use.

```
<%@ Register TagPrefix="cmsnet" TagName="Header" Src="Header.ascx" %>
```

It contains three attributes:

- *TagPrefix:* An alias to associate the User Control with a namespace. Basically, it allows multiple User Controls with the same TagName to be unique.

- *TagName:* An alias to associate the User Control with its class. In other words, it is the class name used in the Codebehind.

- *Src:* The source code location (relative or absolute) of the User Control.

The second new thing is the actual User Control element that you add where you want the User Control to be displayed. Basically, it is TagPrefix:TagName, any id you want, and the runat="server" attribute.

```
<cmsnet:Header id=Header Level="home" runat="server">
```

The code generated by the design tool does not include any properties that may be required by the User Control. As you see in the preceding line, Level="home" had to be added manually.

Designing the Home Page

Listing 13-11 shows the entire ASP.NET home page design code. The design tool generated most of the code automatically. To make the code more specific to CMS.NET, I changed the TagPrefix from the generic uc1 to cmsnet. I also set the Level property to home. As you will see when you look at the Codebehind, you can also set properties there.

Listing 13-11. The Home Page Design Code

```
<%@ Page language="c#" Codebehind="HomePg.aspx.cs"
                       AutoEventWireup="false"
                       Inherits="CMSNET.CDA.HomePg" %>
<%@ Register TagPrefix="cmsnet" TagName="Header" Src="Header.ascx" %>
<%@ Register TagPrefix="cmsnet" TagName="NavBar" Src="NavBar.ascx" %>
<%@ Register TagPrefix="cmsnet" TagName="Footer" Src="Footer.ascx" %>
<HTML>
  <HEAD>
    <title>CMS.NET Home</title>
  </HEAD>
  <body MS_POSITIONING="FlowLayout">
    <form id="HomePg" method="post" runat="server">
```

```
<TABLE cellSpacing=8 cellPadding=1 width="100%" border=0>
  <TR>
    <TD colSpan=2>
      <cmsnet:Header id=Header Level="home" runat="server">
      </cmsnet:Header>
    </TD>
  </TR>
  <TR>
    <TD width="20%" style="WIDTH: 150px" bgColor=#8cd3ef valign=top >
       <br>
      <cmsnet:NavBar id=MainNavBar runat="server">
      </cmsnet:NavBar>
    </TD>
    <TD width="80%">
      <H1><FONT color=darkslategray>Welcome to CMS.NET!</FONT></H1>
      <P>(Add home page stuff here)</P>
    </TD>
  </TR>
  <TR>
    <TD colSpan=2>
      <cmsnet:Footer id=Footer runat="server">
      </cmsnet:Footer>
    </TD>
  </TR>
</TABLE>
    </form>
  </body>
</HTML>
```

The Home Page Codebehind

The NavBar User Control, which you previously created, has an optional property called Domain. When set, it changes the hyperlink of the specified domain to a literal. This does two things. First, it's another visual clue of the user's location, and second, it stops the user from clicking the redundant, current domain hyperlink.

The Codebehind for the home page is very simple (see Listing 13-12), but it has one catch. The definition of the User Control, unlike intrinsic controls, is not automatically added to the Codebehind. You have to add it manually, so you have to know what class is called. Fortunately, that is provided by the ASP.NET design code, as is its namespace.

Setting User Control Properties in the Codebehind

The current Domain is passed with the Request, except when CMS.NET is accessed the first time and thus is set to the home page domain of 1. You set the Domain property just as you set any other property.

Listing 13-12. The Home Page ASP.NET Codebehind

```
public class HomePg : CMSNET.Common.PageEx
{
    protected CMSNET.CDA.NavBar MainNavBar;

    private void Page_Load(object sender, System.EventArgs e)
    {
        int Domain = Convert.ToInt32(Request.QueryString["Domain"]);

        // First Time in no Domain specified
        if (Domain == 0)
            Domain++;

        MainNavBar.Domain = Domain;
    }
}
```

The HeadlineTeaser User Control

CMS.NET's Content-Domain and Zone Web forms both use one additional User Control called HeadlineTeaser. You will see shortly that, unlike the previous User Controls, HeadlineTeaser is dynamically added to Web forms. Dynamically creating User Controls is not difficult to do. It is just not obvious how it is done.

But first, you need to create the User Control.

HeadlineTeaser User Control Design

There is nothing special about HeadlineTeaser's design (see Listing 13-13). It is simply five labels, an image, and a hyperlink.

Listing 13-13. The HeadlineTeaser User Control Design Code

```
<P>
  <STRONG>
    <asp:Label id=lbHeadline runat="server"></asp:Label>
  </STRONG>
  <BR>
  <asp:Label id=lbSource runat="server"></asp:Label>
  <BR>
  <EM>
    <FONT size=2>
      <asp:Label id=lbBy runat="server">by</asp:Label>
    </FONT>
    <asp:Label id=lbByline runat="server" Font-Size="X-Small">
    </asp:Label>
  </EM>
  <BR>
  <asp:Label id=lbTeaser runat="server"></asp:Label>
</P>
<P>
  <asp:Image id=imgPlus runat="server"
      Height="11px" Width="11px" ImageUrl="Images/plus.gif">
  </asp:Image>
   
  <asp:HyperLink id=hlReadMore runat="server">Read More</asp:HyperLink>
</P>
<HR align="center" width="60%" SIZE=1>
<br>
```

The HeadlineTeaser Codebehind

The Codebehind for HeadlineTeaser starts by defining two properties: ContentID and Version. If these properties are not set before accessing the User Control, a "No Stories" message is displayed instead of the expected header, source, author, teaser, and hyperlink.

When valid ContentID and Version properties are set, the HeadlineTeaser grabs the content out of the Content database table and displays it. It also creates a hyperlink to a Story Web form so that the user can read the entire story if she chooses. There's no rocket science here, so let's move on.

Listing 13-14. The HeadlineTeaser User Control Codebehind

```
private int m_contentid = 0;
private int m_version = 0;

public int ContentID
{
    get
    {
        return m_contentid;
    }
    set
    {
        m_contentid = value;
    }
}

public int Version
{
    get
    {
        return m_version;
    }
    set
    {
        m_version = value;
    }
}
```

```
private void Page_Load(object sender, System.EventArgs e)
{
    if (!IsPostBack)
    {
        AppEnv appEnv = new AppEnv(Context);
        Content content = new Content(appEnv.GetConnection());
        AccountProperty property = new AccountProperty(appEnv.GetConnection());

        DataRow dr = content.GetContentForIDVer(m_contentid, m_version);

        if (dr != null)
        {
            lbHeadline.Text = dr["Headline"].ToString();
            lbSource.Text = dr["Source"].ToString();
```

```
                lbByline.Text = property.GetValue(
                            Convert.ToInt32(dr["Byline"]), "UserName").Trim();
            lbTeaser.Text = dr["Teaser"].ToString();
            hlReadMore.NavigateUrl = "StoryPg.aspx?ID=" + m_contentid +
                                "&Ver=" + m_version;
        }
        else
        {

            lbHeadline.Text = "No Stories";
            hlReadMore.Visible = false;
            lbBy.Visible = false;
            imgPlus.Visible = false;

        }


    }
}
```

The Default Content-Domain Web Form

Like all the default Web forms, the Content-Domain Web form (from now on just called the Content Web form) has a header, a NavBar, and a footer (see Figure 13-12). The code is identical to that of the home page, which you have already covered and will not cover again here.

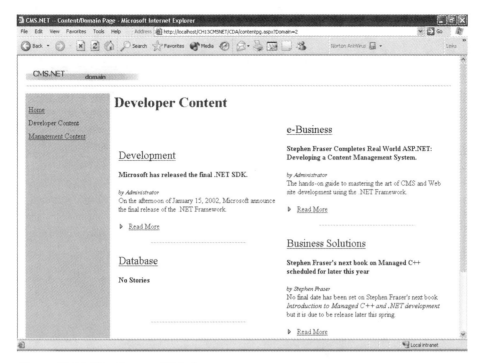

Figure 13-12. The Content Web form

The Content Web Design

The only difference between the Content Web design and the Home Page Web design is found in the main body section of the Web form, which contains a label to hold the domain name and a two-column table. You should note that the two columns or `TableCells` have IDs, which you will use in the Codebehind.

Listing 13-15. The Content Page Design Code

```
<H1>
  <asp:Label id=lbDomain runat="server" ForeColor="DarkSlateGray"></asp:Label>
</H1>
<P>
  <asp:Table id=tblDomHeadlines runat="server" CellPadding="8" Width="100%">
  <asp:TableRow>
      <asp:TableCell Width="50%" ID="tcLeft"></asp:TableCell>
      <asp:TableCell Width="50%" ID="tcRight"></asp:TableCell>
  </asp:TableRow>
  </asp:Table>
</P>
```

The Content Codebehind

Like most Codebehinds in ASP.NET, all the action happens in the Page_Load()
method (see Listing 13-16). The first thing the method does is grab the domain
that is sent along with the Request, select the Domain name using this value out of
the Domain database, and then place the value on the lbDomain. Next, it selects out
of the Zone database all zones for the domain. This is pretty standard stuff.

Now comes the fun stuff. The method counts the number of zones and
divides it in half. The first half of the zones will be placed into the tcLeft
TableCell and the remainder into the tcRight TableCell. Note that you have to
manually add to the code for the declaration of the TableCells because the design
tool does not generate them.

On the Content Web page, only the lead story of each zone is displayed, so
what gets placed in each row is a hyperlink to the Zone Web page and
a HeadlineTeaser to the lead story. To do this, you need to be able to create the
HeadlineTeaser control dynamically.

Listing 13-16. The Content Web Page Codebehind

```
protected System.Web.UI.WebControls.TableCell tcLeft;
protected System.Web.UI.WebControls.TableCell tcRight;
...
private void Page_Load(object sender, System.EventArgs e)
{
    int curDomain = Convert.ToInt32(Request.QueryString["Domain"]);

    if (curDomain == 0)
        Page_Error("No domain specified");

    MainNavBar.Domain = curDomain;

    Domain domain = new Domain(appEnv.GetConnection());
    DataTable dt = domain.GetDomainForID(curDomain);
    lbDomain.Text = dt.Rows[0]["Title"].ToString();

    Zone zone = new Zone(appEnv.GetConnection());
    dt = zone.GetZonesForDomain(curDomain);

    Distribution dist = new Distribution(appEnv.GetConnection());
```

```
int i;
HyperLink link;
for (i = 0; i < (int)Math.Ceiling((float)(dt.Rows.Count) / 2.0); i++)
{
    link = new HyperLink();
    link.Text = dt.Rows[i]["Title"].ToString();
    link.NavigateUrl = "ZonePg.aspx?zone=" + dt.Rows[i]["ZoneID"];
    link.Font.Size = new FontUnit(FontSize.Large);
    tcLeft.Controls.Add(link);

    DataTable dtd = dist.GetOrdered(Convert.ToInt32(dt.Rows[i]["ZoneID"]));
    HeadlineTeaser hlt =
        (HeadlineTeaser) LoadControl("HeadlineTeaser.ascx");
    if (dtd.Rows.Count > 0)
    {
        hlt.ContentID = Convert.ToInt32(dtd.Rows[0]["ContentID"]);
        hlt.Version = Convert.ToInt32(dtd.Rows[0]["Version"]);
    }
    tcLeft.Controls.Add(hlt);
}

for ( ; i < dt.Rows.Count; i++)
{
    link = new HyperLink();
    link.Text = dt.Rows[i]["Title"].ToString();
    link.NavigateUrl = "ZonePg.aspx?zone=" + dt.Rows[i]["ZoneID"];
    link.Font.Size = new FontUnit(FontSize.Large);
    tcRight.Controls.Add(link);

    DataTable dtd = dist.GetOrdered(Convert.ToInt32(dt.Rows[i]["ZoneID"]));
    HeadlineTeaser hlt =
        (HeadlineTeaser) LoadControl("HeadlineTeaser.ascx");
    if (dtd.Rows.Count > 0)
    {
        hlt.ContentID = Convert.ToInt32(dtd.Rows[0]["ContentID"]);
        hlt.Version = Convert.ToInt32(dtd.Rows[0]["Version"]);
    }
    tcRight.Controls.Add(hlt);
}
}
```

Creating a User Control Dynamically

Creating a User Control dynamically, though easy, is far from obvious. First, you have to load a copy of the User Control for every instance you place on the Web page using the Page.LoadControl() method, as shown here:

```
HeadlineTeaser hlt = (HeadlineTeaser) LoadControl("HeadlineTeaser.ascx");
```

Next, you need to set all the properties of the User Control before it is used. I like to do this right after it is loaded, but you can choose to do it later in the Page_Load() method if you want. The following is how the Content Web page sets the properties:

```
hlt.ContentID = Convert.ToInt32(dtd.Rows[0]["ContentID"]);
hlt.Version = Convert.ToInt32(dtd.Rows[0]["Version"]);
```

Finally, you have to add the control to the Web page. In the Content Web page's case, it is added to the TableCell as follows:

```
tcRight.Controls.Add(hlt);
```

You might be wondering why you don't just create an instance using the following:

```
HeadlineTeaser htl = new HeadlineTeaser();  // ERROR do not do this!!!
```

The reason is that User Controls are abstract classes, which cannot be created independently. Because they can only be called from the page that contains them, they need to be loaded first through the Web page.

The Default Zone Web Form

The Zone Web form (see Figure 13-13) provides the users of CMS.NET with the capability to see a list of all the stories that fall within a single zone. Code-wise, this Web page is very similar to the Content Web page discussed previously.

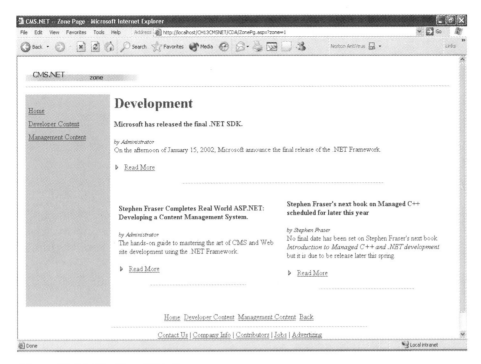

Figure 13-13. The Zone Web form

The unique part of this Web page is that it shows that a User Control can be used statically and dynamically within the same page. Not that this should come as any big surprise. Listing 13-17 shows the ASP.NET design code for the main body of the Zone Web page.

You have probably noted that it is very similar to the Content Web page. In the design code, I added a statically declared HeadlineTeaser User Control because all zones will have at least one story or the message "No Stories," both of which HeadlineTeaser can display.

Listing 13-17. The Zone Page Design Code

```
<%@ Register TagPrefix="cmsnet" TagName="HeadlineTeaser"
            Src="HeadlineTeaser.ascx" %>

...

<TD width="80%">
  <H1>
    <asp:Label id=lbZone runat="server" ForeColor="DarkSlateGray">
    </asp:Label>
  </H1>
  <cmsnet:HeadlineTeaser id=htLead runat="server">
  </cmsnet:HeadlineTeaser>
```

```
  <P>
    <asp:Table id=tblDomHeadlines runat="server" CellPadding="8" Width="100%">
      <asp:TableRow>
        <asp:TableCell Width="50%" ID="tcLeft"></asp:TableCell>
        <asp:TableCell Width="50%" ID="tcRight"></asp:TableCell>
      </asp:TableRow>
    </asp:Table>
  </P>
</TD>
```

The Codebehind has nothing new in it. As Listing 13-18 shows, the Page_Load() method gets the ZoneID from the Request and then gets all the content for that zone, which it displays using the HeadlineTeaser User Control. It is very similar to the Content Codebehind, except that it gets all the content from one zone instead of getting one piece of content from many zones.

One thing to note is that you have to manually add the declaration of both TableCells and the HeadlineTeaser classes.

Listing 13-18. The Zone Web Page Codebehind

```
protected System.Web.UI.WebControls.TableCell tcLeft;
protected System.Web.UI.WebControls.TableCell tcRight;
protected CMSNET.CDA.HeadlineTeaser htLead;

private void Page_Load(object sender, System.EventArgs e)
{
    int curZone = Convert.ToInt32(Request.QueryString["Zone"]);

    if (curZone == 0)
        Page_Error("No zone specified");

    Zone zone = new Zone(appEnv.GetConnection());
    DataTable dt = zone.GetZone(curZone);
    lbZone.Text = dt.Rows[0]["Title"].ToString();

    Distribution dist = new Distribution(appEnv.GetConnection());
    DataTable dtd = dist.GetOrdered(Convert.ToInt32(dt.Rows[0]["ZoneID"]));

    if (dtd.Rows.Count > 0)
    {
        htLead.ContentID = Convert.ToInt32(dtd.Rows[0]["ContentID"]);
        htLead.Version = Convert.ToInt32(dtd.Rows[0]["Version"]);
```

```
    int i;
    for (i = 0; i < (int)Math.Ceiling((float)(dtd.Rows.Count-1)/2.0); i++)
    {
        HeadlineTeaser hlt =
            (HeadlineTeaser) LoadControl("HeadlineTeaser.ascx");
        hlt.ContentID = Convert.ToInt32(dtd.Rows[i+1]["ContentID"]);
        hlt.Version = Convert.ToInt32(dtd.Rows[i+1]["Version"]);
        tcLeft.Controls.Add(hlt);
    }
    for ( ; i < dtd.Rows.Count-1; i++)
    {
        HeadlineTeaser hlt =
            (HeadlineTeaser) LoadControl("HeadlineTeaser.ascx");
        hlt.ContentID = Convert.ToInt32(dtd.Rows[i+1]["ContentID"]);
        hlt.Version = Convert.ToInt32(dtd.Rows[i+1]["Version"]);
        tcRight.Controls.Add(hlt);
    }
}
}
```

The Default Story Web Form

The Story Web form (see Figure 13-14) is one of the most important Web pages, from the user's perspective, in all of CMS.NET because it is where the actual content is displayed. Believe it or not, it is also one of the easiest Web pages to create.

As you can see from the Story design code (see Listing 13-19), the Web page is simply a set of labels of the database columns you want to display. You've done similar things since way back in Chapter 6.

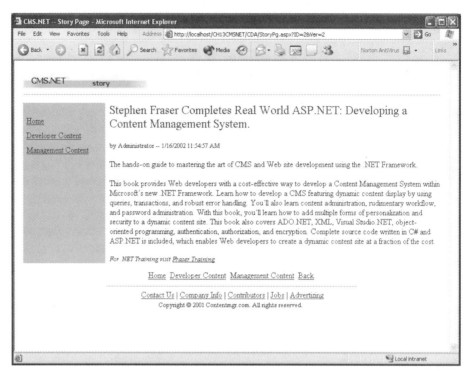

Figure 13-14. The Story Web form

Listing 13-19. The Story Page Design Code

```
<TD width="80%">
  <FONT color=darkslategray>
    <P>
      <asp:label id=lbHeadline runat="server" Font-Size="Large">
      </asp:label>
    </P>
    <P>
      <STRONG>
        <asp:Label id=lbSource runat="server">
        </asp:Label>
      </STRONG>
    </P>
  </FONT>
  <P>
```

```
  <asp:label id=lbBy runat="server" Font-Size="Smaller">by</asp:label>
   
  <asp:label id=lbByline runat="server" Font-Size="Smaller"></asp:label>
   
  <asp:label id=lbDashes runat="server" Font-Size="Smaller">--</asp:label>
   
  <asp:label id=lbDate runat="server" Font-Size="Smaller"></asp:label>
</P>
<P>
  <asp:label id=lbTeaser runat="server"></asp:label>
</P>
<P>
  <asp:label id=lbBody runat="server"></asp:label>
</P>
<P>
  <EM>
    <FONT size=2>
      <asp:label id=lbTagline runat="server"></asp:label>
    </FONT>
  </EM>
</P>
</TD>
```

The Codebehind for the Story Web page (see Listing 13-20) simply gets the ContentID and Version. With that, it selects the story out of the Content database and then matches up each column with its appropriate label.

In a case in which the content is not found in the database, a "No Stories" message is displayed instead. This should actually never happen, but it is possible that an inquisitive user might try to search for stories by entering content IDs and versions manually in the Address edit field of the browser.

Listing 13-20. The Story Web Page Codebehind

```
private void Page_Load(object sender, System.EventArgs e)
{
    int curId  = Convert.ToInt32(Request.QueryString["ID"]);
    int curVer = Convert.ToInt32(Request.QueryString["Ver"]);

    Content content = new Content(appEnv.GetConnection());
    AccountProperty property = new AccountProperty(appEnv.GetConnection());

    DataRow dr = content.GetContentForIDVer(curId, curVer);

    if (dr != null)
```

```
    {
        lbHeadline.Text = dr["Headline"].ToString();
        lbSource.Text = dr["Source"].ToString();
        lbByline.Text = property.GetValue(Convert.ToInt32(dr["Byline"]),
                                          "UserName").Trim();
        lbDate.Text = dr["ModifiedDate"].ToString();
        lbTeaser.Text = dr["Teaser"].ToString();
        lbBody.Text = dr["Body"].ToString();
        lbTagline.Text = dr["Tagline"].ToString();
    }
    else
    {
        lbHeadline.Text = "No Stories";
        lbBy.Visible = false;
        lbDashes.Visible = false;
    }
}
}
```

Deploying Content

All the code in this chapter is quite useless if you can't load it with the content from the repository. Content that is in the process of being created should not be accessible for viewing on the Web site. Only after it is completed and approved should content be available. It is ultimately the job of the deployment process to make content available to users of the Web site. Deploying content is the last step of CMS.NET's workflow.

Because workflow is the topic of the next chapter, I am going to delay covering this until then. For those of you who want to add content and see it displayed, however, a simplified version of the source code for deploying content (see Figure 13-15) is included on the Apress Web site (www.apress.com) in the Downloads section. Using this is easy. Submit the content from the content development area and then deploy it from the site maintenance area. It is also possible to see all the stories deployed to all zones, or to a particular zone, and shift the viewing order of the stories.

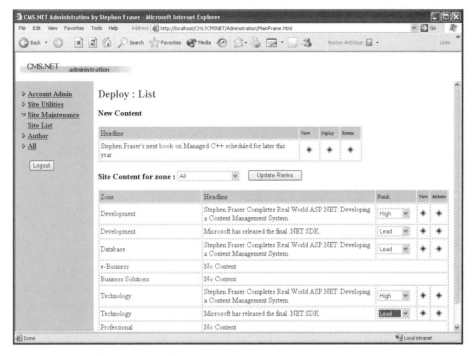

Figure 13-15. The Deploy Web page

Summary

This chapter covered the displaying of dynamic content.

It started by covering the basics of what dynamic content is and how it uses a three-level approach to dynamic content. Next, it took a little side trip and covered stopping and starting CMS.NET so that the user never gets the ugly "The page cannot be found" error. It then got back on topic and described the new database tables needed to handle three-level navigation. Next, it covered User Controls and you created a few. Finally, you implemented the default dynamic Web pages using these User Controls.

The next chapter returns to the content management application (CMA), which you started building in Chapter 11, and adds a simple workflow.

Using a Workflow to Enter Content

WORKFLOW IS ONE OF THE MOST IMPORTANT FEATURES of a content management system (CMS), so much so that Chapter 3 was devoted entirely to covering the theory behind it. In this chapter, on the other hand, you get to have some fun and actually develop the workflow for CMS.NET.

CMS.NET's workflow isn't the most elaborate, but it does have all the pieces needed to develop a content management application (CMA) that supports the following:

- Multiple users

- Internet maintainability

- Multiversion content

- Interstate communication

- State change e-mail events

- Role-based content development

- Role-based security

- Repeatable process

It supports a few other features that I'm sure I missed, but I'd say this isn't too bad for one chapter's worth of work.

CMS.NET Content Workflow

Most of the more expensive CMSs on the market support a fully dynamic work-flow generator. These systems enable the Web system developer to generate a workflow however she wants. I suppose that having this capability could merit a little higher price tag than, say, the hard-coded workflow supported by CMS.NET. Not the few hundred thousand dollars difference but maybe a few thousand dollars at least. On the other hand, these systems don't provide full source code so that you can change the workflow to suit your exact needs.

Figure 14-1 shows CMS.NET's content development workflow. It starts with the author creating the content. When the author is happy with the content, he passes it to an editor who edits it. When the editor is happy, it is passed to an approver, who gives the final rubber stamp and passes it on to the deployer for deployment.

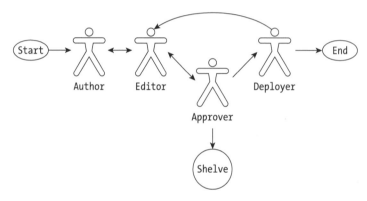

Figure 14-1. The content development workflow

Each piece of content can maintain a running commentary or audit using dated notes attached to it. This facility also can be used to handle all communication between the roles when the content moves from state to state. Keeping the notes separate from the content means no cleanup of the document is needed at the end to remove all unwanted commentary.

When a piece of content migrates from one state to another, CMS.NET will automatically send e-mail notification of the content's availability to all persons that fill the next role in the workflow. As soon as a specific person is designated to that role, only she will get the e-mail notifications. This helps people manage their time better because they no longer have to continually monitor the CMS for new content. Instead, they will be alerted by a simple e-mail.

Content is available on a first-come first-served basis for each role. In other words, the first user to start processing the content when it becomes available is given complete control of it until he relinquishes it to the next role in the workflow.

Unlike many content workflows, nothing enforces an author review, but the editor can handle this procedurally by returning the content to the author before she forwards it for approval. Forcing this review into the workflow would only require a few minor changes to the code, which I will leave to the reader as an exercise.

It is assumed that testing in this workflow is done throughout the process. Adding an additional role to handle testing should not be difficult. As you will see, much of the functionality in each role is repeated. This will also be the case for the tester role.

CMS.NET Roles

CMS.NET only uses four roles to handle content development:

- Author

- Editor

- Approver

- Deployer

Author

The author's role is to create the original content that the Web site will provide. Unlike the more expensive CMSs on the market, authors for CMS.NET have to be HTML knowledgeable so that they can format their content. For example, paragraphs require the <P> tag, images use the <img> tag, and boldface uses the <B> tag. In fact, all HTML formatting tags are supported.

All text entered into the edit boxes ignores spaces and new lines, so any manual formatting that the author does (that isn't done using HTML) is ignored when it finally displays on the Web site.

It is true that a good CMS enables an author to not worry about HTML when creating content. To keep the program simple, I overlooked this fact, but nothing is stopping you from augmenting the editor. An easier solution (and the one that I use) if you need any elaborate formatting is to use FrontPage or an equivalent tool and just cut and paste the HTML generated within the <body></body> tags into the edit boxes.

Figure 14-2 shows a little of what is available to an author in the way of HTML formatting. By the way, I created this Web page first using FrontPage to save time.

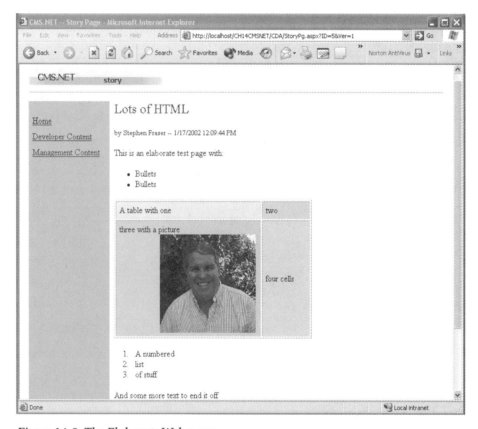

Figure 14-2. The Elaborate Web page

As you can see in Listing 14-1, which shows the actual HTML used to create the Elaborate Web page, the code contains bullets, a table, two images, and a numbered list. You might have noted the <BR Clear="all"> tag at the end. This little nifty tag makes sure that all subsequent HTML is placed after this visually on the Web page. If you leave it off, sometimes you might find that the tagline is embedded in the middle of your body.

Listing 14-1. The Elaborate Web Page's HTML

```
<p>This is an elaborate test page with:</p>
<ul>
  <li>Bullets</li>
  <li>Bullets</li>
</ul>
<table border="1" width="60%" cellpadding="6">
  <tr>
    <td width="75%" bgcolor="#CCFFFF">A table with one</td>
    <td width="25%" bgcolor="#FFCCFF">two</td>
  </tr>
  <tr>
    <td width="75%" bgcolor="#FFCC99">
      three with a picture
      <img border="0" align="right"
           src="http://localhost/CMSNET/Images/steph.gif"
           width="180" height="180">
    </td>
    <td width="25%" bgcolor="#99FFCC">four cells</td>
  </tr>
</table>
<ol>
  <li>A numbered</li>
  <li>list</li>
  <li>of stuff</li>
</ol>
<p>And some more text to end it off</p>
<BR clear="all">
```

Editor

The editor does have a more specific role in most content management systems, but in CMS.NET it is simply a second person to look over the piece of content with the authority to update as she sees fit.

Again, to keep things simple, I merged many roles into the editor role. In CMS.NET, the editor fills all the roles normally broken up into editor, copy editor, proofreader, compositor, and so on. Nothing is stopping you from adding these roles, and I'm sure you will find that much of the code is already provided.

If you have authors who are not HTML savvy, the editor's role could be used to add HTML formatting to the author's content.

As you can see, having a dynamic way of creating a workflow can come in handy. Here's a note to managers reading this: It took me only one week to write this entire workflow. If your software developers are saying it will take months to update it, they are yanking your chain, or you need better developers.

Approver

This role has the last say before the content is deployed in the Web site. CMS.NET only needs one person to approve the content, but it will not take much effort to change it to require more than one.

This role does not have the ability to make any changes to the content. He approves it, sends it back to the editor for more revisions, or withdraws it altogether. As I said in Chapter 3, this workflow has a chance of being wasted effort if the approver withdraws the content at this point. Hopefully, the editor and approver have already had some communication about the content before it gets to this point.

Deployer

This role simply takes the content and places it into the Web site repository. At this point, all the deployer does is place the content into its default content zone(s). If you were to add personalization to the Web site, this role would most likely expand.

The deployer also, frequently, takes content off the main Web site and places it into an archive. Since CMS.NET does not support archiving, the archive process just sends the content back to the editor for more revisions. (I did this so that I could test content workflow without having to keep creating new content.)

Interrole Communication

Let's get back to some coding. CMS.NET uses two methods to handle communication between roles in the workflow: notes and e-mails. CMS.NET uses notes as a means to provide a running commentary on the content and its development. E-mails, on the other hand, are used as an instant notifier of content availability.

Content Notes

Notes are simply time-stamped messages attached to a piece of content. They contain almost any kind of information. They are free format and, unlike content formatting that is manually typed in, will remain. HTML tags do not work.

The ContentNotes Database Table

This is the only new database table in this chapter. It is designed to hold content notes for a specific Content ID. The design of the database table, as shown in Table 14-1, is purposely simple in nature. It enables almost any type of textual information to be stored as a comment to the content.

Table 14-1. The ContentNotes Database Table Design

COLUMN NAME	DATA TYPE	LENGTH	KEY	DESCRIPTION
NoteID	int	4	true	Note identifier
ContentID	int	4	false	ContentID for which this content addresses
Note	text	16	false	The note text
Author	int	4	false	Author of the note
ModifiedDate	datetime	8	false	Date domain was last changed
CreationDate	datetime	8	false	Date domain was created

Notes Implementation

The implementation of content notes simply involves the standard CURVe processes. For those of you who don't remember, the CURVe processes are creating, updating, removing, and viewing. As you can see in Figure 14-3, the design of the notes process closely resembles that of the author's content development process covered in Chapter 11.

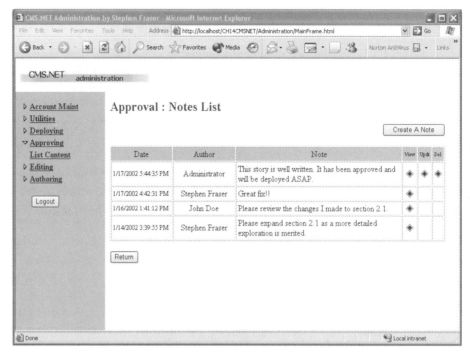

Figure 14-3. The NotesList Web page

No new coding is used to develop the notes process. It is really just a simplified cut and paste of the author's CURVe process. Because there is nothing new, none of the code will be displayed, but like all the source code, it can be found on the Apress Web site (www.apress.com) in the Downloads section.

The thing to remember about the notes process is that there is only one copy of the source. All the roles will use the exact same code to handle the maintenance of notes, unlike much of the rest of the common functionality shared by the roles, which have their own copy.

E-mail

CMS.NET automatically sends an e-mail whenever the content is sent to another role for processing. If the person fulfilling the role has already been determined, that person will be the only one receiving the e-mail. Otherwise, when the role changes, all persons in the next role in the process will be notified.

Creating e-mails is extremely easy using .NET. In fact, it can take as few as six lines of code. The first five build the e-mail message, and the final one sends the e-mail on its way.

```
MailMessage mail = new MailMessage();

mail.To      = "target_email@address.com";
mail.From    = "your_email@address.com";
mail.Subject = "Subject of the email";
mail.Body    = "Main body of the email";

SmtpMail.Send(mail);
```

The implementation of the e-mail process for CMS.NET is localized in the EmailAlert class (see Listing 14-2). Most of the class is simply little utility functions to help populate the e-mail message without the help of the Web page developer.

Only the Send() method actually does the work of sending the e-mail. Basically, the Send() method populates the e-mail with a subject line based on the alert code passed to it. Then, it checks to see if the e-mail is addressed to a specific person. If so, it addresses the e-mail only to him. If it is addressed to user zero, this means it should be sent to all users of a role specified by the alert code found. The process of getting all the accounts of a specified role is done by a simple select of the AccountRoles database table.

Listing 14-2. The EmailAlert Class

```
public class EmailAlert
{
    private int m_code;
    private int m_towho;
    private string m_body = "";
    private HttpContext m_context;

    public int Code
    {
        get { return m_code;   }
        set { m_code = value; }
    }

    public int ToWho
    {
        get { return m_towho;   }
        set { m_towho = value; }
    }
```

```csharp
public string Body
{
    get { return m_body;  }
    set { m_body = value; }
}

public EmailAlert(HttpContext context, int code, int towho)
{
    m_context = context;
    m_code    = code;
    m_towho   = towho;
}

public void Send()
{
    AppEnv appenv = new AppEnv(m_context);

    string SMTPServer = appenv.GetAppSetting("smtpserver").Trim();
    if (SMTPServer.Length <= 0)
        return;  // do not use email notifications

    SmtpMail.SmtpServer = SMTPServer;

    Account account = new Account(appenv.GetConnection());

    MailMessage mail = new MailMessage();

    DataRow dr = account.GetAccountForID(1); // Admin account
    mail.From = dr["Email"].ToString().Trim();

    mail.Subject = generateSubject();
    mail.Body = m_body;
    mail.BodyFormat = MailFormat.Text;

    if (m_towho != 0)
    {
        dr = account.GetAccountForID(m_towho);
        mail.To = dr["Email"].ToString().Trim();
        SmtpMail.Send(mail);
    }
    else
    {
```

```
            AccountRoles roles =
                new AccountRoles(new AppEnv(m_context).GetConnection());
            DataTable dt = roles.GetAllRole(getRoleForCode());

            foreach (DataRow drr in dt.Rows)
            {
                dr =
                  account.GetAccountForID(Convert.ToInt32(drr["AccountID"]));
                mail.To = dr["Email"].ToString().Trim();
                SmtpMail.Send(mail);
            }
        }
    }
}

private string getRoleForCode()
{
    switch (m_code)
    {
        case StatusCodes.RequiresUpdate:
            return "Author";

        case StatusCodes.AwaitingEdit:
        case StatusCodes.Editing:
        case StatusCodes.RequiresEditing:
            return "Editor";

        case StatusCodes.AwaitingApproval:
            return "Approver";

        case StatusCodes.Approved:
            return "Deployer";

        default:
            return "";
    }
}

private string generateSubject()
{
    switch (m_code)
    {
        case StatusCodes.AwaitingEdit:
            return "New content available for editing";
```

```
            case StatusCodes.Editing:
                return "Updated content available for editing";

            case StatusCodes.AwaitingApproval:
                return "Content available for approval";

            case StatusCodes.RequiresUpdate:
                return "Content requires updating";

            case StatusCodes.RequiresEditing:
                return "Content requires editing";

            case StatusCodes.Approved:
                return "Content available for deployment";

            case StatusCodes.Discontinued:
                return "Content has been discontinued";

            default:
                return "";
        }
    }
}
```

If you were observant you may have noticed the new AppSetting: smtpserver. When this value in empty, no e-mail notification is sent. The population of this AppSetting was added to setup/setup2.aspx. Basically, the change was adding a new text field and then making sure that the AppSetting is set along with all the others. The code involved is simply a cut and paste of any of the other AppSettings on the Web page.

To implement the alert, simply add two lines to the Web page where you want the alert sent, one to create the EmailAlert and the second to send it.

```
EmailAlert ea = new EmailAlert(Context, code, user);
ea.Send();
```

In the case of CMS.NET, you add this code to the submittal, approval, and return content Web pages. All of these pages are state transition Web pages because, once executed, the user no longer controls the content.

The Authoring Phase

Chapter 11 covered the author's process, but then there was only one user, the administrator, and roles had not been covered. A major problem with the earlier implementation of the author process was that the author had the right to access all content. When you later added more users and roles, the author was able to access content that was not even his own.

This may not seem too bad until you sit down and think of the ramifications, the worst of which is the complete lack of coordination in the development of content because many authors could work on the same piece of content at the same time without being aware of it. It is very dangerous to allow this in a CMS without careful monitoring and control. CMS.NET provides no special tools to monitor or control content entry.

Restricting Author's Content

An author should be able to access only his own content. In this situation, only one person at a time would be able to update any particular piece of content. Only when the author is finished and has passed the content on to the editors would someone else have write access to the content.

Limiting access in this fashion is easy enough to do. You only need to change the content retrieval method in the AutList Page_Load() method (see Listing 14-3) from the Content database helper GetHeadlines() method to the new GetHeadlinesForAuth() method (see Listing 14-4). This new method selects and retrieves headlines only for the user specified as a parameter, in this case the current user.

As a special condition, CMS.NET still wants to be able to get all the content if the user is the administrator, which in the case of CMS.NET is always account 1. In this scenario, CMS.NET continues to use the old GetHeadlines() method to retrieve content because it selects and retrieves all content in the Content database table.

Listing 14-3. Restricting Content to the Current Author Only

```
private void Page_Load(object sender, System.EventArgs e)
{
    ...

    DataTable dt;
    int accountNo = account.GetAccountID(User.Identity.Name);

    if (accountNo == 1)  // Admin sees all content
    {
        dt = content.GetHeadlines();
    }
    else
    {
        dt = content.GetHeadlinesForAuth(accountNo);
    }

    ...
}
```

As you can see in Listing 14-4, there really isn't anything special about the Content database helper method GetHeadlinesForAuth(). It is virtually the same as the GetHeadline() method, except it has the additional WHERE clause added to the stored procedure.

Listing 14-4. Content Database Helper GetHeadlinesForAuth Method

```
public DataTable GetHeadlinesForAuth(int Byline)
{
    //   SELECT ContentID, Version, Headline, Status
    //     FROM Content
    //    WHERE Byline=@Byline

    SqlCommand Command =
        new SqlCommand("Content_GetHeadlinesForAuth", m_Connection);
    Command.CommandType = CommandType.StoredProcedure;

    Command.Parameters.Add(new SqlParameter("@Byline", SqlDbType.Int));
    Command.Parameters["@Byline"].Value = Byline;

    SqlDataAdapter DAdpt = new SqlDataAdapter(Command);
```

```
    DataSet ds = new DataSet();
    DAdpt.Fill(ds, "Content");


    return ds.Tables["Content"];
}
```

Reducing Viewable Content

Over time, the number of articles will become overwhelming because nothing in CMS.NET actually gets deleted from the repository. So, CMS.NET, as shown in Figure 14-4, provides a drop-down box that reduces what an author views on the AutList Web page.

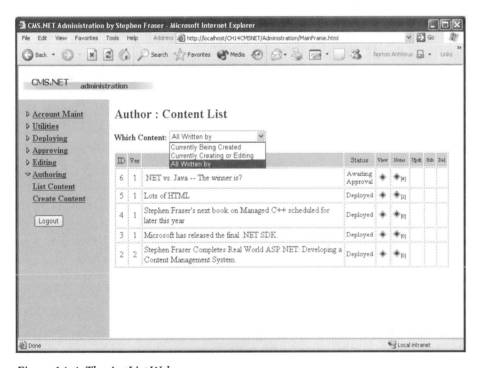

Figure 14-4. The AutList Web page

There are three levels, provided by CMS.NET, of the amount of content listed on the AutList Web page. As you can see in the AutList ASP.NET design code shown in Listing 14-5, the first option of the drop-down list displays only content currently being written. The next option displays active content, content that is being written or edited. The final option displays all content that an author has ever written.

Listing 14-5. The AutList Web Page Drop-Down List

```
<P>
  <STRONG>Which Content: </STRONG>
  <asp:dropdownlist id="ddlWhichContent" runat="server" AutoPostBack="True">
    <asp:ListItem Value="0">Currently Being Created</asp:ListItem>
    <asp:ListItem Value="1">Currently Creating or Editing</asp:ListItem>
    <asp:ListItem Value="2">All Written by</asp:ListItem>
  </asp:dropdownlist>
   
</P>
```

The AutList Codebehind to handle the amount of content viewed can be found, as usual, in the Page_Load() method (see Listing 14-6). As you can see, it is just a simple if statement. The complexities of this if statement are actually hidden within the IsTypeRequested() method, which checks the user-selected value of the drop-down box to see the amount of content the user wants to see. Depending on the level requested, the method then compares each piece of content to see if it falls into the desired level. If so, it is displayed; otherwise, it is simply ignored.

Listing 14-6. User-Determined Reduction of Visible Content in the AutList Method

```
private void Page_Load(object sender, System.EventArgs e)
{
    ...

    foreach (DataRow dr in dt.Rows)
    {
        cur = Convert.ToInt32(dr["ContentID"]);

        if (cur != prv)
        {
            prv = cur;

            if (IsTypeRequested(dr["Status"].ToString()))
            {
                ...
            }
        }
    }
}
```

```
private bool IsTypeRequested(string status)
{
    switch(Convert.ToInt32(ddlWhichContent.SelectedItem.Value))
    {
        case 0:
            return StatusCodes.isCreating(status);
        case 1:
            return (StatusCodes.isCreating(status) ||
                        StatusCodes.isAwaitingEdit(status) ||
                        StatusCodes.isEditing(status));
        case 2:
            return true;
        default :
            return false;
    }
}
```

Other Changes to the AutList Web Page

The AutList Web page also has two additional columns added to it: Status and Notes.

AutList Status Code

Status is a helpful column that enables an author to see where his content is in the workflow. Implement it simply by adding a new heading to the table on the AutList Web page and then, as CMS.NET is looping through the columns to display each headline, place the status in a literal control (see Listing 14-7). The status retrieved from the Content database is of type integer, which must be converted using the ToString() method of the StatusCodes class (see Listing 14-8) to a readable text string.

Listing 14-7. Adding the Status to AutList Web Page

```
lit = new LiteralControl(StatusCodes.ToString(Convert.ToInt32(dr["Status"])));
cell = new TableCell();
cell.Font.Size = new FontUnit(FontSize.XSmall);
cell.HorizontalAlign = HorizontalAlign.Center;
cell.Controls.Add(lit);
row.Cells.Add(cell);
```

Listing 14-8. The StatusCodes Common Utility Class

```
public class StatusCodes
{
    public const int None          = 0x00000000;
    public const int Creating      = 0x00000001;
    public const int AwaitingEdit  = 0x00000002;
    public const int RequiresUpdate = 0x00010001;
    public const int Editing       = 0x00000004;
    public const int AwaitingApproval = 0x00000008;
    public const int RequiresEditing = 0x00010004;
    public const int Approving     = 0x00000010;
    public const int Approved      = 0x00000020;
    public const int Deployed      = 0x00000040;
    public const int Archived      = 0x00000080;
    public const int Discontinued  = 0x00100000;

    public static string ToString(int val)
    {
        switch (val)
        {
            case Creating:
                return "Creating";
            case AwaitingEdit:
                return "Awaiting Edit";
            case RequiresUpdate:
                return "Requires Update";
            case Editing:
                return "Editing";
            case AwaitingApproval:
                return "Awaiting Approval";
            case RequiresEditing:
                return "Requires Editing";
            case Approving:
                return "Approving";
            case Approved:
                return "Approved";
            case Deployed:
                return "Deployed";
            case Archived:
                return "Archived";
            case Discontinued:
                return "Discontinued";
            default:
                return "None";
        }
    }
}
```

```
}

public static bool isCreating(string val)
{
    return (Convert.ToInt32(val) & Creating) == Creating;
}

public static bool isAwaitingEdit(string val)
{
    return (Convert.ToInt32(val) & AwaitingEdit) == AwaitingEdit;
}

public static bool isRequiresUpdate(string val)
{
    return (Convert.ToInt32(val) & RequiresUpdate) == RequiresUpdate;
}

public static bool isEditing(string val)
{
    return (Convert.ToInt32(val) & Editing) == Editing;
}

public static bool isAwaitingApproval(string val)
{
    return (Convert.ToInt32(val) & AwaitingApproval) == AwaitingApproval;
}

public static bool isRequiresEditing(string val)
{
    return (Convert.ToInt32(val) & RequiresEditing) == RequiresEditing;
}

public static bool isApproving(string val)
{
    return (Convert.ToInt32(val) & Approving) == Approving;
}

public static bool isApproved(string val)
{
    return (Convert.ToInt32(val) & Approved) == Approved;
}

public static bool isDeployed(string val)
{
```

```
            return (Convert.ToInt32(val) & Deployed) == Deployed;
    }

    public static bool isArchived(string val)
    {
            return (Convert.ToInt32(val) & Archived) == Archived;
    }
}
```

AutList Notes

The Notes column enables the author to add comments about his content without changing the content directly. He might use notes to provide information to the editor about what needs to be looked at or to help explain why it was written in a certain way.

To implement this, simply add a call to the notes process. This was discussed earlier.

Submitting Content to Editors

The only other thing of note about the author's process that wasn't covered in Chapter 11 is that AutSubmit (see Listing 14-9) now sets the content status to AwaitingEdit if it is a new content submit or to Editing if the editor is already known. Plus, it builds and sends an EmailAlert to the next role in the workflow, which in this case is the editor.

Listing 14-9. The AutSubmit New Codebehind

```
private void bnSubmit_Click(object sender, System.EventArgs e)
{
    int code;

    content.SetStatus(Convert.ToInt32(dt.Rows[0]["ContentID"]),
        Convert.ToInt32(dt.Rows[0]["Version"]),
        (code = (Convert.ToInt32(dt.Rows[0]["Editor"]) == 0)?
        StatusCodes.AwaitingEdit : StatusCodes.Editing));

    EmailAlert ea =
        new EmailAlert(Context, code, Convert.ToInt32(dt.Rows[0]["Editor"]));
    ea.Send();

    Response.Redirect("AutList.aspx");
}
```

The Editing Phase

There are a lot of similarities between the editor's process and the author's process. Obviously, there is no create procedure because that is the job of the author. Three of the other differences you see on the editor's list Web page, EdList.aspx (see Figure 14-5), are the Edit (instead of the Update) option plus the two new options of Withdraw and Rtn Updt (return to the author for an update).

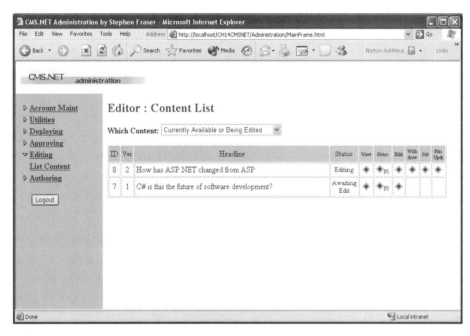

Figure 14-5. The EdList Web page

Restricting and Reducing Listed Editor Content

Just like the author, the editor can reduce the amount of content that is visible. The code to handle this is virtually the same as that of the author. As you can see in the Codebehind for EdList (see Listing 14-11), reducing the code to only that of the editors is done by the GetHeadlinesForEdit() method (see Listing 14-12).

The editor can reduce the content further by selecting what type of content he wants displayed using the drop-down box generated by the EdList ASP.NET design code (see Listing 14-10).

Listing 14-10. The EdList Web Page Drop-Down Box

```
<P>
  <STRONG>Which Content: </STRONG>
  <asp:dropdownlist id="ddlWhichContent" runat="server" AutoPostBack="True">
    <asp:ListItem Value="0">Currently Available or Being Edited</asp:ListItem>
    <asp:ListItem Value="1">Currently Editing or Awaiting Approval
    </asp:ListItem>
    <asp:ListItem Value="2">All Edited by</asp:ListItem>
  </asp:dropdownlist>
   
</P>
```

Listing 14-11. The EdList Codebehind

```
private void Page_Load(object sender, System.EventArgs e)
{
    ...
    DataTable dt;
    int accountNo = account.GetAccountID(User.Identity.Name);

    if (accountNo == 1)  // Admin sees all
    {
        dt = content.GetHeadlines();
    }
    else
    {
        dt = content.GetHeadlinesForEdit(accountNo);
    }
    ...
    foreach (DataRow dr in dt.Rows)
    {
        ...
        if (IsTypeRequested(dr["Status"].ToString(),
        Convert.ToInt32(dr["Editor"])))
        {
            ...
        }
    }
}
```

```
private bool IsTypeRequested(string status, int editor)
{
    switch(Convert.ToInt32(ddlWhichContent.SelectedItem.Value))
    {
        case 0:
            return (StatusCodes.isAwaitingEdit(status) ||
                    StatusCodes.isEditing(status));
        case 1:
            if (editor == 0)
                return false;
            return (StatusCodes.isAwaitingEdit(status) ||
                    StatusCodes.isRequiresUpdate(status) ||
                    StatusCodes.isEditing(status) ||
                    StatusCodes.isAwaitingApproval(status));
        case 2:
            if (editor == 0)
                return false;
            return true;
        default :
            return false;
    }
}
```

Something to note about the GetHeadlinesForEdit() method is the OR condition added to the WHERE clause. Before an editor selects a piece of content to be edited, it is assigned the value of 0. CMS.NET, knowing this, is able to display for the editor a list of all unselected content, as well as content that is specific to the current editor, by selecting both the content with the editor's ID as well as content that has no ID assigned to it.

You might have noticed in the IsTypeRequested() method that if the editor is zero, the second two options return false. This is because those options don't want to view unassigned content.

Listing 14-12. Content Database Helper GetHeadlinesForEdit Method

```
public DataTable GetHeadlinesForEdit(int Editor)
{
    //   SELECT ContentID, Version, Headline, Status
    //     FROM Content
    //    WHERE Editor=@Editor
    //       OR Editor=0

    SqlCommand Command = new SqlCommand("Content_GetHeadlinesForEdit",
                                        m_Connection);
    Command.CommandType = CommandType.StoredProcedure;

    Command.Parameters.Add(new SqlParameter("@Editor", SqlDbType.Int));
    Command.Parameters["@Editor"].Value = Editor;

    SqlDataAdapter DAdpt = new SqlDataAdapter(Command);

    DataSet ds = new DataSet();
    DAdpt.Fill(ds, "Content");

    return ds.Tables["Content"];
}
```

Differences Between Author and Editor Processes

There is no difference between the author and editor's ID, Ver, Headline, Status, View, and Notes columns. In fact, they use almost exactly the same code.

Editor Version Control

The first major difference happens when the editor selects a piece of content to edit. Unlike the author process, in which the only person who has access to a piece of content is the author, in the edit process, all editors have access to the piece of content when it first becomes available. The first thing the edit process must do is restrict the piece of content that is to be edited to one editor.

In CMS.NET, this happens immediately when an editor selects a piece of content for editing within the EdEdit.aspx Web page (see Figure 14-6). The restricting of the content is accomplished by simply setting the editor column in the database to the current author and then setting the status to Editing. If you remember from Chapter 2, this process is how CMS.NET handles version control. This whole process is completely transparent to the editor.

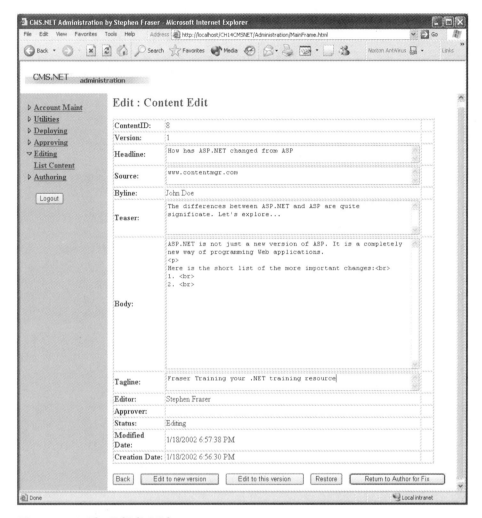

Figure 14-6. The EdEdit Web page

It is a little tricky to handle record locking. You have to remember that more than one person can access the content at exactly the same time. It also is possible to select the content at nearly the same time. It is also possible for an editor to select a piece of content that may be in the process of being selected by another editor. Thus, it is necessary to make sure that an editor who selects content is, in fact, the editor of that content.

CMS.NET takes the simple approach in the EdEdit Codebehind shown in Listing 14-13. The first thing the Page_Load() method does is check to see if the content has been assigned to an editor. If it has not, the SetAsEditor() method is called. This method simply calls the Content database helper method SetEditor() (see Listing 14-14) to assign the current content to the current editor. It then makes one final check to make sure it successfully allocated this content to the current editor.

451

Listing 14-13. The EdEdit Codebehind

```
private void Page_Load(object sender, System.EventArgs e)
{
    int cid = Convert.ToInt32(Request.QueryString["ContentID"]);

    if (cid == 0)
    {
        Page_Error("ContentID Missing");
    }
    dt = new Content(appEnv.GetConnection()).GetContentForID(cid);

    if (!IsPostBack)
    {
        if (StatusCodes.isAwaitingEdit(dt.Rows[0]["Status"].ToString()))
            SetAsEditor();

        BuildOrigPage();
    }
}
```

```
private void SetAsEditor()
{
    int id;
    Content content = new Content(appEnv.GetConnection());
    Account account = new Account(appEnv.GetConnection());
    DataRow dr = dt.Rows[0];

    content.SetEditor(Convert.ToInt32(dr["ContentID"]),
            Convert.ToInt32(dr["Version"]),
            (id = account.GetAccountID(User.Identity.Name)));

    dt = new Content(appEnv.GetConnection()).GetContentForID(
                                        Convert.ToInt32(dr["ContentID"]));

    // Only one person can edit a piece of content
    if (id != Convert.ToInt32(dt.Rows[0]["Editor"]))
        Page_Error("<h3>Too Slow!!</h3>Someone is editing this already");
}
```

The SetEditor() method shown in Listing 14-14 is not quite as simple as it first seems, as the key to only one editor having access to the content is hidden in it. Databases allow only one user to update a database table one row at a time. Thus, by only allowing the Content table row to be updated, if the editor is equal to zero, this basically eliminates two editors from updating the content. Once one of them has updated the content, the value of the editor column no longer will be zero.

This also shows the reason for the final if statement in the SetAsEditor() method in Listing 14-13. If SetEditor() returns without being able to update the content of the Content database, it will have the value of the other editor who snuck in before. This, of course, will cause this error to be presented to the editor.

Listing 14-14. The Content Database Helper SetEditor Method

```
public void SetEditor(int ContentID, int Version, int Editor)
{
    // UPDATE Content
    // SET
    //         Status       = @Status,
    //         Editor       = @Editor,
    //         ModifiedDate = @ModifiedDate
    // WHERE   ContentID = @ContentID
    //    AND  Version = @Version
    //    AND  Editor = 0

    SqlCommand Command = new SqlCommand("Content_SetEditor", m_Connection);
    Command.CommandType = CommandType.StoredProcedure;

    Command.Parameters.Add(new SqlParameter("@ContentID", SqlDbType.Int));
    Command.Parameters.Add(new SqlParameter("@Version", SqlDbType.Int));
    Command.Parameters.Add(new SqlParameter("@Editor", SqlDbType.Int));
    Command.Parameters.Add(new SqlParameter("@Status", SqlDbType.Int));
    Command.Parameters.Add(new SqlParameter("@ModifiedDate",
                                            SqlDbType.DateTime));

    Command.Parameters["@ContentID"].Value    = ContentID;
    Command.Parameters["@Version"].Value       = Version;
    Command.Parameters["@Editor"].Value        = Editor;
    Command.Parameters["@Status"].Value        = StatusCodes.Editing;
    Command.Parameters["@ModifiedDate"].Value = DateTime.Now;

    try
    {
        m_Connection.Open();
        Command.ExecuteNonQuery();
    }
    finally
    {
        m_Connection.Close();
    }
}
```

Giving Other Editors Access to Content

At times, an editor will need to relinquish control over the content she is editing because she is unable, for some reason, to complete the editing process. Because CMS.NET allows only one editor at a time, CMS.NET needs to add Withdraw to the editor list of functions (see Figure 14-7).

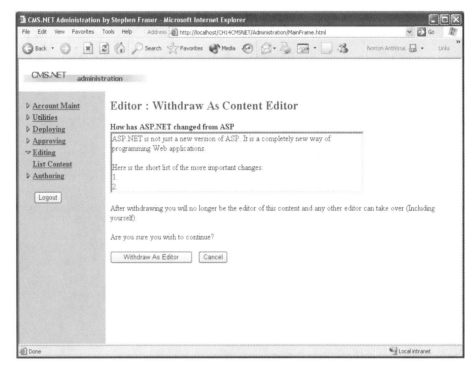

Figure 14-7. The EdWithdraw Web page

Basically, Withdraw sets the editor back to zero and sets the status back to AwaitingEditing. It also creates a new version of the content so that a record of the previous editor's work is maintained. As you can see in the EdWithdraw Codebehind (see Listing 14-15), the code to handle the editor relinquishing control is very similar to all the submit Codebehinds.

First, it displays the content so that the editor can verify that this is indeed the content of which she wants to relinquish control. Then, when the editor clicks the Withdraw As Editor button, a new version of the content is created with an editor of zero and a status of AwaitingEdit. Next, an EmailAlert is sent so that the other editors will be notified of the content's availability. Finally, it jumps back to the list Web page where the content should be listed as available again.

Listing 14-15. The EdWithdraw Codebehind

```
public class EdWithdraw : PageEx
{
    protected System.Web.UI.WebControls.Label lbWhichBody;
    protected System.Web.UI.WebControls.Label lbWhichHeadline;
    protected System.Web.UI.WebControls.Button bnWithdraw;

    private Content content;
    private int cid = 0;
    private DataTable dt;

    private void Page_Load(object sender, System.EventArgs e)
    {
        cid = Convert.ToInt32(Request.QueryString["ContentID"]);

        if (cid == 0)
        {
            Page_Error("ContentID Missing");
        }

        content = new Content(appEnv.GetConnection());

        dt = content.GetContentForID(cid);
        lbWhichHeadline.Text = dt.Rows[0]["Headline"].ToString();
        lbWhichBody.Text = dt.Rows[0]["Body"].ToString();
    }

    private void bnSubmit_Click(object sender, System.EventArgs e)
    {
        try
        {
            int code;
            Content content = new Content(appEnv.GetConnection());
            Account account = new Account(appEnv.GetConnection());

            DataRow dr = dt.Rows[0];
```

```
                content.Insert(cid, Convert.ToInt32(dr["Version"]) + 1,
                    dr["Headline"].ToString(), dr["Source"].ToString(),
                    Convert.ToInt32(dr["Byline"]),
                    dr["Teaser"].ToString(), dr["Body"].ToString(),
                    dr["TagLine"].ToString(), 0,
                    Convert.ToInt32(dr["Approver"]),
                    account.GetAccountID(User.Identity.Name),
                    (code = StatusCodes.AwaitingEdit));

                EmailAlert ea = new EmailAlert(Context, code, 0);
                ea.Send();

            Response.Redirect("EdList.aspx");
        }
        catch (Exception err)
        {
            Page_Error("The following error occurred: " + err.Message);
        }
    }

    private void bnCancel_Click(object sender, System.EventArgs e)
    {
        Response.Redirect("EdList.aspx");
    }
}
```

Returning Content to the Author

The final difference between the author and editor processes is that an editor can return the content back to the author for updating using the EdReturn Web page (see Figure 14-8).

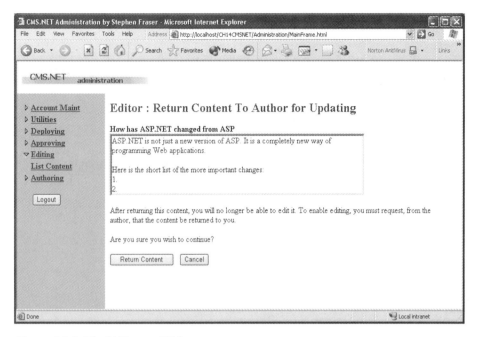

Figure 14-8. The EdReturn Web page

Code-wise, this process is no different than submitting the content to the next phase of the workflow. In fact, it *is* sending it to the next phase. It just happens that the next phase is back to the author. The code is very similar to Listing 14-15 except for the bnSubmit_Click() method (see Listing 14-16). This method only sets the status to RequiresUpdate (leaving the editor unchanged) so that when the author resubmits the updated content, it gets routed immediately back to the same editor.

Listing 14-16. The EdReturn Codebehind

```
private void bnSubmit_Click(object sender, System.EventArgs e)
{
    int code;

    content.SetStatus(Convert.ToInt32(dt.Rows[0]["ContentID"]),
        Convert.ToInt32(dt.Rows[0]["Version"]),
        (code = StatusCodes.RequiresUpdate));

    EmailAlert ea = new EmailAlert(Context, code,
                            Convert.ToInt32(dt.Rows[0]["ByLine"]));
    ea.Send();

    Response.Redirect("EdList.aspx");
}
```

The Approval Phase

The approval process is actually very simple. As you can see in the `AppList` Web page (see Figure 14-9), the approver can only view, add a note to, approve, return (to the editor), or cancel the content. The code to handle these (except View and Notes) is very simple because all they deal with is changing status codes and updating the approver on the content database record.

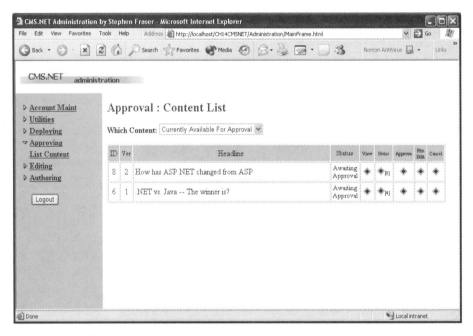

Figure 14-9. The AppList Web page

Approving Content

The `AppApprove` Web page, as you can see in Figure 14-10, is virtually the same as the submit Web page of the author or editor. It has the standard headline, body, warning, and buttons that you found on the other submit Web pages.

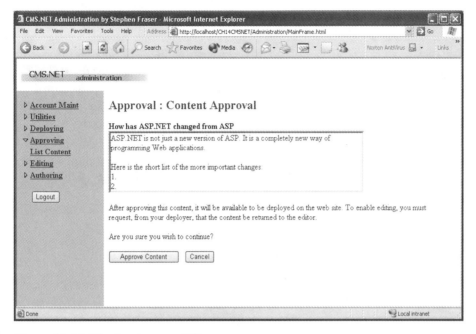

Figure 14-10. The AppApprove Web page

The only difference between AppApprove and the other submits is that the status code is set to Approved and the Approver ID is set to the current approver. As the AppAppove Codebehind shows (see Listing 14-17), there is little new in the way of code.

Listing 14-17. The AppApprove Codebehind

```
private void bnApprove_Click(object sender, System.EventArgs e)
{
    Account account = new Account(appEnv.GetConnection());

    content.SetApproval(Convert.ToInt32(dt.Rows[0]["ContentID"]),
        Convert.ToInt32(dt.Rows[0]["Version"]),
        account.GetAccountID(User.Identity.Name));

    EmailAlert ea = new EmailAlert(Context, StatusCodes.Approved, 0);
    ea.Send();

    Response.Redirect("AppList.aspx");
}
```

Returning Content to the Editor

The AppReturn Web page (see Figure 14-11) is nearly a clone of the EdReturn Web page. In fact, the code is nearly identical. The only difference is that the status is changed to RequiresEditing instead of RequiresUpdating, and the page jumps back to the AppList Web page instead of the EdList Web page, for obvious reasons.

The AppReturn Web page's purpose is to return the page back to the editor because he is unhappy with something about the content.

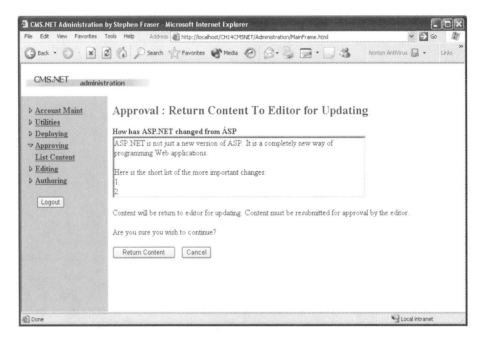

Figure 14-11. The AppReturn Web page

Canceling or Discontinuing Content

The last thing an approver can do is cancel the content. In other words, the approver has the option to discontinue or can the content altogether. There are times when a piece of content simply does not belong on the Web site. For example, the story may be a duplicate.

The AppDiscont Web page (see Figure 14-12) is a little more elaborate than the other submit-type Web pages. This is due to CMS.NET's belief that the editor and author should be given an explanation of why their efforts were canceled. As you can see, two edit boxes are provided: one for an explanation to the editor and the other for the author. Thus, it is possible to provide different levels of detail in the explanations provided to the editor or author.

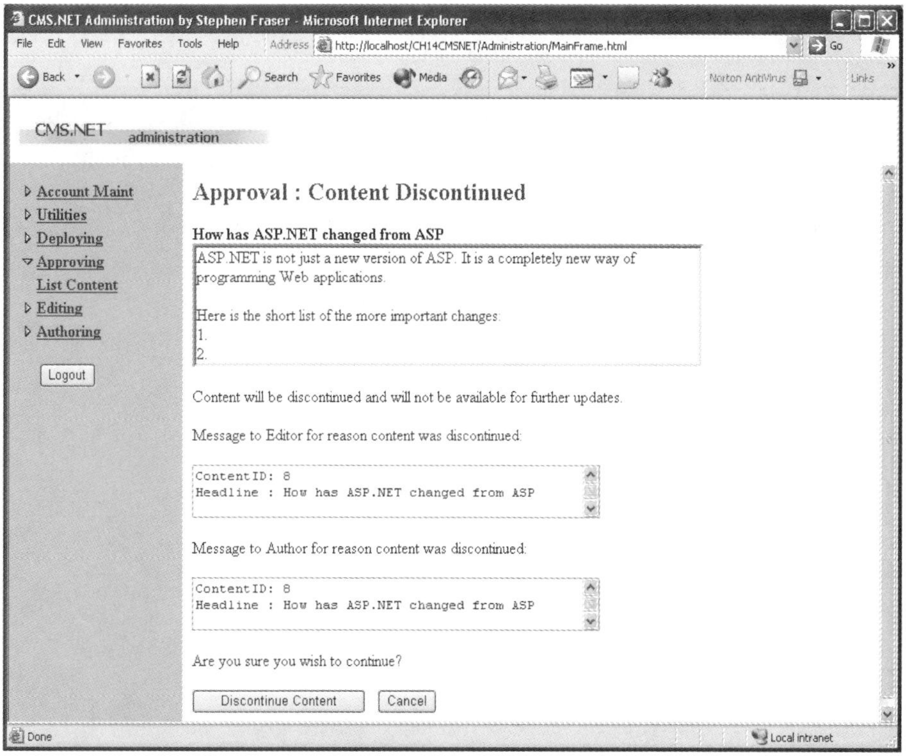

Figure 14-12. The AppDiscont Web page

The main thing the AppDiscont Page_Load() method (see Listing 14-18) does differently from the standard submit-type Web page is that it fills in the edit boxes with default information, saving the approver time. It then displays these edit boxes.

When the approver clicks the Discontinue Content button, it sets the approver column in the Content database to the current user and then sets the status to Discontinued. Next, it sends out different EmailAlerts to the editor and author. Finally, it returns to the AppList Web page.

Listing 14-18. The AppDiscont Codebehind

```
private void Page_Load(object sender, System.EventArgs e)
{
    cid = Convert.ToInt32(Request.QueryString["ContentID"]);

    if (cid == 0)
    {
        Page_Error("ContentID Missing");
    }
```

```
        content = new Content(appEnv.GetConnection());

        dt = content.GetContentForID(cid);
        lbWhichHeadline.Text = dt.Rows[0]["Headline"].ToString();
        lbWhichBody.Text = dt.Rows[0]["Body"].ToString();

        tbEdReason.Text = "ContentID: " + cid + "\nHeadline : " +
                          dt.Rows[0]["Headline"].ToString() + "\n";
        tbAutReason.Text = "ContentID: " + cid + "\nHeadline : " +
                           dt.Rows[0]["Headline"].ToString() + "\n";
}
```

```
private void bnDiscontinue_Click(object sender, System.EventArgs e)
{
        int code;
        Account account = new Account(appEnv.GetConnection());

        content.SetApproval(Convert.ToInt32(dt.Rows[0]["ContentID"]),
            Convert.ToInt32(dt.Rows[0]["Version"]),
            account.GetAccountID(User.Identity.Name));
        content.SetStatus(Convert.ToInt32(dt.Rows[0]["ContentID"]),
            Convert.ToInt32(dt.Rows[0]["Version"]),
            (code = StatusCodes.Discontinued));

        EmailAlert ea = new EmailAlert(Context, code,
                            Convert.ToInt32(dt.Rows[0]["Editor"]));
        ea.Body = tbEdReason.Text;
        ea.Send();

        ea = new EmailAlert(Context, code,
                            Convert.ToInt32(dt.Rows[0]["ByLine"]));
        ea.Body = tbAutReason.Text;
        ea.Send();

        Response.Redirect("AppList.aspx");
}
```

The Deployment Phase

Providing the content to the users is probably one of the most important phases
of the CMS.NET workflow. Without this phase, you wouldn't have much of a Web
site. In fact, you wouldn't have a Web site at all.

The deployment process of CMS.NET is designed to be as simple as possible, but this simplicity in use causes a lot more complexity in development. CMS.NET makes a few assumptions when deploying content that are designed to simplify the process:

- There is only one lead per zone.

- Ranking of content is done on a four-level scale.

- A piece of content can be placed in more than one zone.

- Ranking can be unique for each zone.

- Maintenance of the content is handled manually. (This assumption on a large site would definitely not be acceptable. This book makes this assumption to simplify the process.)

- When a piece of content gets archived, it is done in all zones in which it is deployed.

As you can see, the DeployList Web page (see Figure 14-13) is actually broken up into two lists. The first list contains all the new content that is yet to be deployed. The second list contains all deployed content.

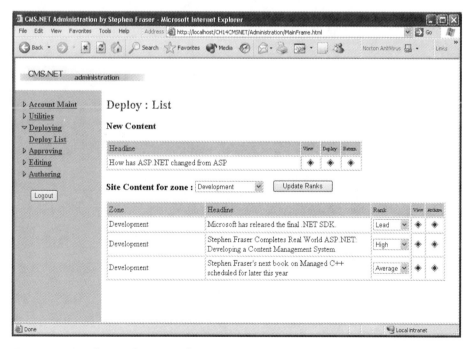

Figure 14-13. The DeployList Web page

Viewing Previously Deployed Content

Creating the previously deployed list looks complicated but, if broken into its parts, is really very straightforward. The first time the Web page is posted, a drop-down list of zones is built and displayed with an empty table. Then, when the user selects a zone from the drop-down list, the Web page immediately gets posted. The result of this post is that all the deployed content for the selected zone is displayed.

The DeployList Codebehind (see Listing 14-19) for selecting all content from a zone is straightforward. The Page_Load() method simply cycles through all the distribution records, looking for any record with the same ZoneID as selected by the user. When a matching record is found, a subsequent lookup in the Content database is done to retrieve the corresponding content record.

Each record in the Distribution database has a ranking that specifies the order in which it gets displayed to the user. This rank is displayed using a drop-down list of all ranks, where the content rank is the selected value of the drop-down list.

To update the rank of any piece of content, the user simply has to select a different ranking for the content from the drop-down list and then click the Update Ranks button. The code in the bnUpdtRanks_Click() method will then proceed and process the change in rank. First, it counts the number of lead stories. If the number of leads is greater than one, an error is posted. Otherwise, the method cycles through each distribution record a second time, updating Distribution database table rankings as appropriate.

Listing 14-19. The DeployList Codebehind

```
private void Page_Load(object sender, System.EventArgs e)
{
    zone = new Zone(appEnv.GetConnection());
    dist = new Distribution(appEnv.GetConnection());
    content = new Content(appEnv.GetConnection());

    LiteralControl lit;
    TableCell cell;
    DropDownList ddlRank;
    DataTable AllRanks = null;

    DataTable dtz = zone.GetAllZones();
    DataTable dt = content.GetHeadlines();

    ...

    if (!IsPostBack)
```

```
{
    ListItem item;

    ddlZones.Items.Add(new ListItem("None"));
    ddlZones.Items.Add(new ListItem("All"));

    foreach (DataRow dr in dtz.Rows)
    {
        ddlZones.Items.Add(new ListItem(dr["Title"].ToString()));
    }
}
else
{
    foreach (DataRow dr in dtz.Rows)
    {
        DataTable dtd = dist.GetOrdered(Convert.ToInt32(dr["ZoneID"]));

        if (ddlZones.SelectedItem.Text.Equals("All") ||
            ddlZones.SelectedItem.Text.Equals(dr["Title"]))
        {
            if (dtd.Rows.Count == 0)
            {
                TableRow row = new TableRow();
                tblSiteContent.Rows.Add(row);

                lit = new LiteralControl(dr["Title"].ToString());
                cell = new TableCell();
                cell.Controls.Add(lit);
                row.Cells.Add(cell);

                lit = new LiteralControl("No Content");
                cell = new TableCell();
                cell.ColumnSpan = 4;
                cell.Controls.Add(lit);
                row.Cells.Add(cell);
            }
            foreach (DataRow drd in dtd.Rows)
            {
                TableRow row = new TableRow();
                tblSiteContent.Rows.Add(row);

                lit = new LiteralControl(dr["Title"].ToString());
                cell = new TableCell();
```

```
            cell.Controls.Add(lit);
            row.Cells.Add(cell);

            DataRow drc =
                content.GetContentForIDVer(
                    Convert.ToInt32(drd["ContentID"]),
                    Convert.ToInt32(drd["Version"]));

            lit = new LiteralControl(drc["Headline"].ToString());
            cell = new TableCell();
            cell.Controls.Add(lit);
            row.Cells.Add(cell);

            if (AllRanks == null)
            {
                AllRanks =
                    new ContentRank(appEnv.GetConnection()).GetRanks();
            }

            cell = new TableCell();
            ddlRank = new DropDownList();
            foreach (DataRow drr in AllRanks.Rows)
            {
                ddlRank.Items.Add(
                    new ListItem(drr["Rank"].ToString(),
                                 drr["RankID"].ToString()));
            }
            ddlRank.Items.FindByValue(
                drd["Ranking"].ToString()).Selected = true;

            cell.Controls.Add(ddlRank);
            row.Cells.Add(cell);

            BuildImageButton(row, "DeployView.aspx?ID=" +
                                  drd["ContentID"] +
                                  "&Ver=" + drd["Version"]);
            BuildImageButton(row, "DeployArchive.aspx?ID=" +
                                  drd["ContentID"] +
                                  "&Ver=" + drd["Version"]);
        }
      }
    }
  }
}
```

```
private void bnUpdtRanks_Click(object sender, System.EventArgs e)
{
    int crow;
    DataTable dtz = zone.GetAllZones();
    DropDownList ddl;

    crow = 1;  // row 0 is titles
    foreach (DataRow dr in dtz.Rows)
    {
        DataTable dtd = dist.GetOrdered(Convert.ToInt32(dr["ZoneID"]));

        if (ddlZones.SelectedItem.Text.Equals("All") ||
            ddlZones.SelectedItem.Text.Equals(dr["Title"]))
        {
            if (dtd.Rows.Count <= 0)
                crow++;

            int LeadCount = 0;
            foreach (DataRow drd in dtd.Rows)
            {
                TableCellCollection tcc = tblSiteContent.Rows[crow++].Cells;
                ddl = (DropDownList)tcc[2].Controls[0];

                if (ddl.SelectedItem.Text.Trim().Equals("Lead"))
                    LeadCount++;
            }
            if (LeadCount > 1)
                Page_Error("<h2>**Error** Multiple Leads found</h2>" +
                            "Only allowed one lead per zone");
        }
    }

    crow = 1;  // row 0 is titles
    foreach (DataRow dr in dtz.Rows)
    {
        DataTable dtd = dist.GetOrdered(Convert.ToInt32(dr["ZoneID"]));

        if (ddlZones.SelectedItem.Text.Equals("All") ||
            ddlZones.SelectedItem.Text.Equals(dr["Title"]))
        {
            if (dtd.Rows.Count <= 0)
                crow++;
```

```
    foreach (DataRow drd in dtd.Rows)
    {
        TableCellCollection tcc = tblSiteContent.Rows[crow++].Cells;
        ddl = (DropDownList)tcc[2].Controls[0];

        if (ddl.SelectedIndex+1 != Convert.ToInt32(drd["Ranking"]))
        {
            dist.UpdateRank(Convert.ToInt32(dr["ZoneID"]),
                Convert.ToInt32(drd["ContentID"]),
                Convert.ToInt32(drd["Version"]),
                ddl.SelectedIndex+1);
        }
    }
    }
}
}
```

NOTE *The code in the Downloads section of the Apress Web site (www.apress.com) is different from the code in Listing 14-19. There is a bug in the current version of ASP.NET that causes the Rank drop-down lists to be cached between posts so that the selected values in them turn up all wrong. The solution used in the code on the Apress site is to redirect to the* DeployList *whenever a new zone is selected, instead of the correct posting method of Listing 14-19. This causes the page to be regenerated from scratch each time. This is not as efficient, but it does seem to work.*

Deploying Content

The new content list provides three functions: view content, deploy content, and return content for editing. The code for viewing and returning content has already been covered in previous phases. The deploy content code has a few new interesting features.

The core of the deployment process is assigning a piece of content to a content zone(s) as appropriate. As you see in the DeployDeploy.aspx Web page (see Figure 14-14), the form is basically broken up into two parts. The top verifies the identity of the piece of content you want to deploy. The bottom is made up of a multiselect list box of all the zones where it is possible to place the content.

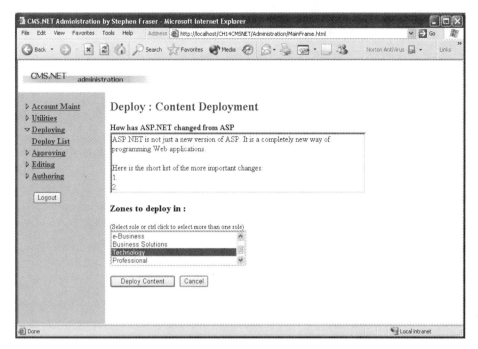

Figure 14-14. The DeployDeploy Web page

The code to handle deployment is actually quite easy, as you can see in the DeployDeploy Codebehind (see Listing 14-20). First, the Page_Load() method loads all the zones into the list box. Then, when the user has selected all the zones for the content, the bnDeploy_Click() method iterates through the list to see which have been selected. When a list entry is selected, a Distribution database table row is created.

Listing 14-20. The DeployDeploy Codebehind

```
private void Page_Load(object sender, System.EventArgs e)
{
    cid = Convert.ToInt32(Request.QueryString["ID"]);
    ver = Convert.ToInt32(Request.QueryString["Ver"]);

    if (cid == 0)
    {
        Page_Error("ContentID Missing");
    }
```

```
    if (ver == 0)
    {
        Page_Error("Version Missing");
    }

    dtz = new Zone(appEnv.GetConnection()).GetAllZones();

    foreach (DataRow dr in dtz.Rows)
    {
        lbZones.Items.Add(new ListItem(dr["Title"].ToString(),
                                       dr["ZoneID"].ToString()));
    }

    content = new Content(appEnv.GetConnection());
    drc = content.GetContentForIDVer(cid, ver);

    tbWhichHeadline.Text = drc["Headline"].ToString();
    tbWhichBody.Text = drc["Body"].ToString();
}

private void bnDeploy_Click(object sender, System.EventArgs e)
{
    Distribution dist = new Distribution(appEnv.GetConnection());
    content.SetStatus(cid, ver, StatusCodes.Deployed);

    int avgRank = new ContentRank(appEnv.GetConnection()).GetRankID("Average");

    for (int i = 0; i < lbZones.Items.Count; i++)
    {
        if (lbZones.Items[i].Selected)
            dist.Insert(cid, ver, Convert.ToInt32(lbZones.Items[i].Value),
                        avgRank);
    }

    Response.Redirect("DeployList.aspx");
}
```

Summary

This chapter covered adding a workflow to the CMS.NET's content management application (CMA).

First, it described the workflow and the roles provided by CMS.NET. Then, interrole communications and e-mail alerts were covered. It finished up by covering the four phases of the CMA workflow:

- Authoring

- Editing

- Approval

- Deployment

The next chapter examines user registration and displaying protected user content.

CHAPTER 15

Registered Users and Protected Content

SOME ADVOCATES SAY THE INTERNET should be free and available to all. If you are one of those people, you might consider skipping this chapter because it is going to go against everything you believe. This chapter will show you how to stop people from seeing parts of your Web site. It does not cover the process of charging people to access these restricted areas because that is the domain of e-commerce and would require an entire book of its own.

There are many ways to protect content. The protection method can range from a retinal scan in a locked room with no outside access to the more lenient method presented in this book: letting users request access and immediately get it without any form of background check.

The first question you should ask yourself as a Web site administrator is "Why am I protecting this content?" If there is no real reason to restrict the content, you probably shouldn't waste your time (and the user's) in protecting it. If a user doesn't see any value in your protected content, she most likely won't register to get access anyway. Or if the user spends time registering only to find nothing of value, she will probably remove herself from the registered users list and never return.

Once you know why you are restricting the content, it should be a simple process of selecting or determining some criteria for allowing access. Your next concern should be figuring out a way for users to register so as to not scare them away from the site with too many questions, but on the other hand, you need to include enough questions so that you know you have a valid user who meets the criteria for accessing the site.

Finally, you have to make logging into the Web site as painless as possible. Many users dislike logging into new Web sites because it means one more login ID and password to remember.

Why Protect Content?

Many Web sites give users complete access to the information provided by the sites. Other Web sites allow users to browse a good portion of the sites to entice them into wanting access to the restricted parts.

Quite often, the restricted portions of a Web site are available for some monetary amount. On the other hand, some Web sites with protected areas, such as CMS.NET, restrict content for the sole reason of wanting to attain more information about their users. For example, an e-mail address can be worth quite a lot to marketing and sales people, especially the e-mail address of someone who has already shown interest in the site.

In some Web sites, the content is restricted to specific people known to the Web administrator or who formally request access to the Web site. Usually, for these types of Web sites, the user does not get immediate access to the site. Instead, the Webmaster or an automated process e-mails the user back to verify his identity. The e-mail usually includes the username and password needed to access the Web site. Other Web sites, such as CMS.NET, provide immediate access after users register. With these sites, the users often pick their own usernames and passwords.

The method chosen usually is determined by how valuable the Web site's information is.

Privacy Policy

No matter what the reason is for restricting content, if the Web site requires personally identifiable information to access the protected content, some type of privacy policy should be available for the users to read. This privacy policy should be detailed, and a lawyer probably should look at it.

Without a privacy policy, you might find that some users will be very leery about entering their private information into your Web site. Some users might decide not to register at all because they are afraid that their private information will be used in a manner that they do not want. Basically, the privacy policy is designed to make users feel more confident that you will keep their personal information confidential.

The CMS.NET privacy policy (see Listing 15-1) provides the user information about the following:

- What personally identifiable information is collected

- How the information is used

- Who has access to the information

- How to update, change, or delete information

- How cookies are used

As you can guess, this is hardly an all-inclusive list of what to include in your privacy policy. Most likely, your policy is not going to be anything like CMS.NET's.

Listing 15-1. The CMS.NET Privacy Policy
```
Privacy Policy


What personally identifiable information does CMS.NET collect?


Over a period of time, CMS.NET may collect personal information, including your
name, address, email address, birth date, gender, and zip code. After providing
CMS.NET with any of this information, you are no longer anonymous.
You do not have to provide any personal information to use the CMS.NET service.
The only information that you are required to provide is a username and
password, which are not linked to you in any way unless you click on the
"Remember Login" checkbox, which causes a cookie to be stored on your computer.


How does CMS.NET use personal information?


CMS.NET does not use your personal information in any way. This program is a
demo program only. Feel free to enter any information when requested, even
incorrect information, as it makes no difference to the functionality of the
Web site.
In fact, periodically, the registration information will be deleted.
The information will never be sold, rented, or distributed.


Who has access to your information?


One person--Stephen Fraser, the author of CMS.NET (this site).


Can you update, change, or delete your data?


As the data is not used for any reason whatsoever, there is no reason to
maintain the data's accuracy. In fact, I recommend that you do not enter valid
information. To delete your data, just contact Stephen Fraser; his email
address is below.


How are cookies used by CMS.NET?


CMS.NET uses two types of cookies: Session and Login.
```

Session cookies only remain as long as the current session and do not remain on your computer. They are used to pass session information, which identifies your current session without any personal information (this is done by a random number).

Login cookies store your login authentication information so that you don't have to log in each time you access the site.

To remove the Login cookie from your computer, you simply need to log out of CMS.NET.

For questions about this policy, please contact:

Stephen Fraser
srgfraser@contentmgr.com

What Are User Profiles?

A *user profile* is the set of information about a user that the system has gathered through, hopefully, multiple visits. A user profile can be static and collect a specific set of information, or it can be dynamic and change as time goes on.

At one time, user profiles were made up of simple things such as a user's name, password, and address. Now, with the addition of personalization, more elaborate and complex information is gathered in user profiles. For example, a profile might record the number of times a user has accessed a Web page of a particular content type. It also could record the reverse: Which Web pages does the user continually ignore when presented?

Almost any information can be stored in a user profile. Caution needs to be used with regard to what information is stored because users like their privacy. If they perceive that the Web site is gathering too much personally identifiable information, they may not be too happy.

When you design database tables for user profiles, it is a good idea to allow for dynamic changes. As time progresses, you will probably find that information you gather now might not be important later, and other information you might not have thought of collecting before might become important.

To handle this, you should consider storing data as outlined in Chapter 10, breaking your account or profile information into two parts. The first part is data that is essential to the running of the CMS. The second part is nice-to-have information that has no impact on the operation of the system.

CMS.NET does this by breaking the user profiles, which CMS.NET calls *accounts,* into three parts: the essential information, the account roles/permissions, and the nice-to-have information. Only the data in the essential section, or the Account database table, needs to be present for CMS.NET to function.

Methods of Gathering User Information

You can gather user information using many different approaches. The most common methods fall into one of two schools: the quick blitz and the slow retrieval. In many cases both are used, such as when a quick blitz is used to get the essential information and slow retrieval is implemented for anything else.

The Quick Blitz Method

The quick blitz method simply presents the user with a huge shopping cart of questions when she first registers into the system. Usually, no rhyme or reason is presented to the user as to why much of this information is needed, and in many cases, it actually isn't needed.

Another approach to the quick blitz is the registration wizard. In this approach, the Web site tries to soften the blow of asking all its questions by breaking them up into smaller, more logical pieces. The need for these pieces can then be explained to the users.

When using either of these approaches, the user, after completing the registration process, usually expects some kind of reward for completing the arduous process. To be dumped back into the same old site with a few more options is quite a letdown.

The Slow Retrieval Method

Personally, I dislike sites that use the blitz method. (You probably figured that out when you read my explanation of the blitz method.) My first thought is always "Why do they need all this information?"

My preferred approach is the slow retrieval method, which goes something like this:

- Get the minimum amount of information from the user that will still allow the Web site to function.

- When additional information is needed that the system doesn't yet have, query the user for it.

Why is this approach better? First, users are not threatened by having to give away their life stories. If you were to monitor which are the most common exit pages for first-time users, you probably would find that this occurs somewhere in the registration process. This is because the site has not yet built any trust with the user.

Second, because the registration process is so quick, users don't expect fireworks when they continue using the site after registering. If the registration process is quick enough, the user might not even notice that he registered. If that were the case, why would he expect anything special?

Third, and most important, the user will see immediately after being queried for the additional information why it was needed. For example, if a site queries for your home address, the site had better be sending you something at that address. Trust is built this way. The user knows that what the system is asking for does, in fact, have some importance. As time goes by and trust is established, the Web site can ask (every once in a while) some esoteric question, and the user will not feel threatened in any way.

You might be thinking that continually querying the user could get annoying to the user, and you would be correct. You will usually find that you do not need as much information as you think you do, and you will be able to get the information in different, less direct ways. For example, instead of asking a user what her favorite sport is, the site could maintain the number of times she accesses a particular sport's Web page. In fact, this information will probably be more accurate. A user might think that he likes baseball, but in reality, he reads the racecar news much more frequently. Capturing data this way also enables seasonal preferences because it is possible to maintain data based on the time of year.

It is true that the slow retrieval method is far more complex, but the trust built by using it is well worth the effort.

Registration Using the Slow Retrieval Method

As I pointed out earlier, the first stage in registration (using the slow retrieval method) is to capture only the information needed about the user to run the CMS successfully. In the case of CMS.NET, as you can see in Figure 15-1, this information is only the username and password. CMS.NET also requests the user's e-mail address, but it doesn't demand it because this is a demo with no real need for it.

Figure 15-1. The Register Web page

NOTE *Being asked for an e-mail address is so commonplace that I decided to throw it into CMS.NET to simplify your CMS development. In the case of CMS.NET, because it is not needed at the time of registration, it should not have been included in the initial registration Web form.*

An e-mail address is normally one of the first things that a Web site requests from a user because it is the most common means of communication. Users are used to the idea of being asked for it, so they usually have little problem supplying it when requested.

The Register Codebehind (see Listing 15-2) to handle the registration has a few new things that I should go over. The first thing you should note is that Page_Load() does absolutely nothing. If you remember, when you create a button (or, in this case, an image button) event for ASP.NET to process, it executes the event after the Page_Load() method. When you use two buttons, as in the

Register Web page, you have to be careful with what you place in the `Page_Load()` method because it will be executed before the button even. In the case of the registration Web page, there is no common code that you want to be run for both the register and cancel events. Therefore, nothing is placed in the `Page_Load()` method; instead, all logic is placed in the appropriate event handlers.

The next thing of interest is the `FormsAuthentication.SetAuthCookie()` method. This method adds an authentication cookie to the session. In effect, this logs the user on without forcing her to fill in a login screen. This seems like a logical thing to do. You know at this point that the user has been authenticated because you just added her to the repository. It also saves the user some unnecessary steps.

The last thing of interest is in the Cancel process. Here, you add a `LiteralControl` containing JavaScript. The JavaScript is the standard `history.go()` method, which is one of the most common ways to implement a Back button, with one catch: You go back two pages instead of one. I'm sure you have the glassy-eyed stare I had when I finally figured it out. Why two pages? I'm not really sure, but I'm sure there is a good explanation. All I know is that when you go back one page, you return to the current page.

Listing 15-2. The Register Codebehind

```
private void Page_Load(object sender, System.EventArgs e)
{
}


private void ibnRegister_Click(object sender, ImageClickEventArgs e)
{
    Account account  = new Account(appEnv.GetConnection());

    if (Page.IsValid)
    {
        try
        {
            if (account.GetAccountID(tbUserName.Text) > 0)
                lblError.Text = "UserID already in use";
        }
        catch (Exception)
        {
            try
            {
                account.Insert(tbUserName.Text, tbPassword.Text, tbEmail.Text);

                FormsAuthentication.SetAuthCookie(tbUserName.Text, false);
```

```
                Response.Redirect("../Default.aspx");
            }
            catch (Exception err)
            {
                Page_Error("The following error occurred " + err.Message);
            }
        }
    }
}
```

```
private void ibnCancel_Click(object sender, ImageClickEventArgs e)
{
    this.Controls.Add(new LiteralControl("<script language=javascript>" +
                                        "history.go(-2);" +
                                        "</script>"));
}
```

At this point, you now have a Web page to create a user profile with CMS.NET essential information. Now, if you were to need more information, at a later time, you would present a small query Web form requesting the needed information. Then, immediately, use the information in a fashion as to prove to the user that there was a need for the information.

Logging into a Restricted Area

A Web user can go about logging into CMS.NET in two ways. First, the user can consciously request to log onto the system. Second, the system can intercept a user's attempt to access an area for which she does not have authorization.

Because the first method should appear on every Web page until the user finally logs in, it only seems appropriate that it be made into a User Control. The second method, on the other hand, is handled by ASP.NET and requires the use of an authentication Web page.

You might be surprised to find out that although both the User Control and Web page serve the same purpose, they actually have quite a few differences.

Login User Control

The Login User Control (see Figure 15-2) is placed in the NavBar of each Web page until the user logs in. After the user successfully logs in, the Logout User Control should be displayed.

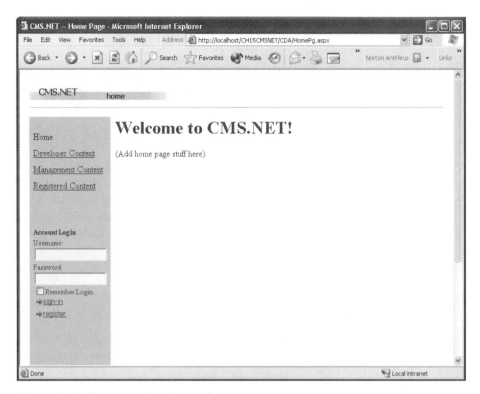

Figure 15-2. The Login User Control

As you can see in the Login User Control design (see Listing 15-3), it takes up as little room as possible yet is clear and functional at the same time.

Another thing you might notice when you look at Figure 15-2 is that the sign-in and register buttons appear to be hyperlinks, but as you can see by the code in Listing 15-3, they are in fact image buttons. I could have used buttons, but I felt that buttons were bulky and distracting and that the hyperlinks better matched the look of the NavBar used by CMS.NET. I could have used a real hyperlink to jump to the registration Web page, but using the image button kept things consistent in the code.

Listing 15-3. The Login User Control Design

```
<P>
  <B>
    <FONT color="darkslategray" size="2"> Account Login</FONT>
  </B>
  <BR>
  <FONT color="darkslategray" size="2">  Username:</FONT>
  <BR>
   
  <asp:TextBox id="tbUsername" runat="server" Width="90%"
      BackColor="LightCyan">
  </asp:TextBox>
  <BR>
  <FONT color="darkslategray" size="2"> Password:</FONT>
  <BR>
   
  <asp:TextBox id="tbPassword" runat="server" Width="90%"
      TextMode="Password" BackColor="LightCyan">
  </asp:TextBox>
  <BR>
   
  <FONT color="darkslategray">
    <asp:CheckBox id="cbPersist" runat="server"
        Text="Remember Login" Font-Size="X-Small">
    </asp:CheckBox>
  </FONT>
  <BR>
   
  <asp:ImageButton id="ibnSignIn" runat="server"
      ImageUrl="Images/signin.gif">
  </asp:ImageButton>
  <BR>
   
  <asp:ImageButton id="ibnRegister" runat="server"
      ImageUrl="Images/register.gif">
  </asp:ImageButton>
</P>
<P>
   
  <asp:Label id="ErrorMsg" runat="server" ForeColor="Red">
  </asp:Label>
</P>
```

The logic of the Login User Control Codebehind (see Listing 15-4) is handled in the two button event handlers. Because there is no common code that needs to be run by this User Control, the Page_Load() method is empty.

The ibnSignIn_Click() method handles the signing in of a Web user. First, it verifies that the user is authentic (or, in other words, has previously registered). If the Web user is authenticated, a temporary session Authentication cookie is created for the user. Also, if the user checked the Remember Login check box, an authentication cookie is placed on the Web user's machine so that the user will not have to log in each time he returns to the site. The method ends by redirecting back to itself. This causes the Web page to reset with any changes due to being authenticated.

The ibnRegister_Click() method is simply a redirect to the registration Web page.

Listing 15-4. The Login User Content Codebehind

```
private void Page_Load(object sender, System.EventArgs e)
{
}


private void ibnSignIn_Click(object sender, ImageClickEventArgs e)
{
    Account account = new Account(new AppEnv(Context).GetConnection());

    if (account.Authenticated(tbUsername.Text, tbPassword.Text))
    {
        FormsAuthentication.SetAuthCookie(tbUsername.Text,
                                            cbPersist.Checked);
        Response.Redirect(Request.RawUrl);
    }
    else
        ErrorMsg.Text = account.Message;
}


private void ibnRegister_Click(object sender, ImageClickEventArgs e)
{
    Response.Redirect("Register.aspx");
}
```

Multipurpose Login.aspx

CMS.NET took the approach that the entire CMS is one system. As a result, CMS.NET was forced to do some magic with the Authentication Web page because only one Authentication Web page is allowed per Web application, and you had already used it to build your administration system.

Another perfectly valid approach would have been to separate the administration application from the content display application and thus get a fresh Authentication Web page to work with.

As you can see in Figures 15-3 and 15-4, the Authentication Web page, better known as the Login page, has two distinct looks, yet they both derive from the same Web page. The Administration Login screen is a little more stark, while the Web User Login provides an explanation of where the user is as well as a way to register if he got here and doesn't have an account to proceed any further.

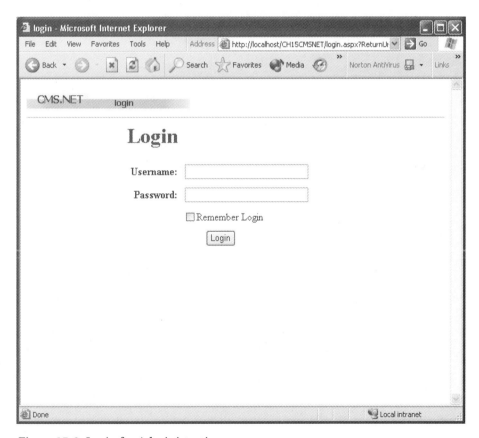

Figure 15-3. Login for Administration

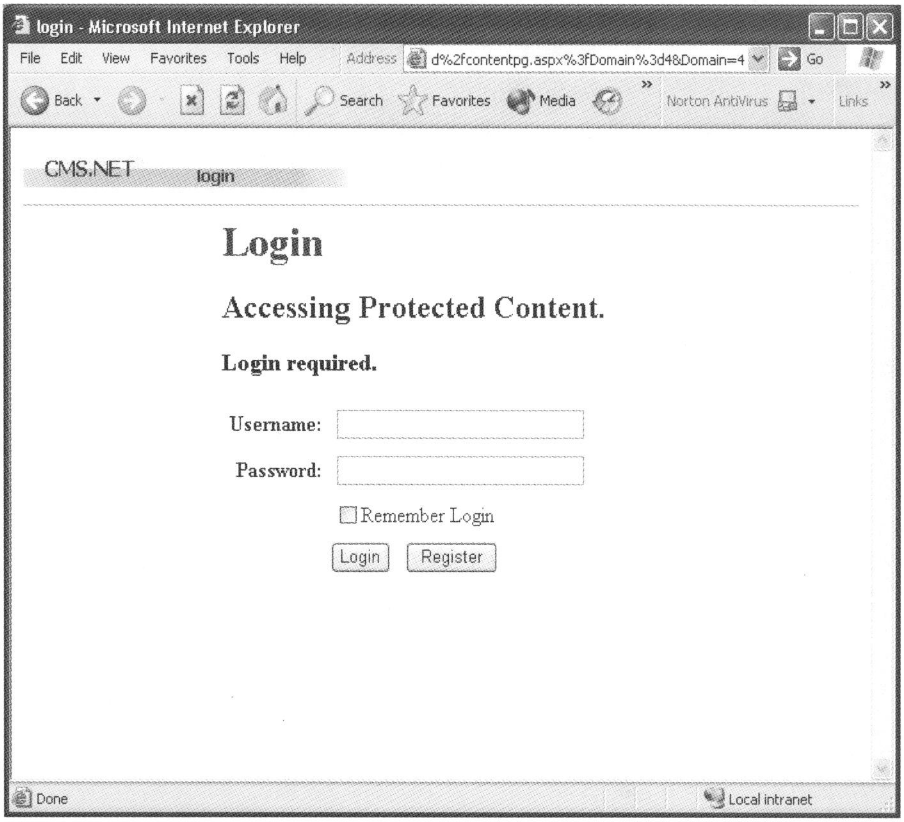

Figure 15-4. Login for Web site user authentication

Chapter 12 covered the first version of the Login.aspx (see Listing 15-5). If you glance back to that chapter, you will see that not much has been changed in the way of Web design. As you will see, however, significant changes are needed in the Codebehind to allow for this dynamic Login Web page.

The design has only two changes. The first change is the addition of a label so that the Login Web page will be able to provide an explanation of where the user has been teleported. You need to remember that the user is expecting to go to a specific Web page, and all of a sudden, she is presented with this Login screen. Without a little bit of explanation, some users may get flustered and leave, and of course, that is the last thing you want to happen.

The other change to the Web design is the addition of the Register button; when clicked, it will cause the user to jump to the registration Web page. This button is a little different than the others you have seen so far. If you take a quick peek at the design code, you will notice two unusual attributes. The first is the `Visible` attribute. This attribute is a way of adding a button that you may not want to display right away or that usually isn't displayed. It is safe to place a button like this on a Web page because an invisible button is not created by the ASP.NET parser and thus is not even placed on the Web page. Because it is not on the Web page, the user has no way to access it. Chapter 11 showed how you can set the attribute in the Codebehind—this is how you do it in the design code.

The second attribute, CauseValidation, is new to CMS.NET. This handy attribute tells the Web page whether or not to perform form validations on the Web page. The default value is true, which is why you have not seen it until now. With the Login Web page, on the other hand, if you don't set this attribute to false for the Register button, validation occurs when the button is clicked. Because the username and password are empty, the validation will fail, and the button will not execute its code to go to the registration Web page. Instead, the Login page will be presented again, asking for a username and password. This is, obviously, not what you want to happen.

Listing 15-5. The Login Web Page Design

```
<form id="login" method="post" runat="server">
  <IMG src="Images/login.jpg">
  <HR width="100%" SIZE="1">
  <TABLE cellSpacing="1" cellPadding="1" width="95%" border="0">
    <TR>
      <TD width="25%">
      </TD>
      <TD>
        <H1>
          <FONT color="darkslategray">Login</FONT>
        </H1>
        <P>
          <asp:label id="lbPrompt" runat="server"></asp:label>
        </P>
        <P>
          <asp:validationsummary id="ValidationSummary1" runat="server"
              HeaderText="The following error(s) occurred while logging in:">
          </asp:validationsummary>
        </P>
        <P>
          <asp:label id="ErrorMsg" runat="server" ForeColor="Red">
          </asp:label>
        </P>
        <TABLE cellSpacing="1" cellPadding="5" width="300" border="0">
          <TR>
            <TD width="15%">
              <P align="right">
                <STRONG>Username:</STRONG>
```

```
        </P>
      </TD>
      <TD width="85%">
        <asp:textbox id="tbUsername" runat="server" Width="100%">
        </asp:textbox>
      </TD>
      <TD width="2%">
        <asp:requiredfieldvalidator id="RequiredFieldValidator1"
            runat="server" ControlToValidate="tbUsername"
            Display="Dynamic"
            ErrorMessage="You must enter a Username">*
        </asp:requiredfieldvalidator>
      </TD>
    </TR>
    <TR>
      <TD>
        <P align="right">
          <STRONG>Password:</STRONG>
        </P>
      </TD>
      <TD>
        <asp:textbox id="tbPassword" runat="server"
            Width="100%" TextMode="Password">
        </asp:textbox>
      </TD>
      <TD>
        <asp:requiredfieldvalidator id="RequiredFieldValidator2"
            runat="server" ControlToValidate="tbPassword"
            Display="Dynamic"
            ErrorMessage="You must enter a password">*
        </asp:requiredfieldvalidator>
      </TD>
    </TR>
    <TR>
      <TD colSpan="3">
        <P align="center">
          <asp:checkbox id="cbPersist" runat="server"
              Text="Remember Login">
          </asp:checkbox>
        </P>
      </TD>
    </TR>
    <TR>
```

```
        <TD colSpan="3">
          <P align="center">
            <asp:button id="bnLogin" runat="server" Text="Login">
            </asp:button>
             
            <asp:button id="bnRegister" runat="server" Text="Register"
                Visible="False" CausesValidation="False">
            </asp:button>
          </P>
        </TD>
      </TR>
    </TABLE>
  </TD>
</TR>
</TABLE>
</form>
```

The Login Web page can be accessed in three distinct ways:

- Automatically by ASP.NET in the administration system

- Automatically by ASP.NET in the content display application

- Directly called by CMS.NET in the content display application

The Login Codebehind (see Listing 15-6) handles these three ways differently.
The Page_Load() method is mainly in charge of figuring out in which of the
three ways the Web page was accessed. It then displays the Login in the appropriate fashion for that access method. It does this in a two-part process. First, it
checks to see if it received a URL in the Request. When this happens, it means that
Login was called directly by CMS.NET.

Second, it checks to see what Web page caused the redirect to the Login Web
page using the FormsAuthentication.GetRedirectUrl() method. This method
returns the full URL of the Web page that was supposed to be the destination of
the last request, before it was trapped and sent to the Login Web page due to the
user not being authenticated. If Login.aspx was called directly and was not
the result of a user authentication trap, the GetRedirectURL() method returns
Default.aspx.

CMS.NET knows that the Login Web page was automatically called from the
administration system when the GetRedirectURL() method returns a URL containing the string admin.aspx.

Now that CMS.NET knows how it was called, the Page_Load() method can continue and display the Login Web page appropriately.

The bnLogin_Click() method's job is to authenticate the user (by checking the username and password) and then create an authentication certificate (cookie). How the cookie is created depends on how the Login Web page was called. If it was automatically called by ASP.NET, CMS.NET uses the RedirectFromLoginPage() method, which creates the authentication cookie and then redirects it to the Web page that it was originally going to before it was intercepted by ASP.NET. On the other hand, if the Login Web page was called directly from CMS.NET, it uses the SetAuthCookie() method, which only creates the cookie. CMS.NET then uses the value of the URL variable that is received in the Request to redirect the Web page to its intended destination.

Listing 15-6. The Login Web Page Codebehind

```
private void Page_Load(object sender, System.EventArgs e)
{
    URL = Request.QueryString["URL"];

    if (URL != null)
        URL.Trim();

    if (!IsPostBack)
    {
        if (FormsAuthentication.GetRedirectUrl("",
            false).IndexOf("admin.aspx") < 0)
        {
            lbPrompt.Text = "<h2>Accessing Protected Content.</h2>" +
                            "<h3>Login required.</h3>";
            bnRegister.Visible = true;
        }
    }
}

private void bnRegister_Click(object sender, System.EventArgs e)
{
    Response.Redirect("CDA/Register.aspx");
}
```

```csharp
private void bnLogin_Click(object sender, System.EventArgs e)
{
    if (Page.IsValid)
    {
        Account account = new Account(new AppEnv(Context).GetConnection());

        if (account.Authenticated(tbUsername.Text, tbPassword.Text))
        {
            if (URL != null && URL.Length > 0)
            {
                FormsAuthentication.SetAuthCookie(tbUsername.Text,
                                                    cbPersist.Checked);
                Response.Redirect(URL);
            }
            else
                FormsAuthentication.RedirectFromLoginPage(tbUsername.Text,
                                                    cbPersist.Checked);

        }
        else
            ErrorMsg.Text = account.Message;
    }

}
```

Logging Off

Because it is possible for the user to log in and store his login authentication cookie on his machine, it is a good idea to provide a way to remove this cookie. CMS.NET does this with the Logout User Control. As you can see in Figure 15-5, the Logout User Control is simply an image button that replaces the Login button on the NavBar after the user has logged in.

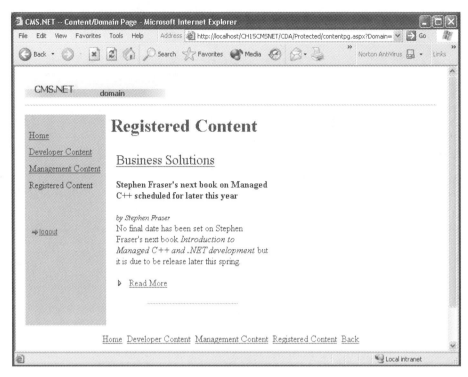

Figure 15-5. The Logout User Control

The Logout Codebehind (see Listing 15-7) has nothing you have not covered before. It calls the FormsAuthentication.SignOut() method, which deletes the authentication cookie and then redirects the user back to the home page.

Listing 15-7. The Logout User Content Codebehind

```
private void ibnLogout_Click(object sender, ImageClickEventArgs e)
{
    FormsAuthentication.SignOut();
    Response.Redirect("Default.aspx");
}
```

Restricting Content to Registered Users

The changes required to add protection to the current version of CMS.NET are actually very minor. In all cases, it is just a few lines of code. This is no coincidence, though, because I designed CMS.NET with protection in mind.

To implement protection, CMS.NET uses ASP.NET's built-in authentication functionality. Basically, whenever a user accesses protected content, he is forced to run Web pages in a new directory with authentication enabled. Because authentication is on, only users who are authenticated can continue and view the content; all others will be interrupted with a Login screen that asks for a user-name and password.

Database Updates

The first things that need to be updated are the Content, Zone, and Domain data-base tables. Each needs a way to specify whether a row in its table should be protected or not. To do this is actually very easy. All you need to do to each of these database tables is add a Protected column, similar to what is shown in Table 15-1.

Table 15-1. The Protected Database Column

PROPERTY	VALUE
Column Name	Protected
Data Type	int
Length	4
Key	false
Allow Nulls	false
Description	When this value is greater than 0, the column is protected.

Adding the column sounds easy enough; the only problem is the Allow Nulls property. If you already have data in the table, adding this column causes an error when being saved because null values are found in the new Protected col-umn. This happens because when a new column is added to a database, it is null filled.

To fix this problem, you have to create the column in three steps:

1. Create the Protected column with Allow Nulls set temporarily to a value of true.

2. Manually set all Protected columns in the database table to a value of 0 (or 1 if you want it protected).

3. Update the database definition of the Protected column by setting Allow Nulls to its proper value of false.

Updating the Domain and Zone Databases

The final version of CMS.NET will have an automated way to create and maintain Domain and Zone databases, but for now, the only way to populate these tables is via Visual Studio .NET's Server Explorer (see Figure 15-6).

	DomainID	DomainType	Protected	Title	Description	ModifiedDate	CreationDate
▶	1	homepg	0	Home	The domain is the home page of the web site	1/1/2002	1/1/2002
	2	contentpg	0	Developer Content	This domain handles all developer content	1/1/2002	1/1/2002
	3	contentpg	0	Management Content	This domain handles all management content	1/1/2002	1/1/2002
	4	contentpg	1	Registered Content	This domian handles content for register users only	1/1/2002	1/1/2002
✳							

Figure 15-6. Updating the Domain database table

The only difference (as far as a Domain or Zone database table is concerned) between a protected row and an unprotected row is that the Protected column of the row will have a value other than zero. For future explanation, I thought it a good idea to allow more than just a true/false value in this column. This will allow different levels of protection or different areas of access, depending on the user or group of users.

Automatic Protection of Content During Deployment

There is no way to protect a particular piece of content in CMS.NET. Instead, CMS.NET makes the assumption that if a piece of content is deployed to a zone that is protected, the piece of content is also protected. This assumption also stipulates that if it is protected in one zone, it is protected in all zones. I think this seems logical because allowing it to be read in one place while it is protected in another defeats the purpose of protecting the content in the first place.

The content protection process takes place in the DeployDeploy Codebehind method (see Listing 15-3). There is nothing much to the code. All the method does is check to see if the zone to which it is distributed is protected. If the zone is protected, it sets a flag that is later checked and, if true, protects the content but sets the Protected column to 1.

Listing 15-8. The DeployDeploy Codebehind, Protecting Content by the Zone's Protection Value

```csharp
private void bnDeploy_Click(object sender, System.EventArgs e)
{
    bool protectedZone = false;
    int  zoneVal;

    Distribution dist = new Distribution(appEnv.GetConnection());
    content.SetStatus(cid, ver, StatusCodes.Deployed);

    int avgRank = new ContentRank(appEnv.GetConnection()).GetRankID("Average");

    for (int i = 0; i < lbZones.Items.Count; i++)
    {
        if (lbZones.Items[i].Selected)
        {
            zoneVal = Convert.ToInt32(lbZones.Items[i].Value);
            dist.Insert(cid, ver, zoneVal, avgRank);

            if (!protectedZone)
                protectedZone = zone.IsProtected(zoneVal);
        }
    }

    if (protectedZone)
        content.SetProtected(cid, ver, (protectedZone ? 1 : 0));

    Response.Redirect("DeployList.aspx");
}
```

The code for checking to see whether a zone is protected is found in the Zone database helper IsProtected() method (see Listing 15-4). As you can see, it simply checks to see whether the selected row has a Protected value greater than zero. CMS.NET could have written its own stored procedure to handle this method, but because it is so similar to the GetZone() method, it was far easier just to call that instead.

Listing 15-9. The Zone Database Helper Methods Checking for a Protected Row

```
public bool IsProtected(int ZoneID)
{

    DataRow dr = GetZone(ZoneID);


    return (Convert.ToInt32(dr["Protected"]) > 0);
}


public DataRow GetZone(int ZoneID)
{
    // SELECT *
    //    FROM Zone
    //   WHERE ZoneID=@ZoneID

    SqlCommand Command = new SqlCommand("Zone_GetZone", m_Connection);
    Command.CommandType = CommandType.StoredProcedure;
    Command.Parameters.Add(new SqlParameter("@ZoneID", SqlDbType.Int));
    Command.Parameters["@ZoneID"].Value = ZoneID;


    SqlDataAdapter DAdpt = new SqlDataAdapter(Command);


    DataSet ds = new DataSet();
    DAdpt.Fill(ds, "Zone");

    if (ds.Tables["Zone"].Rows.Count > 0)
        return ds.Tables["Zone"].Rows[0];
    else
        return null;
}
```

Protected CDA Directory

As previously pointed out, protected content is accessed through its own set of
Web forms. These forms are in their own directory and use ASP.NET authentication. If you recall from Chapter 12, to implement ASP.NET authentication, you
simply have to add a web.config file to that directory.

This web.config file is virtually the same as any other you have already implemented from this book, as you can see in Figure 15-5. It basically denies all
unauthenticated users. The only difference between this version and the previous ones you have seen is that it doesn't use the <allow roles> element.
CMS.NET's CDA doesn't restrict Web site users by roles. It simply cares that the

user is authenticated. This doesn't mean, though, that you can't add roles to this file in the future, restricting content to specific roles or, more accurately in this case, groups of users.

Listing 15-10. The CDA/Protected web.config File

```xml
<?xml version="1.0" encoding="utf-8" ?>
<configuration>
    <system.web>
        <authorization>
            <deny users="?" />
        </authorization>
    </system.web>
</configuration>
```

Protected Default Web Forms

CMS.NET does not display protected content any differently than unprotected content. This is not to say that your CMS can't have additional things displayed with protected content or maybe even a completely different look and feel.

Because what is displayed is identical, all CMS.NET did to create protected Web forms was copy the default `ContentPg`, `ZonePg`, and `StoryPg` Web pages to the Protected directory.

Obviously, in the Web design code of each Web page, the `<#@ Page Inherits="">` attribute had to be changed to reflect the new namespace of the Codebehind that is now in the Protected directory.

A little less obvious, though, is the need to change every occurrence of a User Control to a reference to its location in the parent directory because the User Controls were not copied to the Protected directory. For example, here is how it needs to be done in a Web design and a Codebehind:

```
<%@ Register TagPrefix="cmsnet" TagName="Header" Src="../Header.ascx" %>
```

```
HeadlineTeaser hlt = (HeadlineTeaser) LoadControl("../HeadlineTeaser.ascx");
```

There was no need to copy the User Controls to the Protected directory because a user can't access them directly anyway. They can only be called from within a Web page. Thus, they are protected indirectly because they are called by a protected Web page.

Copying the User Controls to the Protected directory would only mean more redundant code. As it is, CMS.NET has very similar Web page code in two places. But, as you will see, the code is not identical. Plus, in the future, it is very possible that protected content will display more information than unprotected content and thus will be even more different than their unprotected equivalents.

Updates to Default Web Forms

Each of the original default content display Web forms needs minor changes to support protected content. Most of the changes revolve around populating navigation URLs to reflect the new, protected content and to stop a sneaky user from trying to view protected content using the unprotected content display Web forms.

HomePg Web Page

No coding changes are needed on the HomePg Web page to protect content. The home page should be visible to all, at the very least to say that you need permission to access the rest of the site.

The following changes are, in fact, to add the Login and Logout User Controls to the NavBar (see Figure 15-7 and Figure 15-8). This book will only show this change once here in the HomePg, even though the change needs to be done in all Web forms—protected and unprotected.

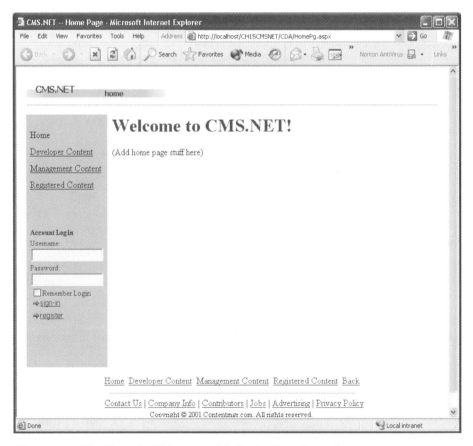

Figure 15-7. The HomePg Web page with Login User Control

Figure 15-8. The HomePg Web page with Logout User Control

The HomePg Web design (see Listing 15-11) shows the simple addition of the Register directive for Login and Logout and their tags being added to the NavBar cell of the HomePg layout table.

You might also note that the User Controls both have their Visible attributes set to false, which means that the Codebehind needs to change one of them to true to be visible to the Web user.

Listing 15-11. The HomePg Web Page Design

```
<%@ Page language="c#" Codebehind="HomePg.aspx.cs"
                     AutoEventWireup="false"
                     Inherits="CMSNET.CDA.HomePg" %>


<%@ Register TagPrefix="cmsnet" TagName="Header" Src="Header.ascx" %>
<%@ Register TagPrefix="cmsnet" TagName="NavBar" Src="NavBar.ascx" %>
<%@ Register TagPrefix="cmsnet" TagName="Login" Src="Login.ascx" %>
<%@ Register TagPrefix="cmsnet" TagName="Logout" Src="Logout.ascx" %>
<%@ Register TagPrefix="cmsnet" TagName="Footer" Src="Footer.ascx" %>
```

```
<!DOCTYPE HTML PUBLIC "-//W3C//DTD HTML 4.0 Transitional//EN" >
<HTML>
  <HEAD>
    <title>CMS.NET Home</title>
  </HEAD>
  <body MS_POSITIONING="FlowLayout">
    <form id="HomePg" method="post" runat="server">
      <TABLE cellSpacing="8" cellPadding="1" width="100%" border="0">
        <TR>
          <TD colSpan="2">
            <cmsnet:Header id="Header" Level="home" runat="server">
            </cmsnet:Header>
          </TD>
        </TR>
        <TR>
          <TD vAlign="top" width="20%" bgColor="#8cd3ef">
            <br>
            <P>
              <cmsnet:NavBar id="MainNavBar" runat="server">
              </cmsnet:NavBar>
            </P>
            <P>
              <cmsnet:Login id="ucLogin" runat="server" Visible="False">
              </cmsnet:Login>
              <cmsnet:Logout id="ucLogout" runat="server" Visible="False">
              </cmsnet:Logout>
            </P>
          </TD>
          <TD width="80%" vAlign="top">
            <H1>
              <FONT color="darkslategray">Welcome to CMS.NET!</FONT>
            </H1>
            <P>
              (Add home page stuff here)
            </P>
          </TD>
        </TR>
        <TR>
          <TD colSpan="2">
            <cmsnet:Footer id="Footer" runat="server">
            </cmsnet:Footer>
          </TD>
        </TR>
```

```
        </TABLE>
      </form>
    </body>
</HTML>
```

The HomePg Codebehind (see Listing 15-12) is pretty self-explanatory. First, you have to manually add the User Controls to the Codebehind because the Visual Studio .NET code generator doesn't do it for you. Then, within the Page_Load() method, examine the Request.IsAuthenticated property to see if the user has been authenticated. If the user is not authenticated, display the Login User Control. Otherwise, display the Logout User Control.

Listing 15-12. The HomePg Codebehind for Viewing Login and Logout User Controls

```
public class HomePg : CMSNET.Common.PageEx
{
    protected CMSNET.CDA.NavBar MainNavBar;
    protected CMSNET.CDA.Login ucLogin;
    protected CMSNET.CDA.Logout ucLogout;

    private void Page_Load(object sender, System.EventArgs e)
    {
        int Domain = Convert.ToInt32(Request.QueryString["Domain"]);

        // First Time in no Domain specified
        if (Domain == 0)
            Domain++;

        MainNavBar.Domain = Domain;

        if (!Request.IsAuthenticated)
            ucLogin.Visible = true;
        else
            ucLogout.Visible = true;
    }
}
```

NavBar User Control

The NavBar Codebehind coding change to handle the redirect of protected content is really very simple (see Listing 15-13). All you need to do is place the string "Protected/" in front of every navigation URL that has a destination of a protected domain.

In other words, the Page_Load() method checks to see whether the Protected column in the Domain database is greater than zero. If it is, place "Protected/" in front of the NavigateUrl property.

Listing 15-13. The NavBar Codebehind for Referencing Protected domains

```
private void Page_Load(object sender, System.EventArgs e)
{
    ...
    foreach (DataRow dr in dt.Rows)
    {
        ...
        if (m_domain != Convert.ToInt32(dr["DomainID"]))
        {
            link = new HyperLink();
            link.Text = dr["Title"].ToString();
            link.NavigateUrl = buildDirectory(dr) +
                               dr["DomainType"].ToString().Trim() +
                               ".aspx?Domain=" + dr["DomainID"];

            cell.Controls.Add(link);
        }
        ...
    }
}

private string buildDirectory (DataRow dr)
{
    if (Convert.ToInt32(dr["Protected"]) == 0)
        return "";

    return "Protected/";
}
```

This same code change needs to be done to the HeadlineTeaser User Control and the unprotected versions of the ContentPg and ZonePg Web pages. The only difference in each of these is that they are checking different databases for their protected NavigationUrls. The code is so similar that there is no need to include it here, but if you need it, you can find it on the Apress Web site (www.apress.com) in the Downloads section with all the other code in this book.

StoryPg Web Page

The final change is that you need to stop sneaky users from using the unprotected versions of the content viewers to view protected content. Until now, CMS.NET has been relying on the idea that the user will run the correct version of the viewer to view the content. This will enable ASP.NET to trap unauthenticated users.

Unfortunately, there is nothing stopping the user from manually accessing the same piece of content using the unprotected version of the Web form and thus bypassing the ASP.NET-imposed authentication security.

To combat this, one further check must be made within the unprotected version of the ContentPg, ZonePg, and StoryPg Web forms to verify that the content is not protected. This check is not needed in the protected versions because ASP.NET will not allow the Web page to run until the user has been authenticated.

The StoryPg Codebehind (see Listing 15-14) shows this final check. If the content is protected, check to see whether the user has been authenticated. If the user has not been authenticated, redirect to the Login Web page. Note the following code:

```
"?URL=" + HttpUtility.UrlEncode(Request.RawUrl));
```

This code places the current URL onto the Response. You need to use the UrlEncode() method because the current URL contains reserved characters that, later on down the line, wreak havoc. In particular, the ampersand (&) in "&ver=" is interpreted as a separate parameter when the Login Web page tries to grab the URL out of the Request using Request.QueryString["URL"].

Listing 15-14. The StoryPg Codebehind for Verifying Content Protection

```
private void Page_Load(object sender, System.EventArgs e)
{
    ...

    DataRow dr = content.GetContentForIDVer(curId, curVer);

    if (Convert.ToInt32(dr["Protected"]) > 0)
    {
        if (!Request.IsAuthenticated)
        {
            Response.Redirect("../Login.aspx" +
                            "?URL=" + HttpUtility.UrlEncode(Request.RawUrl));
        }
    }
    ...
}
```

Summary

This chapter covered registering users and restricting content.

It started by describing some reasons why a Web site might protect its content. Then it covered what a Web page privacy policy is, discussed why you need one, and then showed the CMS.NET policy. Next, it covered user profiles and the two most common methods of populating them: the quick blitz and the slow retrieval. It then showed the registration portion of CMS.NET's implementation of the slow retrieval method. It followed this up by showing logging in and out of CMS. Finally, it covered the changes that need to be implemented to add protected content to CMS.NET.

INDEX

Apress Titles

ISBN	PRICE	AUTHOR	TITLE
1-893115-73-9	$34.95	Abbott	Voice Enabling Web Applications: VoiceXML and Beyond
1-893115-01-1	$39.95	Appleman	Dan Appleman's Win32 API Puzzle Book and Tutorial for Visual Basic Programmers
1-893115-23-2	$29.95	Appleman	How Computer Programming Works
1-893115-97-6	$39.95	Appleman	Moving to VB. NET: Strategies, Concepts, and Code
1-59059-023-6	$39.95	Baker	Adobe Acrobat 5: The Professional User's Guide
1-893115-09-7	$29.95	Baum	Dave Baum's Definitive Guide to LEGO MINDSTORMS
1-893115-84-4	$29.95	Baum, Gasperi, Hempel, and Villa	Extreme MINDSTORMS: An Advanced Guide to LEGO MINDSTORMS
1-893115-82-8	$59.95	Ben-Gan/Moreau	Advanced Transact-SQL for SQL Server 2000
1-893115-91-7	$39.95	Birmingham/Perry	Software Development on a Leash
1-893115-48-8	$29.95	Bischof	The .NET Languages: A Quick Translation Guide
1-893115-67-4	$49.95	Borge	Managing Enterprise Systems with the Windows Script Host
1-893115-28-3	$44.95	Challa/Laksberg	Essential Guide to Managed Extensions for C++
1-893115-39-9	$44.95	Chand	A Programmer's Guide to ADO.NET in C#
1-893115-44-5	$29.95	Cook	Robot Building for Beginners
1-893115-99-2	$39.95	Cornell/Morrison	Programming VB .NET: A Guide for Experienced Programmers
1-893115-72-0	$39.95	Curtin	Developing Trust: Online Privacy and Security
1-59059-008-2	$29.95	Duncan	The Career Programmer: Guerilla Tactics for an Imperfect World
1-893115-71-2	$39.95	Ferguson	Mobile .NET
1-893115-90-9	$49.95	Finsel	The Handbook for Reluctant Database Administrators
1-59059-024-4	$49.95	Fraser	Real World ASP.NET: Building a Content Management System
1-893115-42-9	$44.95	Foo/Lee	XML Programming Using the Microsoft XML Parser
1-893115-55-0	$34.95	Frenz	Visual Basic and Visual Basic .NET for Scientists and Engineers
1-893115-85-2	$34.95	Gilmore	A Programmer's Introduction to PHP 4.0
1-893115-36-4	$34.95	Goodwill	Apache Jakarta-Tomcat
1-893115-17-8	$59.95	Gross	A Programmer's Introduction to Windows DNA
1-893115-62-3	$39.95	Gunnerson	A Programmer's Introduction to C#, Second Edition
1-59059-009-0	$39.95	Harris/Macdonald	Moving to ASP.NET: Web Development with VB .NET
1-893115-30-5	$49.95	Harkins/Reid	SQL: Access to SQL Server
1-893115-10-0	$34.95	Holub	Taming Java Threads
1-893115-04-6	$34.95	Hyman/Vaddadi	Mike and Phani's Essential C++ Techniques
1-893115-96-8	$59.95	Jorelid	J2EE FrontEnd Technologies: A Programmer's Guide to Servlets, JavaServer Pages, and Enterprise JavaBeans
1-893115-49-6	$39.95	Kilburn	Palm Programming in Basic
1-893115-50-X	$34.95	Knudsen	Wireless Java: Developing with Java 2, Micro Edition
1-893115-79-8	$49.95	Kofler	Definitive Guide to Excel VBA
1-893115-57-7	$39.95	Kofler	MySQL
1-893115-87-9	$39.95	Kurata	Doing Web Development: Client-Side Techniques
1-893115-75-5	$44.95	Kurniawan	Internet Programming with VB

ISBN	PRICE	AUTHOR	TITLE
1-893115-38-0	$24.95	Lafler	Power AOL: A Survival Guide
1-893115-46-1	$36.95	Lathrop	Linux in Small Business: A Practical User's Guide
1-893115-19-4	$49.95	Macdonald	Serious ADO: Universal Data Access with Visual Basic
1-893115-06-2	$39.95	Marquis/Smith	A Visual Basic 6.0 Programmer's Toolkit
1-893115-22-4	$27.95	McCarter	David McCarter's VB Tips and Techniques
1-893115-76-3	$49.95	Morrison	C++ For VB Programmers
1-893115-80-1	$39.95	Newmarch	A Programmer's Guide to Jini Technology
1-893115-58-5	$49.95	Oellermann	Architecting Web Services
1-893115-81-X	$39.95	Pike	SQL Server: Common Problems, Tested Solutions
1-59059-017-1	$34.95	Rainwater	Herding Cats: A Primer for Programmers Who Lead Programmers
1-59059-025-2	$49.95	Rammer	Advanced .NET Remoting
1-893115-20-8	$34.95	Rischpater	Wireless Web Development
1-893115-93-3	$34.95	Rischpater	Wireless Web Development with PHP and WAP
1-893115-89-5	$59.95	Shemitz	Kylix: The Professional Developer's Guide and Reference
1-893115-40-2	$39.95	Sill	The qmail Handbook
1-893115-24-0	$49.95	Sinclair	From Access to SQL Server
1-893115-94-1	$29.95	Spolsky	User Interface Design for Programmers
1-893115-53-4	$44.95	Sweeney	Visual Basic for Testers
1-59059-002-3	$44.95	Symmonds	Internationalization and Localization Using Microsoft .NET
1-893115-29-1	$44.95	Thomsen	Database Programming with Visual Basic .NET
1-59059-010-4	$54.95	Thomsen	Database Programming with C#
1-893115-65-8	$39.95	Tiffany	Pocket PC Database Development with eMbedded Visual Basic
1-893115-59-3	$59.95	Troelsen	C# and the .NET Platform
1-893115-26-7	$59.95	Troelsen	Visual Basic .NET and the .NET Platform
1-59059-011-2	$39.95	Troelsen	COM and .NET Interoperability
1-893115-54-2	$49.95	Trueblood/Lovett	Data Mining and Statistical Analysis Using SQL
1-893115-16-X	$49.95	Vaughn	ADO Examples and Best Practices
1-893115-68-2	$49.95	Vaughn	ADO.NET and ADO Examples and Best Practices for VB Programmers, Second Edition
1-59059-012-0	$49.95	Vaughn/Blackburn	ADO.NET Examples and Best Practices for C# Programmers
1-893115-83-6	$44.95	Wells	Code Centric: T-SQL Programming with Stored Procedures and Triggers
1-893115-95-X	$49.95	Welschenbach	Cryptography in C and C++
1-893115-05-4	$39.95	Williamson	Writing Cross-Browser Dynamic HTML
1-893115-78-X	$49.95	Zukowski	Definitive Guide to Swing for Java 2, Second Edition
1-893115-92-5	$49.95	Zukowski	Java Collections
1-893115-98-4	$54.95	Zukowski	Learn Java with JBuilder 6

Available at bookstores nationwide or from Springer Verlag New York, Inc. at 1-800-777-4643; fax 1-212-533-3503. Contact us for more information at sales@apress.com.

Apress Titles Publishing SOON!

ISBN	AUTHOR	TITLE
1-59059-022-8	Alapati	Expert Oracle 9i Database Administration
1-59059-015-5	Clark	An Introduction to Object Oriented Programming with Visual Basic .NET
1-59059-000-7	Cornell	Programming C#
1-59059-014-7	Drol	Object-Oriented Flash MX
1-59059-033-3	Fraser	Managed C++ and .NET Development
1-59059-038-4	Gibbons	Java Development to .NET Development
1-59059-030-9	Habibi/Camerlengo/Patterson	Java 1.4 and the Sun Certified Developer Exam
1-59059-006-6	Hetland	Practical Python
1-59059-003-1	Nakhimovsky/Meyers	XML Programming: Web Applications and Web Services with JSP and ASP
1-59059-001-5	McMahon	Serious ASP.NET
1-59059-021-X	Moore	Karl Moore's Visual Basic .NET: The Tutorials
1-893115-27-5	Morrill	Tuning and Customizing a Linux System
1-59059-020-1	Patzer	JSP Examples and Best Practices
1-59059-028-7	Rischpater	Wireless Web Development, 2nd Edition
1-59059-026-0	Smith	Writing Add-Ins for .NET
1-893115-43-7	Stephenson	Standard VB: An Enterprise Developer's Reference for VB 6 and VB .NET
1-59059-032-5	Thomsen	Database Programming with Visual Basic .NET, 2nd Edition
1-59059-007-4	Thomsen	Building Web Services with VB .NET
1-59059-027-9	Torkelson/Petersen/Torkelson	Programming the Web with Visual Basic .NET
1-59059-004-X	Valiaveedu	SQL Server 2000 and Business Intelligence in an XML/.NET World

Available at bookstores nationwide or from Springer Verlag New York, Inc. at 1-800-777-4643; fax 1-212-533-3503. Contact us for more information at sales@apress.com.

books for professionals by professionals™

About Apress

Apress, located in Berkeley, CA, is a fast-growing, innovative publishing company devoted to meeting the needs of existing and potential programming professionals. Simply put, the "A" in Apress stands for *"The Author's Press"*™ and its books have *"The Expert's Voice"*™. Apress' unique approach to publishing grew out of conversations between its founders Gary Cornell and Dan Appleman, authors of numerous best-selling, highly regarded books for programming professionals. In 1998 they set out to create a publishing company that emphasized quality above all else. Gary and Dan's vision has resulted in the publication of over 50 titles by leading software professionals, all of which have *The Expert's Voice*™.

Do You Have What It Takes to Write for Apress?

Apress is rapidly expanding its publishing program. If you can write and refuse to compromise on the quality of your work, if you believe in doing more than rehashing existing documentation, and if you're looking for opportunities and rewards that go far beyond those offered by traditional publishing houses, we want to hear from you!

Consider these innovations that we offer all of our authors:

- **Top royalties with *no* hidden switch statements**
  Authors typically only receive half of their normal royalty rate on foreign sales. In contrast, Apress' royalty rate remains the same for both foreign and domestic sales.

- **A mechanism for authors to obtain equity in Apress**
  Unlike the software industry, where stock options are essential to motivate and retain software professionals, the publishing industry has adhered to an outdated compensation model based on royalties alone. In the spirit of most software companies, Apress reserves a significant portion of its equity for authors.

- **Serious treatment of the technical review process**
  Each Apress book has a technical reviewing team whose remuneration depends in part on the success of the book since they too receive royalties.

Moreover, through a partnership with Springer-Verlag, New York, Inc., one of the world's major publishing houses, Apress has significant venture capital behind it. Thus, we have the resources to produce the highest quality books *and* market them aggressively.

If you fit the model of the Apress author who can write a book that gives the "professional what he or she needs to know"™," then please contact one of our Editorial Directors, Gary Cornell (gary_cornell@apress.com), Dan Appleman (dan_appleman@apress.com), Peter Blackburn (peter_blackburn@apress.com), Jason Gilmore (jason_gilmore@apress.com), Karen Watterson (karen_watterson@apress.com), or John Zukowski (john_zukowski@apress.com) for more information.